W9-AGE-285

Uniting the Tribes

Uniting the Tribes

THE RISE AND FALL OF PAN-INDIAN COMMUNITY ON THE CROW RESERVATION

Frank Rzeczkowski

University Press of Kansas

© 2012 by the University Press of Kansas
All rights reserved

Published by the University Press of Kansas (Lawrence, Kansas 66045), which was organized by the Kansas Board of Regents and is operated and funded by Emporia State University, Fort Hays State University, Kansas State University, Pittsburg State University, the University of Kansas, and Wichita State University

Library of Congress Cataloging-in-Publication Data

Rzeczkowski, Frank.
Uniting the tribes : the rise and fall of pan-Indian community on the Crow reservation / Frank Rzeczkowski.
p. cm.
Includes bibliographical references and index.
ISBN 978-0-7006-1851-4 (cloth : alk. paper)
1. Crow Indians—Montana—Crow Indian Reservation—History. 2. Crow Indians—Montana—Crow Indian Reservation—Ethnic identity. 3. Crow Indian—Social networks—Montana—Crow Indian Reservation. 4. Indians of North America—Montana—Crow Indian Reservation—History. 5. Indians of North America—Montana—Crow Indian Reservation—Ethnic identity. 6. Indians of North America—Social networks—Montana—Crow Indian Reservation. 7. Crow Indian Reservation (Mont.)—Ethnic relations. 8. Crow Indian Reservation (Mont.)—Social conditions. 9. Crow Indian Reservation (Mont.)—Politics and government. I. Title.
E99.C92R94 2012
978.6004'975272—dc23

2012005830

British Library Cataloguing-in-Publication Data is available.

Printed in the United States of America

10 9 8 7 6 5 4 3 2 1

The paper used in this publication is recycled and contains 30 percent postconsumer waste. It is acid free and meets the minimum requirements of the American National Standard for Permanence of Paper for Printed Library Materials Z39.48-1992.

To Amy

CONTENTS

A photo section appears following page 115

ACKNOWLEDGMENTS

During this project's long gestation period, it has acquired an equally long list of people to whom I am indebted. Thanks first must go to those people who welcomed me into their homes and supported my efforts to learn more about their community's history. At Crow, this list includes elders Joseph Medicine Crow and Barney Old Coyote—paragons of knowledge, generosity, and kindness. Thanks also go to Tyrone Ten Bear for sharing his knowledge on early Crow peyotism, to Gordon Sees the Ground Jr. and his family for their hospitality, and to the staff at Little Big Horn College, particularly archivists Magdelene Medicine Horse and Carson Walks Over Ice, and to college librarian Tim Bernardis (who put me up for several days after my truck's engine blew up during an early research trip to Crow), and to faculty member and former Little Bighorn Battlefield National Monument historian Tim McCleary, who not only shared his own research with me but also fed a hungry graduate student and unknowingly bequeathed to me a cat named Rufus.

What eventually became this book began as a master's thesis at the University of North Dakota investigating Crow responses to the Bozeman Trail. During this project, I became intrigued by the connections I was finding between the Crows and their putative Lakota adversaries. In addition to history professors Richard Beringer and Barbara Handy-Marchello, both of whom served on my master's thesis committee, I owe particular thanks to two individuals at UND: former communications professor James Smorada, for convincing me that I could write, and to history professor Jim Mochoruk, for convincing me that I could do history. At Northwestern University, the dissertation this book is based on was guided through successive stages by James Merrell, Steven Hahn, Mary Weismantel, and Josef Barton. Though he was only at Northwestern for my first year, the influence and wisdom of Frederick Hoxie is reflected in nearly every page of this book. Fred's own study of Crow history was an essential guide for my own work, and he continued to be an unfailingly generous mentor even after moving on to the University of Illinois. What good there is in this book is largely due to their guidance and wisdom; any flaws or omissions are entirely my own.

While at Northwestern, I was fortunate to enjoy not only the support of the history department and graduate school, but also to receive funding from the Phillips Fund Grant for Native American Research from the American Philosophical Society. I probably would never have reached Northwestern at all without the assistance of the Montana Historical Society's Merrill G. Burlingame–K. Ross Toole Award, which opened doors that otherwise might have remained closed to a North Dakota grad student. The research upon which this book is based was also made possible through the assistance of staff members at the Montana Historical Society, Montana State University, Plenty Coups State Park in Pryor, Montana, Little Bighorn Battlefield National Monument, the National Archives in Washington, D.C., and the Rocky Mountain Branch of the National Archives in Denver, Colorado, the Newberry Library in Chicago, the Buffalo Bill Historical Center in Cody, Wyoming, the American Heritage Center at the University of Wyoming, the Jesuit Archives at Gonzaga University in Spokane, Washington, and the National Anthropological Archives at the Smithsonian Institution, as well as those at Little Big Horn College.

Any graduate student relies as heavily on the kindness of friends and fellow students as on faculty members and institutions. At Northwestern, I was fortunate to count Wallace Best, Christopher Tassava, and Brett Gadsden among my friends. Beyond Northwestern, Jerry Mercier, Deborah Hoffman, and Greg Deyak were constant sources of encouragement and enthusiasm. Since leaving graduate school I have been equally blessed by the support of colleagues and friends at Northwestern and DePaul universities, and particularly at Xavier University, which has been kind enough to provide me with employment during the time this book was written. Ranjit Arab, acquisitions editor for the University Press of Kansas, has always been an enthusiastic supporter of this project and a reliable guide, while production editor Larisa Martin answered my many queries with patience and unfailing good humor. I am also indebted to Alexandra Harmon of the University of Washington, Colin Calloway of Dartmouth College, and Kathleen Sherman of Colorado State University, who all read the manuscript and whose questions, critiques, and suggestions immeasurably improved the final product.

The most profound thanks, of course, must be reserved for family. In my case, this includes my sister, Anne (who is interested in everything), and her husband, Greg Fox, and my mother, Rosemarie Rzeczkowski, and my father, Henry Rzeczkowski (who never completely understood what I was doing, but who never failed to support my doing it). Finally, there is my wife, Amy, who has brought me more joy and happiness than I ever imagined was possible in life; this book is dedicated to her with love.

Uniting the Tribes

Young Man Afraid of His Horses's Letter

Young Man Afraid of His Horses lived in a tribal world. Born to a prominent Oglala Lakota family, he grew to manhood at the apex of the Lakotas' mid-nineteenth-century push for new hunting grounds on the Northern Plains, taking part in battles against the Crow, Shoshoni, and Pawnee. As a result of his deeds and his personification of the four cardinal Lakota virtues of generosity, bravery, fortitude, and wisdom, he became one of four Oglala shirtwearers—individuals charged with protecting and providing for the Oglala people—as well as an *itancan,* the leader of an Oglala *tiyospaye,* or band. With the mounting incursions and demands of the United States in the 1860s, Young Man Afraid of His Horses participated in Lakota resistance against the U.S. Army. Although he later eschewed armed resistance to the Americans, he continued to serve in the role of protector, trying to shield his people from the worst effects of U.S. Indian policy. In the 1870s and 1880s, he became an intermediary and negotiator for the Oglalas, attempting to smooth their transition to life on what would become the Pine Ridge Indian Reservation. But despite this seeming resignation to U.S. domination, Young Man Afraid of His Horses, as one biographer puts it, "did not intend to become a white man and give up being a Lakota." Until his death in 1893 at age fifty-six, he never spoke English and sought to live according to Lakota values.[1]

Seen from this angle, Young Man Afraid of His Horses's life appears neatly circumscribed within an ever-smaller series of concentric circles: from the broader Lakota community to the smaller Oglala subset of that community, to his own *tiyospaye* and family. In a similar fashion, the geographic boundaries of his world also seemingly grew smaller with time, as the vast expanses of the Lakotas' mid-1800s homelands were reduced to smaller, separate, isolated reservations by the late 1800s. Beyond these boundaries, Young Man Afraid of His Horses seemingly dealt with outsiders only as adversaries, or at best as unwelcome but unavoidable intruders into the Lakota world. In January 1889, however, Young Man Afraid of His Horses composed a remarkable letter to General George Crook. Written though the amanuensis of a young army officer, the letter explained Young Man Afraid of His Horses's reasons for wanting to travel to the Crow Indian Reservation in Montana.

Young Man Afraid of His Horses began his letter with a question: "Is it right to stop us Indians from visiting each other?" After diplomatically praising Crook for his role in ending intertribal warfare, he complained of the treatment he had received from the Crows' government agent during a previous visit. Despite permission from Pine Ridge agent Hugh D. Gallagher to travel to the Crow Reservation, "I had no sooner reached there than I was surrounded by the military, made a prisoner, and put off the reservation." Such treatment, he suggested, interfered with the process of turning former enemies into friends.

But as Young Man Afraid of His Horses made clear, more was on his mind than mere friendship. "I want to visit the Crows and plan with them for the protection of our people," he stated, "for the white man is crowding us, and will want to crowd us still more." Not only had different tribes become friends, they had become "as one nation, related to each other." As one nation, Crows and Lakotas needed to meet "to talk of things that are of interest, and what is best for our common welfare." Such items of interest included land claim issues like the Black Hills and compensation for lost resources like the deer and the buffalo. Finally, Young Man Afraid of His Horses justified the journey in terms even a Euro-American could understand: direct kinship and personal property. "I have relatives among the Crows by the marriage of my aunt," he said. "They gave me three horses and I want to get them."[2]

Young Man Afraid of His Horses's letter is remarkable on a number of levels. It reveals, among other things, a much broader sense of identity and community than the tribal world Young Man Afraid of His Horses lived in seemingly permitted. Despite his self-serving praise for Crook, what linked Young Man Afraid of His Horses to the Crows was not anything the general had done, but rather direct and personal ties via his aunt's marriage. And in citing the need for Crows and Lakotas to meet to discuss their "common welfare" as peoples "related to each other," Young Man Afraid of His Horses asserted a shared identity that not only included his aunt's Crow relatives but all Crows and Lakotas—even, potentially, all Native peoples living under U.S. domination. This was not, it should be emphasized, the U.S. government–sponsored rhetoric that envisioned Native tribal identities and cultures being replaced by assimilation into mainstream American society; as his biographer points out, Young Man Afraid of His Horses had no intention of becoming a white man. It was instead an assertion of a pantribal Indian identity, with interests, attitudes, and experiences that were separate and distinct from those of Anglo Americans. Young Man Afraid of His Horses was a Lakota by birth, affiliation, and residence, but as his letter makes clear, by 1889 he also thought of himself as an Indian, and of Crows and Lakotas as "us Indians." Seen from this angle, the dimensions of Young Man Afraid of His Horses's world expanded far beyond the confines of Oglala Lakota society and Pine Ridge.

Young Man Afraid of His Horses's letter raises many questions. How did his (and his aunt's) connection to the Crows come about? How was that connection maintained, despite the hostility that had often characterized Crow–Lakota relations prior to the reservation era? Perhaps most significantly, how and why did he come to see Crows and Lakotas "as one nation," with shared interests and concerns? However, the letter is also suggestive of larger, more fundamental issues that extend well beyond Young Man Afraid of His Horses himself. How did Lakotas, Crows, and other Native peoples on the Northern Plains relate to and interact with one another before the reservation era? To what extent did those interactions persist, and to what extent did they change, after the onset of reservation life in the 1880s? Finally, what implications did those interactions—both before and after the establishment of reservations—have for Native American understandings of concepts such as identity and community during an era marked by massive changes and dislocations in Native life? Was Young Man Afraid of His Horses simply a unique individual, or does he (and his letter) illustrate a dimension of Native American history that we have yet to fully understand?

The tribal world Young Man Afraid of His Horses lived in has proven exceptionally problematic for scholars. Though still a dominant theme in the field of Native American history, the entire concept of tribalism has come under increasing scrutiny—and criticism—in recent decades. Some historians and anthropologists have argued that the entire notion of tribes was a fundamentally European creation foisted on Native American communities as a means of colonial domination; others have argued for the abandonment of the term altogether.[3] The scholarly squabbles over how Native American communities should be defined and understood has even led one anthropologist to state, "I do not know what is meant by 'tribal societies.'"[4] (For discussion of my use of the terms "tribe" and "tribalism," see the "Note on Terminology" at the end of the Introduction.)

Part of the problem with the concept of tribalism lies in its legacy as an element in evolutionary anthropology, in which tribal peoples were slotted into a lower level on the scale of cultural and political evolution and defined as primitive, in contrast to more advanced, modern peoples.[5] One result of this was the tendency to view tribes as primordial entities frozen in time; "people without history," to use Eric Wolf's phrase.[6] Though the overtly pejorative connotations of this typology have long since been jettisoned, the perceived cultural distinctions between being tribally minded—parochial, rigidly bounded, hostile to outsiders, and constrained by tradition—and being modern—with its emphasis on fluidity, diversity, and openness to change—has persisted in some areas, particularly with regard to concepts of Indianness.[7]

As a result, when historians and anthropologists have attempted to trace the origins of an Indian identity, they have usually turned their attention away from tribes, reservations, and individuals like Young Man Afraid of His Horses, and toward younger generations in nontribal, nonreservation environments. The perceived dichotomy between being tribal and being modern suggested that in order to become Indian, Native Americans had to surrender older, limiting tribal identities. From this perspective, a collective sense of Indian ethnicity could emerge only in places where tribal lines had either blurred or dissolved entirely. Indeed, in the 1950s and 1960s, studies of pan-Indianism were typed as a branch of acculturation studies.[8]

Over the years, historians and anthropologists have identified a number of places where the transformation from tribal to Indian took place, including Indian Territory, off-reservation boarding schools, cities, and in the activities of educated, acculturated elites such as Charles Eastman or Carlos Montezuma in organizations like the Society of American Indians. In these locations, so the argument goes, Native peoples could redefine themselves and find common ground with other Indians. In Indian Territory, Plains peoples like the Kiowa and Cheyenne came into contact with Creeks and Cherokees from the Southeast and Delawares, Winnebagos, and Miamis from the Midwest, with intermarriage and cultural borrowing between these socially, culturally, and geographically diverse groups eventually producing what James Howard described as the "pan-Indian culture of Oklahoma."[9] Similarly, boarding schools became places where "an inter-tribal, 'Indian' identity emerged as an important cohesive concept."[10] Later in the twentieth century, emerging communities of urban Indians also possessed boundaries that one scholar describes as "far less absolute" than the "rigid, geopolitical, and culturally circumscribed boundaries that define tribal communities."[11] According to Thomas Cowger, all of these developments "advanced the use of English, supplying individuals from different tribes with a common language. It brought together in one location a multitribal population. In the process, intertribal dating relationships produced marriages across tribal lines and fostered Native American solidarity."[12] There is little room in any of this for Young Man Afraid of His Horses, who never attended school, much less an off-reservation boarding school, and never lived outside a tribal or reservation environment.

In contrast, the geographically isolated, federally supervised reservations imposed on (it seems disingenuous to say "negotiated with") Northern Plains tribes by the United States in the late nineteenth century were regarded as unlikely sources for the emergence of a sense of pantribal Indian identity. Subject to the hegemonic power of the U.S. government, and confined by pass systems that required explicit permission to travel beyond the limits of one's home reservation (and even with a pass, Young Man Afraid of His Horses was still turned away by the Crow agent), Indians were often regarded as effectively marooned on landlocked reservation islands, with both friendly and hostile contact interdicted by American officials. During this era, as one scholar puts it, Indians on reservations "languished in poverty and isolation, their prospects dim for any kind of development, growth, or improvement, much less an ethnic resurgence."[13]

Yet alongside these themes in Native American historiography are parallel threads that have begun to modify many of the assumptions that once informed the search for the origins of a Native American identity. Chief among them is the growing recognition that tribal communities like the Crow and Lakota were never ahistorical, essentialized, and unchanging bodies, but were instead dynamic inventions of the people who created and comprised them. Long before Europeans arrived in the Americas, Native societies repeatedly emerged, collapsed, disappeared, merged, and reformed and reshaped themselves in response to social, environmental, cultural, and technological changes, in what scholars have come to call ethnogenesis.[14] Part of the problem with tribalism, it turns out, was that the concept itself—as least as it used to be defined and understood—simply did not accurately reflect the fluid, flexible, often heterogeneous, innovation-embracing communities it was supposed to describe.

The arrival of Europeans in the Americas accelerated and intensified many of these processes. Trade, diplomacy, warfare, and even rituals prompted migrations and human exchanges that created what Patricia Albers has called "geographically far-ranging and ethnically mixed social formations" on the Plains and elsewhere.[15] Buffeted by the impact of newly introduced European diseases and heightened intertribal conflicts sparked by disputes over territory and access to trade, many Indian communities turned to wholesale adoption of war captives to augment shrinking populations. (Young Man Afraid of His Horses's aunt, as it turns out, was herself a former war captive.) From the adoption of hundreds, even thousands, of captives into Iroquois communities during the late 1600s, to the incorporation of fugitive African American slaves into Creek and later Seminole communities in the 1700s, to the ritual taking of captives by the Pawnee for the Morning Star ceremony in the early 1800s, to the more prosaic intermarriages and adoptions that cemented alliances, tribes never were hermetically sealed, neatly bounded entities.[16] In some cases, as members of different communities intermarried or adopted mixed residency patterns as a means of forging political alliances and trade networks, originally distinct ethnic groups merged into one single community.[17] Viewed in this light, Young Man Afraid of His Horses's connections to the Crows and his willingness and ability to see Crows and Lakotas as being linked in ways that transcended linguistic or cultural difference begins to seem less extraordinary, and tribes themselves begin to resemble the polyglot, ethnically messy modern urban Indian communities they have often been counterpoised to—"new" peoples living in new ways, often in new places.

On the Great Plains, where Native peoples ranged widely in pursuit of the buffalo (and ranged even more widely after the introduction of horses), and where the vastness of the region led to the development of equally vast trade networks, these same phenomena manifested themselves.[18] Examining the region straddling the U.S.–Canadian border, both Albers and Susan Sharrock have found evidence of the intermixing and merging of formerly distinct Cree and Assiniboine bands during the late eighteenth and early nineteenth centuries.[19] Extending his inquiry farther back in time and farther to the west, Theodore Binnema documented similar patterns. Originally conceived as a history of the Siksika Blackfeet in the late 1700s and early 1800s, Binnema's *Common and Contested Ground* became instead a regional history of Native peoples on the northwestern Great Plains, after Binnema found it impossible to ignore what he called "the reality of intraethnic communities and interethnic connections" that linked the peoples who defined themselves as Blackfoot, Cree, Assiniboine, Crow, Shoshoni, and Flathead. Indeed, Binnema stated that tribal affiliation "was only one way in which people identified themselves—and the evidence gave me no reason to believe that it was usually the most important."[20] In an environment charged with new technologies, means of living, and economic opportunities—as well as repeated, devastating epidemics and recurring warfare—the ability to create links to other people was vital to survival. It was these ties that Young Man Afraid of His Horses sought to use in 1889 to consult and plan with the Crows "for the protection of our people."

In 1889, of course, Young Man Afraid of His Horses's efforts to meet with the Crows ran afoul of the Crow agent's intransigence. Yet here too, recent scholarship has begun to suggest limits to federal officials' ability to exert complete domination over their Indian wards, and Young Man Afraid of His Horses himself provides an instructive case in point. Young Man Afraid of His Horses's reference to the three horses previously given him by the Crows suggest that his 1889 journey was not his first trip to the Crow Reservation. When did Young Man Afraid of His Horses first begin to visit the Crows? And how had he obtained permission (or circumvented Office of Indian Affairs regulations) to do so?

Ironically, it was Pine Ridge agents' need for support from influential Oglalas such as Young Man Afraid of His Horses that helps explain the latter's ability to travel to Montana in the first place. It was to court his influence and gain his backing for government initiatives—particularly as a counterweight to the resistance of other Oglalas like the aging Red Cloud—that then–Pine Ridge agent Valentine McGillycuddy began granting permission for Young Man Afraid of His Horses to visit the Crows as early as 1883.[21] And despite the rebuff from the Crows' agent that prompted the letter to Crook in 1889, Young Man Afraid of His Horses would return to the Crow Reservation the following year and continue to travel there on a nearly annual basis until his death in 1893—a death that occurred while en route to Montana to visit his Crow kin.[22]

Young Man Afraid of His Horses's ability to use McGillycuddy (and his successor, Gallagher) for his own ends illustrates a point made by Nicholas Thomas: far from being monolithic, stable, and hegemonic, colonialism exists and functions in multiple, shifting, and unstable forms. "Colonial projects are construed, misconstrued, adapted, and enacted by actors whose subjectivities are fractured," Thomas writes. "Half here, half there, sometimes disloyal, sometimes almost 'on the side' of the people they patronize and dominate, and against the interests of some metropolitan office."[23] Within these cracks and interstices in the foundations of American Indian policy, Young Man Afraid of His Horses found space to maneuver, setting conditions on and demanding concessions and privileges in return for his cooperation. Even when the Crow agent called in the military to meet the disruptive threat Young Man Afraid of His Horses evidently posed to good order at Crow, Young Man Afraid of His Horses was able to dodge the Office of Indian Affairs' bureaucracy entirely by appealing directly to the military high command in the form of George Crook, the man who ultimately commanded the soldiers the agent had relied on.

Young Man Afraid of His Horses was not, of course, an ordinary Oglala. His status and prestige opened doors for him—particularly to the Pine Ridge agent's office and George Crook's mailbox—in ways that may not have been the case for less influential individuals. However, he was not alone in using what political scientist James Scott has called "weapons of the weak."[24] At Pine Ridge, Crow, and elsewhere, Indians of more humble backgrounds proved equally adept at manipulating, dodging, selectively adapting to, or simply ignoring federal policies designed to restrict their movement and autonomy. At nearly the same time that Young Man Afraid of His Horses was writing to Crook, for example, Agent Gallagher reported to his superiors that nearly 200 Pine Ridge Lakotas were absent from the reservation, traveling with Wild West shows. Some had obtained consent from the agent to leave the reservation to take jobs with the shows, but fully half, Gallagher noted, were "absent . . . without permission."[25]

In the late 1800s and early 1900s, federal Indian policy was fraught with contradictions and limitations. The government's goal of "individualizing" Indians and freeing them from the limits of tribalism (which ironically demanded that the government assert almost total control over its charges to control their behavior), also occasionally required allowing Indians to leave the reservation to work, or to reward good behavior, or even simply to attempt to encourage good behavior in the future. At the same time, chronic shortages in funding and manpower further hamstrung the ability of agents to restrain their subjects. Under such circumstances, federal control often proved to be unexpectedly feeble. Studying late nineteenth-century Kiowa history, Jacki Thompson Rand has argued that previous generations of scholars "have exaggerated historic colonial power and granted it a uniformity of purpose and action that is assumed rather than an accurate reflection of local conditions."[26]

None of this, of course, is to say that government policies were not spectacularly successful in certain areas, particularly in transferring valuable resources such as land from Indian to non-Indian hands. It cannot be emphasized too strongly that individuals (and groups) who defied government regulations and resisted government control too brazenly could face severe and sometimes even lethal consequences, as would be demonstrated by the killing of several hundred Lakotas during the suppression of the Lakota Ghost Dance in 1890.[27] Yet even in the face of these threats, Indians continued to act to maintain and defend cultural beliefs and values, and assert a degree of control over their lives. Whether it be Lakotas sneaking off their reservations to sign up with touring Wild West shows, Nez Perces preserving existing community relationships in accepting allotments, or Cheyenne tribal judges refusing to fully implement government prohibitions on polygamy, Native Americans repeatedly demonstrated their ability to evade, thwart, or limit the stated objectives of those assigned to control them.[28] Nowhere was this resistance more visibly successful than in the continued survival of Indian communities themselves, but in the late 1800s, resistance to federal domination was also visible in the determination of individuals like Young Man Afraid of His Horses to not only maintain existing ties with other Indian communities, but forge new ones as well.

Despite the regulations and restrictions the U. S. government attempted to enforce, the late 1800s and early 1900s proved to be an era of exceptional cultural and social vitality on the Northern Plains. From the rise and spread of religious movements such as the Ghost Dance and peyotism, to more secular developments such as the rise of powwow dancing, Native Americans across the region regularly defied their federal overseers to travel, communicate, and exchange information, ideas, rituals, beliefs, and even people across tribal lines. However, though a rich literature has emerged on these subjects, most studies of these developments have tended to take a fairly narrow focus, either through anthropological analysis of one single phenomenon (peyotism, for example) or though historical study of the impact of one of these developments on a single tribal group (such as the Lakota Ghost Dance).[29] Relatively few of these studies, however, have investigated the bigger, broader, preexisting networks of people and tribes that made the diffusion of these movements possible or examined the impact that those networks and those developments had on how Native peoples thought about themselves and each other.[30] Likewise, most of the numerous tribal histories that have appeared in recent decades take as their main focus the relationship between a particular tribe and the United States, particularly during the reservation era, rather than closely examining their subjects' relationships with other Native peoples and the way those relationships shaped Indians' perceptions of themselves and each other.[31]

Uniting the Tribes takes as its focus the people Young Man Afraid of His Horses claimed kinship with: the Crows. It is not, however, a tribal history of the Crow people, or a history of the Crow Indian Reservation.[32] Instead, it focuses outward on the history of the contacts, connections, and relationships that were forged between the people who would become the modern Crow tribe—eventually residing on the Crow Indian Reservation in south-central Montana—and other native peoples. In a sense, it is an intellectual history of Native American thinking about the nature of community on the Northern Plains in the 1800s and early 1900s. It does not purport to speak for Young Man Afraid of His Horses, but it does seek to understand how he and other Native Americans interacted with each other and the consequences those interactions had on their sense of identity and community. It documents those moments when people from different tribes came into contact, and the possibilities and limitations revealed by those incidents. It is a history of pathways explored, roads not taken, and avenues begun and then abandoned.

In doing so, it follows the call made by historian Robert Berkhofer a generation ago for more studies of Indian–Indian relationships, including ones that transcended village or tribal boundaries.[33] It is also inspired by Gregory Evans Dowd's *A Spirited Resistance,* which examined the efforts of Native peoples throughout eastern North America to unite in the face of European— and later U.S.—colonization during the late 1700s and early 1800s. Dowd documented how prophets among Native communities inspired a cultural rebirth that called upon people from all tribes to join together spiritually and politically, from Delawares, Miamis, and Shawnees in the north to Creeks and Cherokees in the south. Dowd provocatively argued that "Native Americans themselves, unlike many of their historians, could think continentally"—a sentiment Young Man Afraid of His Horses might well have endorsed.[34]

Far from dividing people, tribalism on the Northern Plains in the early to mid-nineteenth century actually provided a means to bring people of diverse origins together. Young Man Afraid of His Horses may not have been a typical Oglala in terms of his family's status within Lakota society, but the milieu within which he was raised—where community boundaries were by definition and by necessity flexible and inclusive—was entirely typical of Northern Plains communities at the time. The same ability to incorporate and absorb outsiders that created the ties between Young Man Afraid of His Horses and the Crows also facilitated exchanges of ideas, information, culture, and material goods between individuals, families, and communities—even among those normally hostile toward one another.

Nineteenth-century tribalism, in other words, carried within it the latent potential for the growth of a larger sense of Indian identity, a potential that flowered during the early reservation period. The establishment of reservations removed old sources of tension and conflict between Northern Plains peoples while fostering a sense of solidarity among members of different tribes by giving all a common, shared relationship with the United States. And though the destruction of tribal autonomy closed off certain aspects of Native life, these dense networks of kinship, communication, and exchange became, if anything, even more relevant, encouraging the maintenance of old and the growth of new patterns of intertribal contact for Native Americans—like Young Man Afraid of His Horses—determined to resist American domination.

As it turns out, Young Man Afraid of His Horses was not the only non-

Crow Indian to come to the Crow Reservation during this period. Other Indians came to Crow to work and for sustenance at a time when poverty and economic instability afflicted many Indian communities. Some came temporarily; others settled permanently or married into the Crow community—and Crows, true to their concepts of kinship and community, would adopt or propose to adopt many of these people well into the twentieth century. Still others came for more social reasons: to visit relatives, or simply to maintain traditions of travel and visiting that remained vibrant even within a reservation context. As they did so, these people too shared ideas, beliefs, and culture with their hosts as their ancestors had done. A history that ignores these people ignores a central element of life on the Crow Reservation in the late nineteenth and early twentieth centuries.

The sense of Indianness that emerged as a result of these processes was not a harbinger of acculturation or assimilation to non-Indian norms. Nor did it signify the disintegration of separate and distinct tribal communities or cultures. It coexisted with rather than eroded discrete tribal identities. However, just as reservations allowed these older elements of Plains Indian life to flourish and gain new meaning, they also contributed to their eventual downfall.

The need to conserve increasingly scarce reservation resources like land, jobs, and the associated benefits that came with tribal membership would eventually lead many Crows to embrace a more restrictive definition of identity that would exclude people like Young Man Afraid of His Horses and others of mixed tribal heritage, as well as individuals and families with no preexisting ties to Crows who came to the Crow Reservation for the opportunities it had once offered. What eventually emerged from all this in the early twentieth century was a narrow, bureaucratic, and exclusive form of tribalism—the tribalism that still legally defines Plains tribes today. It was far different from the flexible, expansive, and permeable community structures that dominated the Northern Plains before and during the early reservation era. The transformation of tribalism that took place on the Crow Reservation and elsewhere on the Northern Plains did carry certain benefits for those who could fit under the new definition of who could be—and what it meant—to be Crow, or Oglala Lakota, or Northern Cheyenne, but it also compromised efforts to bring tribal peoples together to collectively challenge their subordination to U.S. rule.

The narrative structure of this book is broken into two parts. Part I examines Crow relationships with other peoples on the Northern Plains during the prereservation period. It focuses on the events occurring in the region during this era that led to conflict, cooperation, communication, and exchange—sometimes all at once. It also examines how those interactions were structured by and shaped the structure of Crow culture and society, as well as that of the peoples the Crows interacted with.

The two chapters comprising Part I of this book consist of case studies examining Crow contacts with the Blackfeet and Lakota before the 1880s. Although much of the existing scholarly literature on Crow–Lakota and Crow–Blackfeet relations focuses on war and conflict, the emphasis in these chapters is on what anthropologist Raymond Fogelson has called "peacefare." Chapter 1 analyzes patterns of interaction between Crows and Blackfeet, particularly cultural and social exchanges. It documents how shifts in economic patterns on the Northern Plains, such the rise of the European fur trade, brought members of these two communities closer together, even as it intensified competition for valuable resources. Chapter 2 examines Crow–Lakota relations during the 1860s, more specifically during the conflict between the United States and the Lakotas and their allies sparked by the Bozeman Trail, an emigrant route to Montana that ran squarely through one of the richest remaining game regions on the Northern Plains. During this conflict, the Crows—who had seen the region largely usurped by the Lakota, but who still claimed it as part of their homeland—informally allied themselves with the United States, but nevertheless pursued objectives that often saw them siding with their putative Lakota enemies. In this delicate political balancing act, preexisting ties between the two groups (particularly those between the Man Afraid family and Crows) played a vital role in Crow–Lakota interaction and communication.

In Part II, the setting shifts to the Crow Reservation during the 1880s and beyond. Chapter 3 examines the continued vitality of intertribal contact, and the covert—and sometimes overt—political dimensions of visiting between Crows and other Native peoples in the late 1800s and early 1900s. Chapter 4 looks at one of the most significant changes wrought by reservations: the destruction of autonomous hunter-gatherer economies and their replacement by increasingly wage labor–oriented economic systems. At Crow, these developments, symbolized most vividly by the Crow Irrigation Survey, a massive irrigation construction project, served as a new conduit for contact, bringing Indian workers from across the Northern Plains to the Crow Reservation, but also generated disputes over who was entitled to work at Crow. At the same time, wage labor contributed to the creation of entirely new strains of pan-

Indianism at Crow, mainly through the introduction of peyotism by Southern Cheyenne irrigation workers.

Chapter 5 studies the Indian community that existed on the Crow Reservation at the beginning of the twentieth century, finding it to be far more diverse and heterogeneous than the reservation communities so often found in tribal histories. Far from being the exclusive residence of officially recognized Crow Indians, the Crow Reservation was in many senses a multiethnic community, including not just Crows of mixed descent who preserved their ties and affiliations with other tribal communities, but also non-Crow Indian workers, long-term residents, and individuals and families who found at Crow both a comfortable Indian environment and a place of refuge from social discord, unhappy marriages, or poverty on their home reservations. As such, the Crow Reservation reflected not just new currents and elements in Indian life during the reservation era, but also older traditions of flexible, permeable community boundaries that readily incorporated and accepted outsiders.

The final chapter tracks the breakdown of this inclusive community at Crow in the early twentieth century and its replacement by a more rigid and bureaucratically defined definition of community, the process by which the modern Crow tribe came into existence. Government officials and Crows themselves played a key role in this process of attempting to define who belonged at Crow and was entitled to a share of tribal resources. In the process of doing so, the criteria for acceptance as a Crow shifted from a bottom-up construction of community marked by acceptance and incorporation into a family to a top-down construction requiring approval from the Crow tribal government and Office of Indian Affairs officials. Ultimately this narrowing of community led to the rejection of pantribal political activism by the Crow tribal council in the 1920s, even as older, more flexible concepts of identity continued to flourish in cultural and spiritual movements such as powwows and peyotism. The book's Conclusion examines the significance and implications of these changes for Native Americans at the time, and for our understanding of Native American history.

A NOTE ON TERMINOLOGY

As noted above, the terms "tribe" and "tribalism" have become increasingly contentious in recent decades, with some historians and anthropologists preferring to refer to groups like the Crow and Lakota as "band societies," a term

I myself will make use of. However, I do still believe there is a place for concepts such as "tribe" and "tribalism." Although groups like the Crow and Lakota lacked a formal, centralized governing structure during the prereservation period, there is no question that individuals like Young Man Afraid of His Horses (and Crows, Lakotas, and other Native peoples on the Northern Plains) regarded themselves as belonging to a society or community larger than that of the particular band with which they were affiliated at any particular time. Among the Lakota, these communities included intermediate groups such as the Oglala, Hunkpapa, and Sicangu, as well as the larger Lakota society that encompassed all these groups. The same was true for Crows who recognized their affiliation with the Mountain, River, or Kicked-in-the-Belly Crows, as well as the larger Crow community. The difficulty scholars have had in classifying and creating models for these groups does not necessarily invalidate the reality of their existence.

Nor does the historically constructed nature of these communities—the fact that their boundaries, composition, and relationships with one another (both internally and externally) varied over time—necessarily invalidate the concept of such a thing as the Crow tribe. To admit that tribes were (and are) historically constructed communities—"imagined," to borrow a term from Benedict Anderson—is not to say they are not real.[35] Tribalism, like tribes themselves, has to be understood as a dynamic, historical concept. Just as different tribal communities differed from each other, so too did each change over time. Part of this book's agenda is to explore what tribalism (or, to use a less loaded word, community) and identity meant to Native peoples on the Northern Plains at different times and in different contexts, and in particular its shift from a kinship-based society open to outsiders via intermarriage or adoption and without a centralized governing body, to a society possessing a centralized government and closed to official entry by individuals of foreign birth. To discard the terms "tribes" and "tribalism" altogether is to risk throwing the baby out with the bathwater. What is required instead is an increased sensitivity to the inherent complexity of such entities—a complexity shared by nearly all human social units.

There is an important caveat here. My use of the term "tribe" is *not* meant to imply that these entities were the sole source of an individual or group's identity, affiliation, or connections. As Binnema and others have pointed out, abundant evidence exists of individual members or subgroups within a particular tribe having ties to other individuals or groups within other tribes, as indeed was the case with Young Man Afraid of His Horses.[36] Native Americans, like most people throughout history, were (and are) complex people capable of juggling or maintaining several different identities or affiliations at the same time. This book explores the ways in which differing, multiple, competing, and coexisting concepts of community, both within tribal communities and beyond the boundaries of those communities, emerged and either persisted, changed, or were discarded in response to the changing conditions of life on the Northern Plains in the nineteenth and early twentieth centuries.

PART ONE

Intimate Enemies

In the early 1920s, while narrating his life story to ethnographer William Wild-schut, the elderly Crow Two Leggings recounted an episode in which inter-tribal hostility unexpectedly gave way to peaceful interaction. After the killing of a Crow hunter by Piegans, a young Two Leggings joined a party of war-riors bent on revenge. After several days' pursuit, Two Leggings and the other Crows finally caught up to the killers. "As we raced over a ridge they were forc-ing their tired horses up a high hill," he recalled. "When I reached the top I and three others were a few horse lengths away. I put an arrow in my bow and yelled as I chased them down the other side."

In their haste the Crows ignored their surroundings and suddenly found themselves nearly in the middle of a Piegan camp. Roles reversed as pursuers became the pursued. While the Crows retreated back up the ridge, a Piegan with a white-painted face and knotted hair put an arrow into the shield slung across Two Leggings's back. As Two Leggings prepared to loose his own arrow, "another Piegan stood beside this man as I was aiming and shouted in our language for me not to shoot. When he asked about his brother, Poor Wolf, I recognized him." The Crow-speaking Piegan, named Strap, was one of several Piegans (including Poor Wolf) who had been captured as children by the Crows several years earlier. The captives had escaped just before the Piegan raid, and now Strap sought to use this unexpected meeting to get infor-mation about his sibling. Two Leggings told Strap that Poor Wolf had also left the Crow camp and had not been seen or heard from since then.

Tensions were slow to dissolve as the two groups came together. After shooting the arrow at Two Leggings, the white-faced Piegan aimed a gun at him, only to have it broken against a rock by Strap. "As we drew near, a Pie-gan asked if I had been wounded and I said no," Two Leggings remembered. "If they had not gathered about me so quickly I would have killed the man who had shot at me." Despite these lingering animosities, Strap's intervention succeeded in defusing a potentially deadly confrontation. "We made friends with those Piegans," Two Leggings said. "Many times they promised they would not shoot our buffalo or steal our horses. But they always lied and soon afterwards we found them again in our country."[1]

Two histories collide in the story of Two Leggings's unexpected encounter with Strap. The first, much better-known history is that of the apparently intractable, unending cycle of hostility between Native communities. On the surface, the setting of this episode and its postscript—the killing of a Crow hunter by Piegans and the eventual resumption of Crow–Piegan conflict—seem to reinforce images of irreconcilable hostilities between Crows and "traditional" or "hereditary" enemies such as the Piegan and Lakota. The second, lesser-known history, concerns the startling frequency with which Native peoples, even from communities normally hostile to one another, met peacefully on common ground to exchange information, ideas, rituals, goods, and even people—a history exemplified in this case by Strap's presence and actions.

Strap succeeded in turning enmity into friendship by crossing ethnic and linguistic boundaries. He altered the context of the encounter so radically that both sides had little choice but to put down their weapons. Through Strap's use of the Crow language and his invocation of kinship, Two Leggings was forced to realize that one of his adversaries was someone who had lived for several years with the Crows; indeed, in all likelihood both Strap and Poor Wolf probably had been adopted into a Crow family at some point, making them potential clan or kin relatives to members of the Crow war party. Conversely, the Piegans accompanying Strap were forced to defer to their fellow tribesman's desire for information about his brother, as well as to Strap's very real connection (linguistic and potentially filial) to the men they had been attempting to kill just moments before.

Throughout the nineteenth century, Crows maintained complex, dynamic relationships with other Indian communities on the Northern Plains. Though some of these relationships tended to be marked by conflict and others by amity, these conditions were not fixed. Circumstances both large and small—the need to gain or defend hunting territories, the desire for revenge or information about a relative, even the desire for spiritual power—dictated interactions between Crows and other Indians. Circumstance in particular marked Crow relations with both the Piegan (and the larger Blackfeet community the Piegan were a part of) and the Lakota. Though rivals for trade, territory, and wealth, Crows and Piegans found themselves drawn to each other on the basis of shared beliefs regarding the cultural and supernatural origins of individual and community power, as well as by the exchanges of people like Strap that occurred as a natural result of conflict. Similarly, the need to protect the valued hunting grounds of the Powder River Country after the blazing and military occupation of the Bozeman Trail by Americans in the 1860s would bring Crows and Lakotas—formerly rivals for control of that region—together.

In these interactions, people such as Strap would play a crucial role. The transfer of people between communities created individuals ideally suited to serve as intermediaries and conduits for the exchange of information, ideas, rituals, and goods, and who also acted as liaisons in large-scale tribal and smaller-scale personal diplomacy. Though this process did not lead to the merger of or even the creation of enduring alliances between Crows and their Lakota and Piegan neighbors, people who possessed ties to multiple communities also possessed the ability to cross ethnic boundaries and bring otherwise antagonistic people together, at least temporarily, even in the cases of war captives like Strap who did not remain permanently with their adoptive community. Paradoxically, on the Northern Plains in the prereservation era, personal, often intimate ties linked enemies as much as allies. The legacies thus created— like the memory of Two Leggings's encounter with Strap—would linger long after the establishment of American hegemony in the region.

CHAPTER ONE

Symbiotic Enemies:
Crows and Blackfeet, 1800–1885

At the close of the eighteenth century, Crows and Blackfeet were relative strangers to one another culturally, socially, and geographically. Originally from the northern fringes of the Canadian plains, the peoples of what would later become known as the Blackfeet Confederacy—Piegans, Bloods, and Siksikas (or Blackfeet proper)—had slowly migrated southwest, completing the expulsion of the Kutenai and Shoshoni from the northwestern Plains by the end of the eighteenth century.[1] The Crows, meanwhile, had split off from the horticultural, semisedentary Hidatsa, leaving the Missouri River valley to become buffalo-hunting nomads in what would become south-central and southeast Montana and northeastern Wyoming.[2] In contrast to the three main Blackfeet groups, the Crow were split into two main divisions, the Mountain Crows and the River Crows. The River Crows ranged mostly north of the Yellowstone River, while the Mountain Crows occupied the Yellowstone valley itself and the Bighorn and Powder River basins to the south. By the early 1800s, an offshoot of the Mountain Crows called the Kicked-in-the-Bellies had begun to emerge, ranging south of the Bighorn Mountains in the vicinity of the Shoshone and Wind rivers.[3]

These migrations—of Siouan-speaking former horticulturalists and Algonquian-speaking parklands/plains dwellers—were just two elements in a broader pattern. The Northern Plains was in a state of flux in the late eighteenth century, increasing in both population and diversity. In part this marked a continuation of a trend that began as early as 1500, with the end of a 300-year droughty period, known to archeologists as the Pacific climatic episode, that most likely led to a resurgence in buffalo numbers in the region and an expansion of horticultural settlements northward along the Missouri River. The northward spread of horses in the late 1600s and early 1700s served to accelerate this trend. By the early eighteenth century, "new" Plains peoples were becoming a significant presence, creating an environment where newcomers, existing residents, and peoples in the midst of social and cultural transformations jostled for position, prestige, and power.[4]

Despite anthropologists' retrospective description of the Plains as a "culture area," these developments brought widely disparate peoples together in the region. By 1800 no fewer than four major linguistic groups were represented among Northern Plains peoples, including Algonquian speakers such as the Blackfeet, Plains Cree, Cheyenne, and Gros Ventre; Siouan-speaking Crows, Hidatsas, Mandans, and Lakotas; Athabaskan-speaking Sarcees; and Caddoan-speaking Arickaras, to say nothing of differences in specific languages and dialects.[5] Culturally and geographically, the origins of Northern Plains residents ranged from early inhabitants like the Kiowa, Shoshoni, Mandan, and Hidatsa, to former horticulturalists turned nomads such as the Cheyenne from the Midwest; the prairie and tallgrass plains-dwelling Lakota from what would become Minnesota and the eastern Dakotas; and the horticultural Arickara migrating up the Missouri River, in addition to the Crows and Blackfeet, each group with its own distinct history and cultural, social, and religious practices.[6]

The relative foreignness and unfamiliarity of Crows and Blackfeet with one another is reflected by the absence of mutual references to both groups in the accounts of early European traders and explorers in the late 1700s. While Blackfeet informants frequently spoke of Shoshonis, Flatheads, Kutenais, and other tribes to British traders operating in the Saskatchewan River basin, references to Crows remained conspicuously absent. Similarly, though the Crows themselves did not come into regular contact with Europeans until around 1800, the first European to travel with and write about the Crows, Francois Antoine Laroque, a French Canadian trader with the Northwest Company and a careful chronicler of intergroup relations on the Northern Plains, also recorded no mention of the Blackfeet.[7] The two groups seem not to have come into sustained, close contact with one another until the end of the eighteenth century, a by-product of the Blackfeet migration and the eviction of the Shoshoni from the Plains that opened up new hunting ranges in central Montana that both the Blackfeet and Crow moved to exploit.[8]

Both groups impressed early European observers with their wealth and power. North West Company fur trader Alexander Henry the Younger described the Blackfeet as a proud and haughty people. Aided by firearms obtained first through Cree middlemen and later directly from British traders, the Blackfeet had not only driven their enemies south, but had also amassed large numbers of horses, a critical tool for hunting and tracking the bison herds in the new Plains lifestyle and thus a key measure of wealth and status. In 1809 Henry claimed that some Siksikas owned up to fifty horses, while the number of horses owned by individual Piegans—the vanguard of the Blackfeet migration, and thus best positioned to acquire horses from more southerly groups by

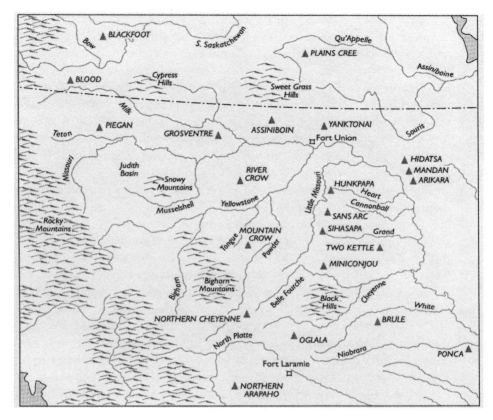

Map 1. The Northern Great Plains, circa 1850.

either raids or trade—could number in the hundreds.[9] At the same time, the establishment of permanent trading posts on the northern fringes of Blackfeet territory in the late 1700s by the North West Company and Hudson's Bay Company increased their importance as primary producers of furs and food (primarily buffalo meat) for traders, while giving them greater access to European goods.[10]

Although they lagged behind the Blackfeet in acquiring direct connections to European traders, the Crows were tied into a Native trade nexus that gave them a middleman role between horticultural villagers on the Missouri River and the horse-rich tribes of the Plateau and central Plains. Every year Crow traders, and even whole villages, traveled east to trade dried meat, robes, and horses for corn and other foodstuffs at the villages occupied by the Mandans and the Crows' Hidatsa relatives; the opposite process occurred in the other direction as Crows traded the fruits of their hunts (along with Missouri River corn) to the Shoshoni, Nez Perce, or Kiowa for horses. By the early 1800s, the Crows' Native trade links had given them considerable wealth in horses and a reputation as some of the finest judges of horseflesh on the Plains.[11] A trader who met the Mountain Crows in 1833 noted that "their trade was all in substantial goods, which kept them always well-dressed, and extremely rich in horses." He added that the Crows were savvy negotiators who accepted only the "finest and highest-priced goods" and shunned the tainted liquor offered them by European traders.[12]

The burgeoning wealth of the Crows and Blackfeet did more than make them objects of European traders' attention. It also made them natural targets for attacks, both from other tribes and from each other. Hunting territories greatly expanded by the availability of horses and the demands of the fur trade had to be defended or augmented. And despite their utility, horses themselves proved to be distressingly vulnerable to the ravages of Northern Plains winters, requiring frequent restocking by trade, or, more frequently, raids on neighboring communities.[13] As a partial result of this, the subsequent history of Crow–Blackfeet relations has rarely been understood in forms other than that of conflict. However, as Strap's story indicates, conflict was only one dimension of a complex, multifaceted relationship that often brought Crows and Blackfeet together, and whose ramifications extended into the realms of individual status and prestige, community demographics, and the unending quest for spiritual power and access to material resources that underlay tribal life in the nineteenth century.

During the early and mid-1800s, both Crows and Blackfeet lived in band societies. Each band was a collection of affiliated families who chose to live, hunt, and travel together. Although members of a band were connected to other bands in a larger tribal community by language, culture, and kinship, each band possessed political autonomy in conducting its own affairs. Neither the Blackfeet nor the Crows (or their major subdivisions, such as the Piegan and River Crow) possessed the formal, centralized leadership structures that typified European nation-states. Band membership was fluid, with individuals and families able to leave their old band and join a new one at any time. The autonomy possessed by both a band and its members placed formidable demands on individuals aspiring to leadership positions, who were expected to exercise good judgment and discretion in forging consensus among their followers.[14]

Among the Crows, eligibility for band leadership was open only to men holding the status of a *batse'tse* ("good man"). The definition of a *batse'tse* reflected the growing importance of warfare as a means of gaining wealth and status in Crow communities. Criteria for becoming a *batse'tse* included successfully leading a war party, capturing a horse picketed inside an enemy camp, being the first to touch (or count coup on) an enemy, and seizing a weapon from an opponent in hand-to-hand combat.[15] The qualities that becoming a *batse'tse* required—courage, wisdom, and the ability to lead a group in a dangerous and uncertain environment—closely mirrored those of a capable band leader. In contrast, the Blackfeet in the late eighteenth century possessed a parallel leadership structure consisting of civil chiefs and war chiefs, in which civil chief status appears to have been at least partly hereditary. However, as warfare shifted away from ritualized, large-scale encounters to more individualized raiding with the introduction of guns and horses, leadership qualifications in Blackfeet society also began to emphasize individual merit and achievement. The more egalitarian social structures and distribution of wealth that typified pedestrian hunters began to fade as differentials in horse ownership allowed some individuals to amass and transport greater amounts of material goods.[16] Although early nineteenth-century Crow and Blackfeet tribal institutions retained many of the pre-horse-era components that promoted community well-being and unity, increasing individual and group wealth and power were working subtle changes among both communities.[17]

The rise of the European fur trade was a major factor in these developments. Both the Crow and Blackfeet were well positioned to serve as major suppliers for the trade, able to exploit game-rich regions on the Northern Plains, the Rocky Mountain front, and outlying ranges such as the Bighorns, Crazy Mountains, and Cypress Hills. In 1829 William Ashley claimed that the Blackfeet beaver trade alone was "more valuable than one half of all the other tribes" west of the Missouri, while beaver hides from Crow country were rated as equal to the best "Mountain Beaver" and superior to "Missouri Beaver" in the thickness and quality of their fur.[18] Equally important, the ability to tap mountain and grassland ecotones enabled both groups to survive the collapse of the beaver trade in the 1830s and transition to its successor trade in buffalo robes.[19] However, in occupying adjacent territories, hunters from each group routinely transgressed into boundary regions claimed by the other, as Two Leggings suggested. The likelihood of such collisions was magnified by the fact that, being too dangerous for entire bands to live in and exploit on a permanent basis, such boundary regions often contained the richest game resources.[20]

Besides being brought into competition as producers of furs, initially Crows and Blackfeet were tied into competing trade networks. In general, trade systems on the Northern Plains took the form of parallel chains running from east to west. Communities usually maintained amicable relations with contiguous links in their chain but more hostile relationships with competing groups possessing similar specializations in parallel chains.[21] In the early 1800s, Crow trade flowed through Mandan and Hidatsa middlemen in villages on the Missouri River in present-day North Dakota to French, and later American, traders operating out of St. Louis. By the 1830s these connections were supplanted by the opening of American fur trading posts on the upper Missouri and Yellowstone rivers to the north and on the North Platte River to the south.[22] In contrast, early Blackfeet links to Cree middlemen were eventually replaced by ties to British traders located on the North Saskatchewan River. Not until Fort Piegan was established at the mouth of the Marias River in 1831 would the Blackfeet (and particularly the Piegan) begin to be drawn into the American orbit. Even then, however, Crows and Blackfeet remained rivals as producers of furs.[23]

The rise of new economic patterns based on the availability of horses and the Euro-American fur trade intersected with culture in shaping both Crow and Blackfeet society. For Native peoples, the significance of horses and the fur trade lay not only in the opportunities for gaining wealth and status that they provided, but in the way they shifted perceptions of the most efficacious sources of the spiritual power necessary for attaining those ends—the spiritual capital required for gaining material and social capital. A *batse'tse*'s authority, for example, derived not only from his personal character and abilities, but ultimately from the spiritual guardians whose powers he could tap for the well-being of himself and his followers. For Crows and Blackfeet, the most powerful forces shaping these perceptions were the parallel rise of equestrianism and the fur trade, and the sometimes cataclysmic decline of horticultural villagers (such as the Mandan, Hidatsa, and Arickara) and nomads (such as the Cree and Assiniboine) less well positioned to amass and exploit the advantages conferred by horses in the early nineteenth century.

Among Crows and Blackfeet (as among Native Americans in general), wealth and status were viewed less as a sign of individual skill or ambition than as evidence of the efficacy and power of one's spiritual helpers. "In Blackfoot eyes," Gerald Conaty notes, "success is not necessarily expressed as possession of material goods or the means of production. Success comes from access to spiritual power which, if honored and respected, may result in material wealth."[24] In a similar vein, a recurring motif in Crow mythology is that of the orphan, a child "without relatives," who, abandoned by the community of his birth, earns the favor and protection of the Above Ones to become powerful and return to his people in triumph.[25]

Before the arrival of horses, the Mandan and Hidatsa in particular had been viewed as possessing the most powerful cultural and spiritual capital among tribes in the region. Though not immune to the vicissitudes of climate or other circumstances, the horticulturalists' ability to grow crops and store surpluses of food and other goods in their earth-lodge villages meant that they generally lived farther from the knife-edge of subsistence than pedestrian buffalo hunters. These same surpluses (and the predictable, relatively stable locations of their villages) also made them a magnet for trade.[26]

Given the spiritually oriented worldview of Plains peoples, economic strength led to cultural emulation and borrowing. Many scholars, including Leslie Spier, Clark Wissler, Preston Holder, Alice Kehoe, and Howard Harrod, have argued for the village cultures of the Middle Missouri as the ultimate progenitors of much of what has become known as typical Plains Indian culture, including the Sun Dance. Among both the Blackfeet and the Crow, the Sun Dance seems to predate European contact to a time when the villages on the Middle Missouri were the center of Native trade, and when the relative wealth of the horticulturalists (and thus the influence of their spiritual practices and religious rituals) was much greater than that of pedestrian buffalo-hunting groups.[27] The arrival of horses and the rise of the European fur trade changed this equation. Both opened new routes to wealth and status, affecting the way Crows and Blackfeet viewed those tribes who had formerly been central not just to trade, but also to cultural and spiritual sources of power—and, concomitantly, the ways Crows and Blackfeet perceived and interacted with each other.

It is difficult to overstate the impact the introduction of horses had on people on the Northern Plains. Before horses, pedestrian hunters either bore their meager possessions on their backs or on travois hauled by dogs. People too badly injured, elderly, or otherwise unable to keep up with the group sometimes had to be abandoned to ensure the survival of the larger community. As the Crow woman Pretty Shield, born in the mid-1800s, put it, "All this was changed by the horse. Even the old people could ride. Ahh, I came into a happy world. There was always fat meat, glad singing, and much dancing in our villages. Our people's hearts were then as light as breath-feathers."[28] Though scholars have debated the relative impact horses had on individuals and gender roles within Native societies, at the community level, they greatly expanded the territory bands could cover and the ability to track and keep up with buffalo herds, enlarged the amount of goods they could possess and carry, and marginally decreased their exposure to epidemics.[29]

Historians' ability to recognize the cultural implications of this shift, however, has been hindered by the sources available to them. To early European traders concerned with markets and material exchange, shifting cultural trends were not a matter of interest and were masked, in any case, by seeming continuities in economic patterns. Initially, European traders mimicked their customers and suppliers by locating their posts at existing trade centers, particularly the Mandan and Hidatsa villages along the Missouri River, and interpreted the drawing power of those villages as an indication of the horticulturalists' continued dominance. After his first meeting with the Crows at a Hidatsa village in 1806, Canadian trader Alexander Henry recorded his impression that the Hidatsa kept "those poor inoffensive Crows in subjection, making their own price for horses and everything else."[30]

Beyond the villages, however, a different dynamic was at work. As horses became increasingly available—and crucial—to hunter-gatherer lifestyles, the last moorings of older patterns of cultural influence were broken. As the wealth and power of the villagers declined and that of the nomads rose, the perceived value of the cultural and religious capital possessed by the former communities dropped, and the spiritual stock of the latter increased in proportion. Although older rituals such as the Sun Dance remained important for maintaining community cohesion, on an individual level, ambitious Crows and Blackfeet began to look to other sources for the spiritual power necessary to attain individual success, including each other. Rituals and objects perceived as possessing the spiritual power requisite for individual success became particular objects of desire and articles of trade and exchange. By the early 1830s, despite the frequent hostilities between the two groups, a trade in Crow war shields embossed with designs representing visionary experiences and the spiritual power they conveyed had developed with the Blackfeet.[31]

The logic of trading with one's enemy, particularly trading objects used in warfare, requires some explanation. For Blackfeet men, the cachet of Crow war shields derived at least partly from the Crows' perceived ability to cope with adverse demographic and geographic circumstances. Significantly smaller in size than surrounding communities such as the Blackfeet and Lakota, the Crows nonetheless proved able to survive, even prosper, in the dangerous environment of the Northern Plains.[32] From a Blackfeet perspective, such an achievement was less a mark of martial prowess than a sign of spiritual favor. Paradoxically, the very success of one's opponent provided a powerful incentive to engage in trade to acquire the physical objects (and the spiritual powers they manifested) that made such success possible. Possession of a spiritually powerful object such as a war shield represented an investment in the future, giving the promise of protection in one's quest for status.

For Crows, a different logic applied. Blessed with a homeland rich in resources desired by others, both Indian and European, Crows nevertheless faced significant obstacles in capitalizing on these advantages. By the 1830s key trading centers—the Mandan and Hidatsa villages on the Missouri River, or newly established European posts on the North Platte River or at the junction of the Yellowstone and Missouri rivers—were increasingly on the periphery of Crow territory, requiring trips that were becoming more difficult and dangerous by the year. Although American traders had repeatedly attempted to establish trading establishments in Crow territory along the Yellowstone River in the early 1800s, these posts, far beyond the limits of steamboat navigation at the time, proved to be too remote, too dangerous, and their returns too limited to survive for more than a few years.[33] For Crow men, trading an essentially defensive item such as a war shield, even to a putative enemy, could be an attractive proposition, depending on the amount of European merchandise it could bring in return, or for the access to trading posts it could provide.

Nor were peaceful exchanges of spiritually powerful commodities limited to individual items such as shields. The Blackfeet, either through purchase or simple adoption, also incorporated other Crow rituals, including tobacco ceremonialism, into their own culture. The rituals of the Crow Tobacco Society, which commemorated the Crows' separation from the Hidatsa and movement onto the Plains, represent what might be called the origin story of the Crows as a separate, distinct people. Beyond that, tobacco ceremonialism (involving the planting and harvesting of a specific variety of tobacco) celebrated the Crows' status as a people spiritually favored by the intercession and gift of tobacco to the Crow culture hero No Vitals, thus carrying meaning for Crows beyond that of the Sun Dance or other rituals.[34] As a distinctive marker of a powerful and independent people, Crow tobacco ceremonialism carried an obvious attraction for rivals like the Blackfeet. In Blackfeet hands, the historically contingent and group-specific elements of the ritual were modified by incorporating tobacco ceremonialism into the existing Blackfeet Beaver Bundle complex. During this same era, other rituals, like the Crow Medicine Water ceremony, that lacked the group-specific elements of Crow tobacco ritual were incorporated in toto into Blackfeet culture.[35]

Although raiding and warfare led inevitably to social and cultural contact between communities, the exchanges occurring between Blackfeet and Crows in the early to mid-1800s are notable for their spiritually charged nature, an attribute not nearly as visible in interactions with other groups. Both the Crows and Blackfeet also adopted rituals and dances from other, more horse- and trade-poor tribes during this era, but these ceremonies, such as the Grass Dance of the Gros Ventre and the Horse and Tea dances of the Assiniboine, were primarily social in nature and carried few, if any, spiritual connotations.[36]

Increasing inequalities in wealth among Crows and Blackfeet gave added impetus to this process. Although Native ethos of redistribution, reciprocity, and extended kinship sought to ensure that even the poorest members of the community did not suffer from want, not all shared equally in the benefits of the fur trade and the new equestrian lifestyle. Individual members of both groups could amass spectacular wealth, as expressed in horses and items of European manufacture. In 1833 the aristocratic European traveler Alexander Philip Maximilian claimed that a recently deceased Piegan chief had owned between 4,000 and 5,000 horses.[37] Although almost certainly an exaggeration, his report illustrated the extreme wealth a few Blackfeet attained through warfare and the fur trade. Trader Charles Larpenteur made the connection between horse wealth and the fur trade explicit: "It is a fine sight to see one of those big men among the Blackfeet, who has two or three lodges, five or six wives, twenty or thirty children, and fifty to a hundred horses; for his trade amounts to upward of $2,000 a year."[38] Although the distribution of horses and wealth appears to have been slightly more equitable among the Crows, disparities remained. A rich Crow family could own a hundred or more horses; fur trader Edwin Denig commented that "an individual is said to be poor when he does not possess at least 20."[39] Wealth and the opportunities for redistribution it represented created alternative avenues to status even for Crow men who did not meet the requirements to be a *batse'tse*. The mid-nineteenth-century Mountain Crow Iron Bull was not particularly renowned as a warrior, but his generosity in redistributing the wealth he gained via participation in the fur trade gave him considerable prestige and authority.[40]

Even as conflict between them mounted in the early 1800s, then, Crows and Blackfeet found themselves inextricably drawn toward each other, not just geographically, but also socially and culturally. Although still remaining distinct and different communities, Crows and Blackfeet increasingly faced "others" who increasingly resembled themselves, the end result of a process fueled by shifting perceptions of power, wealth, and status, by exchanges of ritual and—as will be seen—people.

For materialist-minded Euro-American observers, the increasing cultural connections linking Crows and Blackfeet in the early 1800s were less obvious than
the recurring hostilities between them. The American adventurer Zenas
Leonard typified this attitude in describing a chance meeting between his Crow
companions and a Blackfeet party in 1834. "War," he wrote, "was now their
only desire."[41] Native-generated records, in contrast, provide a more nuanced
view of Crow–Blackfeet relations during the turbulent 1830s and 1840s. Blackfeet winter counts—calendrical devices, usually drawn on a buffalo hide, which
depicted the major event of each year—document both conflict and coexistence. In 1838, two winter counts recorded fighting between Crows and Blackfeet, but another winter count for that year reported a Siksika band and a Crow
band holding a mutual Sun Dance.[42] Two summers later, a Crow named Cut
Nose visited the Siksika and received horses and other gifts from his hosts.
However, the very next year, the Siksika killed a Crow chief (quite possibly
Cut Nose himself), and a Blood man named Walking Crow was killed by the
Crows.[43]

A few hints of the complex nature of Crow–Blackfeet relations do crop up
in white records, however, although usually those of ethnographically minded
missionaries, army officers, or European travelers rather than those of trap-
pers or fur traders. In 1836, Crows and Piegans managed to establish a truce
for purposes of trade that lasted several months. The peace disintegrated after
a party of Crows en route to a Piegan camp killed and scalped a pair of Piegan hunters. The scalps were discovered while the Crows were in the village,
and the killers were immediately put to death, effectively ending the truce.[44]
Failure to follow established patterns of trade could also lead to breakdowns
in amity. According to Maximilian, the trade in Crow war shields during the
1830s ended when the Blackfeet failed to reciprocate for Crow gifts of shields,
horses, and headdresses, an act that "incensed" the Crows.[45]

Attempts to establish peaceful contact were never risk-free, and even when
successful, they most often resulted in only temporary truces, but the rules
regulating the reception and treatment of visitors opened avenues for intertribal trade and diplomacy, even for strangers who lacked prior ties to another
community. According to Thomas Leforge, a white man who lived for nearly
twenty years with the Crows, an "open and announced" approach to a foreign
camp "in broad daylight and without the least appearance of stealth" carried
with it an assumption of amicable intent. Only someone bent on peace—or
a crazy person—would behave in such a fashion, and killing such an individual was an act that bestowed no honor on the killer.[46]

Trade and diplomacy, whether with Europeans or between members of Native communities, were not the only factors shaping the internal dynamics of Crow and Blackfeet society and their relations with outsiders. The arrival of European traders in the late 1700s and early 1800s was paralleled by a demographic crisis brought about by the increased intensity of warfare and the arrival of European-introduced infectious diseases. Both the Crow and Blackfeet suffered heavy losses from smallpox and other pathogens, with epidemics striking with appalling frequency in the 1830s and 1840s. The massive Plains smallpox epidemic of 1837 killed an estimated 6,000 Blackfeet, and a similar epidemic reportedly reduced the Crow from 600 to 360 lodges.[47] With a relatively small population base, and located between expansionist-minded rivals like the Piegan to the north and the Lakota to the south and east, the very survival of the Crows seemed to be threatened at times. By the mid-1800s, Euro-American observers freely predicted their eventual extinction. Fur trader Denig claimed that, "situated as they now are, the Crows cannot exist long as a nation," while the artist George Catlin suggested in 1832 that the Crows would be "entirely destroyed" by the Blackfeet within a few years.[48]

Yet here too, the combined impact of disease and warfare led to the intensification of ties between Crows and Blackfeet. One response to demographic crisis was an attempt to rebuild community numbers through taking and adopting captives, primarily women and children. In the early 1830s the River Crow leader Sore Belly led a strike against a Piegan camp on the Musselshell River that reportedly resulted in the capture of 230 women and children. Although the Crows also captured more than 500 horses and large quantities of camp equipment, the attack seems to have been motivated primarily by a desire for captives.[49] In 1845 Crows staged a similar attack on the Piegan Small Robes band, destroying fifty families and capturing 160 women and children. Ironically, the victorious Crows contracted scarlet fever from the captives and suffered heavily in the ensuing epidemic.[50] Although the Blackfeet do not seem to have launched large-scale attacks against the Crows for the express purpose of obtaining captives, they too adopted women and children taken prisoner from the Crows and other tribes. The presence of these captives and adoptees was sometimes indicated in their names: Nez Perce Woman, Cree Woman, Last Captured Woman, Capturing Woman, and Snake Woman.[51]

The treatment of captives varied by community and individual circumstance. Among the Blackfeet in the early 1800s, captives could either be kept as slaves or incorporated fully into a family as kin or a spouse. Even adopted captives could still face abuse or death, especially in the case of captured women taken as wives by Blackfeet men, because they initially lacked kin ties to and the protection of birth families available to native-born Blackfeet women. It also appears clear, however, that many captives were adopted and incorporated fully into Blackfeet society, and were treated and regarded no differently than individuals who had been born into the community.[52] The Crows' more precarious geographic and demographic position may have encouraged better treatment of captives; the Crow woman Pretty Shield bragged that because female captives among the Crows enjoyed the same rights as Crow women, "they never tried to get away."[53] The story of Strap, however, suggests similar variability in the experiences, attitudes, and actions of Crow captives.

The incorporation of outsiders was eased by the flexible kinship structures, permeable community boundaries, and the bottom-up construction of community that characterized both the Crow and the Blackfeet. Among the Crow, as with most Plains communities, families provided the basic building blocks of society. When the Crows devastated the Small Robes band in 1845, the captives were not incorporated into Crow society en masse but instead were adopted individually by families.[54] Membership in a family, whether by virtue of actual descent or adoption, enmeshed one in a web of relationships that branched out through the band and tribe and conferred acceptance in the larger community. Most importantly, membership in a family automatically gave an individual membership in one of the thirteen matrilineal clans in Crow society. Crows termed their clans *ashammaleaxia,* meaning "as driftwood lodges." Anthropologist Rodney Frey has discussed the significance of the term as a metaphor for Crow society:

> As driftwood lodges together along the banks of the river, so the members of a clan cling together, united in a turbulent stream. Each individual is like a piece of driftwood, orienting himself or herself around, and depending on, the others of the prescribed group. . . . An individual would find it exceedingly difficult to float alone, confronting adversaries at every bend. To maintain the group's integrity and his or her membership within it, each individual participates in gift exchanges with others; each gives to the others, and in return the driftwood lodges.[55]

Kinship thus signified more than internal relationships between members of a family or clan; it signified appropriate codes of conduct and social relationships among members of an entire community, linking Mountain Crows to River Crows to Kicked-in-the-Bellies. In contrast to European notions of descent and community membership, which often emphasized an individual's status and rights vis-à-vis a centralized governing body, for Crows and other

Plains peoples "identity encompassed inner qualities that were made manifest through social action and cultural beliefs" among "widely-spread networks of differentially connected individuals having reciprocal rights and duties toward one another."[56] As Frederick Hoxie puts it, "One was not a Crow because of particular political rights or economic standing, but because one belonged to a household and was willing to assume the obligations associated with family living."[57]

The proliferation of Crow clan and kin ties meant that the average Crow counted far more relatives than a Euro-American. The Crow term "father," for example, embraced not only one's biological father, but also the father's brothers, the father's maternal uncles, the paternal aunt's sons, and adoptive and ceremonial fathers. All these connections were fundamental to establishing a person's place and status in the community. As the anthropologist Robert Lowie put it, "No worse insult could be hurled at a Crow than to say, 'You are without relatives': it meant that he was a person of no account."[58] However, it went farther than that: to be without relatives suggested that one was not really even Crow.

Such a social structure was ideally suited to the assimilation of individuals though adoption or marriage. Genealogy, prior affiliation, and European concepts of race did not constitute barriers to incorporation. The Crow phrase for "they were going to adopt him," *bici'tse-wiak,* literally means "they were going to cause him to be born," suggesting the irrelevance of the adopted individual's past affiliations.[59] In 1868, for example, after a young Crow named Three Irons befriended the teenage, Ohio-born Tom Leforge, Three Iron's father, Yellow Leggings, decided to formally adopt the young man. In honor of the occasion, Yellow Leggings sponsored a dance and a giveaway for the other Crows in his band. During the ceremony, Leforge was brought into Yellow Leggings's lodge and his new status formally proclaimed. "I know this young man's true mother and father," Yellow Leggings said. "They are my friends; they have eaten at my lodge and I have had food given to me at their home. Now this young man is going to be my son. His name is Horse Rider." Leforge's new mother then gave him a drink of water. "Thus I became a Crow Indian," Leforge recalled, "a brother of Three Irons and a son of Yellow Leggings"—and, of even greater importance, the son of Yellow Leggings's wife, and through her, kin to all members of her clan.[60] Although previous friendly interactions between Leforge and his family with Yellow Leggings certainly played a role in his adoption, the process by which war captives from tribes like the Blackfeet were adopted by families and became Crow was most likely similar.

Nor was foreign or mixed birth an impediment to the ability of individuals to rise to positions of prominence in Crow society. Several Crow chiefs were of mixed descent, including the Mountain Crow headman Plenty Coups, whose father was Crow but whose mother was a Shoshoni who had been captured and adopted.[61] In his study of Native communities on the northwestern Plains in the 1700s, Theodore Binnema makes the provocative suggestion that "persons with a mixed heritage were well suited to leadership roles, especially in contexts where diplomacy became important."[62] In 1861, Medicine Prairie Chicken, a half-Piegan Crow headman, visited the Bloods and was received with presents of trade goods and horses.[63] In August of the following year, a band of several hundred Crows arrived at Fort Benton, then the center of Blackfeet trade on the Missouri, and attempted to conclude a peace with the Piegan. Writing from a European perspective, the Jesuit missionary Pierre-Jean De Smet called it "a bold as well as hazardous step on the part of the Crows, as they and the Blackfeet had not been on friendly terms for a long time."[64] Although it is impossible to draw any conclusions from this sequence of events, and De Smet failed to record the outcome of the Fort Benton meeting, it is tempting to speculate on the role that Medicine Prairie Chicken may have played in opening a dialogue between the two communities.

In certain instances, the origin of Crow men who had entered the community as captives was remembered, because a vital role in the Crow Sun Dance was reserved for men of foreign birth.[65] However, on a practical, day-to-day level, such distinctions were meaningless, particularly given the cumulative impact of adoption and intermarriage over decades of demographic exchanges with other Native communities, especially for a relatively small community such as the Crow. By the 1870s one observer claimed that "it is probably a safe assertion that at the present day there are scarcely a hundred Crows in the entire tribe that possess the original [Crow] blood in the purity it existed in even 100 years ago."[66]

To many non-Native observers, pluralities of fathers and the ease with which individuals were incorporated into new communities were signs of the weakness of Native kinship, rather than strength—and evidence of the cultural, if not racial, inferiority of indigenous societies.[67] Drawing on images of Indians as deficient in "normal" kin affinities, fur trader Edwin Denig simultaneously commented on what he perceived as the ability of Crows in particular to absorb outsiders while remaining hostile to the groups those individuals came from: "It is also worthy of remark that the women, after a year's residence, and understanding of the language, will not return to their people when given their liberty. . . . The male children become Crow warriors, and carry the tomahawk and scalping knife against their relations, often murdering their own fathers or brothers without knowledge or remorse."[68]

At times, Crows and Blackfeet themselves wondered about the affinities of former tribespeople who had joined another community. The Blood Eagle Plume told James Schultz of the time a war party he was a member of spied on a Crow village, and how his companions speculated on the sympathies of former captives among the Crows: "We knew the Crows had captured many winters back a few women of our kind when a large party of them had ambushed a number of our hunters out after buffalo, on Yellow (Judith) River. We wondered if they were happy, contented. Black Elk said they had probably become Crows in all but their blood."[69]

In reality, of course, kin and community allegiances were not a tabula rasa to be written over at will. Some captives, like Strap, returned to their birth communities, even after a number of years. And while many individuals chose to remain with their new kin, older ties were not forgotten. The Blood headman Red Crow recalled an occasion when his war party was spotted spying on a Crow village by a young girl. Instead of alerting the Crows to their presence, the girl—evidently a Blood who had been captured by the Crows—called out to them softly in their language, "My friends, go away, you will be killed," and "My friends, you are watched."[70] Unlike Strap, the girl apparently had no desire to escape from the Crow village, but capture and adoption had not destroyed the affinity she felt toward members of her old tribe.

As was the case with Strap, the presence of individuals with ties to both communities created openings for peaceful contact and exchange by increasing the familiarity of Crows and Blackfeet with each other's language, social structures, and cultural institutions. Children, of course, would have been unlikely to possess much information about rituals of social or spiritual significance, but the movement of women from one society to another was a different matter. Women played key roles in both the Crow Tobacco and Medicine Water ceremonies, and may well have been responsible for their transmission and adoption by the Blackfeet. In the case of the Crow Medicine Water society, a Piegan woman named Good Captures who had been captured and adopted by the Crow as a child later helped teach the ritual to her Blackfeet relatives when she returned to visit them.[71] Contemporary Euro-Americans, prone to emphasizing exclusivity rather than hybridity in their classification schemes (and equally prone to emphasizing the importance of men rather than women in intergroup relations), were not likely to recognize or record such nuances.

Despite the presence of intermediaries like Medicine Prairie Chicken and the proliferation of social and cultural ties, warfare between Crows and Blackfeet continued throughout the 1840s, 1850s, and 1860s. Skirmishes and raids regularly occurred, costing each tribe upward of 100 men annually, according to one observer.[72] Yet with the exception of occasional events such as the Small Robes massacre, warfare remained constrained within the boundaries established by Crow and Blackfeet culture. In a typical incident in February 1856, a party of Blackfeet stole seventy ponies from a Crow camp at the mouth of the Yellowstone River. When the theft was discovered, some 100 Crows pursued, each mounted and leading a spare horse. After three days, the Crows caught up to the raiders, who had been slowed by the need to break a trail through deep snow. Instead of attacking the Blackfeet, however, the Crows circled the camp and recovered their horses, then ambushed a pair of Blackfeet sent out to track down the missing animals, killing one. "No further attempt was made on the rest hard by," fur trader Denig reported. "They had accomplished what they set out to do—got back their horses and killed a man without losing any of their own party, which is a better coup than killing several enemies with the loss of a man on their side."

For Denig, the raid and the Crow response were more evidence of the irrationality of Native warfare and the intractable nature of Crow–Blackfeet hostility. Denig identified the Blackfeet and the Lakota as the Crows' "natural and eternal enemies . . . with both of whom war has continued from time immemorial without being varied by even a transient truce."[73] Beyond his erroneous assessment of the constancy of intertribal rivalries, what Denig missed was the cultural dynamics of Crow and Blackfeet warfare—warfare that was necessary not just for survival but as a means of accumulating wealth and demonstrating one's spiritual power, but that was also limited by the decentralized nature of both societies, making the complete destruction or subjugation of another community not only difficult or impossible to achieve, but superfluous to the individual motivations of many Crows and Blackfeet.

However mistaken it might have been, Denig's impression was furthered by the seeming failure of U.S.-sponsored peacemaking efforts. Although Crows participated in the 1851 treaty councils at Fort Laramie, no Blackfeet leaders attended—not particularly surprising given Laramie's remoteness from Blackfeet territory. American officials did regard the presence of Father De Smet and fur trader Alex Culbertson (married to the Blood Snake Medicine Woman) as a proxy for the Blackfeet, but it is unlikely the Blackfeet felt themselves bound by treaty provisions calling for an end to intertribal warfare.[74]

Similarly, when U.S. officials arranged the Judith River council in October 1855, Blood, Piegan, and Siksika leaders were present, along with representatives from the Flathead, Pend d'Oreille, Nez Perce, and Cree, but no Crow headmen.[75] Even though fourteen Piegans, eight Bloods, and four Siksikas signed the document, which stipulated both an end to intertribal hostilities and the establishment of a common hunting ground for all the signatory tribes, the Blood chief Seen From Afar warned the U.S. commissioners not to expect too much from the treaty: "I wish to say that as far as we old men are concerned we want peace and to cease going to war; but I am afraid that we cannot stop our young men. The Crows are not here to smoke the pipe with us and I am afraid our young men will not be persuaded that they ought not to war against the Crows."[76]

American peacemaking efforts were complicated by the political autonomy of Blackfeet and Crow bands. Leaders of two bands might forge a peace, with or without American assistance, but such an agreement did not extend to other Crow or Blackfeet bands. Without signatures from every Crow and Blackfeet band leader, such truces were unlikely to be effective or enduring, particularly because members of different bands were still linked by kin (and in the case of the Crows clan) ties, meaning a raid against one band might well provoke retaliation not just from members of the targeted group, but also from kin in other bands. If a headman lost his position or his adherents for whatever reason, any agreement he had made was no longer binding on his former followers. Not surprisingly, neither the Fort Laramie treaty nor the Judith treaty accomplished the goal of permanently ending conflict between Crows and Blackfeet. Siksika winter counts record a battle in which the Blackfeet defeated the Crows in 1851, and a fight the following year in which the Blackfeet were defeated and the Siksika warrior Old Prairie Chicken killed.[77] In 1855, a Blood war party departed for a raid on the Crows less than ten days after the signing of the Judith treaty.[78]

The inability of older chiefs such as Seen From Afar to control their young men was symptomatic not only of the complexity of band and kin politics, but also of young men's desire for status, and—among the Blackfeet—the progressive fissioning of bands and tribes themselves. Throughout the mid-nineteenth century, the number of Blood, Siksika, and especially Piegan bands grew as family and kin groups hived off from existing groups. By 1831 the Small Robes Piegan were distinct enough from their parent community that one writer classed them as a separate, fourth Blackfeet tribe in their own right.[79] The near destruction of the Small Robes in 1845 was probably all that prevented them from becoming a separate community on the same level as the Piegan themselves. By 1860 the Piegan may have included as many as twenty-three bands; the Blood and Siksika were divided into seven and six bands, respectively.[80]

There is a clear correlation between the wealth of different Blackfeet groups and the number of bands they contained. By almost any measure, the Piegan were the wealthiest Blackfeet group, particularly in horses, and they continued to enjoy a preeminent position in the fur trade.[81] This wealth also spawned an inordinate number of individuals with claims (or at least plausible pretensions) to leadership. Competition for status, and the rivalries that ensued as a result, produced dissension that often led to the splitting of bands. The fission of one band into two or more was one of the few means available to cope with the political and social tensions that could occur in such situations.[82] Population pressures were not a factor; indeed, Piegan bands were, in general, significantly smaller than their Blood or Siksika counterparts.[83]

In contrast to the Blackfeet pattern, Crow political and social structure remained more stable throughout the nineteenth century, with the Mountain Crow, River Crow, and Kicked-in-the-Bellies continuing as the three major divisions, and with less evidence of bands within these three groups proliferating and becoming smaller in size over time. External and internal factors, in particular the need to maintain band sizes large enough to defend against aggressive neighbors like the Blackfeet and Lakota, combined with the Crows' relatively small population base, militated against the sort of extreme fissioning apparent among the Piegan, and may have contributed to a greater sense of community cohesion that helped to mitigate and defuse internal conflicts. Indeed, in contrast to the Blackfeet, who themselves recognized social distinctions between the Blood, Siksika, and Piegan, Crows often grouped River Crows, Mountain Crows, and Kicked-in-the-Bellies together, referring to all as *bi'ruke* ("we"), a closeness intensified by widespread intermarriage and mixed residential patterns, with River Crows residing among Mountain Crows and Kicked-in-the-Bellies and vice versa.[84]

Yet in other ways, the convergence of Crow and Blackfeet culture—marked not by a merging of the two but by development and change along separate but parallel lines—continued throughout the mid-nineteenth century. As was the case with the trade in Crow war shields and the adoption of Crow rituals by the Blackfeet, one of the most significant manifestations of this process occurred in the means by which young men sought the spiritual power necessary for gaining success and status in their respective societies, particularly in the increasing commodification and proliferation of spiritually powerful items and rituals.

Among the Blackfeet, medicine bundles constituted the physical form through which spiritual power was embodied and brought forth. The bundles had their origins in visions and contact with supernatural beings who granted access to their powers to favored individuals. The most common avenue through which this access was gained was the vision quest, a solitary endeavor in which a person separated himself from his community and fasted, depriving himself of food, shelter, and clothing for several days in an attempt to gain the attention and sympathy of powerful spiritual beings. Items representing significant elements of a vision or a person's spiritual helper would be assembled and kept in a bundle, and would be used in rituals to assure success in a particular endeavor.[85]

As late as the 1830s, observers described Blackfeet bundles as being individually held and rarely alienated from their original owners. Many Blackfeet guarded their bundles so zealously that they would not even divulge the contents of them to others. As the artist George Catlin put it, "The value of the medicine-bag to the Indian is beyond all price; for to sell it, or give it away, would subject him to such signal disgrace in his tribe, that he could never rise above it; and again, his superstition would stand in the way of any such disposition of it, for he considers it the gift of the Great Spirit." According to Catlin, bundles were frequently buried with their owners when they died, rather than being passed down to an heir or some other individual.[86] There were exceptions to this rule, particularly in the case of bundles of tribal rather than individual significance, such as the Thunder Pipe and Beaver bundles, which were transferred and added to by various custodians—not owners—over the years.[87]

The importance of obtaining strong visions, medicine bundles, and rituals lay not only in their spiritual power, but also in the wealth and status that they could potentially confer. Material wealth such as horses and other possessions were transitory and subject to loss in a single hard winter or a raid. Spiritual power, manifested through bundles, represented a form of wealth that could not be taken away, and that could enable an individual, through success in war, hunting, or other endeavors, to gain (or regain) material prosperity. Moreover, provided the proper rituals and deference were observed, even individual bundles and the rights to ritual knowledge and spiritual power they represented potentially retained their efficacy indefinitely, a trait that, combined with the desire for status and wealth within increasingly individualist and competitive Blackfeet bands, helps explain shifts in the acquisition and treatment of spiritual power.[88]

The treatment of spiritual items as commodities had precedent in the purchasing of Crow war shields by Blackfeet men in the 1830s, but the purchasing and proliferation of bundles themselves were occurring within Blackfeet society by the 1860s and 1870s. Young men still went on vision quests, but many hedged their bets by obtaining proven medicine to augment or even replace those gained through their own visions. Increasingly, bundles could be purchased from elders whose spiritual helpers had acknowledged and recognized powers, and individuals were not limited to obtaining spiritual aid from only one source. Of twenty-one elderly Blackfeet interviewed by anthropologist John C. Ewers in the 1940s, only the Blood man Weasel Tail had obtained his medicine (a wolf cap and robe) through his own vision. All the rest had obtained their medicine from others, often, but not always, a relative.[89] Such medicine had to be paid for, usually in horses, which favored young men from wealthier families. The Siksika Bad Old Man explained how the urge to obtain spiritual power and status contributed to intertribal conflict and bore unequally on young men from poorer backgrounds, noting that "the poorer class of men have to get out on the warpath often to get horses in order to buy these fine clothes and medicine bundles which honor such owners"—a factor that helped drive conflict and contact with groups like the Crow.[90]

The vision quest process itself also changed in subtle but significant ways. As late as the 1830s, Blackfeet men were restricted to one vision quest attempt, possibly a holdover from Woodland Algonquian traditions, where the vision quest was a rite of passage to be performed at a certain age, rather than an undertaking to be performed at the individual's discretion.[91] By the 1870s, however, Blackfeet men were undergoing multiple vision quests in an attempt to obtain the strongest possible spiritual protectors. One Siksika man, Tearing Lodge, fasted seven times.[92]

Similar patterns emerged among the Crows. Although it is not known whether Crow men were ever limited to a single vision quest, it is clear that young men, particularly young men from poorer families who could not obtain strong spirit helpers through purchase, were subjecting themselves to multiple vision quests by the mid-1800s. According to anthropologist William Wildschudt, "a Crow might fast five, six, seven, or even more times during his lifetime. White-Man-Runs-Him fasted a staggering fourteen times."[93] Two Leggings, a River Crow from a poor family, went on a second vision quest after the first was inadvertently interrupted: "I did not think my dream was powerful, but at least I had some medicine songs I had dreamt myself." Two Leggings had purchased medicine earlier, but because of his poverty, the only medicine he could afford came from a man "who had never been a real warrior and preferred to live in camp." Two Leggings also participated in a Sun Dance in hopes of obtaining a vision, but failed to receive one.[94]

Other Crows, including men from more prominent families such as Plenty Coups and Medicine Crow, also went on more than one vision quest. Medicine Crow's father, a man with renowned spiritual power, could have given him a strong bundle, but he encouraged his son to obtain his own medicine to ensure that he would remain powerful after the father died.[95] Some Crow bundle owners claimed permission from their spiritual guardians to make full or partial copies of bundles to sell or give to others—up to twenty in the case of one man's war medicine. Such duplication was more common with war-related bundles than with any other class of medicine bundles, reflecting the importance of warfare as a route to wealth and distinction.[96]

The proliferation of bands and the commodification of spiritual power were not the only changes taking place in Crow and Blackfeet society. Hunting and food procurement patterns also shifted from cooperative community endeavors to more individualistic techniques. Before the introduction of horses, both Crows and Blackfeet relied heavily on buffalo drives to supply them with food. Drives involved herding a band of buffalo over a cliff or into a pound, crippling or corralling the animals so they could be easily killed and butchered. Conducting a successful drive required the coordinated action of a large group of people, from the scouts and runners who located the buffalo and drove them toward the chosen spot, to the people at the terminal end of the drive who funneled the buffalo over the precipice or into the enclosure.[97] The introduction of horses made such elaborate strategies less necessary, while the shrinking size of bands among the Blackfeet made conducting a successful drive more problematic.

By the early 1800s, the use of pounds and drives was already dying out among the Piegan; the more northerly and less horse-rich Bloods and Siksikas continued to use pounds until the mid-1870s, albeit with decreasing frequency. According to John C. Ewers, the Piegan made their last bison drive in the 1850s, a story that carries its own eloquent commentary on the shifting nature of spiritual power and the increasingly fragmented nature of Blackfeet society. While camped on the Teton River in northern Montana, the Never Laughs band made three attempts to drive a herd over an embankment and into a corral, failing each time. That night, a young man named Many Tail Feathers burned the corral, earning the enmity of his people. In a subsequent vision quest, the buffalo came to him and asked him if he was the individual who had burned the corral. In thanks for his act, the buffalo presented Many Tail Feathers with a red war bonnet, which enabled him to build an impressive military record. However, to achieve individual status, Many Tail Feathers had sacrificed the good of the group.[98]

Increasing inequality in wealth was also changing the functioning of Blackfeet age-set men's groups, called the All Comrades societies. Unlike warrior societies in other Plains tribes, including the Crow, membership in Blackfeet age-grade societies was not a matter of individual choice; instead, entire age sets of young men entered the society designated for novice warriors and would progress together over the years from one society to another. Movement from group to group entailed the collective purchase of a society's regalia, songs, and rituals by members of a particular age set. At one time the All Comrades had been the dominant factor in Blackfeet tribal organization, regulating hunts, policing camps, and playing a role in the selection of headmen. In the 1850s a new society was added at the low end of the age-grade scale, but by the 1870s the inability of all of the members of an age set to purchase the rites and rituals of the preceding groups was leading to a breakdown of the entire system. The Dogs, a society of mature warriors, last sold their ritual in 1860. By 1874 the Doves, Flies, Tails, and Raven-Bearers had all sold their rites for the last time. Not only did inequalities in wealth make it difficult (if not impossible) for all the members of an age set to move up, but changes in Blackfeet society itself, particularly among the Piegan, were eliminating many of the functions of the All Comrades, rendering several societies obsolete. In prehorse days and the early nineteenth century, the Catchers society had regulated communal buffalo drives, but the gradual disappearance of such hunts rendered the Catchers superfluous by midcentury. During the 1850s, the Piegan Catchers society passed out of existence when the members of the group sold their rites to a party of Bloods.[99]

In contrast to the Blackfeet age-grade societies, membership in Crow warrior societies cut across all age levels of adult men, with the various societies competing against one another for members and prestige. Like the Blackfeet All Comrades societies, Crow warrior societies policed camps and regulated marches and communal hunts. Like the Crows' matrilineal clans, the Lumpwoods, Foxes, and other warrior societies also cut across tribal divisions, with members treating one another as brothers irrespective of Mountain, River, or Kicked-in-the-Belly origin and affiliation, thus reinforcing the sense of unity in Crow society.[100] However, as was the case with the All Comrades, over time, most Crow warrior societies became defunct. In 1833 Maximilian reported the existence of eight warrior societies. By 1870, the number had fallen to four—or perhaps only two, with the most successful and prominent societies, the Foxes and Lumpwoods, either dominating among new members or absorbing other clubs entirely.[101]

Ironically, these changes in Crow and Blackfeet culture were reaching an apex just as both communities were facing renewed challenges to their homelands. Continued Lakota aggression during the 1860s drove Mountain Crows and Kicked-in-the-Bellies west across the Powder and Bighorn rivers, threatening to separate them from their River Crow relatives to the north and east. In response the River Crows, themselves increasingly menaced by Yanktonai and Assiniboine bands pressing west along the Missouri River, forged closer relations with the neighboring Gros Ventre. The Blackfeet experienced similar pressures, in the north from Canadian Cree bands whose former homelands were now largely denuded of buffalo, and in the south by the same westward movement of Siouan groups such as the Assiniboine that imperiled the River Crows. For Crows and Blackfeet alike, the 1860s and 1870s marked a time of contraction, with both being pressed into what one scholar describes as "a tightening geographic circle."[102]

All of these developments traced their ultimate origin to the rapidly shrinking range of the buffalo. The retreat of the buffalo—resulting not only from Native American hunting for the fur trade but also from the onset of droughts marking the end of the Little Ice Age and, potentially, the introduction of diseases from domesticated cattle—accelerated in the 1860s and 1870s with the westward extension of transcontinental railroads like the Union Pacific and Northern Pacific and the arrival of professional hide hunters. By the mid-1870s the central plains were essentially denuded of buffalo, sending groups like the Oglala and Brule Lakota and the Northern Cheyenne and Arapaho north and west in search of bison.[103] In Canada, even without the presence of railroads, these same factors (combined with the activities of Metis hunters and the establishment of Metis settlements along the North Saskatchewan River by the 1860s) resulted in a similarly rapid diminution of the herds.[104] These events led several white observers to predict a final battle over the buffalo between tribes desperate for food.[105]

Two of the logical antagonists in this confrontation were, of course, Crows and Blackfeet themselves, and two of the anticipated battlegrounds were the Judith and Musselshell river basins that Crows, Blackfeet, and transmontaine peoples like the Nez Perce, Flathead, and Kutenai had been exploiting for decades.[106] As far back as 1846 Father De Smet had predicted that this region, "the plains of the Yellowstone and Missouri and as far as the forks of the Saskatchewan, occupied today by the Blackfeet," would become "the last retreat of the buffalo."[107]

Small-scale raiding and violence between the Crow and Blackfeet did arguably increase in the 1870s and early 1880s. With the destruction of the buffalo herds, horse raiding actually became easier, as Crow and Blackfeet bands tended to cluster more predictably around agencies for the government-issued rations that were becoming increasingly vital to survival. According to Crow agent Henry Armstrong, Piegans alone stole more than 500 horses from the Crow in 1882, 200 to 300 more in 1883, and more than 100 in the first two months of 1884.[108]

Ironically, the persistence of family ties between Crows and Blackfeet may have contributed to this phenomenon. As Leforge put it, "Intermarriages between Crows and Piegans created a situation regarded as helpful to raiders." In particular, Leforge identified the marriage of the half-Piegan Bob Jackson, a former army scout, to the Crow widow of the government physician at the Crow agency as a subject of speculation. "Jackson's Piegan friends came for prolonged and frequent visits with him," Leforge noted. "As guests they were held inviolable, but it was thought they used this immunity for horse-stealing activities."[109]

A similar increase in violence, however, did not occur over access to rapidly dwindling hunting grounds. In general, both Crow and Blackfeet leaders sought to avoid a large-scale confrontation over territory. When River Crow bands migrated to the Judith River basin (a game-rich area that the Piegan also frequented) in the 1860s, the Blackfeet made no concerted effort to drive them out. When the River Crows left the area to join their Mountain Crow brethren on the Yellowstone in 1870, it was smallpox rather than Blackfeet that prompted the move.[110] The only major engagement between Crows and Blackfeet over hunting territory took place in 1866, when a band of River Crows, accompanied by their Gros Ventre allies, attempted to move into Blackfeet territory near the Cypress Hills in present-day southern Alberta. The strategy backfired in a disastrous battle in which Piegan warriors ambushed the combined force, inflicting 100 to 300 casualties.[111]

The reluctance to press too closely against other communities was perfectly expressed by the Mountain Crow leader Blackfoot (also known as Sits in the Middle of the Land) in 1873, when U.S. officials proposed moving the Crows from their established reservation south of the Yellowstone River to a new one located in the more northerly Judith basin. Although the proposed move promised to give the Crows some much-needed relief from Lakota aggression, Blackfoot protested that the region was regarded as a common hunting ground by local tribes, and that moving the Crows there would only stir up conflict:

> We have gone to the Judith Basin a great deal, and you wish us to take it for a reservation. All kinds of men go there. . . . The Sioux Indians,

Crees, Santees, Mandans, Assiniboines, Gros Ventre, Piegans, Pend d'Oreilles, Flatheads, the Mountain Crows, the River Crows, Bannacks, Snake, and Nez Perce Indians and white people, all go there. You wish us to take the Judith Basin for a reservation. All these Indians will come, and we will likely quarrel; that is what we think about it. Judith Basin is a small basin; a great many people go there.[112]

Although Crows already used the basin as a hunting ground, Blackfoot feared that moving the Crows there permanently would destabilize existing relationships. That Crows and Blackfeet already warred against one another was, in his eyes, immaterial. By the late 1800s, Crow and Blackfeet patterns of conflict were motivated more by individuals' desire for status, rather than the attainment of group goals. As deadly and destructive as that warfare was, it could be accommodated in ways that a direct confrontation over territory could not.

As it turned out, there would be no apocalyptic showdown over the buffalo, even though the rapid depletion of herds in the late 1870s forced bands from rival tribes to roam more widely and hunt in closer proximity to each other. Around 1876, some Crows and Piegans made a peace agreement near the Sweetgrass Hills, most likely with regard to hunting rights.[113] Three years later, the disappearance of buffalo from their home hunting grounds forced desperate Blood bands to migrate south to the Judith River basins for the winter—without serious interference from Crows.[114] The next year, Bloods under the leadership of White Calf and Medicine Calf traveled south to the Yellowstone near present-day Billings. Encountering a camp of Crows, the two held a council with the Crow headmen Was Kicked and Pregnant Woman, and agreed to camp and hunt together for the remainder of the summer. With the final disappearance of the buffalo from the Yellowstone Valley in 1881, the Bloods parted from the Crows amicably and returned to their reserve in Canada.[115]

In 1885, in response to continued horse raids, American officials finally brokered what they regarded as a final peace agreement between Piegans and the Crows, shepherding a Crow delegation to the Blackfeet Agency in northern Montana. However, the significance of this council, as was often the case with U.S.-sponsored negotiations, may be less important that it appears to be in government records. Small-scale raiding by young men persisted for several years after 1885, but the larger conflict feared by army officers and Office of Indian Affairs officials had already been rejected by Crow and Blackfeet lead-

ers, who, as survival became more tenuous, chose coexistence and accommo-
dation over mutual destruction.[116]

In his old age, the River Crow Two Leggings would lament that after the end
of intertribal warfare, "there was nothing more to tell."[117] It was a sentiment
that resonated with turn-of-the-century ethnographers and anthropologists
obsessed with documenting what they regarded as swiftly vanishing cultures
and people.[118] When viewed in isolation, the warfare that so often characterized Crow–Blackfeet relations could appear endemic and at times aimless. If
conflict alone were the sine qua non of Crow–Blackfeet interaction, there
would indeed be little room for the continuation of meaningful contact after
reservation life replaced autonomous existence. However, when placed in a
larger context of demographic, material, and spiritual exchange, and the evolution of Crow and Blackfeet society and culture, new possibilities emerge. As
federal officials asserted more and more power over tribal affairs during the
reservation era, status and power would prove more and more difficult to
attain. But the need for spiritual power to thrive—or simply survive—would
not disappear. Similarly, exchanges of people, ideas, and goods produced links
that would not simply disappear with the last raiding party. The evolution of
Crow and Blackfeet culture, as well as the connections members of each community forged with the other, during the second half of the nineteenth century permitted both societies to flourish while threatening the survival and
integrity of neither. The cultural and human dynamics of Crow–Blackfeet
interaction would provide a basis for continued contact and exchange in the
1880s and beyond. Similar dynamics would be at work in Crow relations with
other Native peoples, perhaps most notably in Crow relations with their other
principal adversary, the Lakota, both before and after the onset of the reservation era.

CHAPTER TWO

Crows, Lakotas, and
the Bozeman Trail, 1863–1868

The Crow wealth that created both conflict and connections with the Black-feet during the first half of the nineteenth century was the product of more than just horse ownership, the European fur trade, or access to spiritual power. It was also the result of Crow possession of what American Fur Company trader Edwin Denig called "the best game country in the world." As Denig put it:

> From the base of the mountains to the mouth of the Yellowstone buffalo are always to be found in immense herds. Along that river elk may be seen in droves of several hundred at a time; also large bands of deer both of black-tailed and white-tailed species. Antelope cover the prairies, and in the badlands near the mountains are found in great plenty bighorn sheep and grizzly bear. Every creek and river teems with beaver, and good fish and fowl can be had at any stream in the proper season.[1]

Mountain Crow headman Rotten Belly put it more succinctly to trader Robert Campbell. "The Crow country is in exactly the right place," he said. "Everything good is to be found there. There is no country like the Crow country."[2]

The heart of this homeland was the Powder River country, the basin south of the Yellowstone River watered by the Powder, Tongue, Little Bighorn, and other streams flowing north from the Bighorn Mountains. Occupied primarily by Mountain and Kicked-in-the-Belly bands, whites associated this region with the Crows so strongly that several mistranslated "Apsaalooke," the Crows' name for themselves, as the name of the region itself.[3] Beyond game, the region contained nearly every resource and environment desired by roaming hunter-gatherers. Mountain pastures were invitingly cool when the sun scorched the plains in summer, while the forested mountains and foothills offered plentiful supplies of lodgepole pine for teepee poles and travois. In spring and autumn, Crow bands exploited the plains' rich buffalo herds, and in winter took shelter in the wooded river bottoms. According to trapper Joe Meek, the Powder River country was a "Land of Canaan" and a hunter's paradise.[4]

As was the case with territories to the north claimed by both the Crow and Blackfeet, however, Crow title to the Powder River country was not uncontested. In the eyes of the United States, the Fort Laramie Treaty of 1851 confirmed Crow possession of that portion of the Powder River country lying west of the Powder River.[5] But the same qualities that made the area invaluable to the Crows also made it irresistible to other tribes. Increasingly, as midcentury approached, Lakotas and Northern Cheyennes challenged Crow control of the region.[6]

The Lakota–Cheyenne push was impelled partly by fur trade economics but also by changing buffalo demography on the Northern Plains. Throughout the 1840s, the hunting grounds of the Oglala, Minniconjoux, and Brule Lakota near the North Platte River and the emerging Oregon Trail had been progressively denuded of buffalo. By 1859, buffalo were no longer seen near the North Platte, and other game such as antelope, elk, and deer had also become scarce. Similarly, buffalo grew scarce along the middle Missouri River hunting grounds formerly relied on by more northerly bands of Hunkpapa, Blackfoot, and Sans Arc Lakotas. In their search for new hunting grounds, the Lakota and Cheyenne looked north and west to the Powder River country.[7]

The Lakota–Cheyenne quest for new hunting territory crossed paths with an increasingly desperate Crow need for reliable access to manufactured goods, either in the form of trade goods or government annuities promised by the Treaty of 1851. Until the mid-1850s, Fort Laramie on the North Platte River had served as the main southern contact point for Mountain and Kicked-in-the-Belly Crows engaged in the fur trade, and as a primary location for the disbursement of treaty annuities. However, as Lakota and Cheyenne bands pressed farther north and west into the Powder River country, Fort Laramie became increasingly remote and dangerous for Crows to visit. In 1858, Deer Creek, some 100 miles west of Fort Laramie, was described as the boundary between Lakota and Crow country. Three years later, the resident government agent found it impossible to distribute goods to the Crows, who were unwilling or unable to travel to the North Platte to receive them. Instead, the agent distributed the Crows' goods to 200 lodges of Lakotas, Cheyennes, and Arapahoes who came in "from their hunting grounds to the north, on Cheyenne and Powder River"—the Crows' former domain.[8]

At the same time that the Oglala, Minniconjoux, and Brule surge was making it difficult for the Crows to trade along the North Platte, the westward movement of Hunkpapa, Blackfoot, and Sans Arc Lakota bands farther north was making travel to Fort Union on the upper Missouri, the eastern portal for Crow trade, equally hazardous. Other options for trade and supplies were also dwindling. As early as 1807, fur companies had attempted to tap the Crow trade directly by establishing posts in the Yellowstone Valley, but in 1859, the last such post, Fort Sarpy II, was abandoned, a casualty of poor profits and repeated Lakota and Blackfeet attacks against the Crows.[9] In 1863, Lakotas repeatedly attacked the steamboats *Robert Campbell Jr.* and *Shreveport,* both bearing annuity goods for the Crows, as they moved up the Missouri River. Low water and Crow reluctance to come any farther east than the mouth of the Milk River forced Agent Samuel N. Latta to cache the goods indefinitely at Fort Union.[10] The following year, annuity goods also had to be left at Fort Union, where some of the items were distributed to small bands of Crows who made the perilous journey to the post. Special agent Henry Reed undertook to deliver some of the goods to the Crows in person, noting that "as they [the Crows] dare not go up into their own country on the Yellow Stone, arrangements were made for them to receive them [the annuity goods] at such time and place as would suit their convenience."[11] "Convenience" was hardly the right word. That same year, the Crows' regular agent reported that the tribe had lost most of its horses and a third of its people to the Lakota. In 1865, just eight Crows dared make the trip to Fort Union.[12]

From a Crow perspective, the loss of contact with the fur trade and treaty annuities was potentially disastrous. As the Crow leader Plenty Coups noted, the bow was unrivaled as a tool for hunting buffalo but inferior to the gun in warfare. In this respect, he claimed, the Crows were virtually unarmed compared to their enemies. "The northern tribes [Blackfoot and Piegans] could easily trade with the Hudson's Bay people, while the tribes eastward of us [Sioux, Cheyenne, and Arapaho] traded furs and robes to the American Fur Company for guns, powder, and lead."[13] The annuity issues that Crows increasingly lacked access to, and that occasionally came into the hands of the Crows' adversaries, also frequently included weapons and ammunition. In 1858 alone, Blackfeet agent Alfred J. Vaughn distributed 108 trade guns, sixteen kegs of powder, and twenty-nine bags of bullets to the Piegan.[14]

In the Yellowstone and Powder River country in the 1850s and 1860s, to be unarmed was to be at the mercy of one's enemies. In a meeting with the leaders of an army exploration expedition in 1860, the Crow headman Great Bear vented his frustration:

> The white man has set our enemies upon us; some of our warriors have been killed and we have lost many horses. They have taken our trading post away from us. We could go there and trade with the whites without being killed by our enemies the Sioux; but now we have no presents; we

cannot trade our robes and blankets anywhere. The Sioux will not let us trade at Fort Union; and now our hearts are black.[15]

By 1865, the Crows had been pushed more than 100 miles to the north and west, beyond the Bighorn and Yellowstone rivers.[16]

As was the case with the Blackfeet, the years of conflict between the Crows and the Lakota and Cheyenne produced more than just casualties. Decades of hostilities interspersed with occasional truces yielded innumerable links and connections—political, economic, and social. Crows adopted Cheyenne and Lakota captives; Cheyennes and Lakotas did the same with Crows. After counting his first coup against a Crow raiding party, a young Northern Cheyenne received the name Wooden Leg in honor of his favorite uncle, who had been born Crow but was captured and adopted by the Cheyennes as a boy. On the other side, the wife of the Crow Kicked-in-the-Belly headman Blackfoot (also known as Sits in the Middle of the Land) was not only a Lakota captive, but also the sister of the Oglala Lakota band leader (*itancan*) Man Afraid of His Horses.[17]

The common needs of the Crows and the Lakotas and their allies for access to hunting grounds and trade outlets also produced occasional attempts at conciliation and coexistence. After the Fort Laramie Treaty of 1851, Minniconjoux bands under Red Fish and Lone Horn managed to establish a fairly stable peace with Kicked-in-the-Belly Crows under Big Robber. The truce permitted Lakota use of southern portions of Crow hunting grounds along the upper Powder River, while the Crows gained access to trading posts along the North Platte.[18] Except for a few isolated incidents, other Oglala and Cheyenne bands also apparently maintained amicable relations with the Crows until about 1857. The effects of the peace extended as far as the Nez Perce and the Shoshoni, both of whom entered the area occasionally for purposes of hunting and trade. However, increasing tensions and the refusal of the Crows to grant the Lakota use of more extensive hunting territory led to renewed hostility, including numerous raids by the Crows and retaliatory attacks by Lakotas and Cheyennes, one of which resulted in the death of Big Robber in 1858. As the Cheyenne chief Black Horse explained to an army officer in 1866, "We stole the hunting grounds of the Crows because they are the best. . . . We fight the Crows, because they will not take half and give us peace with the other half."[19]

The opening of the Bozeman Trail added a new ingredient to this unstable situation. Gold had been discovered in Montana as early as 1852, and later strikes at Alder Gulch and Emigrant Gulch produced a full-scale gold rush in the early 1860s. In 1863, disappointed gold-seeker John Bozeman and fron-tiersman John Jacobs left Montana to blaze a new emigrant trail, connecting with the old Platte Road just west of Fort Laramie. From the Platte Road, Bozeman's route traversed the headwaters of the Powder River and its tribu-taries, skirting the east face of Bighorn Mountains to a crossing of the Bighorn River just below where it emerges from its namesake range. From the Bighorn, the trail continued north to the Yellowstone River near present-day Livingston, Montana, before turning west through the Gallatin Valley to its ultimate ter-minus in Virginia City. Despite its length, Bozeman's road cut some 400 miles off the existing land route to Montana via Salt Lake City. Undeterred by an encounter with a party of Indians (usually identified as Crows) who stripped the pair of their clothes and equipment and ordered them out of the country, Bozeman advertised his shortcut to emigrants the next summer and led a train up the trail to the gold camps without incident. Two other trains followed, bringing an estimated 1,000 people to Montana via the trail in 1864.[20]

Together with the massacre of Cheyennes and Arapahos at Sand Creek in 1864, the opening of the Bozeman Trail, which ran squarely through some of the best remaining hunting grounds on the Northern Plains, provoked intense opposition from Lakota, Cheyenne, and Arapaho bands in the region.[21] How-ever, despite their potential role in looting Bozeman and Jacobs, the trail appears to have attracted much less opposition from the Crows, who by now controlled little of the land it traversed, except for the final leg west of the Bighorn River. Significantly, the Crows Bozeman and Jacobs met were not part of a village but were apparently a war party on a raid against Lakota and Cheyenne villages in the region.

Indeed, for the Crows, the creation of the trail held potential benefits, not the least of which were the possibilities for renewed contact with independent traders such as John Richard, Mac McKenzie, John Baptiste "Big Bat" Pourier, and Matthias "Cy" Mounts, operating out of newly established towns like Bozeman in the Gallatin Valley. By fall 1864, several of these men, some of whom had arrived in Montana via the Bozeman Trail, had established trade relationships with the Crows. Trade remained a hazardous venture, but at least the Crows once again had access to a regular flow of manufactured goods, not least among them weapons and ammunition.[22]

Given these factors, a Crow–American alliance against the Lakota and Cheyenne seems natural, even inevitable. However, although Crows welcomed traders, they were also acutely aware of the impact emigrants, miners, and other intruders could have on game and other resources, as demonstrated by their behavior during their encounter with Bozeman, as well as with other whites. In 1859, in a meeting on the Yellowstone just below the mouth of the Bighorn River, a delegation of Crows led by Red Bear firmly told Captain William F. Raynolds of the army corps of engineers that he was welcome to explore the region, but to leave when he was finished. "They occupy the best buffalo ground in the west," Raynolds explained, "and are jealous of intrusion. While they expressed a willingness that I should pass through the country, they were careful to add that they could not consent to my staying."[23] In 1863, besides evicting Bozeman and Jacobs, Crow warriors attacked parties of prospectors on the Yellowstone and Bighorn rivers, stealing horses, killing one miner, and driving the rest out of the area.[24]

Nevertheless, by the mid-1860s at least a few Crows were willing to tolerate, or at least consider, a permanent American presence in the region in return for U.S. aid in recovering their lost territory. Meeting with General Alfred Sully on the Yellowstone River during his campaign against the Lakota in 1864, a Crow delegation offered assistance in return for Sully's promise to drive the Lakota out of the Powder River country. Sully rejected the Crows' offer; he also failed to establish a fort on the lower Yellowstone, despite orders from his superiors to do so.[25]

The government itself recognized the shifting balance of power in the Powder River country in the fall of 1865, when emissaries went out to invite Lakota and Cheyenne bands to Fort Laramie for a council the following summer. Though the purpose of the negotiations was to secure permission for continued use of the trail—and despite the government's prior recognition of Crow ownership of the region in the Treaty of 1851—the Crows themselves were not invited.[26] As it turned out, the government would prove as inept in dealing with the Lakota and Cheyenne as it was negligent in dealing with the Crows. While on the one hand attempting to secure the Bozeman Trail through diplomacy, the government simultaneously moved to occupy the trail militarily. On June 13, 1866, in the midst of negotiations, Colonel Henry Carrington's command of the 18th Infantry arrived at Fort Laramie. Carrington's arrival eliminated any possibility of a successful council. "I was introduced to several chiefs," Carrington later recalled. "Without exception, every chief to whom I was then introduced as the 'White Chief going up to occupy Powder River, the Bighorn country, and the Yellowstone,' treated me coldly." A friendly Brule informed Carrington that Red Cloud and other Lakota leaders "will not sell their hunting grounds to the white man for a road. They will not give you the road unless you whip them." Three days later, after an acrimonious meeting with Carrington and the treaty commissioners, Red Cloud's Oglalas led a general walkout of the Powder River bands of Lakotas and Cheyennes. When

Carrington departed Laramie on June 17, the Bozeman Trail war got under way in earnest.[27]

No Crows were at Fort Laramie to witness the treaty councils and the arrival of Carrington's column, but they learned of events there, and the Lakota response, almost as quickly as Carrington did. After the breakdown of negotiations, Red Cloud, Man Afraid of His Horses, and several other Lakota leaders visited Crow camps not to raid but to seek an alliance. Bearing ceremonial gifts of tobacco and more substantial presents of horses and ammunition, the Lakota leaders asked the Crows to join them in closing the trail and driving the whites out of the region. Although several young warriors declared themselves in favor of an alliance, the Crow chiefs were hesitant. The Crows politely returned the visits, but refused to commit themselves.[28]

At the same time, Carrington dispatched emissaries to gauge the Crows' temperament. On August 4, while the main body of his command halted at the forks of Piney Creek 228 miles out of Laramie to build Fort Phil Kearney, Carrington sent two companies under Captain Nathaniel C. Kinney to construct a second post, Fort C. F. Smith, at the crossing of the Bighorn River ninety-one miles farther up the trail. Accompanying Kinney as guides were former mountain men Jim Bridger and Henry Williams. After aiding Kinney in locating a suitable site for the fort, Bridger and Williams had the dual mission of communicating with Montana's territorial governor and, belatedly, making contact with the Crows. On their way back from Virginia City, Bridger and Williams joined a party of traders at a Crow village of 500 people at the mouth of Clark's Fork of the Yellowstone. Arriving at Fort Phil Kearny on October 27, the two scouts told Carrington of the Lakota visits and the Crow response, adding that "White Mouth, Black Foot, Rotten Tail (chiefs) insisted that they were at peace and wished to be always. The young men in some cases wished to join the Sioux, and compromise their old title to this country."[29]

Even before Bridger reached the camp on Clark's Fork, however, the Crows had initiated their own overtures toward the soldiers. On August 27, seven Crows appeared on the opposite side of the Bighorn from C. F. Smith. More Crows steadily joined the group, until about sixty clustered on the far bank. Though hindered by the lack of an interpreter, the Crows managed to tell the soldiers that they belonged to a large party camped a short distance downstream and wished to talk. The next day, the Crows reappeared, this time accompanied by an interpreter and White Mouth, a prominent Crow leader.

Through the interpreter, a former American Fur Company employee

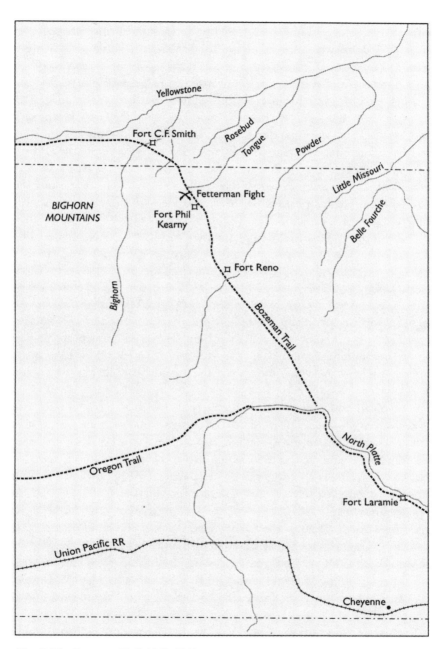

Map 2. The Bozeman Trail, 1863–1868.

named Pierre Chien, White Mouth told of the Lakota alliance proposal, and that 1,500 Lakotas were camped on the Tongue River. According to Lieutenant George Templeton, White Mouth and Chien also spoke of a treaty the Crows had signed at Fort Benton, in which they were promised a reservation. Through Chien, White Mouth told the soldiers that without an agency, "he was like a crazy man—had no place to trade." Echoing the Crow responses to the Lakotas, post commander Kinney replied noncommittally to White Mouth's statements, although he intimated that the government would support the Crows in any conflict with the Lakota. Kinney also provided the Crows with rations and papers that they could present to whites attesting their friendship, as well as permitting them to trade with post sutlers Alvin C. Leighton and John W. Smith.[30]

The context of the meeting suggests that White Mouth, having heard Red Cloud's offer, was now attempting to discern the United States' stance in regard to the trail and the Crows' lost homelands. Several issues were of concern to White Mouth and other Crow leaders before they would commit themselves. On one hand, Crow leaders appear to have been distinctly wary of Lakota offers of friendship, possibly fearing that an alliance would subordinate the Crows to the Lakota, with no guarantee of continuing peace between the two communities when (or if) the army was driven out. Militating against an immediate alliance with the army was the memory of Sully's failure to assist the Crows two years previously.

Even more troubling was the potential split in the Crow community. Even Crow leaders who leaned toward the Americans would be reluctant to move without a broad consensus of opinion among their followers. Though Bridger and Williams characterized the Lakota-leaning Crows as "young men," the divide among Crows was not entirely generational. Although some younger Crows may have been swayed by Lakota presents or warnings of what an American presence would do to game and other resources, others were equally eager to take action against the Lakota. Both Bridger and James Beckwourth, an African American fur trader who had formerly lived with and married into the Crow community, claimed that several hundred Crow warriors would readily volunteer to fight with the army against the Lakota if asked.[31] However, lack of unanimity posed the threat of Crows being pitted against kith and kin in any conflict.

The army's tepid response to Crow overtures also undoubtedly contributed to Crow ambivalence. Authorized to enlist fifty Indian auxiliaries, Carrington believed he lacked the authority to exceed that quota. And instead of enlisting Crows, he sent a representative back to Omaha to enlist either Pawnees or Winnebagos. Carrington explained his choice by noting that unlike the Crows, both the Pawnees and Winnebagos had previously served with the army against the Lakota. Additionally, Carrington said he decided not to enlist the poorly armed Crows because "the necessary delay in procuring their arms, would defeat the object of their employment."[32]

Nor could the army's manner of defending the trail have given Crow leaders much reassurance. Hamstrung by lack of troops, Carrington and Kinney could do little more than defend the forts themselves. Unable to take offensive action, they could not even effectively protect the trail itself beyond gunshot of the forts, let alone drive the Lakota and Cheyenne out of the region. Even near the posts, and particularly at Fort Phil Kearny, troops were subjected to almost daily harassment and attacks. If the futility of trying to protect a 545-mile route with fewer than 1,000 men was evident to the officers and men manning the posts, it was equally evident to the Crows. If the army was unable to protect the trail itself, what could it do for them?

Finally, even Crows friendly to the United States disliked the manner in which the trail had been blazed without permission through a region the Crows claimed as their own. In the camp on Clark's Fork, Iron Shell told Bridger that the Crows had signed a treaty aboard the steamer *Ben Johnson* in which they gave permission for a route that paralleled the Bozeman Trail south and west of the Bighorn Mountains (the so-called Bridger Cutoff). In Iron Shell's opinion, the agreement gave no permission for the Bozeman Trail, but he was willing to remain at peace until the matter could be settled by negotiation.[33]

To many of the officers stationed on the trail, especially at isolated and undermanned C. F. Smith, retaining the friendship of the Crows quickly took priority over safeguarding a trail no emigrants dared use. Among those concerned was Lieutenant George Templeton, who reported after a council with the Crows on October 31,

> From all I can see I am of the impression that if the government does not take decided measures very soon in regard to the Sioux, that the Crows will enter a league and for the first time make war with the whites. If the proper number of troops could be sent out next spring, the Crows would be glad of an opportunity to pitch into the Sioux and give them a good whipping. But as it is now they are so few in number in comparison with the Sioux that they are afraid to make war, but would rather submit to a disgraceful peace.[34]

Part of Templeton's concern was based on the continuing evidence of close contact between Crows and Lakotas. Throughout the fall of 1866, the Crows provided ongoing information to the soldiers on the strength, location, and intentions of the Lakota and their allies. According to Crow informants, it took half a day to ride through Lakota camps on the Bighorn. The Crows also reported a conversation with Red Cloud, who said he would starve the soldiers out by cutting Fort Phil Kearny's communications with Fort Laramie.[35]

Far from becoming Lakota allies, however, the Crows were beginning to realize the advantages they possessed as a neutral party. The Lakota, concentrating their efforts on harassing Fort Phil Kearny, were still trying to convert the Crows to allies. This preoccupation with fighting the Americans and the accompanying peace overtures to the Crows effectively freed the latter from Lakota raids. And because the Lakota had already stopped emigrant traffic on the trail, buffalo and other game remained relatively undisturbed. Taking advantage of the resulting freedom of movement and the abundance of game, a Crow village moved close to C. F. Smith in late October, and in early November, a large buffalo hunt was mounted for robes to trade with Smith and Leighton. The Crows also used their position to shut other tribes out of the trading loop, forbidding a group of Cheyennes from trading without a permit from Kinney. The Crows' insider position as a trade intermediary led a group of seventy-six Arapaho lodges to join their village in order to trade with Smith.[36] In the interest of maintaining friendly relations, the Crows exchanged visits with soldiers from the fort before splitting up in late November. Approximately a third of the Crows remained camped on the opposite bank of the Bighorn, while the remainder moved west to Clark's Fork of the Yellowstone to trade more of their newly acquired robes to the Nez Perce for horses.[37]

The Crows' ability to maintain amicable relations with both warring sides was further demonstrated the following winter, when the Lakota scored their greatest victory over the army in the so-called Fetterman Massacre (referred to by Indians as the Hundred Men Killed Fight) on December 21, 1866. In this engagement, a force sent out from Fort Phil Kearny to relieve a wood train under attack was itself ambushed and destroyed, with all eighty-one men in the detachment killed.[38] The Crows learned of the fight sooner than the soldiers at isolated C. F. Smith. Indeed, at least four Crows, three men and one woman, fought with the Lakota and Cheyenne in the battle.[39] The Crows told the initially disbelieving soldiers at C. F. Smith about the battle within a week, claiming at the time to have received the information from a Crow who had been visiting Lakota camps. Between winter weather and Lakota interdiction of the trail, official word of the disaster would not reach the fort until early February 1867.[40]

The Fetterman fight shocked the army and the nation, but it also marked a watershed for the Crows. The debacle could not have improved their estimate of the army's fighting abilities, but, perhaps fearful that the army would abandon the forts and the region to the Lakota, the Crows resumed their overtures of assistance. At the same time, the Lakota were warning the Crows to move away from the forts before they became embroiled in the conflict.[41] Templeton accurately summarized the Crows' position: "The Crows are in a quandary about the Sioux. They have received orders from them to leave our vicinity and they are afraid to disobey, and yet would like to remain and help the whites."[42] Kinney reported that several Crows had volunteered to act as couriers between C. F. Smith and Phil Kearny before the massacre, but none were willing to do so afterward.[43] For some Crows, however, the Fetterman fight drove a wedge between them and their Lakota suitors. According to the Crow Half Yellow Face, some Crows who had been camping with the Lakota separated from them after the Fetterman fight. To drive the point home, Crow raiders took five Lakota scalps and sent a message via an elderly Lakota prisoner that they would kill every Lakota who fell into their hands.[44]

Although the Crows were unwilling to serve without compensation, Kinney was able to hire ten Crows to serve as scouts and spies in January. The village near C. F. Smith was preparing to leave for the Wind River Valley, and Kinney did not care to lose his only source of reliable intelligence. The move to the Wind River may have been an attempt by the Crows to get their families out of the way of the conflict, or it may simply have been part of their seasonal pattern of movement.[45] Nevertheless, groups of Crows ranging in size from a few individuals to whole villages continued to frequent the area around C. F. Smith for the rest of the winter, hunting and trading. Those Crows who did remain in the area apparently perceived little danger from the Lakota.

The Lakota reaction to the Crows' continuing association with the army, and to the Crows' continued rejection of a Lakota–Crow alliance during the winter of 1866–1867, is difficult to gauge. Although Lakotas continued to warn the Crows to move away from the whites, there are no indications of Lakota aggression against the Crows during the winter; indeed, the Lakota apparently went out of their way to avoid being forced to fight the Crows. Indeed, the Crows' presence near Fort C. F. Smith may well have saved that small post's vulnerable garrison from attack. Post commander Kinney acknowledged as much when he reported that no hostile Indians had been sighted near C. F. Smith during the winter, partly due to the weather, "but chiefly to the fact of the Crows being camped within a few miles."[46]

The Lakota also did not seem overly upset with Crows carrying mail and gathering intelligence for the army, perhaps because the military showed no inclination to use the information to coordinate action or go on the offensive. Given the apparently decisive victory won in the Fetterman fight, it is possible that the Lakota and their allies had decided that they didn't need Crow assistance to drive the troops out and did not wish to fight both the army and the Crows to do so. (In a similar vein, it is possible that the Lakota had decided against putting themselves under any obligations to the Crows in return for their aid.) Finally, it served both Lakota and army purposes to use the Crows as intermediaries to communicate with and gather information about their adversaries. In January, for example, the Lakota sent word via the Crows that they intended to attack C. F. Smith with 3,000 warriors—a threat possibly aimed at encouraging the soldiers to abandon the fort. The promised attack never materialized. Later, Kinney used the Crows to deliver a message to a Lakota chief believed to be wavering between peace and war.[47]

As a result, Crow freedom of movement remained intact through January and February 1867. Despite the Lakota warning, Kinney's Crow scouts continued to gather information, and Blackfoot's band of Kicked-in-the-Bellies arrived in the vicinity of C. F. Smith in early February, with a portion of the village moving west to the Stinking Fork (Shoshone River) and others camping opposite the post. Toward the end of the month, the village moved again, with the women setting up their lodges around the fort while the men traded with the post sutler. Several Crows, including Long Horse, Bear in the Water, The Dog That Bats His Eye, and Iron Bull, also agreed to serve as couriers for $33 per month, although the service was less than reliable in the eyes of some officers. In March, Templeton recorded his exasperation with a pair of couriers carrying mail to Fort Phil Kearny who had turned back upon sighting buffalo at Lodge Grass Creek, writing, "I don't know what kind of ideas they have about running courier."[48]

Actually, the couriers knew exactly what they were doing. For the Indians, reporting the movements of buffalo during the winter, often a season of scarcity, was far more important than delivering messages between forts. The presence of buffalo nearby also called for a heightened state of awareness concerning the Lakota, in case they too were following the herds. The location of the Lakota became an increasing concern as spring approached because it was becoming difficult for the Crows to maintain their dual role. Although the Lakota and their allies had succeeded in closing the trail to emigrant traffic, they had failed to drive or starve the troops out. With another summer of warfare in the offing, they could no longer afford to tolerate either Crow neutrality or assistance to the Americans. A Crow who had visited a Lakota village reported that the Lakota were preparing to fight both the whites and the Crows unless the latter committed themselves to an alliance. According to a correspondent for the *Montana Post,* the Lakota offered the Crows 3,000 horses in return for their cooperation. Although the Crows refused the offer, on March 18, Templeton recorded that eight lodges of Crows had joined the Lakota, and there were rumors that even more planned to join after trading with the whites for powder.[49]

The disappearance of the neutral ground that the Crows had successfully occupied for nearly a year was demonstrated in May. During that month, bands of hostile Lakotas and Cheyenne moved closer to Fort C. F. Smith than ever before, running off some mules belonging to the post sutler, as well as some Crow ponies.[50] Until now, Lakota efforts to woo the Crows had insulated C. F. Smith, and the Crows themselves, from Lakota attacks. For a time, the Crows continued their efforts to play off one side against the other. In late June, when twelve Indians drove off thirty-nine mules and four horses from C. F. Smith, the Crows were accused of helping the raiders. When it appeared that the stampeded stock was headed toward the fort, some of the Crows camped around the post galloped between the animals and the fort, turning them back toward the raiders. The gesture may have been appreciated by the attackers, but not by the post commander, who promptly ordered all Crows away from the fort.[51]

Events in Montana also threatened to compromise the Crows' precarious position. Panicked first by the Fetterman debacle and then by the reported nearby presence of hostile Lakotas, settlers in the Gallatin Valley held an emergency meeting on April 19, calling for the raising of a military force to guard the settlements there. The request was given added impetus by the news that John Bozeman had been killed by Indians on the Yellowstone River near the site of present-day Livingston.[52] In response to the meeting, acting governor Thomas Meagher authorized the raising of a volunteer Montana militia. Volunteers were promised the right to keep any spoils of war they captured from "hostile" Indians.[53]

Despite the report of Bozeman's companion, who identified the killers as either Blackfeet or Bloods, rumors rapidly spread that held the Crows responsible. These rumors were given credence by the first dispatch from General Thomas Thoroughman, commander of the militia, dated May 7 from Bozeman:

I had no idea the Crows were willing en masse to break their peaceful relations with the whites and go to war, but just last night I had a conversation with five men just in from Ft. Smith who say that the Crows will first help take that fort, and then pass on to the northern part of the territory through this valley. It was they who killed Bozeman and wounded Cover. I believe they are the worst of all.[54]

Lesser members of the militia echoed the belligerent sentiments of their commander. Captain John A. Nelson claimed that Bear's Tooth's band of Crows, some eighty lodges, was preparing to go to war against the whites. Another militiaman, writing under the pseudonym Volunteer, alleged that the Crows were stealing horses from the militia and warned, "If Bear Tooth knows what 'the better part of valor' is he will give them up on demand."[55] The *Montana Post* helped fan the flames of suspicion. Earlier in April, the paper had recommended arming the Crows against the Lakota while holding Crow families hostage as guarantees of good behavior. Now the paper printed letters from members of the militia, alleging that the Crows were sheltering Bozeman's killers in their camps. Meagher, citing information from the Nez Perce, reiterated Thoroughman's rumor that the Crows had joined the Lakota in a plot to take the Bozeman Trail forts.[56]

The motive behind much of this warmongering is not difficult to discern. Montanans had long speculated about the mineral wealth that Crow lands might contain. In 1863, the Crows had driven groups of prospectors encroaching on their lands, killing one, and during the Bozeman Trail conflict, the *Montana Post* repeatedly printed reports touting the mineral potential of the area.[57] In 1865 and 1866, Meagher had urged the government to conclude treaties with the tribe to gain legal access to Crow lands, pointing out that hundreds of miners were already exploring and prospecting in the Yellowstone Valley and beyond the junction of the Missouri and Gallatin rivers.[58]

The Crows' efforts to remain neutral in the Bozeman Trail conflict also played into the hands of Montanans eager to open up Crow lands. It was easy to interpret the lack of Crow–Lakota hostilities as a sign that an alliance between the two communities had actually been consummated. In his 1866 letter, in fact, Meagher lumped the Crows together with the Lakota and Arapaho in holding the Yellowstone Valley "defiantly" against the wishes of white Montanans.[59] Finally, an Indian scare could be profitable, with money to be made from freighting supplies and contracting with the government for goods at highly inflated prices. The perceptive Lieutenant Templeton quickly grasped this motive: "It seems they are authorized to raise 800 militia. Every one seems to be trying to see how much he can make off the government in fitting them out."[60]

Under such circumstances the militia, with many miners in its ranks, was unlikely to be a stabilizing force.[61] Though no attack was made on Gallatin Valley settlements by either Lakotas or Crows, the militia did venture to escort a supply train to C. F. Smith in late May and early June. En route to the Bighorn, the militia met parties of Crows and Lakotas, none of whom offered any resistance. In spite of this, Lieutenant Hazlett of the militia reported that the militia hanged one Indian and shot two others during the trip. Hazlett did not explain why the three were killed or indicate which tribe or tribes they belonged to.[62]

Then, on August 13, a prospecting party consisting of A. F. Weston, his son, William, and Thomas Mann left Bozeman to prospect on Boulder River and Clearwater Creek, both in Crow territory. After being joined by Frank Hodges on August 23, the four were prospecting four miles up Stillwater River when they were surrounded by an estimated 200 Indians. William Weston and Hodges were both killed and the survivors driven out of the area. A force of militia sent to rescue the elder Weston and Mann and recover the bodies of the dead encountered a band of Crows, killing one and recovering items identified as belonging to William Weston and Frank Hodges.[63] That the Crows had been defending their own territory and had apparently allowed the two survivors to escape was ignored in letters and reports from the militia. Colonel Neil Howie reported that "everything in the deserted camp goes to prove they were a war party of FRIENDLY Crows," while Captain Isaac F. Evans wrote that "there is now but no question but what the Crows have joined the Sioux and Blackfoot and are bent on a war of extermination against the whites."[64]

By spring 1867, the Crows appeared trapped between increasingly hostile white Montanans on one side and increasingly insistent Lakotas on the other, with an impotent army and seemingly unresponsive U.S. government either unable or unwilling to effectively intercede on their behalf. However, events in the region, including the Fetterman fight and the formation of the Montana militia, finally spurred the government to action. Scrambling to maintain friendly relations with one of the few communities in the region not in active conflict with Americans, both the army and Office of Indian Affairs condemned the creation and actions of the militia. Influenced by memories of the 1864 Sand Creek Massacre, in which a unit of Colorado militia had helped spark a war by slaughtering a village of friendly Cheyennes, Lieutenant General William Tecumseh Sherman, rarely an advocate of softness toward Indians, castigated Meagher for threatening to bring on a conflict with the Crows "when he knew very well that the government desired very much to retain peaceful relations with them."[65] Representatives from the Office of Indian Affairs, which rarely found itself in harmony with Sherman, wholeheartedly agreed, commenting that the militia's actions "would have involved us in an almost interminable war with the Crows but for the interference of the military authorities."[66] Then in February, the secretary of the interior, Orville H. Browning, ordered the formation of a six-member commission to gather information about the Fetterman fight and investigate the causes of the Bozeman Trail conflict.

The creation and the composition of the commission boded well for the Crows. Unlike the Fort Laramie councils of 1866, this time the Crows would have the opportunity to have their voices heard, with commission member Judge John F. Kinney specifically assigned to meet with them.[67] The commission also included the Crows' old acquaintance, General Alfred Sully. Even before reaching Laramie, Sully outlined his views in a letter to Secretary Browning. In the letter, Sully claimed that maintaining friendly relations with the Crows would not only be good policy but "an act of justice." He reiterated the history of Lakota conquest of the region and his own belief that Lakota hostility "forfeited all claim on our Government to any recognition of their rights and title to that country to the exclusion of the Crows." Backed by the rest of the commission, Sully advocated sending a sufficient military force into the region to drive the Lakota out and reinstate the Crows on their treaty lands. Then the government could negotiate with the Crows for any necessary roads through the region.[68]

Sully's letter carried the promise of everything the Crows sought. It portended a complete reversal of the 1866 negotiations, in which the government had tacitly recognized and legitimized the Lakota conquest of the Powder River country. It proposed to return Crow treaty lands first, then negotiate for trail rights and other concessions sought by the whites, as well as the opportunity for the Crows to seize a central position in the northern Plains fur trade. If the commission held to the views expressed in Sully's letter and the government acted on them, the Crows could be the beneficiaries of a 180-degree turn in the tribal power structure in the region.

Arranging a meeting between the Crows and Kinney proved difficult, however. The Crows refused to make the difficult and dangerous trip through Lakota-controlled territory to Fort Laramie, preferring a meeting at the more congenial surroundings of C. F. Smith.[69] The Crows' reluctance was heightened by the disappearance of three warriors, whom the Crows suspected had been killed by the Lakota.[70] Eventually, General Henry Wessells, Carrington's successor, was able to convince the Crows to make the trip to Phil Kearny, but they remained adamant about not venturing farther south.[71] But by the time Kinney arrived at Phil Kearny on May 31, most of the Crows had decamped. Their departure for a buffalo hunt in the Tongue River valley may have been hastened by a Lakota raid that claimed forty-three Crow ponies. Only a small group led by White Mouth, Bad Elk, and Roman Nose remained behind. Kinney asked Roman Nose to bring the rest back for a council.[72]

In his conversations with Crow leaders, Kinney learned that they had reopened negotiations with the Lakota for a temporary truce. Despite this, he told his superiors, most Crows preferred an alliance with the United States. "Without our protection," he reported, "self-preservation will require them to join the Sioux. They much prefer the former." Kinney recommended that the Crows be given military protection as well as supplies, and included a request by Thin Belly that the Crows be compensated for the loss of ponies incurred while waiting for his arrival. Finally, and most significantly, he continued to advocate returning the Crows' lost lands.[73] Unfortunately, there are no available accounts of this meeting from Crow sources. If Kinney expressed the same sentiments to them that he did to his superiors, they could only have come away from the meeting with heightened expectations. But the Crows' subsequent actions, as well as the Lakota response to Kinney's visit, do provide some clues.

On June 18, Crows cooperated with troops at Phil Kearny to thwart a Lakota horse-stealing raid, an action for which Wessells warmly commended the Crows.[74] At C. F. Smith, a party of Crows under Iron Bull requested permission from the post commander to go out and meet a small group of Lakotas spotted lurking about the fort. After a short fight, the Crows routed the Lakota, taking one captive, who they promptly burned to death.[75] Later, Crows warned C. F. Smith's garrison of an impending attack by the Lakota, a warning fulfilled when the Lakota and their allies fruitlessly attacked a hay contractor's camp (known as the Hayfield Fight) on August 1.[76] Further evidence of the breakdown in Crow–Lakota amity can be seen in changes in the quality and quantity of intelligence the Crows provided the military regarding the Lakota. Throughout 1866 and into 1867, the Crows were able to provide detailed information about the location and size of Lakota camps. Indeed, the Crows often camped in close proximity to the Lakota, taking advantage of their newfound freedom of movement to follow the buffalo herds in peace. By early June 1867, however, the Crows had lost track of Lakota movements and locations, though they did report a small band of Cheyennes camped near the mouth of the Little Powder River.[77]

In the meantime, Kinney had assigned his interpreter, trader John Richard, and Raphael Gallegos to accompany the Crows and prevent them from being influenced by the Lakota.[78] The pair joined Crazy Head's camp on the Little Bighorn, but before the camp could complete a planned move to the Wind River, a Lakota messenger arrived bearing word of an impending Lakota visit—and that the Crows could either trade with them willingly or fight. The messenger claimed that the combined Lakota, Cheyenne, and Arapaho mustered 6,000 warriors, compared to 500 in the Crow camp.[79]

After the emissary's arrival, a hastily called council of headmen and leaders of warrior societies met to consider options. Fighting was quickly ruled out, but even trading was at best a bad bargain because the Crows would have to trade many of their best horses and accept inferior Lakota mules and horses in return. Finally, the council decided to trade with the visitors and then attempt to move out of reach.[80] After the decision was reached, Richard, Gallegos, and about forty Crows slipped out of camp, fearing to remain behind lest they be killed. The group's arrival at C. F. Smith on July 11 with news of the Lakota threats caused a general exodus of Crows from the vicinity of the fort.[81]

When Gallegos returned to Crazy Head's camp, he interrogated the camp headmen about whether the Crows had traded any ammunition to the Lakota. "They told me they did not trade them a single charge of ammunition," he reported. "They said the village was harangued the whole day the Sioux were there against trading ammunition, and the young men and soldiers were forbidden by the Chiefs to trade their ammunition to the Sioux." Gallegos believed the Crows wanted to retain their ammunition for self-defense in case the Lakota attacked them, vividly portraying their precarious situation: "Being so inferior in numbers to the hostile Indians, they were in constant fear of them, expecting every day a fight. . . . While I was with them their village was constantly guarded against their attacks, and their horses kept close about their camps, for fear of their being stolen by the Sioux."[82]

According to Gallegos, the Crows had planned to move up into the mountains immediately after their meeting with Kinney to avoid the Lakota, but the snow in the mountain pastures was still too deep for good grazing and the Crows were desperately short of meat, forcing them to remain in the area to hunt. Still, Gallegos remained convinced that "no nation of Indians can force them to join in a war against the whites."[83]

Gallegos's testimony showed that the Crows' meeting with Kinney had not eased the tribe's situation. Indeed, in some respects, the Crows were worse off than they had been before. Unless the United States abandoned its defensive policy and committed enough troops to take the offensive, the Crows would continue to be vulnerable to Lakota attacks. The breakdown of Crow–Lakota amity would also make it increasingly difficult for the Crows to hunt buffalo and lay in vital stocks of meat for the coming winter.

Moreover, other members of the commission, while questioning the United States' right to the Bozeman Trail, were more inclined to recognize Lakota control of the region via conquest rather than honor Crow treaty rights. Even before the Kinney–Crow meeting, Commissioner Nathaniel Buford had recommended that the trail be given up. Buford regarded the trail as superfluous, given the availability of the Missouri River water route to Montana and the continued extension of the Union Pacific Railroad, which had already reached the town of Cheyenne, directly south of Fort Laramie, by 1867. Commissioner John B. Sanborn added that the government had acted in bad faith in failing to obtain Lakota consent before opening the Bozeman Trail. Both Buford and Sanborn recommended abandoning the trail and creating one massive reservation for use by all the Indians in the region, a proposal that implicitly accepted Lakota hegemony in the Powder River country.

Even Kinney, the Crows' main supporter, was pursing an agenda ultimately incompatible with the tribe's goals. The Crows sought the return of the Powder River country in order to maintain their nomadic, hunt-based lifestyle. Kinney, however, saw assistance to the Crows as the first step in a broader process of transforming Indians into a sedentary, agricultural, Christianized people, with the bonus that the Crows, as American allies, would not need to be conquered first. In the same letter that recommended aid to the Crows against the Lakota, Kinney wrote of the need of the Crows to be "tamed and enlightened."[84] The shift in government priorities from maintaining the Bozeman Trail to conciliating and civilizing Indians was reflected in a message from the commissioner of Indian affairs, Nathaniel Taylor, to Kinney on July 9. In the message, Taylor advised against bringing the Crows to Phil Kearny for their meeting with Kinney. Instead, Kinney was to leave them in their own country on the Tongue River to subsist themselves. If they were driven out by the Lakota, Kinney was to bring the tribe to a railhead or some point on the Missouri River where the government could feed them.[85]

Taylor's instructions were never carried out, for the very good reason that they did not arrive until after Kinney's meeting with the Crows. However, even if they had, it is doubtful that the Crows would have agreed to what essentially would have been the complete abandonment of their homeland and complete dependency on the government for survival. On the other hand, Taylor's directive was admirably suited to a program of "taming" the Crows by divorcing them from their old lifestyle, and in the process avoiding the thorny issue of whether the Lakota or the Crows had a right to possession of the disputed Powder River country.

The Hobson's choice the Crows faced became clearer on July 20, 1867, when Congress appointed a new seven-member peace commission to negotiate an end to the Bozeman Trail conflict. Neither Kinney nor Sully retained their appointments from the old Fetterman commission; the only holdover was John Sanborn. Joining Sanborn was Commissioner of Indian Affairs Taylor, Senator John B. Henderson, Indian agent Samuel Tappan, and generals William T. Sherman, William S. Harney, and Alfred H. Terry.[86] As it organized in St. Louis in early August, the commission dispatched trader Gemien Beauvais and Dr. Henry Matthews to contact the Lakota and Crows, respectively, for a fall council at Fort Laramie.[87]

When Matthews arrived at C. F. Smith on September 12, he found the Crows much more restive and divided than they had been during Kinney's visit. Troubles with the militia had crested in August with the attack on the Weston party, and time for crucial fall hunts was rapidly approaching. At an initial meeting with about a dozen Crow headmen, Matthews received a cordial reception, but he noted that "one or two of their speakers touched upon our occupancy of the country, in such a manner as . . . would lead one to infer that they did not acquiesce in it very cordially." More ominously, the chiefs told Matthews that the young warriors were violently opposed to making the trip to Laramie. One week later, Long Horse led a group of his followers in for an acrimonious talk with Matthews. Long Horse's specific grievances are impossible to ascertain; Templeton reported only that his conduct was "saucy" and that after being ordered to keep quiet, the chief left the fort in a huff.[88]

If Long Horse's words were not recorded, the broader cause of Crow discontent is easier to discern. In truth, the spring decision to reject a Lakota alliance and pin their hopes on the United States had been barren of results for the tribe. Kinney's advice to stay away from the Lakota, while reasonable, also meant that the Crows had been unable to take advantage of the buffalo herds in the Powder River country. By the fall of 1867, the Crows were facing the prospect of starvation.

Throughout the fall and winter, Lieutenant Colonel Luther Bradley, commanding the Mountain District from C. F. Smith, called the government's attention to the Crows' predicament. In a letter to Commissioner Sanborn in October, Bradley wrote that the conflict over the trail, as well as the Crows' friendship with the whites, had impoverished the tribe. "The Crows are poor and are very much in need of substantial aid from our government," he wrote. "They have nothing but their small stocks of ponies and what skins they have dressed this summer. I do not see how they are to get through the coming winter."[89] A fortunate few obtained employment as couriers and scouts, but for most, this was not an option.[90] By January, Bradley estimated that fully half the Mountain Crows would need assistance to prevent suffering.[91] A month later, Matthews reported he had purchased twenty-five head of cattle and 100 sacks of flour from supply officers at C. F. Smith to provision the Crows, who were "clamorous for food."[92]

In subsequent meetings with the Crows, Matthews urged them to stay together for protection against the Lakota, while continuing his efforts to lure a delegation to Laramie to meet with the peace commission. Somewhat paradoxically, Matthews also sent Crow couriers to Lakota camps in an effort to bring them to the council as well. Although none of Matthews's messengers induced the Lakota to come in, one did return with surprising information.

On October 23, White Forehead returned from a Matthews-sponsored mission with news that the Lakota and their Cheyenne and Arapaho allies had agreed to suspend hostilities until after the Laramie negotiations had ended, although they still did not plan to attend. Even more interesting was White Forehead's report that a war party of Lakotas, Cheyennes, Arapahos, *and* Crows was leaving for a raid against the Shoshoni. (Three days later, a supply train arriving at C. F. Smith reported it had met this party, some 300 warriors strong; the raiders had sent a Crow to the train to reassure the soldiers that they had no hostile intent.)[93]

Two weeks before White Forehead's return, the Crows had suddenly announced a willingness to travel to Fort Laramie to meet the commission. Accompanied by Matthews and a military escort, some 300 Mountain Crows and Kicked-in-the-Bellies, led by nearly twenty prominent headmen, including Blackfoot, Bear's Tooth, White Horse, Wolf Bull, and Shot-in-the-Face, left C. F. Smith on October 13 for the 327-mile journey.[94] It seems extremely unlikely that the Crow reversal was due to Matthews's persuasiveness. Instead, it suggests that the most important diplomacy during this period was not taking place between Matthews and the Crows, but between the Crows and the Lakota, as indeed would become apparent during the Laramie councils.

The refusal of the hostile Lakota and Cheyenne to attend made the Crows the focus of the meetings held on November 12–13. Besides the Crows, a few Arapahos were the only Indians from the Powder River area present. The only Lakotas at Laramie were the so-called Laramie Loafers, most of whom had abandoned the hunting life and were more or less permanent residents near the fort. Although the Crows had center stage, their old requests that the United States drive the Lakota out of the Powder River country were conspicuously absent from Crow speeches. Instead, the Crows' main speakers, Bear's Tooth and Blackfoot, demanded the closing of the trail and the abandonment of the forts in the region. Besides being the fastest route to peace, Blackfoot labeled the trail "the cause of all our wars and misfortunes."[95] Far from being an ally of the United States, the Crows now appeared to be serving as a proxy for Lakota and Cheyenne interests.

Or at least appeared to be. In reality, Crow interests had been converging with those of the Lakota and Cheyenne for more than a year. During that time, Crows had steadily seen Lakota predictions regarding the deleterious effects of the trail borne out, while the focus of U.S. policy shifted from treating the Crows as a valuable ally to treating them as a ward in need of cultural and social transformation.

As early as 1866, army officers themselves had observed and commented on the adverse effects of the trail on buffalo and other game. En route to C. F. Smith in August 1866, Lieutenant Templeton reported more than 10,000 buffalo in the valley of the Little Bighorn. Just two weeks later, Templeton noted the absence of buffalo near the Bozeman Trail crossing of the Bighorn River. He speculated that the herds had been frightened off by the emigrant trains that had been backed up at the crossing during previous weeks.[96] Two years later, the commander at C. F. Smith corroborated Templeton's report. "It is certain that since this country has been used for travel, and for troops, that the buffalo is leaving it," he wrote, "why this is so I cannot say. I only speak of the fact, as testified to by the officers who came up here in 1866, by the border men, like Bridger and Richard, and by the Indians themselves."[97]

Lest the commissioners be in any doubt on this point, Bear's Tooth made the Crow perspective clear:

Call back your young men from the mountains of the bighorn sheep. They have run over the country; they have destroyed the growing wood and the green grass, they have set fire to our lands. Fathers, your young men have devastated the country and killed my animals, the elk, the deer, the antelope, my buffalo. They do not kill them to eat them; they leave them there to rot where they fall. Fathers, if I went into your country to kill your animals, what would you say?[98]

Nor were the Crows any more receptive to commissioners' suggestions that, because the buffalo were doomed to disappear, the Crows should sell off their land, begin to farm, and accept schools so that "your children may become as intelligent as the whites." "We want to live as we have been raised, hunting the animals of the prairie," Blackfoot responded. "Do not speak of shutting us up on reservations and making us cultivate the land."[99]

In the view of many whites, both the Crows and the United States sought the defeat of the Lakota. For the Crows, however, that goal had gradually been superseded by the preservation of an environment in which their culture, lifestyle, and integrity as a people could be maintained—an objective that by 1868 was threatened much more directly by the Bozeman Trail and the United States than by the Lakota. Should the buffalo be wiped out and the Crows forced to subsist on the white man's handouts or an agricultural way of life, the retention of the Powder River country would be meaningless.

It was this realization—that in many respects the interests of the hostiles and those of the Crows were identical—that brought Crows together with their former enemies in the fall of 1867. Like the Crows, the Lakota and Cheyenne faced similar problems of subsistence and survival, not to mention unity, during the increasingly drawn-out conflict. During the fall, a runner sent by Gemien Beauvais to contact the Lakota and Cheyenne reported that several Lakota band leaders, or *itancans,* along with the Cheyenne headman Lame White Man, appeared receptive to peace overtures, but were opposed by those allied to war leaders such as Red Cloud. The messenger's arrival sparked a fight in a Lakota camp between war and peace factions in which several people were hurt, horses killed, and property destroyed.[100]

The connections between two prominent families eased Crow–Lakota communication. Taking advantage of the kin ties created through his marriage to the sister of the Lakota *itancan* Man Afraid of His Horses, the Crow leader Blackfoot spoke with both his brother-in-law and Red Cloud before the Laramie council and relayed their refusal to consider a treaty until the trail was abandoned to the commissioners.[101] For his part, Bear's Tooth said the Lakota had asked the Crows to report what was said at the council and had predicted that the whites would lie to and attempt to swindle the Crows.[102]

At the close of the council, the Crows unanimously refused to sign the proposed treaty the commission had brought, citing three main objections. First, the Lakotas were not present to give their consent to the treaty. Second, the treaty made no mention of abandoning the Bozeman Trail. Finally, the Crows declared that all their headmen should be present to sign an important agreement. The best the commission could salvage from the talks was an agreement to meet again at Fort Phil Kearny in the spring.[103]

———————

In the clash of cultures between Indians and Americans in the fall of 1867, Crows and Lakotas stood together—for a time. This united front would not survive the abandonment of the Bozeman Trail, however. When several hundred Lakotas, Cheyennes, Arapahos, and Crows appeared at Laramie for a council with Matthews in late December 1867 and early January 1868, a Lakota speaker piously proclaimed that "the Sioux, Arapahos, Cheyennes, and Crows never fought with one another until the white man came into the country and drove away our game, then drove us away. And we had to fight each other for sufficient ground to hunt upon." When the time came for Blackfoot, the main Crow representative present, to speak, he did not repeat Lakota platitudes about intertribal harmony but instead requested gunpowder. Whether the gunpowder was needed for hunting or defense he diplomatically did not say.[104]

In the spring of 1868, the U.S. government's decision to abandon the trail and the forts along it was confirmed in a series of treaties with area tribes. However, the 1868 treaties represented more than a tacit acknowledgement of American defeat. The agreement between the United States and the Lakota ratified not just the latter's defense of the Powder River Country, but also their conquest of it. In addition to establishing what became known as the Great Sioux Reservation (essentially, that part of the future state of South Dakota west of the Missouri River), the treaty also set aside the areas "north of the North Platte River and east of the summits of the Bighorn Mountain" as "unceded Indian territory" claimed by the Lakota.[105] In contrast, the Crows' treaty severely reduced Crow territorial claims, compared to those recognized in 1851. The treaty set the boundaries of the Crow reservation as the Yellowstone River on the north and west, the Montana border on the south, and the 107th meridian of latitude on the east, well to the west of the Powder, Tongue, and Rosebud rivers. Despite bitter protests that the United States treated their enemies better than their friends, ten Mountain Crow and Kicked-in-the-Belly headmen and one River Crow representative signed the treaty on May 9.[106]

The ink was hardly dry on the treaties before relations between the Crow and Lakota resumed their normal course. Less than a month after the Crows signed their treaty, a Lakota war party killed a Crow returning from Laramie, possibly in an attempt to hasten the Crows' departure from the area. Under the leadership of Thin Belly, fifty Crows quickly formed a war party to seek revenge. In subsequent years, the Crows would continue to serve as scouts for the U.S. Army in their campaigns against the Lakota, and the Lakota would continue their steady encroachment onto Crow lands (the Battle of the Little Bighorn, at which Crows scouted for George Armstrong Custer's 7th Cavalry, would actually take place within the boundaries of the Crow Reservation, just two miles from the future site of Crow Agency).[107]

In later years, the warrior and chief Plenty Coups would proclaim that for the Crows, allying themselves with the Americans was "the only way open to us." However, Plenty Coups added an important caveat: "When I fought with the white man . . . it was not because I loved him or because I hated the Sioux and Cheyenne, but because I saw that this was the only way we could keep our lands."[108] When the threats to Crow lands and society came from the United States, Plenty Coups and other Crows would find ways to consult and collaborate with other Native peoples, both in 1867 and after the onset of the reservation era.

PART TWO

Reimagining Community

In the fall of 1909, Joseph K. Dixon, a former Baptist minister and self-proclaimed Indian expert, and Rodman Wanamaker, a prominent Philadelphia businessman and philanthropist, sponsored what they called the Last Great Indian Council. Twenty-one representatives from thirteen tribes converged at Crow Agency for a week of meetings, speeches, and reminiscences. Afterward, Dixon published the transcribed speeches of participants in a book grandiloquently titled *The Vanishing Race*.[1]

Not surprisingly, Dixon's introduction to the book mirrored the backward-looking, nostalgic tone suggested in the title. To Dixon, the council was an opportunity for "a long and last farewell," not only for a previous way of life, but also for Indians themselves. "The Indian, as a race, is fast losing its typical characters and is soon destined to pass completely away," he wrote, by way of emphasizing the significance of "the last great Indian Council that will ever be held on American soil." After this, Dixon implied, there would be no occasion or reason for Indian peoples from different tribes to meet and talk to each other. On the surface, the speeches of Dixon's cast of "typical characters"— all elderly male warriors—supported this master narrative, replete with tales of warfare, folklore, and yearning for a vanishing past.[2]

At the same time, however, subtle undercurrents cut against this fading into oblivion. Several of Dixon's chiefs failed to play to type, with one proclaiming his status as a tribal policeman, another worrying about the status of his hay crop during his absence from home, and another boasting of his work as a church missionary. Moreover, many of the participants' speeches contained tropes of kinship and amity rather than hostility. Opening the council, the Crow leader Plenty Coups stated, "I am at peace with all the tribes, they are all my brothers, and I meet them all as one man." The Umatilla Tin-Tin-Meet-Sa, shaking hands with Plenty Coups, seconded this statement, saying, "On this day we meet as Indians and as brothers," while others also declared themselves "friends and brothers" and "a brother to all the tribes."[3]

The historian Russell Barsh suggests that such proclamations demonstrated Dixon's willingness to "romanticize and patronize" Plenty Coups and the other council participants. According to Barsh, for Dixon, such statements validated "a triumph of personal power and white supremacy." "In just a few days," Barsh notes with a heavy dose of irony, "Dixon singlehandedly settled centuries of intertribal warfare and brought peace to all Indians."[4]

Barsh's analysis may accurately describe Dixon's fantasies, but less clear (in both *The Vanishing Race* and Barsh's later examination of "The Last Great Indian Council") is the perspective of Barsh's patronized old men. Were the declarations of Plenty Coups and his fellow chiefs merely window dressing, an attempt to mouth the proper words to please a prominent white patron? Or might their professions signify something else, a recognition of a shared identity, built not on white-sponsored events and institutions such as the Last Great Indian Council, but on generations of intertribal contact and shared contemporary circumstances? Could the gathering at Crow Agency have revealed not the passing of a vanishing race, but the emergence of a shared, reservation-based Indian identity? Or, given the contents of Young Man Afraid of His Horses's 1889 letter, the persistence of an already existing, reservation-based Indian identity?

The social, cultural, and political ties forged between Crows and other Indians during the early to mid-nineteenth century did not simply disappear with the imposition of American hegemony and the arrival of the reservation era in the late 1800s. Despite the best efforts of government officials to keep "their" Indians at home, reservations never became the hermetically sealed, isolated islands so often portrayed in tribal histories. Indeed, the emergence of reservations would, paradoxically, help bring Indian communities together. The creation of separate reservations for separate tribes eliminated contests over land and resources that had often placed tribes at odds with one another, while the expansion of railroads and the spread of mail service eased travel and communication. At the same time, the introduction of wage labor–based economies and ongoing threats to native landholdings, cultures, and communities posed by the United States stimulated movement and exchange between reservations, reinforcing old relationships and forming the basis for entirely new relationships founded on broad-based Indian values such as reciprocity, generosity, and extended kinship, often counterposed to American values like thrift, materialistic individualism, and nuclear kinship.

At Crow, these developments would lead to the emergence of a new sense of Indianness, one that extended beyond the direct kin ties of the early to mid-nineteenth century and that asserted a common, shared relationship between Indians of all tribes. Moreover, rather than replacing older, more discrete tribal identities, this emerging Indian identity coexisted with older conceptions of community; indeed, its growth was facilitated by the decentralized, bottom-up construction of community that typified prereservation-era tribalism. Combined with the new elements of reservation life, the flexible and permeable boundaries of traditional tribalism would pave the way for the introduction of new religious beliefs (in the form of peyotism) and eventually to a push for the wholesale incorporation of dispossessed, homeless Crees into the Crow tribe.

However, the circumstances of reservation life would also produce a countervailing movement toward a more limited and impermeable definition of community. The finite amounts of land, jobs, and other resources available on the reservation created pressure from both Crows and the U.S. government to limit access to these resources to "real" Crows. One result of this would be a shift toward a more bureaucratic, corporate, top-down means of determining membership in the Crow tribe. The determination to create a reservation only for Crows would also manifest itself in opposition to government proposals to resettle Northern Cheyennes on a portion of the Crow Reservation; to opposition to peyote as a deviation and departure from traditional Crow spirituality; and eventually to a rejection of the kind of intertribal politics the Crows had engaged in to close the Bozeman Trail in 1867–1868. Ultimately, the Crow tribe that emerged on the Crow Reservation around 1900, although remaining distinctively Crow, would be far different from the Crow community as it had existed in the early and mid-nineteenth century.

CHAPTER THREE

The Politics of Visiting

In early October 1883, Crow agent Henry Armstrong was jolted out of his daily routine by what, to him, was an unprecedented event: a peaceful visit by a delegation of Oglala Lakotas. Led by Young Man Afraid of His Horses, forty-five Lakota warriors attired in full regalia and war paint arrived at Crow Agency. Approaching a group of waiting Crows, the delegation halted, except for Young Man Afraid of His Horses and one other Lakota. The pair dismounted, and in Armstrong's words, "advanced four or five paces in front of their horses, knelt down with their heads bent forward until they almost touched the ground, remained in that position a moment, then arose, returned to their horses, squatted, or sat, down in a row in front of the horses and began shouting and making speeches." One Crow rushed forward and threatened to kill the Lakotas, but was restrained by Crow agency policemen. It was, Armstrong averred, "the first friendly visit we have any word of" from the Crows' "ancient enemies."[1]

Ending intertribal warfare was a key element in the U.S. government's program to civilize Plains Indians in the late 1800s, but Armstrong detected ominous portents in the Oglalas' visit.[2] He treated them less as guests bent on peace than as unwelcome intruders, and refused to issue them rations during their stay at Crow. Nevertheless, on the day set for the Lakotas' departure, they showed no sign of leaving. In response, Armstrong called several of the visitors to his office and told them that "if they did not go at once I would get some troops [from nearby Fort Custer], and round them up, and send them back. Then they went."[3]

Writing to his superiors afterward, Armstrong suggested that the cessation of intertribal hostilities could cause as many problems for the government as continued warfare. He reported that he had told the Lakotas that he "had no feeling of enmity or ill-will toward them; but that I thought that it was not good for them to come here visiting in large parties; [and] that I did not want my Indians to go to their country visiting." Then, in his letter to the commissioner of Indian Affairs, Armstrong penned a much more revealing comment: "I think it is a better policy to keep alive the traditional enmities and jealousies between these tribes (not to the extent of causing or permitting them to make

79

war upon each other however) than for us to try and get them to be friends. The more divided these northwest tribes are the weaker they are and the more easily controlled."[4]

Armstrong's responses to the Lakota visit neatly encapsulated the attitudes that would inform federal Indian policy during the next forty years: the desire to restrict indigenous freedom of movement; the demand that Indians not look to the government for support; and the threat of arrest or the use of force to compel compliance. By and large, these are the same themes scholars have emphasized in what little discussion exists on the subject of intertribal visiting during the early reservation era.[5]

However, other elements also appear in Armstrong's report. As much as he disapproved of and deplored the possible consequences of the visit, he was unable to prevent it from taking place. Armed with a pass from Pine Ridge agent Valentine McGillycuddy, Young Man Afraid of His Horses could make a case for the legitimacy of his presence at Crow.[6] Instead of immediately evicting his unwelcome guests, the best Armstrong could do was negotiate a departure date.

Additionally, far from being the "first friendly visit" between Lakotas and Crows, Young Man Afraid of His Horses's trip was actually the second peaceful contact between the two in the space of a year. During the winter of 1882–1883, ration shortages forced McGillycuddy to allow Young Man Afraid of His Horses to take a party of men off Pine Ridge to hunt buffalo in the Powder River country. While hunting, the Lakotas had encountered a group of Crows and, in McGillycuddy's words, "made peace with them," with Young Man Afraid of His Horses promising to make a formal visit to Crow to confirm the peace the next year. The proposed visit—the same one that caused Armstrong's consternation—received McGillycuddy's blessing. "Considering that these two tribes have been at war for several generations," he wrote, "an exchange of visits would be conducive to the general welfare of the Indians, and also tend to suppress a war-like feeling generally."[7]

Armstrong and McGillycuddy's differing roles in and responses to Young Man Afraid of His Horses's actions illustrate another theme emphasized by historians in recent scholarship: the fragmented, incomplete, ambiguous, and often contradictory nature of American efforts to resolve the country's "Indian problem" in the late 1800s.[8] Armstrong's desire to keep Indians divided and at home crossed paths with McGillycuddy's anxiety to defuse "war-like feeling" as well as the need to prevent the unrest that went with short rations. Despite their seeming positions of power, both found themselves forced to compromise abstract principles as a result of local circumstances beyond their control.

Young Man Afraid of His Horses was fully capable of exploiting such circumstances. Embroiled in disputes with Red Cloud, by now the officially recognized head chief of the Oglalas, McGillycuddy had been cultivating the goodwill of Young Man Afraid of His Horses for four years by 1883. For his part, according to biographer Joseph Agonito, the Oglala used McGillycuddy in an attempt "to restore the Man Afraid family to a position of political prominence within the Lakota community at Pine Ridge and to the white world beyond." McGillycuddy won Young Man Afraid of His Horses's support for the creation of an Indian police force at Pine Ridge (a move opposed by Red Cloud and leaders of the Oglala warrior societies), as well as for the creation of a board of councilmen in 1884 (in which Red Cloud refused to participate). Members of the initial board selected Young Man Afraid of His Horses as its president. During the same period, Young Man Afraid of His Horses also supported McGillycuddy's drive to suppress (publicly, at least) the Sun Dance at Pine Ridge.[9] However, such support did carry a price. In 1884, Young Man Afraid of His Horses requested another pass to visit the Crows, while Little Wound and Blue Horse sought permission to visit the Shoshonis (another so-called traditional enemy of the Lakota). Writing to commissioner of Indian Affairs Hiram Price, McGillycuddy commented, "As all the above Indians are the staunch supporters of the Government, I recommend that pass be granted to them."[10]

As McGillycuddy's letter to Price suggested, Young Man Afraid of His Horses was not alone in being able to manipulate government officials in order to secure permission to visit other reservations. In the early to mid-1880s, even agents like Armstrong, who deplored McGillycuddy's seemingly permissive attitude, found themselves faced with a limited range of options when it came to intertribal visiting. Restricted financial and manpower resources limited their ability to restrain their charges and confronted them with a dilemma: either issue passes for Indians to visit other tribes, or face the prospect that their putative charges would simply travel on their own. Responding to complaints that Crows were leaving the reservation to hunt and to visit other reservations, Armstrong would explain to Commissioner Price (at virtually the same time that McGillycuddy was writing) that persuasion was his only real weapon to keep the Crows at home. "I do everything I can to keep my Indians from leaving the reservation and to keep foreign Indians from coming here," he wrote. However, the shortage of agency personnel, most of whom were engaged in

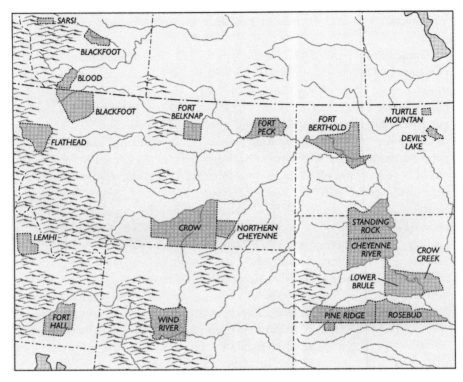

Map 3. Indian Reservations on the Northern Plains, 1890.

teaching the Crows to farm, meant that Armstrong couldn't "possibly patrol more than a hundred miles of the reservation line to prevent the good-for-nothing Indians from getting outside." As Armstrong knew, calling on the troops at Fort Custer was at best an after-the-fact remedy, unless standing orders were instituted to patrol reservation boundaries—a delegation of military control to the Office of Indian Affairs that the army high command was unlikely to endorse.[11]

More often than not, Crows unpersuaded by Armstrong's entreaties simply ignored the agent's orders. Crazy Head and Deaf Bull left the reservation repeatedly in the early 1880s, both to hunt and to visit the Lakota at Pine Ridge and Standing Rock reservations. Bear Wolf, another Crow band leader, also set out for the Lakota agencies in the fall of 1883 but was arrested and incarcerated briefly at Fort Custer. Undaunted, he left the reservation again after his release in the spring of 1884 and spent the summer hunting and traveling between the Pine Ridge and Cheyenne River Lakota reservations in Dakota

Territory and the Northern Cheyenne Reservation at Tongue River just east of Crow.[12]

Although Armstrong (and other agents) were prone to label such roamers as recalcitrant traditionalists unwilling to settle down to farming, the hunters' activities bore little resemblance to stereotypical images of bloodthirsty, savage warriors.[13] Instead, by the early 1880s, the Powder River country, which had been hotly contested territory only a generation ago, had become not only one of the last remaining game refuges on the Northern Plains, but also an arena for intertribal communication and conciliation.

What is particularly striking about all these activities is not only the extent of these encounters, but also the background of the personalities involved. It seems unlikely that Young Man Afraid of His Horses's central role in brokering the initial Lakota visit to Crow Agency was the mere happenstance McGillycuddy portrayed it to be. Indeed, it would be difficult to identify a more likely candidate to lead a friendly party to Crow than Young Man Afraid of His Horses, given his family's kinship ties to the Crows and the role members of the Man Afraid family had played in Crow–Lakota communication during the Bozeman Trail era. Other key participants in this hunters' diplomacy also had ties to both communities, including Bear Wolf, the offspring of a Crow father and a Lakota mother. Even Crazy Head, described as a stalwart warrior in former years who "kept the Sioux away," was also the leader of a camp visited by Lakotas during the late 1860s.[14] Far from being the product of new leaders reversing past patterns of hostility, visiting and intertribal diplomacy during the 1880s had its roots in preexisting legacies of contact, communication, and exchange.

In the early and mid-1880s, the limited and contested nature of government control on Northern Plains reservations was evident. The year after Young Man Afraid of His Horses's first visit, a delegation of thirty Northern Cheyennes led by Two Moons made an unauthorized trip from the neighboring Tongue River Reservation to Crow.[15] The Northern Cheyenne had been allied with the Lakota in their conflicts with the Crow, but as in the Lakota case, years of warfare had also forged numerous ties between the two. Typical of these ties was the family background of the Northern Cheyenne Wooden Leg, named after his Crow-born, Cheyenne-raised uncle. Other Cheyennes, including Bull Thigh and Big Foot, and the headmen Little Horse and Crazy Head (not to be confused with the Crow band leader Crazy Head), were the sons of captured Crow women who had married Cheyenne men.[16]

Armstrong called on the military at Fort Custer to remove his unwanted guests and predicted to the fort's commander that such action would "probably guarantee no more visits from them this season."[17] Unfortunately, Armstrong's actions proved no more effective a deterrent than his jailing of Bear Wolf. Two weeks later, Two Moons's party returned, this time bearing a pass from Northern Cheyenne agent E. P. Ewers.

Writing to Ewers subsequently, Armstrong admitted to tearing up Two Moons's pass but denied calling Ewers "a fool." Armstrong reiterated his dislike of visits from large parties—or any parties—of "strange" or "foreign" Indians. Armstrong pleaded with Ewers to prevent the Cheyennes from coming to Crow "if you could possibly keep them from doing so."[18]

Armstrong's "if" indicated an awareness of the special problem the twenty-four-mile common border between the Crow Reservation and Tongue River posed. It was possible for Northern Cheyennes to travel to Crow (and vice versa) simply by crossing the line, without having to travel through any intervening nonreservation, white-settled territory.[19] Armstrong's "if" may also have indicated a growing awareness of the influence internal reservation politics played in visiting. Like Young Man Afraid of His Horses, Two Moons was a community leader whose goodwill and cooperation were worth courting. Although technically prisoners of war after their surrender at the close of the Great Sioux War of 1876–1877, Two Moons and many of his followers subsequently served as army scouts at Fort Keogh at the junction of the Yellowstone and Tongue rivers in the late 1870s and early 1880s. Both before and after the establishment of the Tongue River Reservation (by executive order rather than treaty) in 1884, Two Moons played a key role in preventing conflict between the Northern Cheyennes and local white ranchers who opposed the creation of a reservation on grazing land they coveted. In the 1890s, Two Moons's son, John, was appointed head of the agency police. Such services merited special consideration; in 1898, Tongue River agent James Clifford wrote to his counterpart at Crow requesting permission for Two Moons and about seventy Cheyennes to visit the Crows before spring plowing. Ordinarily, Clifford explained, he was not in favor of allowing large parties to go visiting, "but in view of Two Moons' past services," he asked the Crow agent to approve the trip.[20]

In such circumstances, all most agents could do was to attempt to maintain a semblance of control by granting formal travel passes to encourage or reward good behavior, a carrot that even less noteworthy individuals could enjoy. In the summer of 1887, the agent at Rosebud Reservation wrote to notify Crow agent Henry Williamson that he had authorized a pass for Two

Strike, agency policeman He Dog, and fourteen other Lakotas to visit the Crows. The agent explained that Two Strike and his party were "not bad Indians though non-progressive," and that the pass was a reward for their good behavior in the past year. Unfortunately, several Indians, including the policeman Turning Bear, had joined the party without permission. The Rosebud agent asked Williamson to arrest Turning Bear and send him and the other hangers-on back to Rosebud.[21]

The Rosebud agent's explanation did nothing to mollify Williamson. Writing to the commissioner of Indian Affairs, the Crow agent fumed that it was wrong to allow "a lot of renegade, taken-for-granted-non-progressive Sioux" to come to Crow in the middle of farming season. Williamson requested that the commander at Fort Custer be ordered to intercept and turn back the entire group, including Two Strike and his fellow pass bearers.[22]

Even Crow agents, however, were forced to issue passes simply to maintain a measure of control over their charges. During the spasm of horse raiding that marked the final years of intertribal warfare in the early 1880s, Crow agents regularly issued passes to Crows to leave the reservation in search of stolen stock, or sent out groups under the supervision of an agency employee to preempt retaliatory raids.[23] Crows also took advantage of a clause in the agreement granting a right of way up the Yellowstone Valley to the Northern Pacific Railroad that allowed them to ride the trains for free. The provision expired on May 1, 1884, but in June, Armstrong complained to a railroad official that Crows "still ride up and down at pleasure."[24] Less than a month later, Armstrong was writing to Northern Pacific officials with a changed tune. Although the railroad was no longer obligated to let the Crows ride free, Armstrong explained that he was sometimes compelled to let Crows travel by train in search of stolen horses, or to visit friends in prison, and requested that the railroad allow Crows bearing passes from the agent to continue to ride without tickets. Occasionally, Armstrong sent Indian police by train to search for unauthorized absentees from the reservation.[25]

From an agent's perspective, the worst effects of visiting were the disruption of daily routines and the setbacks they inflicted on efforts to inoculate American virtues of thrift, diligence, and other standards of civilized behavior. Even the arrival of otherwise "progressive" Indians could promote distinctly unprogressive behavior. In 1886, acting Crow agent M. L. Black wrote to Fort Berthold agent Abram Gifford regarding the passes Gifford had issued to the Hidatsas Wolf Eye, Dog Bear, and Kidney to visit the Crows. Even with passes in hand, the trio had been on the reservation for a week before reporting to the agency. Although they appeared to Black to be "good Indians," the dances the Crows gave their visitors disrupted farming, and the Hidatsas further irritated Black by demanding rations and free railroad passes to return to Fort Berthold. Black asked Gifford not to issue any more passes.[26]

Black's request echoed prior efforts by Armstrong and Williamson to curtail travel, none of which proved very effective. The previous year, Williamson had sent a circular letter to the agents at every Northern Plains reservation requesting them to arrest any Crows found on other reservations without passes, and that passes not be given to other Indians to visit the Crows. Writing to Blackfeet agent Reuben Allen, Williamson elaborated on the situation. He explained that he issued no passes purely for "social visiting," and that he had eight farmers and his agency police watching for Crows leaving the reservation without permission. In spite of this, Williamson admitted, "There has been a great deal of what I consider unnecessary and useless visiting of other Indians to the Crows, and some visits by the Crows to other tribes."[27]

What Williamson, Armstrong, Black, and other agents termed useless, of course, was viewed differently by those immediately concerned. For Indians, visiting was more than a diversion from reservation life and a chance to indulge in what Williamson dismissively called "two or three weeks of dancing, war paint, and feathers."[28] In fact, in addition to establishing peace with former enemies and maintaining existing friendships, much of the interreservation travel during this time was, ironically, a direct result of federal policy decisions and attempts to control Native populations.

Many Lakota trips to other reservations in the early 1880s were motivated by a desire to trade for horses. During the campaigns of 1876 and 1877, the army had seized thousands of horses from both agency Lakotas and hostile bands after their surrender.[29] Though designed as a military measure to curtail Lakota mobility and resistance, the seizures prompted Lakota efforts to rebuild their herds in the 1880s. Harsh Dakota winters also took a periodic toll on the Lakotas' remaining horses; in 1881, an unusually severe winter resulted in the loss of one-third of the stock at Standing Rock.[30] Earlier in the nineteenth century, the Lakota had raided horse-rich tribes like the Crow and Shoshoni; now that same wealth made the Crow and Wind River reservations prime destinations for horse-trading expeditions.[31]

The cultural importance of horses was not the sole motivation for the Lakota on these trips; economic factors also played a significant role. As the buffalo robe trade declined and dependency on other sources of subsistence increased, many Lakotas turned to freighting as a means to earn or augment their livelihood. Pine Ridge Lakotas not only freighted supplies to Pine Ridge from the nearest railhead at Valentine, Nebraska, but also carried freight from

Valentine to white settlements and mining camps in the Black Hills. Though not representing the OIA ideal of Lakotas turned into sedentary, productive farmers, Pine Ridge agent McGillycuddy nevertheless commented approvingly on this use of "animals that in former times were war ponies and are now broken in as draft animals."[32] However, in a large measure, the development of this area of the Lakota economy depended on the perpetuation of old and the creation of new intertribal networks of trade and gifting.

Not surprisingly, Pine Ridge Oglalas were particularly active in this area. In 1883, McGillycuddy allowed a delegation to travel to Wind River after Red Cloud received a letter from the Northern Arapahos there inviting him to visit and trade for horses. Similarly, the trips by Little Wound and Blue Horse to the Shoshoni, and by Young Man Afraid of His Horses to the Crows, appear to have been motivated at least in part by what a Crow agent dismissively described as a desire to "swap money—blue cloth—pipes, and etc. for ponies."[33] The results of these expeditions are amply documented by the stock censuses included by agents in their annual reports. At Cheyenne River, horse numbers increased from only 606 in 1878 to 2,785 by 1887, while at Pine Ridge, the focus of the army's 1870s confiscation campaign, horses numbered more than 6,500 by 1887 and 9,013 in 1889.[34] Horses continued to be a main item of exchange and a prime rationale for visiting until at least the turn of the century. In 1899, for example, Spotted Elk, a Pine Ridge Oglala, wrote to the Crows' agent requesting permission to visit, explaining that during a previous prior visit to the Crows he had obtained forty horses, but that the harsh winter of 1898–1899 had killed off most of them, forcing him to return to Crow to obtain replacements.[35]

Nor were horses and other material goods the only objects exchanged during these visits. News and rumors also traveled with visitors, sometimes creating situations where supposedly isolated Native Americans proved to be better informed than their guardians. In August 1885, a perplexed Armstrong wrote to the commissioner of Indian Affairs, explaining that several Crows had demanded permission to see their children at the Carlisle Indian School in Pennsylvania, claiming that parents from other tribes had been allowed to see their children. "I do not know how they learned this if it is true," he wrote, and requested official guidance on the matter.[36] The Crows' information (accurate, as it turned out) most likely came from Lakota visitors.[37]

Similarly, Northern Cheyennes complaining of the paucity of rations and supplies issued at Tongue River made invidious comparisons to conditions at other reservations, including that of their Crow neighbors. "You can look around you and see that my young men have old faces," Howling Wolf protested to army major Henry Carroll at an 1890 council. "It is hunger that makes them look so." White Shield added, "Whenever I go to the other agencies I see what they have got and it makes me ashamed. We don't get enough to eat."[38] The Cheyennes' agent confessed that he was unaware of what the ration issue on the Crow Reservation was, but he had been informed that the Crows' revenue from grazing leases amounted to more money than the government's entire appropriation for Tongue River Reservation. He noted that the Crows' "revenue has been expended judiciously for their benefit—this naturally presents to these Indians [the Northern Cheyenne] a great contrast." When rations were increased several months later, a new agent stated that the Cheyenne now appeared "happy and contented."[39]

Visiting, as Agent Armstrong recognized, thus represented far more than the mindless, nostalgic, and apolitical "two to three weeks of dancing, war paint, and feathers" that his successor Williamson would dismiss it as. When Indians of different communities came together in the late 1800s, there was no shortage of pressing contemporary issues to discuss between hosts and guests. Although rooted in earlier patterns and precedents and guided by familiar protocols, visiting arguably took on greater importance after Native American political, economic, and social autonomy came to an end with the onset of reservation life. Indeed, in many ways the emergence of reservations encouraged and aided visiting. War parties might find it more difficult to travel through the spaces separating reservations, now filling with non-Indian farmers and ranchers and towns, but on peaceful journeys, roads, railroads, and even the fixed location of reservations themselves made travel faster and more predictable.[40]

On the surface, however, patterns of Native American travel, hunting, visiting, and interaction during the 1880s do not seem to manifest a singular Indian as opposed to tribal consciousness and identity. Lakota horse-trading expeditions can be seen as a peaceful variant, even a legacy, of generations of horse raiding. Indeed, at the same time that Young Man Afraid of His Horses was leading delegations to Crow, Crows were still engaging in violent exchanges of horse raids with the Piegan and Assiniboine.[41] Similarly, the request of Crow parents that they be allowed to visit their children at boarding schools, just as parents of children from other tribes did, may reflect less an assertion of a shared identity than a demand that the Crows be granted the same privileges enjoyed by other tribes.

At the same time, however, countercurrents were emerging—symbols and voices that spoke of a new sort of kinship. The roots of this kinship lay not just in the biological ties that already linked many Indians to other tribes, but as a shared response to the new relationship that existed between Indian peoples and white society. These new ties did not replace or even weaken tribal affiliations, but instead augmented and extended existing values and beliefs. The expression of these ideas did not emerge in a unified, coherent manner, but in myriad forms, like a thermal basin whose waters, superheated far underground, simmered and boiled to the surface through fissured and cracked rock, emerging as a hot spring in one place, exploding as a geyser in another, and bubbling and splatting as a mud pot elsewhere. The manner in which ideas were expressed depended on a multitude of factors, including the degree of pressure and heat applied, the subterranean geography, and surface conditions. Any of these circumstances were subject to change, whether through massive tectonic shifts or through slow erosion or the deposition of sediment. And if the expression of these ideas varied, neither were they uniformly shared. In some places, the heat and pressure failed to work the transformation, and older beliefs and attitudes persisted.

The signs were hard to read and harder to interpret for contemporary white observers. Early in 1885, the commanding officer at Fort McKinney, Wyoming (just south of the Crow and Tongue River reservations), reported that "Indians from the different reservations have been for more than a year past roaming hither and thither, camping here and there, in parties of from one to fifteen lodges." The activity gave rise to rumors of a grand alliance being established between the Crows, Cheyenne, Arapaho, Shoshoni, and Lakota against the Piegan and other Indians in northern Montana. McKinney's commander, Lieutenant Colonel C. C. Compton, doubted the truth of the rumor, although he stated that "there is to be a meeting by invitation to or from the Sioux and Shoshones extended also to the Crows, in the early summer, at some point on the North Platte River, Wyoming. It is supposed that this meeting is merely to talk and trade horses, etc., but its object is not fully known." Compton promised to have a representative at the meeting to find out its purpose.[42]

As interesting as the rumored alliance were the sources of information that Compton and others tapped. A rumor at Crow held that troops were to be sent out on a punitive expedition against the Piegans, and that "some of the young bucks of the Sioux would like to join the troops." Compton doubted this rumor too, noting that "this last statement must be taken with many grains of allowance, as it was given here by a young Sioux who had been at the Crow agency all winter and not with his own people for six months."[43] At the same time Captain Carroll Potter, commanding Fort Assiniboine near the Fort Belknap Reservation (home to the Gros Ventre and Assiniboine), reported an interview with a Gros Ventre who had "returned from the Crows sometime early in February 1885, after a stay there of nearly three months." This man also cast doubt on the rumors of a grand alliance and intertribal war. Potter added casually that "one lodge of Gros Ventres leave this Agency to-morrow for the Crow Reservation, and I am assured by good authority that it would be next to an impossibility to make ill feeling between Indians at this agency" and the Crows."[44]

Potter and Compton's reports shed a different light on the subject of visiting. Although most visits were relatively brief (albeit still too long for agents like Armstrong), others were extended affairs in which visitors, either singly or in small groups, remained with their hosts for several months or even a year or more. Such sojourners most likely attempted to maintain a low profile to remain undetected by agents anxious to keep foreign Indians off their reservations, but they do occasionally appear in official records. For example, writing to Crow agent Williamson for another pass for Young Man Afraid of His Horses in 1887, Pine Ridge agent Hugh Gallagher stated that a Crow woman named Hail would accompany the party, returning home after a stay of two years at Pine Ridge.[45] Stays of six months to two years hardly seem to qualify as visiting; instead they indicate a level of intercultural and interpersonal exchange that could serve as the basis for a larger, shared sense of understandings that could transcend tribal boundaries. During the latter half of the 1880s, this nascent sense of a larger Indian community would become visible on the Crow Reservation.

As in the army's investigation of a rumored Indian alliance, the signs here were blurred, indistinct, and subject to misinterpretation. One reason for this may be that the transformation (at least in the mid-1880s) was most visible among Indians whom agents and other government officials typically classed as traditionalists, whose adherence to older ways seemingly precluded the emergence of a new, broader sense of identity. Notable among these non-progressives were the leaders of hunting parties meeting with old enemies peacefully in the Powder River Country. Also symbolic of this confusion was the figure of Young Man Afraid of His Horses, viewed as a progressive and a staunch supporter of government authority at Pine Ridge, but as a disturber and impediment to good order on the Crow Reservation.[46]

Young Man Afraid of His Horses's visits, of course, were not the only expression of new attitudes toward intertribal contact. Young Man Afraid of His Horses himself pointed toward a vision of the future couched in the language of diplomacy, trade, and kinship. Rooted in a history of intertribal contact reaching back decades, Young Man Afraid of His Horses's stance did not compromise his Lakota identity and affiliation, but looked forward to a relationship with Crows that did not end with the departure of the last war party. As Armstrong's response to Young Man Afraid of His Horses's first visit indicated, this by itself was enough to threaten the goals of the federal officials, missionaries, reformers, and others bent on eradicating tribal identities and merging Indians into American society as individuals rather than Indians. Some Indians would prove unwilling to follow Young Man Afraid of His Horses's lead; others would push beyond it to voice an even broader vision of the future of intertribal exchange, amity, and unity. In the summer and fall of 1886, two representative figures of these approaches would arrive at Crow in the form of the Hunkpapa Lakota leaders Gall and Sitting Bull.

Formerly an active opponent of U.S. colonialism, Gall had by 1886 become an important ally of Standing Rock agent James McLaughlin, one of twenty Lakota "boss farmers" in charge of farming districts on the reservation, and a member of the Episcopal Church. Characterized by Robert Utley as a "shrewd pragmatist," Gall came to Crow in 1886, ironically to participate in an event that fits the existing stereotype of intertribal visiting: as part of a nostalgic commemoration of the past. In this case, however, the occasion—the tenth anniversary of the Battle of the Little Bighorn—had official sanction. Gall, as a notable participant in the battle and a living symbol of the transformative power of civilization, enjoyed the status of an honored guest, and talked freely and amicably with army officers, including several 7th Cavalry survivors. However, when introduced to Curley, a Crow scout in 1876 and already the subject of legend as the sole escapee from George Armstrong Custer's doomed battalion, Gall's attitude changed. According to one account of the meeting, Gall taunted his former enemy, stating, "You were a coward and ran away before the battle began; if you hadn't you would not be here today."[47]

Despite his "progressive" status, Gall's visit, both in its purpose and in the tenor of his conversation with Curley, pointed to the past. Safely neutralized and expressed in retellings of intertribal hostility, Gall's enmity toward a former Crow adversary posed no threat to reservation order in the present. Ironically, it would be the second visitor, Sitting Bull, the staunchest of all adherents to Lakota culture, society, and spirituality, who would speak in the language of shared Indian peoplehood.

Curiously enough, Sitting Bull's visit also received official approval—at least from Standing Rock and Washington, if not from Crow agent Williamson, who pleaded with Standing Rock agent James McLaughlin not to permit Sitting Bull and some fifty other Lakotas to travel to Crow. "My Indians are peculiarly situated at the present time," Williamson wrote. "They are peculiarly susceptible to any outer influence for good or evil." Writing to the commissioner of Indian Affairs, Williamson left no doubt which category Sitting Bull's trip fell into. "Decidedly opposed Sioux visiting," he telegraphed, claiming "some Crows object—no good to be accomplished. Evil might result." In his letter to McLaughlin, Williamson added a thinly veiled threat of retaliation: if Sitting Bull's trip were permitted, "several hundred Crows" would demand permission to return the visit, disrupting McLaughlin's reservation in much the same way Sitting Bull's arrival would disrupt Williamson's.[48] Increasing Williamson's discomfort was the news that some 100 Cheyenne River Lakotas were planning to visit in response to a Crow invitation promising gifts of ponies "to cement their friendship," while Young Man Afraid of His Horses was bringing yet another Lakota delegation from Pine Ridge.[49]

Williamson was less than candid in describing the "evil" to be expected from traveling Lakotas. Calling on the old image of intertribal hostility, he cited recent horse raids by Piegans and "Sioux" against the Crows, although the Sioux in this case were Yanktons from Fort Peck.[50] Crow raiders had also recently killed two Assiniboine women at Fort Peck. Henry Heth, the Fort Peck agent, proposed "a friendly meeting [between the tribes] be arranged to take place either here or at your agency." Williamson, his reservation about to be overrun by friendly Lakotas, wrote back that "such a meeting would be productive of much harm in many ways," and promised to arrest the murderers.[51] Williamson also claimed that "many of my best Indians are opposed to visits from other Indians"—a dubious assertion in light of the Crows' apparent invitation to the Cheyenne River delegation.[52]

Two years earlier, Williamson's predecessor had warned that intertribal peace, no less than intertribal warfare, could imperil the government's control over Indians. That prediction would prove prescient after Sitting Bull's arrival at Crow in September 1886 for a two-week visit, accompanied, as a precaution, by the chief of the Standing Rock agency police.[53] Like Gall, Sitting Bull called on the memory of the Little Bighorn during his visit. Unlike Gall, however, Sitting Bull used the battlefield, with its newly dedicated monument to the dead of the 7th Cavalry, not to denigrate the Crows, but to symbolize the potential of Indian unity: "Look at that monument. That marks the work of our people. See how the white man treats us and how they treat you. We get one and one-half pounds of beef per ration, while you receive but one-half pound. You are kept at home and made to work like slaves, while we do no labor and are permitted to ride from agency to agency to enjoy ourselves."[54]

Sitting Bull might seem an unlikely candidate to build bridges between

Lakotas and Crows, but as with Young Man Afraid of His Horses, the Hunkpapa possessed a long legacy of intertribal diplomacy. In 1875, a year before the Little Bighorn, Sitting Bull had orchestrated a joint Sun Dance ceremony to strengthen ties between the Northern Cheyenne and the Lakota. Two years later in Canada, he joined with the Nez Perce refugee White Bird in sending an invitation to the Crows to join his Lakotas in fighting the United States. That same year, Sitting Bull succeeded in concluding peace between his people and Piegans led by Crowfoot, cementing the alliance by renaming his youngest son after the Piegan leader.[55]

In 1877 the Crows rejected Sitting Bull's overtures, responding to a Hunkpapa gift of tobacco with a horse raid.[56] In 1886, however, Sitting Bull found a more receptive audience with a rhetoric that spoke of shared concepts of Indian rights and government obligations. At this distance it is impossible to determine exactly how Sitting Bull spoke to the Crows, or the sense in which the phrase "our people" was used, intended, or understood, but in addressing problems of common concern to both Crow and Lakota he clearly struck a responsive chord.

The main problem was land. During the 1880s, pressure on the Crows to cede more of their reservation for white settlement intensified. In 1880, the Crows had agreed to cede 1.6 million acres on the western boundary of the reservation, an agreement that also contained a provision for the assigning of individual allotments of land to Crows. The following year, the Northern Pacific Railroad received a right of way for a railroad line running up the Yellowstone River Valley. During this same period, federal officials also negotiated controversial leases with white cattlemen for grazing rights on reservation land.[57]

Like the Crows, Sitting Bull was no stranger to difficulties with whites over land. In the 1870s, he had witnessed the theft of the Black Hills from the Lakota after the discovery of gold there. Then in 1882, a government commission attempted to break the Great Sioux Reservation into six separate reservations. After separate tracts were assigned to each agency, nearly one-third of the old reservation would be thrown open to white settlement. The commission ultimately failed to gather the required signatures of three-fourths of all Lakota men required by the earlier treaty of 1868, but the prospect of future demands hung heavily over all Lakotas.[58]

Sitting Bull's visit to Crow coincided with the arrival of new allotment officers at Crow. Three days after their arrival, the officers met with the Crows on ration day to explain their presence. They reported "not . . . a word of dissent or opposition," noting that the Crows "all expressed satisfaction that their lands were to be allotted to them."⁵⁹ However, the Crows' supposed support for allotment died quickly after the arrival of Sitting Bull. One allotment officer claimed that "the result of his wily counsels were made evident by expressions, growing more and more emphatic, of opposition," and reported a conversation in which the Hunkpapa leader "virtually admitted that he had given this advice to the Crows; and said further that the same system had been proposed to his people, but that he was opposed to it, and had requested his agent to at least defer the matter for the present." He added, "It is therefore morally certain that the frequent attitude of these people is the immediate result of the machinations of and the insidious counsels of Sitting Bull."⁶⁰

In reality, it seems far more likely that Sitting Bull's visit provided Crows with a justification for openly expressing attitudes already festering just below the surface. Although agents described the Crows as anxious to obtain allotments, Crow dissatisfaction predated Sitting Bull's arrival. When George Milburn, an attorney from nearby Miles City, arrived to begin assigning allotments in the fall of 1885, he was met with a distinct lack of enthusiasm. Many of the survey stakes placed earlier had been either destroyed or removed. Milburn reported that he spent ten days surveying and staking out allotments for a village on the Bighorn River, but no sooner had he completed his work than the Crows "deserted their home and camped near the agency . . . and treated with contempt my endeavor to have them send with me sufficient Indians to enable me to put the Indians' names upon the lands blocked out after so much labor."⁶¹

Sitting Bull's claims regarding the willingness of "his" agent to delay allotment also likely increased Crow disenchantment with their own agent. Crows found Henry Williamson to be bullying, belligerent, and threatening, as well as a drunkard. They also disliked Williamson's handling of agency affairs and regarded the ration issue as insufficient—complaints that gained greater impetus (and belatedly received official notice) in the wake of the Hunkpapa's visit.⁶²

Beyond these elements, the visits of Gall and Sitting Bull illustrate both the irony and the limitations of labels such as "progressive" and "traditional" in considering intertribal visiting during the early reservation period. It was Gall the progressive who called upon and reified the tribal rivalries of the past, while it was Sitting Bull, an arch traditionalist according to most standards, who called on a shared Indian identity, much as members of more acculturated, "progressive" Indian organizations such as the Society of American Indians would do after the turn of the century. But though common concerns provided a basis for Indian unity, local circumstances did impose limitations on the ability—or wisdom—of expressing that unity. The year after Sitting Bull's visit, the armed defiance of government authority by some Crows would fail to gather support, not only within the Crow community, but also from neighboring tribes.

On the evening of September 30, 1887, a group of twenty-five Crows led by a charismatic young man named Sword Bearer returned to Crow Agency after a horse raid on the Piegans. The raiders rode through the agency compound, firing their guns into the air and at the roofs and chimneys of the agency buildings before riding off.

A shocked Henry Williamson requested troops from Fort Custer after witnessing the display from the porch of his home. An extended standoff between troops and Sword Bearer's adherents ensued, during which most Crows maintained a studied neutrality. The confrontation ended on November 5 after a brief exchange of fire between troops and Sword Bearer's supporters. Following the skirmish, most of the Crow leader's supporters surrendered, while a wounded Sword Bearer himself was shot and killed by a member of the agency Indian police.[63]

What became known as the Sword Bearer outbreak has usually been understood within the narrow confines of Crow tribal history. Though some scholars note events such as Sitting Bull's visit as a precursor to the episode, most accounts do not fully explore the intertribal dimensions of Sword Bearer's challenge to federal authority. Sword Bearer, also known as Wraps Up His Tail, belonged to the band led by the half-Lakota Bear Wolf and may well have traveled with Bear Wolf to Lakota agencies in the early part of the decade. In June 1887, Sword Bearer was involved in a confrontation with a detachment of troops from Fort Custer that had been sent to intercept and turn back parties of Lakotas from Pine Ridge and Rosebud arriving at Crow for a visit. The Lakotas, led by Young Man Afraid of His Horses and Two Strike, left peacefully under military escort, but not before a brief standoff took place between Crows and the troops. Crazy Head led the Crows protesting the soldiers' actions, but Sword Bearer was also singled out for mention in the report filed by the officer commanding the detachment.[64]

Sword Bearer also had extensive contact with Northern Cheyennes from Tongue River both before and during the outbreak. Before the June encounter with the soldiers, Sword Bearer and several other young Crow men made an unauthorized visit to Tongue River. When Williamson summoned them to his office upon their return, the Crows came to the agency armed. According to the agency physician, Sword Bearer declared that they had done nothing wrong and would not allow themselves to be arrested. Williamson declined to push the issue and allowed the Crows to go, after warning them not to leave the reservation again.[65]

Northern Cheyennes may also have been responsible for the name Sword Bearer. During their visit to Tongue River, Wraps Up His Tail and several other Crow men reportedly participated in a Cheyenne Sun Dance. According to one account, Wraps Up His Tail's performance in this rite apparently so impressed his Cheyenne hosts that they presented him with a sword.[66] Although the presentation of a weapon was not normally a part of the Cheyenne Sun Dance, this does not preclude the possibility that Sword Bearer received his sword and name in this fashion. Cheyennes were not only familiar with swords from their encounters with the U.S. military but on occasion owned and used them themselves; a Cheyenne ledger book from the late 1860s contains several drawings depicting Cheyennes armed with sabers.[67]

Crow participation in a Cheyenne Sun Dance also merits comment. Although the Crow and Cheyenne rituals were called by the same name and were similar in form, they were completely different in purpose. As Robert H. Lowie put it, "Essentially, the Crow Sun Dance was a prayer for vengeance." The pledger who sponsored the ceremony had typically lost a relative and sought to achieve a vision through the dance that would enable him to gain revenge on the group responsible for the death. Unlike many other Sun Dances (including that of the Cheyenne), the Crow Sun Dance was not an annual ritual. Its specific purpose and the elaborate and expensive preparations it required meant that the Crow Sun Dance was performed only sporadically, perhaps once every three or four years.[68]

In contrast to the Crow Sun Dance, the Cheyenne Sun Dance (called the Medicine Tepee Ceremony by Cheyennes) was an annual earth renewal ritual. However, as suggested by Sitting Bull's sponsoring of a joint Lakota–Cheyenne Sun Dance in 1875, the Cheyenne Sun Dance was more than simply a religious rite. According to John Moore, for the Cheyenne, "Politically the Sun Dance was nothing less than a statement of who was in and who was out of the national alliance at any time, and of who the current enemies and allies might be." In other words, it possessed some of the same meaning for Cheyennes that the rituals of the Tobacco Society did for Crows. As guests, Sword Bearer and his fellow Crows would have occupied a special place in the Sun Dance circle.[69] Sword Bearer's participation signified more than an expression of religious belief; on a social and political level, it also established bonds of alliance, community, and perhaps even kinship.[70]

Regardless of whether or not Sword Bearer received his name and distinctive weapon from the Cheyennes, it is clear that Cheyennes were familiar with him and his power. The Cheyenne historian John Stands in Timber described the Crow as riding "a black bobtailed horse that he painted with a crooked lightning line, and he used to paint himself black, with white stripes and spots on his body and face. He tied his hair together in front of his head, so it fell down over his face." While visiting a Crow camp, a Cheyenne man named Austin Texas witnessed a demonstration of Sword Bearer's power: "He rode through a Crow village one time dressed that way, and up onto a high hill. He faced east and south and west, and then clouds came up and a big storm came and blew a lot of teepees down."[71]

Word of Sword Bearer's defiance quickly spread beyond the Crow and Northern Cheyenne reservations and the borders of Montana. On October 20, the agent at Rosebud Agency, home to the Brule Lakota and some 400 miles distant from Crow, reported, "Effect of Crow disturbance plainly discernable here—runners have arrived and my Indians are uneasy, traveling from camp to camp and urgently soliciting passes in large bodies to visit other agencies." The agent added, "Sitting Bull's incendiary talk on the field where Custer fell is recognized as the origin of the present trouble."[72]

Sword Bearer's travels, as well as outward-rippling news of the outbreak, resurrected fears of a larger, intertribal uprising. The arrival at Crow of twenty Indians "mounted and armed" from Fort Belknap Reservation in mid-October further frayed nerves. Explaining their presence, Fort Belknap agent Edwin Fields reported that he had given passes to two different groups. Seven Assiniboines received a pass to visit relatives at Crow as well as to search for two horses that were believed to have been stolen by Crows. Fields explained that he had issued the pass believing that the Indians would be able to recover the horses "without expense to the Indian Department." Another pass was given to Otter Robe, a leading man among the Gros Ventres, to visit the Crows and the Arapahos at Wind River Reservation. According to Fields, "Otter Robe's father, himself and his family have lived with the Arapahos and Crows half their life time and only for the past five or six years have they resided here. Annually since then they have visited either or both of these tribes." Both passes were issued after the trouble at Crow began, but Fields explained that the mail and newspaper service to Fort Belknap was so slow that he was unaware of the situation at the time—another instance of news spreading faster among Indians than their white guardians. "Had I known of trouble at the time of giving passes under no circumstances would I have granted them," Fields wrote apologetically. Field had taken the precaution of sending a letter to Crow agent Williamson explaining the nature of the visits, but as it turned out, the Indians got to Crow before the mail did.[73]

About October 12, the Assiniboines reported to Fort Custer en route to Crow Agency. Learning of their and the Gros Ventres' arrival, Williamson had the post commander arrest them, but the request was countermanded by Department of Dakota commander Brigadier General Thomas Ruger, who had arrived to supervise military operations against Sword Bearer and his followers. The visitors were quickly released and traveled to Crow Agency, where they remained at liberty for nearly two weeks before being taken into custody and returned home.[74]

After the initial confrontation with Williamson and the troops, Sword Bearer returned to the Northern Cheyennes. In mid-October, he and thirty to fifty of his followers (including Deaf Bull, who had somehow wrangled a pass from Williamson) were reported to be at Tongue River, seeking to enlist Northern Cheyenne support. The panicky Northern Cheyenne agent requested military support, and a company each of infantry and cavalry from Fort Keogh was ordered to Tongue River. The army's adjutant general noted nervously that "it is reported that the Cheyennes of Tongue River Agency are themselves unruly, and the influence of these outlaws over them is feared." However, the Crows failed to gather allies at Tongue River and returned to Crow in a few days.[75]

The failure of Sword Bearer to gain the support of either a majority of Crows or the aid of other tribes, followed shortly thereafter by his death and the arrest and imprisonment of eight of his followers, appears at first glance to be a successful demonstration of U.S. power and the weakness not only of Crow unity, but also hopes for intertribal unity. Seen from a broader perspective, however, these broad conclusions stand in need of refinement.

The emphasis on the Sword Bearer outbreak as an episode in Crow tribal history means that the refusal of the Northern Cheyenne to join the disaffected Crows has not been subjected to close analysis. Although most accounts mention Sword Bearer's travels to Tongue River and interactions with the Cheyenne, most either do so without comment or fall back on the enduring canard of intertribal hostility to explain his failure to obtain Cheyenne support.[76] Similarly, although some studies of the Northern Cheyenne during this period mention Sword Bearer in passing, none investigate whether the Crow's actions or claims to spiritual power (which may have had Cheyenne origins, at least in part) had any attraction for them.

The claim that Crow–Cheyenne hostility explains Sword Bearer's failure to attract Cheyenne support does not withstand scrutiny, particularly given his numerous close interactions with them and the Northern Cheyennes' failure to turn him in to the authorities during his visits to Tongue River. Indeed, since

Two Moons's visit to Crow in 1884, there had been no documented instances of hostility between members of the two communities, but many episodes of friendly contact. Both communities were restive under federal control. However, while the Crows faced the prospect of allotment and Williamson's heavy-handed, sometimes abusive administration, the Cheyenne confronted a different danger: a threat to the very existence of their reservation and community.

Ever since President Chester Arthur issued the executive order establishing the Tongue River Reservation in 1884, hostile white Montanans had clamored for its revocation and the removal of the Cheyennes.[77] Moreover, the Northern Cheyenne community itself was physically split, with some residing at Tongue River and others living with the Oglala Lakotas at Pine Ridge.[78] Throughout the early and mid-1880s, the Northern Cheyenne had agitated for the consolidation of the entire community in one location, preferably in Montana. During this time, troops were regularly dispatched to Tongue River to escort visiting Northern Cheyennes back to Pine Ridge, to investigate or intervene in conflicts between Cheyennes and local white ranchers and cowboys, or in response to alleged threats by Cheyennes against their agent.[79] Speaking to a Jesuit priest in 1886, the holy man White Bull expressed Cheyenne complaints in terms Sword Bearer might have endorsed: "Seeing that the Pale Faces were so bad[,] The Great Spirit left the earth never to return, and fixed his abode in heaven. On account of this the Indians who are now unhappy, deprived of game, and their lands are conquered by the white man, who plunders and steals everything, and strive to exterminate the Indian."[80]

Under the circumstances, it should not have been difficult for Northern Cheyennes and Crows to find common ground. Indeed, less than two months before Sword Bearer's ride through Crow Agency, violence nearly broke out during a council between Northern Cheyennes, their agent, and army officers sent to escort some 200 Pine Ridge Cheyennes (who had attempted to emigrate to Tongue River without government permission) back to Pine Ridge. Bull Berry, the first Cheyenne speaker at the council, "harangued for nearly an hour in a speech of the most incendiary character, full of invective against his Agent and the white race generally," according to the ranking officer present. Later in the council, there was "great excitement and tumult of angry expressions, the Indians closing in upon us in a most threatening manner." However, at this point, Cheyenne headmen, including Two Moons, American Horse, Brave Wolf, Black Wolf, Lost Bull, and, notably, White Bull, took charge and forced the crowd back. After a separate all-Cheyenne council later that evening, the Northern Cheyenne agreed to the peaceful departure of the Pine Ridgers.[81]

Despite their philosophical sympathies and friendship with the Crows, powerful material considerations tilted the Northern Cheyenne away from overt support for Sword Bearer. The Northern Cheyenne quest to reunite their community would not be furthered by an open, armed confrontation between them and the army. Paradoxically, the same military that had escorted some Northern Cheyennes to Indian Territory in 1877, bloodily suppressed the 1878 Cheyenne Outbreak (in which the Indian Territory refugees had attempted to return to their northern homeland), and later escorted Pine Ridgers back to Dakota Territory in the 1880s was also the Northern Cheyennes' chief ally in their struggle to maintain their Montana reservation. It had been the enlistment of Northern Cheyennes (including White Bull) as army scouts after their surrender in 1877 that provided the basis for the initial Cheyenne settlement on Tongue River.[82] Cheyenne military service had won them the support of prominent figures such as Nelson Miles, in 1877 a colonel commanding the district of the Yellowstone, by 1887 a brigadier general, and eventually commander of the army by 1895.[83]

In their efforts to have their people reunited in Montana, Northern Cheyenne representatives such as John Two Moons (Two Moons's son) repeatedly invoked past service with the army and the promises made to them as a result. As Northern Cheyenne agent R. L. Upshaw wrote to Miles, "Two Moons, White Bull, and others refer to you on every occasion and say you put them on the Rosebud and Tongue rivers and told them that they were to stay there permanently."[84] In June 1887, John Two Moons told the agent: "When we got back to Fort Keogh [after the Cheyenne surrender in 1877], Gen. Miles called us up—my father too and said—you people have helped me and I will keep you for Scouts—maybe always—There are but few of you here, most of your people are in the Indian Territory, but you shall stay here and I will try to get all of your people here."[85]

The following month, Captain E. P. Ewers, formerly the Northern Cheyennes' agent and now an officer at Fort Keogh, signed as a witness (and possibly helped write) an appeal from Two Moons, American Horse, and White Bull requesting permission to travel to Washington to lay their request for the reunification of the Northern Cheyenne at Tongue River before the president. In reporting on the removal of the 200 Pine Ridge Cheyenne in August 1887, Fort Keogh's commander, Colonel George Gibson, requested "leave to express the hope . . . that their earnest appeal to be again reunited with their relatives (I might almost say brothers, wives, and sisters) at Tongue River Agency, may be granted."[86] The Northern Cheyennes' refusal to openly support Sword Bearer paid dividends in the form of continued army support for their cause. Two years after Sword Bearer's death, Miles reiterated his support for the Northern Cheyennes' effort to remain in Montana:

> These Indians surrendered in good faith in the spring of 1877. . . . During the last twelve years they have been entirely peaceable. . . . They were told that if they remained at peace and did what they were directed to do the Government would treat them fairly and justly. They have fulfilled their part of the compact and it would be but justice for the Government to allow them to remain where it has placed them.[87]

Ultimately, the Northern Cheyennes' determination to side with the military and not support the actions of Indian dissidents like Sword Bearer would yield fruit. During the suppression of the Lakota Ghost Dance in 1890, a unit of enlisted Northern Cheyenne scouts from Tongue River served with the military at Pine Ridge. After the Wounded Knee Massacre, Miles, over the objection of the Indian Department, ordered the removal of the Pine Ridge Cheyennes (who had not participated in the Ghost Dance movement) to Fort Keogh, citing a fear of Lakota retribution. The Indian Office finally approved the transfer of the Pine Ridge Cheyennes to Tongue River in October 1891.[88]

The well-publicized and highly visible activities of Sitting Bull and Sword Bearer have generally been interpreted as marking the climax—and end—of politically significant intertribal contact on the Crow Reservation. As Frederick Hoxie puts it, Sword Bearer's defeat "demonstrated the impossibility of building an intertribal leadership on the diplomacy of the 1880s." Hoxie goes on to claim that by the time the last supporter of Sword Bearer was released from prison and returned to Crow in 1889, "contact with other plains agencies had ceased." Afterward, he suggests, Crows increasingly turned inward, politically and socially.[89]

To a certain extent, this analysis is accurate. More so than his defeat and death, Sword Bearer's failure to gather allies on other reservations revealed the very real limitations of intertribal cooperation. However, the possibility does exist that his defiance took place too early rather than too late. Had Sword Bearer issued his challenge two years later, when the Great Sioux Reservation was broken up (with the concomitant loss of nine million acres of Lakota land), or in 1890 with the spread of the Ghost Dance across the Northern Plains, his actions might have gathered more support elsewhere. The failure of Sword Bearer's power (particularly if that power was seen as having its origins in a non-Crow ritual like a Cheyenne Sun Dance) may provide a stronger explanation for the Crows' rejection of the Ghost Dance than do other hypotheses that emphasize demographic collapse or the impact of allotment.[90]

Though Crows and other Native peoples on the Northern Plains faced broadly similar environments, specific circumstances played a powerful role in shaping responses to invitations such as those offered by Sitting Bull and Sword Bearer. Sitting Bull's statements resonated among Crows, whose concerns over federal land politics at the time paralleled that of the Hunkpapa. In 1887, however, Northern Cheyennes could not afford to alienate federal officials. For the Cheyenne, the most immediate threat to the Tongue River Reservation came not from the government but from the hostility of local whites and the geographic fragmentation of the Northern Cheyenne community. Unlike at Crow, federal land policies were not an issue; the Northern Cheyenne Reservation would not be allotted until the early 1930s.[91]

But however much local circumstances varied, the broader contours of reservation life and tribal experience in the late 1800s and early 1900s continued to converge, particularly as Native peoples across the Northern Plains were faced with more and more onerous and coercive government regulations regarding education, the open expression of Native cultural, social, and spiritual beliefs, and ongoing threats to resources, including land. Even as overt political resistance, particularly on an intertribal level, fell subject to greater repression, Indian leaders and ordinary Indians in the region began to speak in a language that enabled their activities to hide in plain sight while still fostering communication and a collective critique of American hegemony. One sign of this shift was Young Man Afraid of His Horses's 1885 letter. Although still open in its expression of a larger political agenda, the Oglala leader balanced it with invocations of direct kinship and an expression of property rights (the horses the Crows had given him). By framing his request in this fashion, he made it much more difficult for government officials to either deny his request or the legitimacy of his motives for travel.

In the year after the Sword Bearer outbreak, agents at Crow and elsewhere attempted to prohibit visiting. However, the substance of this policy was less significant than it appeared. Though the new Crow agent, E. P. Briscoe, told the Crows that no visiting would be permitted, he did allow several visits between Northern Cheyennes and Crows, including a visit by ten Cheyennes in June 1888 and a visit by American Horse at the end of the year. Crows also traveled east to Tongue River with Briscoe's permission, including a trip by Little Hand to retrieve a horse from a Cheyenne camp. Covert visiting also continued. Briscoe ordered his police to escort unauthorized visitors off the reservation (as in the case of a party of Lakotas reported at Black Hawk's camp in October). Even with regard to the Crows, Briscoe candidly admitted to a correspondent, "I can't always know where they are."[92]

Given the quixotic nature of Briscoe's attempted crackdown, his successor, M. P. Wyman, reinstituted the issuing of passes, requesting that other agents consider only the good character of those seeking passes, the number of visitors, and the annual demands of the farming season.[93] During Wyman's tenure alone, from 1889 to 1893, Crows received permission to visit the Flatheads in northwest Montana, the Northern Cheyenne at Tongue River, the Assiniboine and Gros Ventre at Fort Belknap in northeastern Montana, the Nez Perce in Idaho, the Shoshonis at Wind River in Wyoming, and the Mandan, Hidatsa, and Arickara at Fort Berthold in North Dakota.[94] During the same period, the Crows received authorized visits from the Northern Cheyenne, Hidatsa, Pine Ridge and Cheyenne River Lakotas, Gros Ventres, Nez Perce, Yanktonais, and Shoshoni, to say nothing of the unknown number of unapproved, illegal visits.[95]

In general, later agents followed Wyman's lead. As Crow agent Edward Becker wrote to his counterpart at Rosebud Reservation in South Dakota in 1900, "Consider any pass issued by you accepted at any time."[96] Even the nominal limits suggested by Wyman were honored in the breach as often as not. In September 1891, Wyman notified the Northern Cheyenne agent that he could not permit a visit in the middle of haying season, but the very next week, he approved a pass for five Crows to travel to Fort Belknap.[97] When Deaf Bull, a headman who had been one of Sword Bearer's main supporters in 1887 (and who had been subsequently incarcerated at Fort Snelling, Minnesota, for nearly two years), requested permission to visit the Nez Perce for a month, Wyman dutifully complied, to the extent of writing the Northern Pacific for a railroad pass for the trip.[98] In 1893, the Crows received so many visitors that Wyman asked his counterpart at Pine Ridge to ensure that future delegations brought their own supplies. "There has been during the present year quite a number of visitors from the different tribes visiting with the Crows, covering periods of 30 to 60 days," he wrote. "It has been a tax upon the Crows to provide a plentiful supply of provisions to their friends."[99]

Over time, in other words, many agents began to view visiting as essentially benign—a sign of Indian backwardness and nostalgia for the old days, rather than a real threat to government authority. Yet there was as much rationalization as reality in this perspective. Agents at Crow typically arrived vowing to crack down on the lax administration and regulation of their predecessor, only

to find their resolve compromised by Indian resistance and the very real, per-
sisting ties between Crows and other Northern Plains peoples. Although the
growth of reservation infrastructure, bureaucracy, and workforces during this
period to some degree facilitated the task of keeping track of both resident
Indians and visitors, the sheer size of the Crow Reservation, and other reservations on the Northern Plains, meant that administrative control would never
be completely effective. Most agents eventually came to accept this situation.
As Pine Ridge agent W. H. Clapp wrote to his counterpart at Crow in 1898, "I
shall do all in my power to keep my Indians at home, but fear quite a number
will get away." The ferocious-sounding directives from Indian office head-
quarters in Washington, D.C., and from newly arrived agents themselves, which
were designed to regulate and restrict visiting, need to be read in this light.[100]

Thus, when Black Hair and Pretty Old Man, two elderly Crows, accompanied by two women and four children, showed up at Fort Belknap in the spring
of 1902 with painted faces and a pass to Fort Berthold, the agent at Belknap
allowed them to stay and wrote to the Crow agent only when they requested
an extension to remain longer. The Crow agent replied that the extension was
permissible, then added apologetically that he thought the party had intended
to visit Fort Berthold "but was mistaken." "As for the bright costumes and
painted faces," he wrote with an air of resignation, "they are both harmless
old men. I would suggest you require them to wash their faces and keep them
washed. The children accompanying them are excused."[101] At Crow, even non-
Indians came to look forward to visiting delegations from other tribes as a
break in the monotony of everyday life. In a memoir written years later, one
agent's daughter vividly remembered the arrival of visitors, particularly the
Northern Cheyenne: "When they did come to Crow, their arrival was an event.
They came in force. They brought whole families and dogs."[102]

Even technically illegal visiting met with less than complete repression. A
party of Lakotas from Cheyenne River caught without passes at Crow was put
to work cutting wood for a week, after which they agreed to go home.[103] However, the older problem of ferreting out unauthorized visitors persisted. In
January 1891, Wyman wrote to the commander of Fort Custer regarding a
party of Assiniboines hanging about the agency. The visitors had arrived in
mid-October of the previous year with a group of Gros Ventres "as near as I
can obtain information," he noted. The Gros Ventres departed after a brief
visit, but the Assiniboines—"all young men none over 25"—remained all winter. Wyman said he had sent his police to bring the Assiniboines in, and "unless
I receive satisfactory information I will remove them at once." The resolution
of this particular event remains unclear, although the next day Wyman issued

a pass for three of the Assiniboines to return to Fort Peck, writing that "since they were at Crow Agency they have behaved themselves very well."[104]

The one thing that did attract immediate attention and punitive action from agents was any sign of overtly resistant political activity. In early December 1890, just three weeks before the Wounded Knee Massacre at Pine Ridge, Wyman accused a delegation of forty-four visiting Oglalas led by Young Man Afraid of His Horses of "talking up the messiah craze and dancing Ghost Dances." The agent requested the military at Fort Custer remove the Lakotas, who were camped within a mile of the agency. "The Crows will be more content and satisfied without the presence of such people," he wrote.[105]

Wyman's accusation was curious, to say the least. Young Man Afraid of His Horses was well known as an opponent of the Ghost Dance at Pine Ridge, to such a degree that Ghost Dancers there burned his home and stole some of his livestock.[106] A clue to Wyman's real source of dissatisfaction lies in the fact that Young Man Afraid of His Horses's visit coincided with U.S. negotiations for the sale of nearly two million acres of land on the western end of the reservation. The negotiations came on the heels of a scorching summer that ruined Crow crops and generated a desperate appeal to have the beef ration increased to avoid starvation.[107] For nearly two weeks, U.S. commissioners met with and cajoled Crow leaders, both individually and in council, in an effort to persuade them to acquiesce to the cession.[108]

On December 6, three days before Wyman's demand for the Lakotas' removal, the commissioners held an acrimonious council with Crow leaders. Plenty Coups and Bell Rock led the Crow opposition. Both noted their support for prior land sales, but rejected this one. "The Great Father buys and buys from me, but this time I won't do it," Plenty Coups proclaimed, while Bell Rock added, "I have obeyed the great father up till this time. This land is rich, and I don't want to sell it." Not until the commission increased its purchase price from $830,000 to $900,000, and agreed to purchase 2,500 head of cattle for a tribal herd at a subsequent council two days later, did the Crows assent to the sale.[109]

The timing of the land sale councils with Wyman's letter suggests a much more plausible explanation for the agent's decision to terminate Young Man Afraid of His Horses's visit. With memories of the breakup of the Great Sioux Reservation the previous year and its disastrous aftermath (including the same drought that withered Crow crops, as well as a cut in rations) fresh in their memory, Young Man Afraid of His Horses and his fellow Oglalas undoubtedly discussed the Lakotas' experience and the proposed Crow land sale with their hosts. Though no Crow speaker made direct reference to the 1889 Sioux agreement, several did make veiled references implying that such conversations had taken place. At the December 6 council, Pretty Eagle told the commissioners, "The Crows have never been fools, like other Indians and the great father ought to go and bother them people instead of coming here and bothering us." Old Crow, for his part, raised the specter of the poverty and starvation that had confronted Lakotas in 1890 by suggesting that if the Crows had all the horses and cattle they wanted, "in 2 or 3 winters" they might consent to discussions regarding a land sale.[110]

Few visitors broached politically sensitive topics as openly as Young Man Afraid of His Horses. However, even seemingly innocuous activities served to strengthen the sense of peoplehood and shared Indian identity that both Young Man Afraid of His Horses and Sitting Bull had invoked. Far from being a product of the blurring of tribal identities and culture, this sense of identity built on existing tribal identities and established protocols for turning outsiders into allies—or even kin. Anthropologist Fred Voget has described Crow reservation culture as "old wine in new bottles," and a similar statement can be made for intertribal contact and exchange after 1885.[111] As in buffalo days, ceremonies and rituals, some spiritual, some social, continued to be exchanged between tribes. Around the turn of the century, Half, Little Owl, and two other Crow men purchased the Long Lodge Dance, which became the main dance for many years at Crow New Year's celebrations, from some visiting Nez Perce. In 1902, a Crow man married to a Gros Ventre woman introduced the Woman Chief dance, a Gros Ventre dance named, ironically, after a Gros Ventre woman who had been captured and adopted by Crows as a girl, became a warrior, and was killed by her former tribespeople in 1854.[112]

None of this symbolized a deterioration of a distinct Crow tribal culture or identity, any more than incorporation of Crow rituals into Piegan culture in the mid-1800s compromised Piegan identity. However, the context of reservation life, where tribes no longer competed for territory, access to resources, and trade, but instead faced similar threats to tribal culture and community from the U.S. government and American society, gave added salience to values, attitudes, and beliefs that transcended tribal boundaries, and which could be counterposed against demands that Indians conform to American norms and behavior. Thus, giveaways, an affront to individualistic, materialist economic behavior, still represented "the celebration of community and the traditional Crow value of generosity."[113] Yet Crow generosity toward visitors extended ties of kinship and alliance far further than the boundaries of the Crow tribe itself. Indeed, the Crows' reputation for generosity, as well as their continued relative wealth compared to other tribes, helps explain the vitality of intertribal visiting at Crow. As Cheyenne historian John Stands in Timber noted, when it came to gifts,

> The Crows were good at that. They had the Cheyennes beat. Deer Nose, a Crow chief, gave away a hundred horses one time. He made a special song and danced around, and gave a stick to each of the Cheyennes, sitting in a row there. Next morning he told them to come to a certain corral with the sticks and lead ropes, and every stick was worth a horse.[114]

Conversely, failures on the part of either visitors or hosts to display expected standards of generosity and amity were sure to attract comment.[115]

For the Northern Cheyenne, even the act of traveling to Crow, although creating new bonds between communities, reinforced elements of Cheyenne culture, calling to mind the protocols of moving camp in prereservation times (with some modern additions): "The military societies were in charge, telling everyone how far to go, and keeping order," Stands in Timber remembered. "We had to have permits to go visiting in those days, and on this trip the Indian police caught a bunch of young men who had come along without them. They made them go back. But they sneaked back and rode all night and beat us to Crow."[116]

Even Anglo-oriented events could be turned to Indian purposes in furthering intertribal interaction. Just as the tenth anniversary of the Battle of the Little Bighorn brought Gall and sundry other Lakotas and Northern Cheyennes to Crow, so too did the fiftieth anniversary in 1926. During the 1926 commemoration, Northern Cheyenne agency physician Thomas B. Marquis accompanied the elderly Northern Cheyenne holy man Porcupine to a Crow camp. "Porcupine and his wife visited the Ben Spotted Horse clan tipi," Marquis wrote. "He conversed in sign talk with the old Crows, then with a 35-year-old Bannock, then with a 30-year-old Nez Perce."[117]

The Fourth of July proved an even more popular and reliable occasion for intertribal visiting. When Young Man Afraid of His Horses and Little Wound requested permission to make one of their annual visits in 1893, Agent Wyman, despite his eviction of Young Man Afraid of His Horses three years earlier, suggested he would be "glad to see them on the 4th of July or thereabouts."[118] Cheyennes from Tongue River were also frequent Fourth of July visitors. Such visits could turn into extended affairs; a full five weeks after the 1894 celebration, the Northern Cheyenne agent wrote his Crow counterpart suggesting that any Cheyennes who had lingered after the Fourth be sent home.[119] The following year, some fifty Lakota families from Pine Ridge arrived for the celebration of American independence.[120]

Either the 1895 celebration or the Crows' subsequent work habits proved less than satisfactory, however. In reply to queries from the agents at Tongue River and Cheyenne River, as well as letters directly from headmen Standing Bear and Spotted Elk at Pine Ridge, Wyman's successor, J. W. Watson, announced that the Crows would have no Fourth of July celebration in 1896. Watson said the holiday interfered too much with summer work. As was the norm with new agents, he stated his broad opposition to visiting in general: "I have always been opposed to various tribes exchanging visits as but little good can result therefore and much evil frequently results." To Spotted Elk, Watson made the more dubious claim that the Crows themselves did not want visitors. Watson promised his correspondents, however, that visitors would be welcome in October, when the Crows would have a harvest fair.[121] As in so many other cases, the restriction did not last; in 1897, the Crows again hosted dances for visitors on the Fourth.[122]

Christian holidays and the work of missionaries also provided venues for intertribal contact. Here, too, limiting the freedom Indians exercised during such occasions could be problematic. When the Northern Cheyenne agent invited Big Shoulder Blade and several other Crows to spend Christmas at Tongue River in 1902, Crow agent Samuel Reynolds noted that, left to himself "Big Shoulder Blade would have taken the entire Reno [a reservation district] outfit over." Reynolds told Big Shoulder Blade to pick out a few friends to accompany him and eventually wrote out a pass for thirteen Crow men. In spite of his attempt at control, Reynolds admitted that he had no way of knowing whether Big Shoulder Blade would follow instructions or not.[123] Two years later, newly arrived Baptist missionary William A. Petzoldt requested permission to invite several Northern Cheyennes to "Christmas exercises." Reynolds gave Petzholdt permission to invite two Cheyennes but warned him to "be careful it doesn't turn into a general invitation to [all] the Cheyenne." Petzholdt was anxious to show off his newly established mission day school to the Crows' neighbors (as well as loosen the domination exercised until then by Catholic missionaries at Crow and Tongue River), but Reynolds had a more cynical view of Indian motivations: "Our Indians have usually spent their Christmas holidays in dancing and feasting. They have no more conception of what the day means than they have the Fourth of July."[124]

The Christian competition for souls offered other opportunities for travel as well. Missionaries occasionally took Indians with them on their travels to other reservations, either as exemplars of the faith or as prospective converts.

Soon after founding the Roman Catholic St. Xavier Mission along the Bighorn River in 1887, Father Peter Prando took five of the "more intelligent and influential members of the tribe" on a monthlong visit to the Nez Perce, Flatheads, and Coeur d'Alenes, who had long been the subject of Jesuit missionary activity.[125] Catholic Indians from other reservations also traveled to Crow: the mission house diaries contain references to Catholic Lakota visitors, as well as Catholic Crees attending masses at St. Xavier. On one occasion, two Lakota Catholics invited several Crow Red Gowns (members of a lay Catholic sodality) to visit them in the Dakotas.[126] When a white physician attended Christmas services at the Baptist Church in Lodge Grass in 1925, he noted two Hidatsas from Fort Berthold sitting beside him.[127]

Though the activities of Indian converts can be read as an example of acculturation, evidence suggests that even Christian Indians carried their own agendas along with their Bibles.[128] When a party of Nez Perce Presbyterians spent a week at the Crow community of Pryor holding revival meetings, the local subagent (himself half Lakota) praised them as "earnest, sincere Christians."[129] However, a proposal by the Congress of Catholic Indians to hold a weeklong meeting on the Fort Berthold Reservation in July gained the notation "certainly a fine time for Indians to be leaving the reservation and neglecting crops" in Crow Agency files. Plans for a Catholic convocation for Montana Indians at Fort Belknap in August 1924 received a similar comment: "If we endorse a trip to a Church meeting in the midst of harvest season, other Indians should feel that they should have the same privilege of going to the fair or races in the midst of their crop season."[130] After a missionary trip by the Lakota catechists Redwillow and Black Elk to the Winnebago in Nebraska returned without converts, their frustrated Jesuit superior wrote, "To an onlooker it would appear that I have become a bureau for traveling Indians."[131]

By the early twentieth century, the largest single institutional form of visiting had emerged in the form of the annual Crow fair. As Wyman's invitation to attend a fall harvest fair in the 1890s illustrated, agents were no less susceptible than missionaries to the desire to show off their Indians' achievements and cultural progress to both Anglo-Americans and other Indians. In 1904, Agent Reynolds instituted the first annual event, modeled after a prototypical American county fair, complete with prizes and premiums for exhibitors to encourage agricultural and domestic industry. Reynolds termed the first fair an "absolute failure," but he called the second "satisfactory" and the third "a dandy." The 1906 fair even attracted several pages of favorable comment in the annual report of the commissioner of Indian Affairs.[132]

For Crows and other Northern Plains peoples, the success of the fair carried an added bonus. In the interest of promoting his creation, Reynolds (the same Reynolds who had vowed to crack down on the lax administration of his predecessor) now welcomed delegations from other reservations. When the agent at Cheyenne River queried whether his Indians would be welcome, Reynolds replied enthusiastically that he would be "glad to have them come," adding, "We will try to make their visit pleasant as well as instructive to them." Reynolds even extended a personal invitation to Crazy Bear, a frequent visitor to Crow from Pine Ridge.[133]

For Crows, the principal appeal of the fair was, as one historian puts it, "not the agricultural exhibition, but the opportunity it provided for visiting, dancing, and politicking"—features that proved to be powerful attractions beyond the limits of the Crow Reservation.[134] Visitors to the 1907 fair included Piegans, Crees, Assiniboines, Umatillas, Nez Perces, Shoshonis, Southern Arapahos and Southern Cheyennes, Yankton Sioux, and Indians from Fort Berthold. About 200 Lakotas, led by American Horse and including representatives from Pine Ridge, Rosebud, Crow Creek, and Lower Brule, also attended. According to one Anglo observer, "Practically the whole tribe of Northern Cheyenne (more than 1,200) under Two Moons of Custer battle fame, arrived on Sunday." Teepees were arrayed in camp circles, and dances were held nightly in each of the Crow district camps as well as in the visiting camps. The largest single dance boasted an estimated 1,000 participants. Each morning, parades wended their way through the Crow and visiting camps, "where the usual ceremonies were performed in their honor." At the close of the fair, Lakotas and Cheyennes held dances in Crow camps to honor their hosts; the Crow reciprocated by performing a buffalo dance for their guests. While acknowledging the "industrial tone" of the fair and that the dancing and parades were "supposed to be a minor consideration," the writer noted, "What visitor ever gave it second place?"[135]

During the 1920s, the Crow fair went on a temporary hiatus, replaced by smaller fairs hosted by individual reservation districts. One suspects that Crow agents, having failed to match the decorum and cultural conformity of a county fair, were not displeased to discontinue the big event.[136] However, by this time, a host of tribal fairs had emerged on other reservations, most of which were distinctly intertribal in nature. Crows visited the Fort Belknap fair, and the Northern Cheyenne fair, sixty miles to the east of Crow Agency at Lame Deer, became an annual attraction, as did other off-reservation events such as rodeos, county fairs, and holiday celebrations where Indians from different communities could meet—and were encouraged by local officials to attend.[137]

The rise of tribal fairs contributed to the emergence of intertribal phenomena such as powwow dancing. Thomas Yellowtail, a Crow born in 1903, remembered that less tribally specific social dances gradually replaced some of the sacred dances unique to individual tribes. "By 1910," he observed, "powwow dancing was strong everywhere." Older customs did not completely disappear, however. "Even in those days people remembered the origins of the dances," he added, "and I remember the special pipe ceremonies and prayers that were always observed."[138] New traditions that recognized the continued existence of separate communities—but also forged bonds between them—emerged as well. A visitor to the Northern Cheyenne fair in the 1920s discovered that the Northern Cheyenne and Crows had developed a tradition for alternating responsibility for evening dances. One year, the Crows sang while the Cheyenne danced a circle around them. The following year, the Cheyenne would dance and the Crows sing. Despite this cooperation, Crow and Cheyenne musical styles remained distinct; the visitor noted that Crow music was "different from that of the Cheyennes. I can tell by the sounds."[139]

Occasionally, tensions between Crows and visitors surfaced, most often in the recounting of war exploits that many non-Indian observers and scholars have identified as the chief attraction of visiting. In the midst of one intertribal hand game, a contest in which a team from each tribe attempted to guess the number of markers held in an opponent's hand, Crows and Cheyennes exchanged war stories in an attempt to spur their teams on to victory. One Crow recounted how he had once killed a Cheyenne and displayed the knife he had used. In response, the Cheyenne Mad Bear recalled how he had scalped a Crow on Lodge Grass Creek (a stream located on the current Crow Reservation). Suddenly, a Crow with a handkerchief on his head stood up and began signing, "The Cheyennes are women. They run away. They do not fight." The Crow headman Plenty Coups finally ushered the man out. "This is the man you scalped," he told Mad Bear. "He is still mad about it. But we are even now. Let's drop everything and just play a hand game. No more war talk."[140]

Of course, the persistence of visiting, the growth of tribal fairs and emergence of powwow dancing, even the occasional outbreaks of competitive animosity, tells us little of the explicit political dimensions of these events and processes. Beyond a mere refusal to abandon tribal cultural norms and a rejection of their white equivalents, did continuing intertribal contact have larger ramifications for how peoples from different tribes thought of themselves and each other? Did the travels, visits, dances, and exchanges of gifts and trade represent only a desperate attempt to hold on to a vanishing past, a refuge from twentieth-century realities? Mere descriptions of Crow fairs cannot reveal what was talked about in camp circles. Did the determination of Young Man

Afraid of His Horses to talk with other peoples "for our common welfare" disappear with his death in 1893?[141]

Camp circle conversations at the Crow fair remain unrecoverable by modern scholars. However, by the early 1900s, Crows and other Northern Plains peoples were communicating not only in person, but also by mail. Letter writing marked one area where the acquisition of English skills could supplement or even replace direct contact. However, just as was true for Young Man Afraid of His Horses's conversations with Crows in the 1880s, English literacy was not essential. Friendly whites, priests, traders, and even agents could be called on as secretaries in a process that often involved serial dictation from Indian to interpreter to scribe on one end and from reader to interpreter to addressee on the other. One agent on a Northern Plains reservation estimated that his office had written 300 letters for Indians to friends on other reservations, and even in Canada.[142]

Obviously, the use of white amanuenses placed potential constraints on the ability of Indian correspondents to discuss culturally or politically sensitive issues. Some of these limitations could be avoided, however, through the use of Indian school graduates or literate mixed bloods.[143] From the Crow community of Pryor on the west end of the reservation, Plenty Coups, though not literate himself, exchanged letters with individuals on several reservations. In January 1906, Plenty Coups received a letter from Pine Ridge addressed to him and to other notable Crows in the Pryor community. The letter opened by proclaiming that "all you people on Arrow [Pryor] Creek are well thought of by your Sioux friends," as were the Crows on the Bighorn River and in Good Eagle's camp. During a recent visit to Pine Ridge, the Crows had been liberal with gifts, "and it is this why your friends here think a great deal of you." The Crow agency policeman, Big Medicine, however, had instructed those under his charge not to give anything away, an act that was "talked about so much" among the Lakotas. The Lakotas assured the Crows that "everything OK" at Pine Ridge and requested that the Crows write back, sending a mix of tobacco and roots and informing them whether the Crows would be having a "big time" on the Fourth of July.[144]

Plenty Coups's correspondence reveals how the social aspects of visiting were inextricably linked to the politically charged rejection of Anglo-American cultural or economic norms, and contributed to a shared tribal- and reservation-based sense of Indian identity. A letter to Plenty Coups from the Kiowa Heap of Bears makes this emerging distinction between Indian and white clear. In his letter, Heap of Bears promised to come up to Crow for a visit in the summer after crops had been planted. All the Kiowas, he said, were glad to be invited up from Oklahoma. Heap of Bears's secretary was a twenty-year-old school-educated Kiowa employed at Fort Scott. Despite his scribe's white education, Heap of Bears assured Plenty Coups that the letter writer and his brother "both speak Indian" and proclaimed proudly that "we don't have a white man to do our business for us."[145]

Explicitly political matters, meanwhile, were on the mind of Bull Calf, another of Plenty Coups's correspondents. Writing from Browning, Montana, the Piegan brought Plenty Coups up to speed on the state of affairs on the Blackfeet Reservation: "You know that we have been very badly around here at Browning and our Indian agent has no respect for any one. And we don't like him at all, but I think he will be out pretty so [soon] and we hope any how." Among the problems was the agent's refusal to issue needed supplies out of the agency warehouses. Bull Calf told Plenty Coups that the Blackfeet were forming a delegation "to go to Washington, D.C. to settle up the Indian rights and strengthen up our Reservation." He described the members of the delegation and invited Plenty Coups up to Browning for a visit. If the Crow needed any more information about the situation at Blackfeet, Bull Calf recommended that Plenty Coups talk to Runner Crane, a Piegan then visiting the Crows.[146] One year later, Bull Calf wrote that matters had not improved; the Piegan were having to sell their horses and cattle to get something to eat. The delegation to Washington had not returned, but "I will let you know after [their return] why what we are going to do with our Reservation." Bull Calf asked Plenty Coups to write back: "You must tell me all the news you can." He suggested, however, that the Crow find another scribe because Plenty Coups's last letter had proved illegible. "Next time you must write your name good," he noted.[147]

As in the case of Young Man Afraid of His Horses, Plenty Coups's letters reveal a breadth of vision and affiliation extending far beyond the social and geographic boundaries of the Crow tribe. They also reveal the limitations on the ability of Indians like Plenty Coups and Bull Calf to exert political pressure across tribal boundaries. Plenty Coups and his correspondents could encourage each other and share information, ideas, opinions, even strategies, but there was little space for Plenty Coups to intervene when it came to the stinginess of an agent on another reservation. Broad federal policies such as land sales and the question of allotment in the 1880s and 1890s could call forth a united Indian response, but on more parochial, strictly local matters, intertribal cooperation and unity remained problematic, as Sword Bearer had discovered in his attempt to enlist Northern Cheyenne support in 1887. As a later chapter will illustrate, this was not simply a result of conscious government policy—Armstrong's prescription for keeping Indians "divided"—but a matter of strategic choice by Native peoples. Although Indians from different tribes shared the same relationship to the United States and encountered similar challenges in coping with federal officials, land-hungry whites, and aggressive missionaries and reformers, the legacies of treaty-making and specific federal obligations to individual tribes could also discourage tribes from engaging in cooperative political activism in their relations with the federal government.[148]

However, Plenty Coups's actions, and those of the dancers at the Crow fair, traveling catechists and converts, and visitors of high and low stature, also demonstrated a resiliency and willingness to creatively engage in new forms of dialogue, as well as to explore the potential of intertribal cooperation. Living in a time of radical, sometimes catastrophic change, Crows and other Native Americans on the Northern Plains maintained old and created new relationships with each other in hopes of creating a better future. The ability and determination of Indians to continue to visit each other, communicate, share ideas, beliefs, objects, hope—to outlast their self-proclaimed conquerors—itself represented a victory, one seen not just in Plenty Coups's correspondence but in the utterly prosaic story of Finds Them and Kills Them's lost luggage.

In the fall of 1925, the Crow Finds Them and Kills Them (also known as Maricota Jim) traveled to the Fort Berthold Reservation to visit the Hidatsa. Before boarding the train for the trip from Billings, Montana, to Garrison, North Dakota, he checked a bundle containing his "personal effects, including regalia for the dress parade." The luggage never reached Garrison. Returning to Crow around Christmas, Finds Them and Kills Them notified Crow superintendent Calvin Asbury of his loss and submitted a claim for $137. Asbury wrote to the Northern Pacific Railroad superintendent at Billing that Finds Them and Kills Them was "naturally very concerned" about his lost luggage. He added, "I hope we will be able to locate this property as he seems to value it very highly. It probably contained some of his treasured ceremonial garb." At the end of February, the baggage agent at St. Paul notified Asbury that the bundle had been found and was being forwarded to Crow Agency.[149]

The story would end there, except for a comment Asbury appended to his original letter. "I have referred to this party as a 'he,'" Asbury wrote.

> To avoid any confusion that might occur, I will say that Maricota Jim or Finds Them and Kills Them is a peculiar character. He usually dresses as

a woman, is a very large person, and has a mannish appearance, but usually wears a woman's clothing and would probably be taken as a woman. On his behalf and on behalf of this office, I thank you for any assistance you can give me in locating this baggage.[150]

In other words, Finds Them and Kills Them was a berdache (*bote* or *bade* in Crow), "a man who specialized in women's work, wore women's clothing, and formed emotional and sexual relationships with non-berdache men." Berdaches like Finds Them and Kills Them were honored among Crows and other tribes as craft specialists and for their roles in religious ceremonies, but they were frequently objects of persecution by government agents as "perverts."[151] (Ironically, when the agent at Fort Berthold forced the last Hidatsa berdache to cut his hair and wear men's clothing in 1879, the Hidatsa berdache fled to the Crows.)[152] Finds Them and Kills Them (Osh-Tisch in Crow) was not immune to this persecution, according to Crow tribal historian Joseph Medicine Crow: "One agent in the late 1890s was named Briskow [Briscoe], or maybe it was Williamson. He did more crazy things here. He tried to interfere with Osh-Tisch, who was the most respected *bade*. The agent incarcerated the *bades,* cut off their hair, made them wear men's clothing. He forced them to do manual labor, planting these trees you see here on the BIA grounds [at Crow Agency]."[153]

Born in 1854, Finds Them and Kills Them was by 1925 the last openly practicing Crow berdache, outlasting all the attacks of agents and missionaries. "Eventually," Will Roscoe notes, "he established cordial relationships with Crow agents. At the turn of the century, he called on Agent Reynolds's wife regularly, to sell her grass bags from the Nez Perce."[154] Despite decades of opposition and oppression from government agents, missionaries, and others determined to change his ways and his people's culture, Finds Them and Kills Them not only survived, but maintained his ability to travel and communicate with other Native peoples, even as a berdache, and have his putative overseer recover his lost "ceremonial garb." Lacking the prominence of a Plenty Coups, Sitting Bull, Young Man Afraid of His Horses, or even Sword Bearer, Finds Them and Kills Them nonetheless contributed to preserving the legacy of intertribal contact and exchange and helped keep the road clear for future interaction and cooperation between Indians on the Northern Plains.

Young Man Afraid of His Horses, the Oglala Lakota leader who in 1889 spoke of the need for Crows and Lakotas to meet to plan "for the protection of our people," and who the following year urged Crows to oppose a proposed land cession. National Anthropological Archives, Smithsonian Institution (inventory number 06639900).

The Crow leader Blackfoot (also known as Sits in the Middle of the Land) with his Oglala Lakota wife (aunt to Young Man Afraid of His Horses and interpreter during Crow–Lakota meetings), photographed during a Crow delegation's visit to Washington, D.C., in 1873. National Anthropological Archives, Smithsonian Institution (inventory number 06570300).

Sitting Bull in 1885, one year before he traveled to Crow to tout the advantages of Indian unity. National Anthropological Archives, Smithsonian Institution (inventory number 06526600).

Gall, the "progressive" Hunkpapa Lakota leader who nonetheless held on to
older tribal animosities, in contrast to Young Man Afraid of His Horses and
Sitting Bull. National Anthropological Archives, Smithsonian Institution
(inventory number 06654200).

Crows with Nez Perce visitors at Crow. Buffalo Bill Historical Center, Cody, Wyoming; PN.32.51.

A dance of Cheyennes and Crows. Montana Historical Society.

A Blackfeet camp on the Little Bighorn River photographed by J. H. Sharp in 1904. The incongruous canoe in the foreground is from a movie production of Hiawatha then filming at Crow. Buffalo Bill Historical Center, Cody, Wyoming; gift of Mr. and Mrs. Forrest Fenn, PN.22.531.

An encampment and parade at the Crow fair in the early 1900s. The fair, a showcase for assimilation and acculturation, quickly became an annual destination for Indians from across the Northern Plains. Buffalo Bill Historical Center, Cody, Wyoming; Dr. William and Anna Petzoldt Collection, gift of Genevieve Petzoldt Fitzgerald, Rev. W. A. Petzoldt, D.D., photographer, LS.95.390.

The Crow fair quickly spawned imitations at other Northern Plains reservations. Here, Northern Cheyenne (left) and Crow men (right) compete in a hand game (a hiding and guessing game) at the Northern Cheyenne fair in Lame Deer in the 1920s. Buffalo Bill Historical Center, Cody, Wyoming; Thomas Marquis Collection, PN.165.1.132.

Northern Cheyennes and Crows share the grandstand with non-Indians during a rodeo at Busby on the Northern Cheyenne Reservation in the 1920s. Buffalo Bill Historical Center, Cody, Wyoming; Thomas Marquis Collection, PN.165.3.32.

Plenty Coups, the Crow leader who corresponded with Indians in Oklahoma and Montana and sought to adopt reservationless Crees into the Crow community in the early 1900s, but who also opposed peyotism as a non-Crow religious practice. National Anthropological Archives, Smithsonian Institution (inventory number 06573600).

Finds Them and Kills Them, the Crow berdache whose lost luggage Crow Agent C. H. Asbury sought to recover. National Anthropological Archives, Smithsonian Institution (inventory number 00476300).

Richard Wooden Leg, a Northern Cheyenne veteran of the Little Bighorn and later a teamster and ditch laborer at Crow, but who swore to never again shake hands with a Crow after a 1909 council. Buffalo Bill Historical Center, Cody, Wyoming; Thomas Marquis Collection, PN.165.1.53.

Wagons of Northern Cheyenne freighters lined up in front of the Crow flour mill in 1909. Photograph by Richard Throssel, courtesy of the Braun Research Library, Autry National Center of the American West, Los Angeles, California; photograph A.83.18.

The interior of E. A. Richardson's store at Crow Agency in 1889, a favorite destination for Cheyenne teamsters during their trips to Crow. Montana Historical Society.

Two views of Indian and non-Indian laborers working on the Lodge Grass ditch on the Crow Reservation in 1904. Buffalo Bill Historical Center, Cody, Wyoming; gift of Olive Meinhardt in memory of Alec F. C. Greene, MS328.13/19.

The Southern Cheyenne Leonard Tyler photographed in 1899, one year after the peyote roadman and missionary spent part of a summer working on the Crow Irrigation Survey. National Anthropological Archives, Smithsonian Institution (inventory number 06115800).

The Northern Cheyenne Fred Last Bull, who lived at Crow for more than ten years as a child, camping with his family at the Crow fair in the 1920s. Buffalo Bill Historical Center, Cody, Wyoming; Thomas Marquis Collection, PN.165.1.110.

Sioux visitors to the Crow Reservation during a dance at Pryor Gap photographed on March 13, 1909. The Pryor community, isolated on the western end of the reservation and under the strong leadership of Plenty Coups, remained a stronghold of intertribal visiting and residency well into the 1900s. Museum of the Rockies/Harriet Brayton (Durland).

CHAPTER FOUR

A New World of Work

One of the attendees at Joseph Dixon's Last Great Indian Council in 1909 was the Northern Cheyenne Wooden Leg. A veteran of the Little Bighorn, Wooden Leg accompanied Two Moons and several other Cheyennes from the neighboring Tongue River Reservation to participate in the meeting with representatives of other tribes. Though not prominent enough to have his presence noted in Dixon's book, Wooden Leg later told another biographer how Two Moons "filled the ears of his hearers [primarily Dixon] with lots of lies, while the rest of us laughed among ourselves about what he was saying."[1]

At the council, Dixon held a separate meeting with Crow, Cheyenne, and Lakota survivors of the Little Bighorn to get their stories about the fabled battle. Afterward, wagons arrived loaded with rations. Though the food was only supposed to be for the veterans of the Little Bighorn, according to Wooden Leg, many other Crows came and helped themselves to the feast. At this, a disgusted Wooden Leg burst out: "You—Crows—you are like children. All Crows are babies. You are not brave. You never helped us to fight against the white people. You helped them in fighting against us. You were afraid, so you joined yourself to the soldiers. You are not Indians."[2] Afterward, memories of Crow behavior on this occasion kept Wooden Leg away from subsequent commemorations of the Little Bighorn. As he put it, "I have made up my mind never again to go to any place where I might be called up on to shake hands with a Crow."[3]

Wooden Leg's rancor recalls images of Gall's meeting with Curley at the tenth anniversary of the Little Bighorn in 1886. However, before his off-putting experience at Dixon's 1909 council, Wooden Leg had been a regular visitor to the Crow Indian Reservation, presumably interacting amicably with his hosts on many of those occasions. Just as significantly, many of his trips to Crow in the late 1800s appear to have occurred not in the context of traditional visits celebrating the passage of a bygone age, such as at that so ostentatiously arranged by Dixon, but in the form of wage labor; either as a teamster hauling food and other supplies from Crow Agency to Tongue River, or as a laborer operating a scraper team during construction of a system of irrigation canals at Crow.[4] Even before he traveled to Crow to take part in Dixon's celebration of a "vanishing race," part of Wooden Leg's introduction to the new, modern world of work came on the Crow Indian Reservation.

Indians had always worked, of course, even when that work was not recognized at the time (as in the designation of male hunting and war-related activities as forms of play by European observers—a designation that enabled those same observers to label Indian women as slaves and drudges), or took the form of nonwage labor, such as Native American participation in the European fur trade.[5] However, the place and significance of Native American wage labor has proven difficult for historians to assess, particularly in a reservation context.

Early attempts to analyze reservation labor often focused on the government's generally unsuccessful efforts to turn Native peoples into capitalist agricultural entrepreneurs. Such studies usually emphasized Indian loss of land and other productive resources, and the decline of Native American economic autonomy.[6] Other studies designated reservations as peripheral entities in global capitalist world systems, with reservation labor often dismissed as too ephemeral and unremunerative to have significantly altered Native American social and cultural beliefs and values, in many cases being limited to temporary jobs "to build reservation infrastructure, haul freight, and other menial tasks for the very Indian Service sent to supervise them."[7]

As a result, many early studies of Native American labor tended to assume that Native Americans' most significant wage labor experiences, and the most significant transformative effects of those experiences, occurred off reservations. Indians worked in centers of war production during World War II; they participated in urban relocation programs in the 1950s and 1960s; they worked as migrant day laborers in agriculture and mining; and during the late 1800s and early 1900s, they even worked as participants in the popular Wild West shows that toured the United States and abroad. It was largely through these non-Indian venues, many historians have argued, that Indians of different tribes came together in ways that fostered the growth of a sense of shared Indian identity.[8]

More recently, much more attention has been paid to reservation-based economic activities and the way those activities intersected with off-reservation economic activities. Reservation work has been analyzed in the context of specific tribal cultural and social structures, assessing the changes and adaptations that took place in both directions as Indians attempted to reconcile existing community beliefs and values with the demands of survival in a non-Indian-oriented economy. In doing so, historians, anthropologists, and sociologists have also documented the ways that many Native peoples effectively commuted from their home reservations seasonally, annually, or for even longer spans of time to take advantage of economic opportunities available elsewhere, while still maintaining ties to their community and adhering to established social and cultural practices.[9]

In light of this scholarship, it may sound counterintuitive to suggest that Native Americans might leave their home reservation to travel to another reservation in search of economic opportunity. If poverty forced Indians to leave their own reservations in search of work, why would they leave one impoverished location, only to travel to another, presumably equally impoverished, Indian community? The very idea that a place like the Crow Indian Reservation could have possessed an environment conducive to both economic enterprise and intertribal contact seems to fly in the face of most received knowledge regarding the nature and conditions of reservation life at the end of the nineteenth century.

Not all reservations or reservation communities were created equal, however. Some reservations were located in remarkably barren and unproductive locales; others possessed greater abundance, whether in terms of land, work opportunities, or other resources. The travels of Lakotas to Crow to trade for horses in the late 1800s suggests that Indians of that era were no less capable of discerning differences in wealth and opportunity between tribes than their forebears were in participating in horse raids or in seeking spiritual items and rituals laden with wealth-giving potential in the early to mid-nineteenth century. On the Northern Plains in the late 1800s, the Crow Reservation quickly emerged as a site where Indians from across the region and beyond might find not just horses but also remunerative work, either short or long term, in a setting where entry into the labor force was eased by preexisting ties between Crows and other Native peoples, and where the persistence or development of Indian cultural values and identities provided a comfortable and familiar environment for non-Crow Indian workers.

Not surprisingly, among the first Indians to take advantage of these circumstances would be the Crows' Northern Cheyenne neighbors. Even among other Northern Plains reservations, the Tongue River Indian Reservation stood out for its extreme poverty in the late 1800s. By all accounts, there was little in the way of meaningful work—or any real economic opportunity, for that matter—at Tongue River. For several years after the establishment of the reservation in 1884, the Northern Cheyenne were able to supplement meager government rations through hunting and gathering, but by 1890, local supplies of game had been exhausted. Ideally, farming would have replaced hunting as the main source of subsistence, but even many government officials acknowledged the total unsuitability of the reservation for agriculture. The main portion of the reservation comprised rough and broken uplands, with Tongue River and Rosebud Creek, the two main watercourses, running in narrow valleys. In 1886, Agent R. L. Upshaw noted that the yellowish soil "contained a considerable amount of alkali" but optimistically predicted that it would still produce good root crops and small grain. However, the shortness of the growing season often prevented crops from maturing, even when they were not destroyed first by drought, disease, or insects. During the last years of the nineteenth century, short rations and recurring crop failures combined to produce what one scholar terms "chronic malnutrition and periodic starvation" at Tongue River.[10]

Even when cultivation did prove successful, the lack of local markets or transportation links to more distant ones eroded Cheyenne enthusiasm. "Without a market and with very little taste for vegetable food," Upshaw confessed, "there is very little incentive for these Indians to do any very laborious farm work."[11] Not only were the climate and lack of markets unfavorable for turning the Northern Cheyenne into farmers, but the status of the reservation itself was clouded by uncertainty. Much of the best land and meager water rights available had already been preempted by white settlers before the establishment of the reservation, and the executive order creating the Tongue River Reservation met with determined opposition from local white interests. Confident that the order would eventually be revoked and the Cheyennes removed, white settlers continued to file entries on reservation land for several years. Under circumstances that placed the long-term survival of the reservation in doubt, both Cheyennes and their agents were reluctant to invest too much time, effort, or money on permanent internal improvements, the building of which might have provided the Northern Cheyenne with at least temporary employment and income.[12]

However, Upshaw also discovered that when there was paid work to be done, the Northern Cheyennne took to it "with alacrity." "I find most of them willing, ready, and anxious to work when there is a prospect for certain payment in a short period of time in money or its equivalent," he wrote, "but they are so situated that very few of them can obtain employment outside the small amount afforded by Government work." In 1887, the Cheyenne earned $1,291.41 from wage labor, mainly fencing, cutting hay, and hauling freight, which was not nearly enough to support a population of more than 800 people.[13] Other agents echoed Upshaw's sentiments. In 1895, Agent George

Stouch secured a contract for the Northern Cheyenne to cut 400 cords of wood for the military post at the agency. "I supposed it would take them months to fill the contract," he wrote,

> but a few days after giving the order, while riding over the hills, I came upon a party of wood cutters, and was astonished at the amount they had cut, and saw that if the other parties had cut as much they had already enough to fill the contract. At once I started runners to stop cutting and tell all hands to bring in what they had cut. As a result of their work I received 517 cords of wood, all of it cut and delivered within two weeks.[14]

Such episodic work could not support the entire community on a permanent basis, Stouch noted. "Scarcely a day [goes by] but someone makes an appeal for work, but unfortunately there is no regular work about the agency for more than a few men."[15] Between 1884 and 1900, the most the Northern Cheyenne earned through wage labor on the reservation was $7,028 in 1895—this for a reservation population that now (following the return of the Pine Ridge Cheyennes to Tongue River) totaled just over 1,300.[16]

Upshaw, Stouch, and other agents were not unreserved in their praise. Agents regularly described the Northern Cheyenne as headstrong and hard to control, and they deplored the reluctance of the Cheyenne to adopt white standards of dress, housing, morality, and medicine. It was entirely possible for an agent to describe the Cheyennes as being eager to work in one sentence and denounce their laziness in the next.[17] However they were described, it was abundantly clear in the late 1800s that the Tongue River Indian Reservation and the Northern Cheyennes were unlikely to become economically self-sufficient, at least in the near future. Ironically, it was this fact that increasingly brought Northern Cheyennes to the Crow Indian Reservation in the late 1800s, not just as visitors but also as workers.

In the mid-1890s, the rail stops closest to the Northern Cheyenne agency at Lame Deer were Rosebud Station, sixty-five miles away in the Yellowstone River valley on the Northern Pacific Railroad, and Crow Agency, fifty-five miles to the west on the Chicago, Burlington and Quincy line.[18] Although the trip to Crow Agency required crossing the Wolf Mountains separating the Little Bighorn and Rosebud drainages, the existence of Indian Service warehouses and other facilities at Crow Agency made it the preferred depot for supplies headed for Tongue River.[19] In a sense, Crow Agency supplied the infrastructure that Tongue River lacked. But the distant location of Tongue

River's main freight terminus required both a workforce and a means of moving supplies from Crow Agency to Tongue River, a job quickly assumed by the Northern Cheyenne themselves. At the same time Crow and Northern Cheyenne agents were trying to discourage visiting and travel between their reservations, long trains of wagons driven by Northern Cheyenne teamsters regularly made the trip to Crow Agency to pick up rations, equipment, and other supplies. At a rate of 75 cents per hundredweight in 1905, a freighter with a full wagon could typically earn close to $10 for a five- or six-day trip.[20]

As Upshaw and other Northern Cheyenne agents noted, freighting proved to be a popular realm of employment. Not only did it offer a measure of independence and a guaranteed return not to be found in weeding pumpkin patches or potato fields, but it also carried the attraction of travel and the opportunity for visiting at Crow Agency. Teamsters represented a broad cross section of Cheyenne society, from unreconstructed, Cheyenne-speaking traditionalists to educated, literate boarding school graduates. A typical train might include among its teamsters the shaman and Ghost Dance proponent Porcupine, tribal judge Wooden Leg, mixed-blood agency employees like Willis Rowland, and several women.[21] Enthusiasm for freighting was so high that some Cheyennes occasionally traveled to Crow Agency on their own account, hoping to find a newly arrived load of supplies to haul back to Lame Deer. "So many of our Indians have gone over to Crow without an order, hoping they might find freight there and have been disappointed, and neglecting their crops," a clerk at the agency wrote in 1915. "I want to be very careful that freight is there before an order is sent out."[22]

Most goods traveled east from Crow Agency to Lame Deer, but a few items traveled in the opposite direction. Northern Cheyennes hauled hides from beeves killed at ration issues to Crow Agency to be loaded onto trains for shipment to tanneries.[23] Lumber, one of the few readily available resources on the Northern Cheyenne Reservation, was also carried west from three Indian Service sawmills, much of it destined for use in construction projects at Crow.[24] Although an Indian Service employee (often an agency farmer, interpreter, or policeman) usually accompanied wagon trains, the inevitable delays in loading often necessitated an overnight stay at Crow, permitting extended interaction with local residents. Many teamsters took advantage of this time to purchase supplies from the store of E. A. Richardson and Company, the local trader at Crow Agency.[25]

Over time, Cheyennes also assumed increasing responsibility for maintaining the road and communication network linking the two agencies, including that portion lying within the Crow Reservation itself. In 1907, Northern

Cheyenne laborers constructed the first telephone line between Lame Deer and Crow Agency. Although agency personnel did much of the skilled work, Cheyennes handled most of the manual labor. As a result of this experience, two years later, the War Department hired Bear Comes Out and Abram Yelloweyes to put in a phone line between the superintendent's house at the Custer battlefield and Crow Agency because the Cheyennes knew "how to get out poles and set them properly."[26] In 1913, the superintendent at Lame Deer reported to his Crow counterpart that Ed Harris, "an industrious Northern Cheyenne," had agreed to perform road work on the route connecting Lame Deer with Crow Agency. For $250, Harris agreed to build three bridges and repair the road from the head of Reno Creek to Custer Buttes. Although the entire stretch lay on the Crow Reservation, Northern Cheyenne superintendent John Eddy urged Crow Superintendent W. W. Scott to employ Harris for the work, as the road "is used largely by our [Northern Cheyenne] freighters."[27]

From an economic standpoint, of course, even this work could not offset the desperate poverty that all too often characterized life at Tongue River. But on another level this work took on an importance out of proportion to its actual economic impact. Freighting and other work at Crow brought Northern Cheyennes closer than ever before to their neighbors, reinforcing existing ties and forging new ones. At the same time, working at Crow accustomed many Cheyennes to leaving home and the reservation to find work. In 1907, Superintendent Eddy would boast to a contractor hiring laborers for a Bureau of Reclamation irrigation project near Sidney, Montana, that the Northern Cheyennes were "the best Indian workers in the Northwest."[28] Even allowing for a degree of hyperbole, part of what made Eddy's statement possible was his confidence in Northern Cheyenne workers to acquit themselves in an Anglo-dominated economic world, even when that confidence had been gained through work done in the distinctly Indian environment of the Crow Reservation.

Physical proximity was not the only reason the Crow Reservation took on such a central role in the economic activities of so many Northern Cheyennes. At the close of the nineteenth century, the Crow Reservation was in fact one of the more prosperous reservations on the Northern Plains. At the beginning of the 1890s, slightly more than 60 percent of all Crows still received government rations; by the end of the decade, the number of individuals on the ration rolls had dropped to 25 percent. Although agents across the Northern Plains regularly sought to reduce the number of individuals receiving rations (sometimes regardless of actual circumstances or need), ration issues at Crow fell much more rapidly than elsewhere, and once reduced, generally stayed at a lower level, suggesting that economic dependency, at least at Crow, was actually declining during this period. By 1900, out of all the reservations in Montana, only the Flathead Reservation had a lower percentage of its population receiving rations. In contrast, ration issues at the Blackfeet Reservation fell from 84 percent in 1891 to 50 percent in 1898; at Fort Peck, the number decreased from 90 to 75 percent; and at Fort Belknap, the percentage receiving rations actually increased from 60 percent in 1891 to 70 percent in 1898. Throughout the decade, the Northern Cheyenne remained the most dependent on rations. In 1895 the number of people on the ration rolls fell to a low of 75 percent; but in the following three years, Tongue River agents reported that once again, 100 percent of Northern Cheyennes depended on government rations to survive.[29]

The relative prosperity of the Crow community during this period stemmed from several sources. The Crows' undisputed ownership of their reservation (in contrast to that of the Northern Cheyenne) brought in income from tribal grazing leases sold to white ranchers. The 1891 sale of the western end of the reservation also brought the Crows $552,000 in annuity payments dispersed over twenty years.[30] However, the single most significant factor may have been the rapid increase in agricultural production by Crows themselves during the decade.

In contrast to the rugged, poorly watered Tongue River Reservation, the Crow Reservation possessed broad, fertile valleys containing major watercourses such as the Bighorn and Little Bighorn rivers. Other, smaller valleys such as that along Lodge Grass and Pryor creeks in the eastern and western portions of the reservation, respectively, also appeared promising for agriculture. Though the sporadic and unpredictable nature of Montana rainfall posed a potential obstacle, government officials argued that this could be overcome through the construction of a network of irrigation ditches, assuring prompt and reliable delivery of water to fields. "A more fertile country cannot be found after water is brought upon the land, or a country where the yield is greater," Crow agent M. P. Wyman enthused in 1891. "There will scarcely be a limit to it."[31]

For once, the optimism of government officials did not seem mistaken. In 1895, Crow district farms (cooperative farms worked by Crow laborers under the direction of government farmers) produced nearly 118,000 bushels of wheat, and in 1896, 120,000 bushels. In 1898, construction began on a mill at Crow Agency to supply both Crows and Northern Cheyennes with flour, with a concomitant increase in the number of Northern Cheyenne engaged in hauling from Crow Agency to Tongue River. By the early 1900s, the Crows supplied Tongue River with up to 300,000 pounds of flour annually, all of it hauled by Northern Cheyenne freighters.[32] (After the introduction of dryland farming techniques at Tongue River in the early 1900s, Northern Cheyenne wheat also began to be hauled west, to be ground into flour at the Crow mill and shipped back to Tongue River.)[33]

Even this production paled in comparison to what government officials envisioned once large-scale irrigation was brought into the picture. As Wyman's comment suggests, Crow agents began touting the potential of irrigation almost immediately after the relocation of Crow Agency from the mountainous Stillwater Valley to the Little Bighorn in 1884.[34] Construction on an irrigation ditch off the Little Bighorn began on a small scale that year, and reservation-wide projects picked up speed in 1891, after the Crows agreed to set aside $290,000 from their land sale proceeds for irrigation work. By 1914, a latticework of headgates, canals, and feeder and lateral ditches covered every major valley on the reservation, at a cost of more than $1.2 million in Crow money spent on ditch construction and maintenance.[35]

Eventually, the grandiose scale and spiraling costs of this irrigation network would prove disastrous to the Crow tribe. Construction costs sapped the tribal treasury and accelerated the transfer of Crow lands into white hands, as tribal members with allotments covered by irrigation districts found themselves charged with maintenance fees (collectively in excess of $10,000 annually), regardless of whether or not they actually made use of the system.[36] For the most part, it has been these highly visible, negative long-term consequences of reservation irrigation projects that have shaped both historical perspectives and narratives, both at Crow and elsewhere. As has been the case with Indian agriculture generally, historians have tended to view irrigation on reservations from a long-term, macroeconomic perspective. Whether as examples of social or civil engineering run amok, the angle of vision has most often been that of irrigation's impact on Native peoples rather than Native peoples' motivations, attitudes, and actions.[37] Even those studies that do examine Native responses usually focus on Indian resistance to irrigation, rather than the ways in which irrigation, and the work associated with it, could be redirected toward entirely different agendas than that of the Indian Service.[38] At Crow, however, when the angle of vision is shifted to Indian labor and its consequences rather than of agents, civil engineers, or Native American resistance, new patterns come into view.

Irrigation at Crow represented more than just a colonial project that further deprived Crows of control over their own land and economy, or a failed attempt to convert Crows into modern, mass-producing farmers. During its construction, the Crow irrigation survey represented one of the biggest, longest-running public works projects of its time in Montana. During peak months of the construction season, the project employed more than 300 workers and provided one of the most consistent sources of work on any reservation in the region.[39] And though some Crow tribal leaders questioned the size of the system, the prospect of steady employment and wages provided powerful incentives for Crows to continue to approve appropriations of tribal funds. As Frederick Hoxie puts it, "Most Crows viewed the project from the perspective of day laborers rather than landowners."[40]

Ditch work held the promise of good wages—$3.50 per day for a team scraper driver guiding a team of horses hitched to an excavating rig, $1.75 per day for a filling scraper operator hauling dirt to use as fill in low spots, and $1.50 for an ordinary day laborer in 1893—with immediate pay, compared to labor on reservation farms with the vagaries of weather, insects, and potential crop disease standing between the worker and payday.[41] Gun Chief, a Crow ditch worker, expressed this attitude well in an 1895 council with Office of Indian Affairs officials: "We make some money working on the ditches, and we can buy what we want with it. Last year I started to work on a Big Farm [district farm] after the snow went off, and I worked till snow flew in the fall. I got $4.50 for my year's work. I have never liked the Big Farms since."[42]

The allure of ditch work for Indians at Crow was so strong that it even caused conflicts between agents and those in charge of irrigation construction. In 1895 and 1896, Agent J. W. Watson and irrigation superintendent Walter Graves engaged in a dispute over the merits of Indians working on ditches. Watson complained that too many Crows (like Gun Chief) were leaving the large district farms for the ditch camps, and he recommended to the commissioner of Indian Affairs that Indians be taken off ditch work entirely and replaced by white laborers. Graves responded by stating that the workforce at Crow was large enough to accommodate both irrigation construction and the district farms. He also alleged that Watson was sending agency police to raid the ditch camps "for the sole purpose of levying an excise upon the workers for the privilege of remaining at work undisturbed. In some instances as much as $25 has been paid for this privilege to the police."[43]

Hidden beneath this bureaucratic turf battle are insights into the full significance of irrigation labor for Native workers. For Indians, working on irrigation in the 1890s provided a sense of autonomy and independence that supervised agricultural labor could not. As ditch workers testified, wage labor enabled individuals to make their own decisions about where and how to work, an argument Crows pointedly made part of their critique of district farms. "I want to say here that we would like to work on our own farms," one Crow stated, "instead of on the Big Farms, so that when we had time, we could go and work on ditches if we wanted to."[44] Wage labor on ditches offered the possibility of choice, an element of control and self-determination that seemingly had vanished with the buffalo.

Just how threatening a vision this was becomes apparent in Watson's own reports. At the same time that he hailed the Crows as being "about to make a leap from the condition of a crowd of beggars depending on the Government to an independent community, supporting itself," he suggested that ditch labor was making Crows too independent. Too much money in Indian pockets encouraged nonprogressive behavior, including frivolous spending, gambling, and the support of networks of relatives who, in Watson's view, should be forced to support themselves—and, of course, there was the customary Crow generosity toward visitors.[45] Crows even used money earned from ditch work to travel to other reservations, as Two Leggings, Comes Up Red, and Little Iron did in using their ditch wages to visit the Blackfeet Reservation in 1910.[46] Wage labor threatened to undermine the state of dependency that agents everywhere relied on to maintain a semblance of control over their charges. Ironically, the government's own irrigation program threatened the government's own assumption that Crows "would enter the economic world of twentieth-century America as obedient wards of the state and its minions."[47] Equally ironically, both the work of ditch labor and the money obtained from it strengthened the ties between Crows and other Native peoples that government officials were so anxious to sever in the late nineteenth and early twentieth centuries.

Irrigation construction on the Crow Reservation was seasonal. During the winter months, extending into March or even April in unseasonably wet or snowy years, only a skeleton crew of surveyors, engineers, and laborers (usually all white) remained on the payroll.[48] As the ground dried and the weather warmed, the workforce swelled to several hundred, with most (especially Indian workers) being employed as manual laborers or driving horse teams. During the high season for construction, usually running from April or May through November, work on the Crow Irrigation Survey made the Crow Reservation an oasis of opportunity in an increasingly impoverished world. At a time when government officials were making concerted efforts to reduce the number of individuals receiving rations and other options for subsistence were increasingly limited, irrigation construction at Crow proved to be attractive, not only for Crows themselves, but also for other Native peoples in the region. However, the extent and significance of non-Crow participation in irrigation work is not immediately apparent in the historical record.

Though construction superintendents submitted monthly reports containing rosters of employees and the wages they earned, only partial runs of the reports survive.[49] The most intact runs date from 1893 to 1898, but even here, at least one monthly report is missing for each year, with only seven extant reports available from 1896. Reports for 1899 and the early 1900s are even more sporadic, with only four surviving from each year between 1899 and 1902. Even those reports that do survive have serious limitations as sources. The forms list workers' names, the days they worked and how many hours per day, what type of work they performed, the pay rate for that work, and each worker's monthly earnings. However, even though workers are identified by name, it is not always obvious exactly who a particular worker is. The reports separate employees into four categories—"white," "colored," "squaw men" (white men married to Indian women), and "Indian"—but Indian workers are not subdivided or identified by tribe. In only one instance does a monthly report identify workers on the basis of tribal affiliation. In this case, two individuals named Black Bird are listed as performing ditch labor in September 1897. Behind the first Black Bird is the parenthetical notation "Crow," while the second is identified as Cheyenne.[50]

Another difficulty is that many Crows and whites who had married into the tribe in effect acted as subcontractors for ditch work. The large numbers of horses owned by Crows allowed them to hire out horse teams to others desiring to work on the ditches, but in such situations, it was the owners of the horse teams who were listed on employment reports, rather than the individuals who actually performed the work. Some horse owners subcontracted teams on a large scale: the July 1897 report, for example, lists Henry Keiser, a white man married to a Crow woman, a total of eighteen times. Crows also subcontracted work, although not to the same extent; the July 1893 report lists Crooked Face five times, while Plenty Coups and Little Light are listed four times each.[51] According to irrigation superintendent Graves, a few Crows even subcontracted ditch work out to white men, in an inversion of standard social and economic hierarchies. As Graves noted, "A number of them [Crows] employ white men to drive their teams for them, and in this they seem to find their greatest satisfaction, even though receiving little remuneration out of the transaction."[52] Crows and men like Keiser almost certainly hired teams out to

Indians as well, but the identities of those individuals cannot be gleaned from the employee reports.

The lack of tribal identifications or names of subcontracted workers on employee records makes it impossible in most cases to determine conclusively the identity of Indian workers. Most of the names on the records are identical to or have potential analogues to individuals listed in Crow tribal censuses, and many, like that of Plenty Coups, are distinctively Crow. However, the commonality of names across tribes—there were Crazy Heads, Sharp Noses, and Stump Horns on both Crow and Northern Cheyenne tribal rolls, for example—creates some ambiguity. In most cases, the workers in question were probably Crow. However, there are also names that are clearly not those of Crows, and other sources that illustrate a degree of non-Crow Indian involvement in ditch labor far greater than employment records alone suggest. Despite their limitations, the available monthly employee reports and other irrigation records suggest that Northern Cheyennes in particular participated in and benefited from irrigation construction at Crow in the late 1800s and early 1900s.

On the basis of the available monthly employee reports during the early 1890s (compared to contemporaneous Crow tribal censuses), the Indian work contingent evidently remained overwhelmingly Crow. A few anomalous names appear, including a worker named Red Hat in October and November 1894, who may be the Northern Cheyenne man of the same name.[53] In 1895, however, the first verifiably non-Crow names appear, when Eugene and Arthur Standing Elk are listed as doing ditch work for eighteen days in April. Eugene Standing Elk was the son of the Northern Cheyenne headman Standing Elk and a graduate of the St. Labre Mission School at Tongue River. Arthur Standing Elk is more difficult to place: an Arthur Standing Elk is listed on the 1891 Northern Cheyenne tribal census as the son of the Northern Cheyenne woman Stands Bad, but he is listed as being only one year old at the time. The Arthur Standing Elk listed in the April 1895 employee report was most likely another member of the large and extended Standing Elk family.[54]

The number of Northern Cheyennes coming to work on irrigation at Crow increased considerably the following year. Northern Cheyenne workers in 1896 included another Standing Elk employed as a scraper driver and laborer in August and October (unfortunately, the September 1896 employee report is missing); a Mrs. Limpy (most likely the wife of the Northern Cheyenne of the same name) employed for six and a half days in August at $1 per day, most likely as a camp cook or caretaker; Wild Hog, the leader of the Northern Cheyenne Elkhorn Scraper warrior society, in October and November; an individual listed as Woman Leggings (possibly a mistranslation or misrecording of Wooden Leg) in October; and several other distinctively non-Crow names of uncertain tribal origin over the course of the spring, summer, and fall.[55] Many of the Cheyenne who worked at Crow in 1896 reappear on employee reports the following year, with the addition of Black Bird, Roman Nose, Frank Standing Elk and Wooden Leg, Howling Wolf, Limpy, and Porcupine in September; the latter three (joined by Wild Hog) staying on to work in October; and Porcupine into November. Other Cheyenne workers may be hidden by names that mirror those of individual Crows or by the listing of Crow or white subcontractors who leased horse teams to workers.[56]

Most distinctive of all the names on the 1896 and 1897 reports are those of mixed-blood Northern Cheyennes, particularly that of Jules Seminole and at least four members of the Rowland family: Willis (and/or William), Zach, James, and Sally.[57] The descendant of a Cheyenne mother and French fur trader father, Seminole actually moved with his family to Crow in the 1890s and worked, as best as can be determined, annually on irrigation construction through at least 1903.[58] The appearance of the Rowlands on irrigation employee reports is particularly worthy of note. The Rowlands were all offspring of a prominent mixed-blood family heavily involved in Northern Cheyenne tribal and agency affairs. In 1900, a government inspector characterized the Rowlands as having "an extended relationship which takes in about every Indian employee of both agency and school (including the police)."[59] The fact that even members of such a well-connected family would have come to Crow to work is a demonstration of both the powerful appeal of irrigation construction labor and an eloquent statement of the lack of economic opportunities available at Tongue River.

The work histories of Northern Cheyennes who came to Crow vary widely. Some stayed for only a day or two; others worked steadily for a month or more. Black Bird took home $38.25 for twenty-five days' work as a common laborer, while Porcupine earned $59.25 for his fall's work.[60] Most Northern Cheyennes appear to have worked as laborers at $1.50 per day. Those Northern Cheyennes who drove scraper teams tended to be mixed bloods like Seminole and the Rowlands, whose greater facility with English may have helped them land more coveted and higher-paying jobs, though the possibility exists that non-English-speaking Cheyennes may have found it easier to use sign language or a Native tongue to communicate and obtain scraper work from subcontracting Crows. Perhaps not coincidentally, many of the Northern Cheyennes whose names are found on irrigation employee lists later worked as freighters hauling flour from Crow to Tongue River, a form of employment whose increasing availability may have led to a reduction in the numbers of Northern Cheyennes working in the ditch camps over time.[61]

The employee reports for 1896 and 1897 are the most complete sets of employee lists available for the Crow Irrigation Survey. After 1897, the number of extant monthly reports sharply declines, including for the summer and fall months, when construction was at its peak. However, those reports that do survive, together with other testimony, suggest that the involvement of non-Crow Indians in irrigation construction at Crow did not end with the Northern Cheyenne.

Though not as evident in the monthly reports, Crees stand out as another Native community whose members came to Crow to work on irrigation. Crow agent John Edwards noted that Crows employed Crees to drive horse teams on the ditches, suggesting that many Cree names are hidden behind lists of subcontractors on employee reports. A history of Crow irrigation prepared by the Bureau of Indian Affairs, for example, noted that a three-and-a-quarter-mile long ditch on Soap Creek irrigating 663 acres in the Bighorn River valley was dug by Crees under contract to Richard Wallace, a mixed-blood Crow.[62] Another agent, W. W. Scott, described the Crees as intelligent and industrious workers who often accumulated considerable herds of horses in their business dealing with Crows. In a cash-poor tribal economy, horses continued to serve as a valuable medium of exchange, with Crees selling their recently acquired horses to whites for cash when needed.[63]

Given the proximity of their reservations and the close economic and social ties already forged between them, the presence of Northern Cheyennes in ditch camps should not come as a surprise. The presence and employment of Crees at Crow, however, requires greater explanation. In the late 1800s and early 1900s, Crees in Montana were literally a people without a home. Small numbers of Crees had ranged below the forty-ninth parallel throughout the mid- to late nineteenth century, but Crees as a community lacked an established treaty relationship with the United States comparable to that possessed by the Crows or the Cheyennes. In 1885, the failure of the Riel rebellion in Canada added several hundred Crees and Cree–Metis refugees to the population south of the border. Both the United States and the state of Montana disclaimed any responsibility for resident or refugee Crees, however, considering them all to be Canadian Indians.

Victims of Western notions of cartography and diplomacy, without a reservation or official recognition, Crees by the late 1800s were the closest approximation to true nomads on the Northern Plains, moving wherever prospects for subsistence and survival seemed least bleak. Some moved to the vicinity of U.S. military posts like Fort Assiniboine, while others settled on the out-skirts of Helena, Butte, and other Montana cities, eking out a precarious exis-tence and subject to demands for their removal by white Montanans.[64] Other Crees moved to established reservations, including the Blackfeet, Flathead, and Fort Belknap reservations, in addition to Crow. Given the precarious nature of most reservation economies, they did not always receive a warm wel-come.[65]

At Crow, however, the existence of a large irrigation construction project cushioned the Crees' entry and presence. Both Crows and government offi-cials found Crees useful as workers at various times and for different purposes. When ditch work schedules collided with the seasonal farmwork agents demanded from Crows, Cree labor became invaluable.[66] Meanwhile, Crows, in addition to subcontracting horse teams to Crees for irrigation work, also hired Crees as agricultural laborers at haying and harvest time, and as construction workers building houses.[67] As a result, Crees flocked to the Crow Reservation "by the hundreds," according to one agent.

Despite their occasional usefulness, Crees were not always welcomed at Crow. Agents often considered them to be a destabilizing element, accusing Crees of poaching game and bringing liquor onto the reservation.[68] At the other extreme, the Crees' eagerness to work was seen as an impediment to the Crows' acquisition of Anglo-American virtues. Agent Scott complained in 1912 that Crees "are employed by Crows to do work which [the Crows] them-selves should do."[69] This attitude emerges most clearly in instructions issued to irrigation construction foreman Joseph Dussome in 1910. "Hire Crows in preference to Crees," he was told. "If more Crows apply you may have to lay off Crees to get the Crows on."[70]

Periodically, agents launched sweeps to round up as many Crees as possi-ble and evict them from the reservation. In 1896, troops from Fort Custer gathered up several hundred Crees and shipped them north from Billings by rail over the Canadian line. However, as an agent noted several years later, "the Indians got back to this country as soon as the troops did, and they have remained in this section ever since."[71] As was the case with visiting, the Sisyphean nature of the effort to keep Crees off the Crow Reservation even-tually led to the adoption of essentially laissez-faire attitudes toward their pres-ence on the part of government officials.[72]

Proximity and the lack of a reservation of their own help explain the pres-ence of Northern Cheyennes and Crees as irrigation laborers, but these were not the only non-Crow Indians who found work at Crow. Most probably learn-ing of the work (if not actually seeing it in progress) during visits to Crow,

Lakotas also expressed interest in ditch work. In 1900, the Crow Spotted Rabbit forwarded a letter to Crow agent Edwards from the Pine Ridge Oglala Spotted Elk, requesting permission for himself and several of his friends to visit the Crows. Spotted Rabbit explained that Spotted Elk wanted to recover six horses he had left at Crow during a previous visit, and that several of the Pine Ridge Indians wanted to come to Crow to work on the irrigation ditches.[73] The Oglala Lakota Charles Means may have been one of these Indians; monthly irrigation employee reports show that Means worked on ditches in both June and July 1900. As was the case with several other non-Crow ditch laborers, Means may have benefited from old kinship ties: though enrolled and allotted at Pine Ridge, his mother was a Crow Indian whose siblings still lived at Crow.[74] In addition to Lakotas, Southern Cheyennes from Oklahoma also appear on ditch records from 1898. Given the lack of tribal identifications on irrigation employee reports, this by no means necessarily exhausts the number of individuals and tribes who may have taken advantage of ditch construction labor at Crow.

As with the identities of individual ditch workers, it is difficult to neatly categorize Crow attitudes toward non-Crow Indians working on the Crow Reservation. Although irrigation supervisors estimated that two-thirds of the money spent went to Indian laborers, on occasion, Crows complained about the number of non-Crows working on ditch construction.[75] "I don't want to injure anyone, but I don't like to see strangers here to build our ditches," a Crow spokesman remarked at a ditch camp council in 1895. "This land and this ditch money is ours, and we want to build our own ditches and get some of our money back. I do not like to see strangers come here and get our money."[76] Many of these complaints were aimed primarily at white workers. "We don't want any more white people on the ditches," Plenty Coups told government officials in 1899, "and those white people that are there now, we want them put off."[77] However, foreign Indians could also occasionally attract condemnation, as Cold Wind illustrated at the 1895 council: "We want to put in all the time we can on the ditches, and we don't want any other Indians sent here to do the work."[78]

It may be a mistake, however, to take Cold Wind's statement as a blanket objection to all non-Crow Indians coming to the reservation to work. In 1895 there were few, if any, foreign Indians working in the ditch camps. Cold Wind's comments regarding "other Indians" being "sent" to Crow came in the wake of proposals by government officials to revoke the executive order establishing the Tongue River Reservation and to relocate all Northern Cheyennes to Crow—a proposal opposed by both Crows and Cheyennes.[79] Likewise, the reference to strangers left open room for individuals with ties to Crows, either real or fictive, or who through their actions or values forged a sense of solidarity and identity with their hosts.

The legacies and role that prereservation ties played in shaping work relationships and attitudes toward Indians from other tribes working at Crow may help explain the appearance of Wooden Leg in irrigation construction records. Regardless of his later attitude toward Crows, Wooden Leg's ties to the Crow community though his Crow-born uncle may well have smoothed his entry into the Crow Reservation workforce. Those ties could then be used to introduce others who may have lacked previous connections. One possible manifestation of this process on ditch labor records is the tendency for non-Crow Indians to show up not as individuals but as members of groups who all apparently came to the camps together, as in the employee lists from fall 1896 and 1897.[80]

Where such ties did not previously exist, the flexibility and permeability of Native systems of kinship and community boundaries meant that they could easily be created. Agents professed themselves mystified by the small profit margins Crows were willing to accept in subcontracting horse teams out for ditch work. In the case of Crees and other Indians, the marginal profits earned by subcontracting Crows may well reflect a sense of shared identity, if not kinship, an expression of a noncapitalist Indian value of generosity toward the less fortunate. As reflected by their determination to come to, and stay at, Crow, Crees certainly found living and working in a predominantly Indian community preferable to the racism and patronizing attitudes exhibited by white Montanans. Eventually, the increasing social and cultural ties between Crows and Crees, including but not limited to intermarriage, would lead to proposals for the wholesale adoption and incorporation of Crees into the Crow tribe in the early 1900s.[81]

The new world of work at Crow did more than just provide economic opportunity and bring members of different communities together in new ways, however. It also provided the venue for the introduction of an entirely new belief system, one defined as uniquely Indian despite its links to Christian belief. Before the late 1800s, peyote, a spineless cactus possessing hallucinogenic qualities when ingested, had been used for hundreds of years for medicinal and spiritual purposes by Native Americans in Mexico and as far north as the Lipan and Mescalero Apache and Caddo. By the 1870s and 1880s, the relocation of Southwestern Indians familiar with peyote to Indian Territory (later

Oklahoma) had spread the ritual use of peyote, now blended with elements of Christianity to form a syncretic, nativistic belief system, to Southern Plains groups like the Kiowa, Comanche, and Southern Cheyenne.[82]

Most historians and anthropologists date the introduction of peyote to the Northern Cheyenne to around 1890 and identify the missionary activities of Leonard Tyler, a Southern Cheyenne from Oklahoma and graduate of Carlisle Indian School, as being critical to the growth of the religion among the Northern Cheyenne.[83] In contrast, the arrival of peyote at Crow is dated much later—usually to around 1910—and is shrouded in ambiguous origins. The tardy diffusion of peyotism to the Crows poses a problem, particularly given the swift spread of other spiritual movements among Plains Indians in the late 1800s and early 1900s. Omer Stewart, the most prominent student of peyotism, explained the twenty-year gap between the introduction of peyote at Tongue River and among the Crows by recourse to the theme of traditional unfriendliness between Crows and Cheyennes dating back to the era of intertribal warfare. However, given the history of friendly relations and social and spiritual exchange between Northern Cheyennes and Crows after 1885, including Sword Bearer's participation in a Cheyenne Sun Dance, Stewart's interpretation is suspect.[84]

Indeed, close examination of Crow Agency records suggests that the initial introduction of peyote to the Crow Reservation, if not its permanent adoption, took place not long after its introduction to the Northern Cheyenne. In fact, Crow Agency records indicate that Leonard Tyler spent considerable time on the Crow Reservation in 1898. By itself this is not surprising; the easiest route to Tongue River from Oklahoma involved taking the train to Crow Agency, then a stage to Lame Deer.[85] However, irrigation employee records also indicate that Tyler and Ed (or Ernie) Black, a fellow Southern Cheyenne (and probably Tyler's brother-in-law), also worked on ditch construction in the Bighorn Valley during this period. Black worked as a laborer during the 1897 and 1898 construction seasons; Tyler joined him at Crow in midsummer of 1898.[86]

The pair spent so much time at Crow, in fact, that they arranged to have their annuity checks from Oklahoma delivered to Crow Agency rather than Lame Deer.[87] However, Tyler and Black's presence and activities also attracted the attention of Tongue River agent James C. Clifford and Crow agent Edward Becker. In July 1898, Clifford wrote to Becker, explaining that he had ordered Tyler to leave Tongue River and take the train south from Crow Agency back to Oklahoma. Tyler, Clifford alleged, "endeavored to incite my Indians to dance the Sun Dance and other dances; to eat the mescal bean; and was a dis-

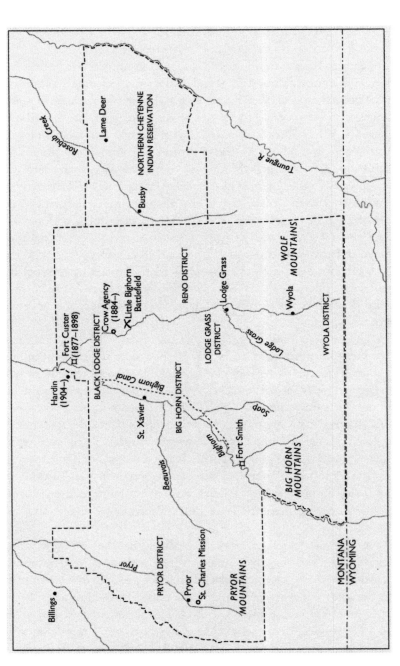

Map 4. The Crow and Northern Cheyenne reservations, 1904.

turbing element in many ways." Clifford added that he had also expelled "Ernie Black," whose "presence on any reservation is bad for the Indians."[88] However, instead of taking the train, Tyler went to the ditch camp on the Bighorn River, where he joined Black (who had already spent the previous summer working at Crow) and signed on as a laborer. "The Indian who took him over," Clifford told Becker, "says Tyler refuses to go to the agency."[89]

The correspondence between Clifford and Becker during this time illustrates perfectly the difficulties agents faced in trying to control both "their" Indians and outsiders from other reservations, as well as the added complications created by wage labor and ditch camps. One month after notifying Becker of Tyler's expulsion from Tongue River, the Northern Cheyenne agent wrote to Becker again, complaining that too many Cheyennes without passes were on the Crow Reservation. "I cannot control my Indians unless you assist me in this matter," he wrote, before reiterating his demand that Tyler and Black, who were both still at Crow, be sent south.[90]

Ditch camps provided a perfect place for Indians like Tyler and Black to hide in plain sight while at Crow. Irrigation laborers did not sign long-term contracts but worked instead on a day-to-day basis. Potential employees could come to the camp, sign on, work for a couple of days, and then vanish, reappearing (or not) a few days, weeks, or months later. Construction supervisors, better versed in engineering than in the nuances and differences in tribal cultures and languages, would have been hard-pressed to pick out individuals deemed undesirable by agents, even with the aid of interpreters and bilingual Indians. Despite the daily record keeping of employee hours and days worked, the relative anonymity of workers and the potential ditch camps posed for social disorder rendered agents understandably ambivalent about the benefits of wage labor in such an environment.

At best, ditch camps were rough places. The highest echelon of the workforce—engineers, supervisors, and clerks—lived in tents, while ordinary workers lived in what Graves described as "dugouts—holes in the ground."[91] The working-class environment of a construction site also exposed Indians to influences and role models unlikely to meet with the approval of agents. In one instance, a ditch worker named Reed, described by an OIA inspector as a "habitual drunkard and bull-dozer," attempted "one bluff too many and was killed a year ago at the ditch construction by one of his own ilk, who after the deed was performed flourished his pistol in the air and declared himself a 'Montana tough,' for all of which he is now doing ten years in prison."[92] In addition to violence, irrigation supervisors also had to defend their work against charges that ditch camps provided havens for gamblers, whiskey runners, and prostitutes.[93]

Ironically, the nature of ditch camps, populated by rough-hewn American workers and Native Americans attempting to negotiate the disorienting transition from autonomy to dependency to wage work, also made them an ideal environment for Tyler and Black to proselytize their new religion. The Peyote Way, with its blend of Christian and Native traditions and its emphasis on fostering "religious feeling and a sense of good fellowship and group respect and understanding," may have had considerable appeal for Native workers on the Crow Irrigation Survey.[94] Certainly the environment of the ditch camps would have given peyotism's doctrines of self-control, hard work, and abstinence from alcohol a high degree of relevance, while the money earned by Tyler and Black would have funded their missionary activities.[95]

Whether Becker ever succeeded in apprehending Tyler and Black and evicting them from the Crow Reservation, or whether the two left of their own accord, is impossible to determine conclusively. In August 1898, however, Black sent Becker a postcard from the Wind River Reservation in Wyoming, stating that he had left Crow after construction on the Bighorn ditch had ended for the season. Black asked Becker to hold on to the ditch money due him until work reopened in the spring and Black returned to Crow. In response, Becker told Black that he was banned from the Crow Reservation and that "if Leonard Tyler is with you on the Shoshone Reservation you will notify him that this letter also applies to him." What happened to Black's uncollected wages is unknown.[96]

Oddly, though Agent Clifford at Tongue River explicitly mentioned Tyler's evangelical work among the Northern Cheyenne (though mischaracterizing it as involving the Sun Dance and the consumption of mescal beans), peyote is not referred to anywhere in the correspondence surrounding Tyler and Black's presence at Crow. In November 1898, however, Crow agent Becker wrote to the commissioner of Indian Affairs, William A. Jones, requesting a face-to-face meeting to discuss reservation affairs at Crow. "There are some matters here in a very peculiar condition," he wrote. "Questions that are necessary to be solved cannot well be taken up by correspondence, and for the interest of the Indians and the prosecution of certain lines of work, policies will have to be outlined for the government of matters on the reservation in the future."[97] Though Jones's reply is not extant, in a subsequent letter Becker promised to follow the instructions given by the Office of Indian Affairs "in relation to one Ernie Black, a Southern Cheyenne Indian, if he makes his appearance on this reservation."[98]

Also impossible to determine, unfortunately, is whether peyote took hold on the Crow Reservation as a direct result of Tyler and Black's efforts. Crow oral tradition holds that Frank Bethune, a mixed-blood Crow from the Little Bighorn, was the first Crow roadman (or peyote ritualist) in the early 1900s. But Crow oral tradition also indicates that Crows were familiar with peyote before Bethune assumed a leadership role in the religion.[99] It does seem clear that whether or not Crows in 1898 embraced the faith Tyler and Black carried with them, they did not object to their presence as Becker did. As Indians, the two apparently enjoyed a sense of commonality with Crows that enabled them to work and live on the Crow Reservation in defiance of official approbation.

Events in the early 1900s gradually reduced the attraction of the Crow Reservation as a destination for Indian laborers. Completion of the centerpiece of the Crow Irrigation Survey—the thirty-five-mile-long Bighorn Canal—in 1905 significantly reduced work opportunities on the reservation. By 1912, chief engineer John Lewis reported that irrigation work employed just 125 men at the peak of the construction season (down from 300 in the late 1890s), mainly Crows "though some Crees and Cheyennes are employed."[100] In 1915, the creation of Rocky Boy's Reservation in northern Montana led to a further exodus of Crees, although a few remained at Crow well into the 1920s.[101] At Tongue River, meanwhile, the commencement of a major irrigation project in 1903 increased work opportunities there.

At the same time, as Eddy's 1907 letter to a Bureau of Reclamation contractor indicated, Northern Cheyenne agents began to actively seek off-reservation employment for their charges, advertising and recruiting Cheyennes as seasonal laborers for the burgeoning sugar beet industry in Montana and Colorado, as railroad workers in Montana and South Dakota, and as laborers on Bureau of Reclamation projects in the lower Yellowstone River Valley.[102] Henry Keiser, the Crow squaw man and labor subcontractor, continued his relationship with the Northern Cheyenne, in 1907 taking a crew of Cheyennes to do railroad work and in 1909 taking another group to the Cheyenne River Reservation in South Dakota (a Lakota reservation, despite the name) for yet another season of railroad construction.[103]

Work patterns shifted further with the elaboration of reservation infrastructure at Tongue River. By the turn of the century, declining optimism regarding the willingness (or ability) of Native Americans to assimilate into white society increasingly led government administrators to accept reservations as essentially permanent features, rather than as the transient "schools for civilization" they had originally been intended to be.[104] In 1898, Indian Service inspector James McLaughlin filed a report recommending that the government buy out the last remaining white settlers on the Northern Cheyenne Reservation. On March 19, 1900, President William McKinley signed an executive order confirming Cheyenne title to Tongue River, ending the threat of removal that had hung over the heads of the Northern Cheyenne since 1884.[105] The buyout of white settlers and their water rights cleared the way for the beginning of irrigation construction and encouraged agents to embark on other projects designed to increase Tongue River's administrative self-sufficiency and lessen its reliance on Crow Agency.[106] Construction of an all-weather road to Forsyth on the Northern Pacific decreased the amount of freight shipped through Crow Agency, while construction of a flour mill at Tongue River in 1915 ended nearly two decades of Northern Cheyenne flour trains to Crow.[107] The purchase of a three-ton truck for the agency in 1921 further pushed Northern Cheyenne freighting into decline.[108] None of these developments lifted the Northern Cheyenne from what one agent in 1907 labeled "depauperate" conditions, but all served to reduce the frequency with which Northern Cheyennes traveled to Crow as laborers, as well as the significance of that work.[109]

It is possible, then, to view the intertribal labor economy at Crow during the late 1800s and early 1900s as a transient event of limited long-term significance. Ultimately, work at Crow failed to pull Northern Cheyennes, Crees, or other Indians from a state of poverty. Yet the new world of work that emerged on the Crow Reservation also illustrated the challenges Northern Plains Indians faced and the strategies they developed to survive.

Like other dispossessed, colonized, and marginalized peoples, Native Americans had to be as economically opportunistic and creative as possible to survive. As Alice Littlefield and Martha Knack have suggested, "Native American wage labor participation . . . was largely self-motivated. Native peoples did not wait for government agents to direct them to wage opportunities; rather, they perceived those openings and sought them out."[110] Yet they also sought out work that permitted them to maintain older, prereservation-era values, which helps explain the popularity of work as show Indians in Wild West productions. It was precisely this ability to fit new patterns of labor and livelihood into a comfortable, familiar Indian milieu that made labor on the Crow Indian Reservation so attractive to so many non-Crow Indians. Although tensions could occasionally exist between Crows and other Indians coming to work at

Crow, this environment also fostered greater intertribal ties and a sense of ethnic solidarity both on an individual and group level.

The intertribal economy that emerged at Crow during this time had important ramifications, both for Crow culture and the Crow community. Work patterns perpetuated and strengthened existing networks of contact and exchange, and fostered the growth of new alliances. Labor served to tie Crows and Northern Cheyennes even closer together on a social level, while irrigation construction proved to be the vehicle for the introduction of an entirely new indigenous belief system. Like the labor economy that provided the setting for (and probably subsidized) Leonard Tyler and Ed Black's missionary work, peyotism itself sought to strike a balance between old worlds and new, to adapt to the radically changed circumstances of reservation life. In the next generation, peyote would introduce new concepts of community that both crossed tribal boundaries and divided Crows internally between adherents and those who condemned the new ritual.[111]

Similarly, the presence of large numbers of Crees as essentially permanent workers as well as residents at Crow raised important questions about the nature of the Crow community itself. During the nineteenth century, Crows had survived demographic crisis largely through the ability to absorb and incorporate outsiders. Whether these inclusive and flexible conceptions of community and identity could survive the darkening economic horizons of Native American life would become a pressing issue for both Crows and government officials in the early twentieth century. The relative wealth of the Crow reservation and the increasingly finite, if not diminishing, nature of that abundance generated questions. Was Crow wealth available to all Indians, including those who lived at but were not enrolled at Crow, or who came to Crow from other reservations for more ephemeral stays, or was it to be restricted only to those who enjoyed official status as Crows, whether in the eyes of the OIA or of Crows themselves?[112] Increasingly in the early 1900s, such economic issues became inextricably bound up in larger questions of who belonged at Crow, or who enjoyed rights to resources there, whether in the form of land, annuities, or work. The answers to these questions would in large measure determine not only the shape of the Crow community, but also the future of the ties that linked Crows and the Crow Reservation to other Indians on the Northern Plains.

CHAPTER FIVE

The Multiethnic Reservation

In the winter of 1898–1899, Office of Indian Affairs officials in Washington, D.C., asked Agent Edward Becker for a full accounting of all the Indians who "belonged at or lived at" the Crow Indian Reservation. In reply, Becker wrote:

> If I am obliged to go into the details and make a correct answer to this question, it means at least 60 days' work for this office force. The Crows, to my certain knowledge, are intermarried with the following tribes, to a more or less extent: Gros Ventre, Sioux, Piegan, Blackfoot, Nez Perce, Snakes, Shoshone, Arapaho, Cheyenne, and Mandans. Well-informed persons tell me that I may as well include every tribe of Indians west of the Missouri River.[1]

Becker's response captured one dimension of the community that existed on the Crow Indian Reservation at the turn of the century: the socially heterogeneous composition of the Crow tribe itself. Much of this mixed heritage was a legacy of generations of trade networks, alliances, and conflict between Crows and other Indians in the years before the end of the free-roaming era in the 1880s. Other elements were products of the reservation era itself, including the creation of new reservation-based labor regimes that brought non-Crow Indian workers to Crow; off-reservation boarding schools that brought Indian children from different tribes together in culturally alien environments; and the unprecedented power of the federal government to craft (if not always effectively enforce) broad policies covering everything from education to land tenure to constraints on social, cultural, and religious freedom that in turn created a new urgency for Indians on different reservations to meet and communicate with one another in devising responses to those policies. All of these factors contributed to the persistence of intermarriage between Crows and members of other tribal communities in the late 1800s and early 1900s. However, after acknowledging the diverse origins of individuals in the Crow community, Becker added the seemingly off-the-cuff yet unequivocal statement that "all the Indians on this reservation are classed as Crows."[2]

Despite its seemingly paradoxical nature, from Becker's perspective and that of the U.S. government such a statement made perfect sense. Over the course of the nineteenth century, the United States had been a party to literally hundreds of treaties and other legal agreements negotiated with various Native communities. Under these agreements, members of those communities were entitled to certain benefits: the distribution of cash payments or material goods in return for land; equipment and technical assistance in adopting elements of Anglo-American culture such as farming; access to educational facilities for one's children; and eventually the right to a parcel of property on one's reservation in the form of an allotment. Logically, regardless of an individual's specific genealogy, one could only lay claim to such benefits as a member of one tribe; one couldn't double-dip, so to speak, and claim allotments, annuities, or rations on more than one reservation. To Becker and the OIA, it was intuitively correct that an Indian could belong at only one reservation and could possess treaty rights and be enrolled as a member of only one tribe.

Added to these legalistic rationales were practical considerations. As Becker's response suggested, most agents did not have the time, staff, or inclination to pursue detailed investigations into the ancestry of the Indians who lived on their reservations. In the 1880s and even into the 1890s, many agents found it difficult to obtain an accurate head count of the number of people under their jurisdiction, let alone probe their personal and family histories.[3] And even if they attempted to do so, obstacles of language and culture interposed themselves as additional barriers to such a project. Among the Crows, such cultural practices included the terming of maternal uncles, the biological father's maternal uncles', and paternal aunts' sons as "father"; the occasional adoption of new names by individuals over the course of their lives; and a reluctance to speak the names of dead people in certain circumstances.[4] As a general rule, agents thus accepted the most outwardly visible aspects of identity—marital and familial ties, and residency in particular—as representing an individual's true legal and social identity. For Becker, a person's prior affiliation or mixed social background was irrelevant and not worthy of further inquiry, unless specific circumstances dictated otherwise.

As so often happened, however, this bureaucratic streamlining of community and identity failed to match more complex realities. As the case of Young Man Afraid of His Horses's aunt indicated, marrying into or simply joining another tribe did not automatically result in the severing of ties between an individual and that person's old community. Additionally, Becker's statement that "all the Indians on this reservation are classed as Crows" ignored another portion of the Crow Reservation's Indian community entirely: those non-Crows who, though not married to or related to Crows, or regarded as belonging to the Crow tribe (even by Crows themselves) nonetheless made their homes at and lived on the Crow Reservation as either long-term or permanent residents. Although their motives varied, with some coming to Crow as a refuge from unhappy marriages or personal conflicts on their home reservations, others in pursuit of economic opportunity, and still others for any of the numberless, nameless reasons that inform individuals' life choices, one common element shaped their decisions: the existence at Crow of an environment within which they were accepted socially, even if not as officially enrolled tribal members, as fellow Indians living in a multiethnic Indian community.

Most scholars examining reservation communities at the turn of the century have followed Agent Becker's lead in describing those communities (at least in terms of ethnicity) as being largely unproblematic, homogeneous, closed entities whose ties to other tribes and other reservations were either minimal to begin with, or were simply not significant enough to warrant investigation.[5] However, an inquiry into the origins and connections of individuals and families on the Crow Reservation, as well as the presence and number of foreign Indians there at the turn of the century, yields a different picture. Whitewashed out of existence by Becker and largely ignored by historians, the Crow Reservation around 1900 remained a diverse community, where Crows of heterogeneous ancestry and non-Crow Indian residents constituted an important part of the social milieu, and whose connections to other tribes and other reservations reached outward like a vast web over the Northern Plains.

Ironically, among the best sources for uncovering the larger dimensions of the Indian community at Crow are government records themselves. Reluctant though they might have been to probe genealogies (even as they sought to enforce regulations governing such minutiae as dress, work habits, religious expression, and other elements of social and cultural behavior and belief), agents found themselves inescapably drawn into the personal histories of the people they supervised. Indeed, one of the first lessons new agents learned upon arriving at Crow was the depth and breadth of kinship connections between Crows and other Native peoples. A few months after assuming office in the spring of 1889, for example, Crow agent M. P. Wyman received a letter from his counterpart at the Fort Belknap Reservation in northern Montana, home reservation for the Gros Ventre and Assiniboine. The Belknap agent claimed to have been told by two visiting Crow tribal policemen that several Gros Ventre families at Crow desired to return "home" to Belknap. Wyman queried both policemen (who denied making the statements attributed to them) and went on to investigate and enumerate all the individuals with Gros Ventre ancestry who lived at Crow.[6]

The Gros Ventres Rides a Horse, Rides by Himself, and Stone were all married to Crow women, had families, and had been with the Crows for at least fifteen years, according to Wyman. A younger Gros Ventre, the incongruously named George Washington, had joined the Crows sixteen years previously, attended school at and later went to Carlisle Indian School from Crow, and after his return married a Crow woman. Calf Robe also had married a Crow woman and lived at Crow for several years; however, in 1887, he traveled to Fort Belknap for a visit from which he did not return until 1889. Despite their Gros Ventre origins, all of the men were listed on Crow tribal rolls, and all had received allotments at Crow, according to Wyman.[7] Gros Ventre women at Crow included two sisters married to The Wolf, whose mother-in-law also lived with them; Pretty Now, who although married to a white man had lived with the Crows for years and was enrolled as a Crow; and a woman married to a Crow man named Walking, who was also a longtime resident and enrolled at Crow. Additionally, Wyman reported (but did not name) other Gros Ventres who were either war captives or who had joined the Crows long ago. Despite the ease with which he was able to identify people with mixed tribal backgrounds, Wyman, like Becker, insisted that "they are to all intents and purposes Crows, and are never mentioned or considered as Gros Ventres."[8] Whether the individuals in question might have been viewed as both Crow *and* Gros Ventre (at least by members of those respective communities) was apparently not a possibility considered by Wyman.

Whether Rides a Horse or the other individuals Wyman listed shared his concept of identity, however, is open to question. In 1898, nine years after being described as a Crow who was "never mentioned or considered as [a] Gros Ventre," Rides a Horse requested permission to visit Fort Belknap to see his father. Crow Agent Edward Becker apologized to his counterpart at Belknap for not providing advance warning of the trip, but said Rides a Horse's "time is limited and could not wait to obtain consent." The actions of other Crows of mixed ancestry provided additional proof that Crows (and other Indians) did not regard one's social identity as being limited by residence on a particular reservation. That same week, Becker requested permission for Bear in the Water (also known as Adlai Stevenson) and his family to travel to Fort Berthold, and for Horse Turns Around and two other Crows to go to Fort Belknap, all to see relatives.[9] In 1891, when Long Bear and six other Crows requested permission to visit the Shoshonis at Wind River, the Crow agent asked the Wind River agent to tell the Shoshoni headman Washakie that "his son is coming." That same year, a delegation of sixty Lakotas led by Young Man Afraid of His Horses was described as "visiting relatives."[10] Eagle Elk, a Pine Ridge resident who arrived at Crow in 1901 without a pass but accompanied by his wife and child, similarly confounded Anglo notions regarding the exclusivity of tribal affiliations. Eagle Elk requested permission to stay at Crow for three months, stating bluntly, "I am a Crow Indian and have relatives here." Despite his assertion of Crow identity, Eagle Elk apparently did not seek to move to Crow permanently or seek enrollment there. To Eagle Elk, residency at Pine Ridge and enrollment as a Pine Ridge Oglala Lakota did not eradicate his links to the Crow community and Crow Reservation.[11]

Though all of the above examples involved temporary visits, agents also had to wrestle with the consequences of long-term (if not always permanent) changes of residency. In 1899, Becker became involved in the case of a woman named Good Owl, who sought to return to Crow from the Fort Berthold Reservation in North Dakota. Some sixteen years previously, Good Owl had traveled with her uncle and his family to Fort Berthold for a visit. Her uncle and his family returned home, but Good Owl stayed, marrying a Hidatsa man and living with him for ten years before the couple separated. Good Owl then remained at Fort Berthold for another five years before requesting permission to return to Crow to live with her parents and receive her share of Crow annuities and issues. After Good Owl's father, One Blue Bead, verified her history, Agent Becker wrote that there was "no question" about her identity and that she would be entered on the Crow annuity rolls.[12]

Good Owl's story demonstrates a far greater degree of personal mobility and autonomy than many scholars have been willing to consider in studying reservation communities during this time. Neither Crow nor Fort Berthold agents apparently challenged Good Owl's move to Fort Berthold or her subsequent marriage to (and separation from) a Hidatsa man. Under Becker and Wyman's reasoning, Good Owl should not have been counted as a Crow at all, given her lengthy residence and marital ties on another reservation. However, in the face of testimony by her family, Becker had no choice but to recognize Good Owl as being legitimately Crow. Despite the putative control that agents like Becker supposedly exercised over "their" Indians, a significant degree of freedom of movement and residence between reservations remained intact in the late nineteenth century, particularly for Indians who could plausibly assert that they belonged in more than one place. Unable to challenge superior Indian knowledge of individual ancestry, Becker could do little but accept the claims of Good Owl and her family at face value.

Nor did marriage prove to be the stable indicator of identity agents envisioned it to be. In Anglo-American culture, marriage was idealized as a permanent bond between two individuals. Yet buried within this definition was an implicit contradiction. People change their minds, and marriages do not remain what they were when they were first contracted. Understood as a contract between individuals in Anglo-American society, state and theological bureaucratic structures nonetheless asserted a central role in legitimizing and upholding marriages. Marriage provided structure to society itself, prioritizing the relationship between husbands and wives and parents and children. As such, marriages could not (in theory, at least) be entered into or ended without the consent of the state or the church. Despite the gradual ascendancy of companionate or romantic marriage over older concepts of marriage as an economic or political linkage of two families, marriage in America was too important to be left up to individuals.[13]

For Native Americans, the institution of marriage was no less important, but patterns and practices were considerably more complex and less immutable. Because kinship practices supplied individuals with a far larger array of relatives (often including multiple "mothers" and "fathers"), the separation of two parents was far less problematic within tribal communities. Though the far broader definition of family and kin in Native American cultures gave marriage a political and economic dimension it had steadily lost in American culture, no state or theological structures existed to formalize or dissolve marriages. Because of this, marriages among Crows and other Northern Plains peoples could be entered into or ended far more easily (and frequently) than in Anglo-American society. Even in the absence of polygamy, what might be described as serially monogamous marriages were common, with an individual being married to a number of different people over the course of his or her life. In the tribal censuses taken in 1900 and 1910, 20 percent of the Crows listed reported having been married at least four times.[14]

The greater flexibility of Native American marriage did not, of course, eliminate the occurrence of unhappy unions, or abusive or unfaithful spouses. It did mean that under such circumstances, a marriage could be ended more readily and with less social stigma attached. However, resentment and hostility between former partners could still remain.[15] In prereservation days, when tribal bands acted and moved independently of one another for much of the year, an individual could simply move to another band or division of the tribe, knowing that contact with a former spouse would be occasional at best.

The grouping of tribes on reservations far smaller than those communities' former ranges changed these dynamics, however. Even though reservations were hardly the prisons they have been understood as in terms of geographic mobility, members of a tribe nonetheless spent much of the year in much closer proximity and contact with other bands and other tribal members than had previously been the case. It is impossible to gauge whether the creation of reservations led to greater conflict between divorced individuals than before, but it did increase the potential for such conflicts to emerge. In such circumstances, relocation to another reservation could become an attractive option.

As a result, agents found themselves not only attempting to enforce Anglo-American marital norms (such as prohibitions against polygamy) but also intervening in cases where individuals abandoned their spouse and fled to another reservation. In 1901, an Indian living at Crow named Harry Eaton claimed that his wife had abandoned him and run off to live at Lame Deer on the neighboring Northern Cheyenne Reservation. When Eaton complained, the chief clerk at Crow wrote to the agent at Tongue River requesting her arrest and return, presumably to the custody of her legally recognized husband. (In an additional twist, both Eaton and his wife were Hidatsas who had moved to Crow in the mid-1880s. At the time, the Crow agent had told Eaton that he had no objection to Eaton and his family coming to Crow, provided he was "of good disposition and willing to aid the Crows.")[16]

Six years later, in the summer of 1907, Crow agent Samuel Reynolds found himself further embroiled in domestic affairs, when the Piegan Pretty Bird Woman, visiting the Crow Reservation with her in-laws, eloped with a Crow man. Her husband on the Blackfeet Reservation deposited $20 with the Blackfeet agent to pay the rail fare for her return, but the disaffected spouse remained at large until the Crow fair in the fall, leaving a trail of romantic wreckage behind her, if Reynolds's correspondence is any indication. At least one Crow man apparently abandoned his own wife to live with her, and the harried Crow agent noted that she had "wanted to marry a number of Crows and a number have wanted to marry her." After finally being apprehended by Crow police, Pretty Bird Woman stated that she feared for her life if returned to her husband and requested to be allowed to live at Crow permanently. By this point, her husband had withdrawn the $20 deposit and reportedly remarried. An exasperated Reynolds told his Blackfeet counterpart, "I want to be rid of this girl; either allow her to marry one of our boys or have her taken home. But I don't want her to marry unless properly divorced." Eventually Reynolds put her on a train for Helena under guard, there to be met by Blackfeet tribal police.[17] Similarly, in 1909 Reynolds refused to issue a marriage license for the Crow Joe Martinez to marry a Shoshoni woman until he could investigate rumors that Martinez's betrothed already had a husband at Wind River.[18]

As the above examples suggest, agents could and did intervene in cases where the presence of outsiders posed the potential, real or imagined, for social disruption. More often than not, however, agents displayed a surprising degree of permissiveness in dealing with such individuals. Even Reynolds—a former Billings banker described by one OIA inspector as having a "forceful personality," and whose no-nonsense attitude and heavy-handed administration regularly brought him into conflict with the Crows—tolerated the presence of the Fort Berthold Indian Plenty Dogs (whom Reynolds termed a "big nuisance") for several years before finally asking him to leave the reservation.[19] Indians whose behavior met basic standards of decorum could live at Crow with little interference, and sometimes even get jobs on the agency payroll. During the early 1900s, the Northern Cheyenne Elmer Little Chief and his family moved to Crow, where his wife obtained a job as a cook at a boarding school, and Little Chief himself was appointed night watchman, a job he was unable to take due to illness. Eventually the Little Chief family left the reservation, perhaps moving to Tongue River, the Crow agent speculated, given the presence of Little Chief's relatives there.[20]

On occasion, agents actually encouraged people to relocate to another reservation, particularly in situations where personal conflicts posed potential threats to social harmony. The Crow Reservation in particular became a haven for Northern Cheyennes who, for one reason or another, became subjects of controversy and sometimes targets of hostility at Tongue River. Ditch worker Jules Seminole moved to Crow in the late 1890s after fatally shooting another Northern Cheyenne during a beef issue. Seminole claimed the killing was accidental—that an errant shot had ricocheted off a steer's skull—but feared revenge from the man's family.[21] The Northern Cheyenne Last Bull also shifted his residence to Crow during this time. Many Northern Cheyennes held Last Bull responsible for the destruction of Dull Knife's village by U.S. troops in the winter of 1876. Despite reports of soldiers nearby, Last Bull had prevented the camp from moving and staged an all-night dance that left the people exhausted when the soldiers attacked the following morning. As leader of the Kit Fox warrior society, Last Bull had also become known as a high-handed, arrogant individual with a reputation for stealing other men's wives.[22] Eventually deposed as head of the Kit Foxes, Last Bull, either exiled or of his own volition, moved his family from Tongue River to the Crow Reservation. Last Bull's son, Fred (who later became the temporary custodian of the Cheyenne Sacred Arrow medicine bundle), grew up speaking Crow.[23]

Unfortunately, with the exception of well-documented cases like that of Seminole, Pretty Bird Woman, and to a lesser extent Last Bull, non-Crow Indians living on the Crow Reservation did not leave a significant documentary trail either in government records, the works of ethnographers, or in the latter-day memoirs of Indians themselves. Instead, individual cases and people pop up briefly and then vanish without comment or explanation for their presence or disappearance, as in the case of a Lakota man named Little Horse, who resided at Crow for at least four years in the mid-1890s, but whose place of origin, reason for being at Crow, and eventual fate remain unknown.[24] Unless they attracted attention by their personal behavior or by formally seeking adoption into the Crow tribe, as Seminole and several others eventually did, they received little notice from overworked or culturally unaware Anglo officials, or from Indians for whom such individuals were a familiar and unexceptional part of the community.[25]

Certain patterns do crop up, however. Individuals and families could find a place to live virtually anywhere at Crow, but for larger groups and fugitives more likely to find themselves subject to the critical gaze of agents, distance tended to influence patterns of residence. By the 1900s, for example, Crees coming to Crow increasingly tended to cluster on the western edge of the reservation, particularly in the Pryor district originally settled by Plenty Coups's band in the 1880s. Pryor's relative closeness to Billings and the transportation network, including trains, that radiated out from there made it a convenient base for Crees who continued patterns of migration throughout Montana and southern Canada.[26] Additionally, Pryor's geographic isolation from Crow Agency—seventy-five "rough and roadless" miles distant, according to the Crow agent in 1913—and the strong leadership provided by Plenty Coups gave both Crows and resident Crees an unparalleled degree of autonomy and security.[27] It comes as little surprise to discover that other Indians interested in maintaining a low profile, like Pretty Bird Woman, also came to Pryor.[28]

For Crees, the availability of work further increased Pryor's attractiveness. As irrigation ditch construction in the eastern and central portions of the reservation along the Bighorn and Little Bighorn rivers wound down, work increasingly shifted to smaller projects such as those along Pryor Creek on the reservation's western end, to which Crees added employment building homes and as farm laborers.[29] Crees also provided other services as well, most notably those of a Cree "doctor" (most likely a shaman or traditional healer), who provided medical services to Plenty Coups. Although the practice of medicine men was officially proscribed by the OIA, Pryor's isolation made it difficult for the government physician stationed at Crow Agency to visit on a regular basis, and apparently this enabled the Cree healer to minister to Plenty Coups without sanction. Afterward, Crow agent George Stouch plaintively asked district farmer A. A. Campbell to "please try to impress on Plenty Coups that our white doctor can do him much more good," and promised to send the agency physician on the several-day round-trip to Pryor if Plenty Coups requested it.[30]

In the late 1890s and early 1900s, most of the Crees on the reservation (whose population was estimated at 250 by 1912) lived in a semipermanent village whose location changed from year to year, but that was usually located along Pryor Creek.[31] The size of the Cree community at Crow is perhaps the best indicator of the degree to which the Crow Reservation really was a multiethnic Indian community in the late nineteenth and early twentieth centuries. A population of 250 Crees would have represented nearly one-eighth of all Indians living on the reservation. (For purposes of comparison, the 1912 Crow tribal census recorded a population of 1,731 enrolled Crows.) In the Pryor district, which in 1907 had an estimated population of 400 Crows, Crees may have comprised up to one-third of the district's Indian residents.[32] When other non-Crow Indians living at Crow are taken into account, up to 15 percent of the Crow Reservation's Indian population may have been Indians who were not enrolled members of the Crow tribe.

Of course, had all these individuals, families, and communities remained socially and culturally aloof from their Crow neighbors (or vice versa), their presence would be far less significant. Over time, however, the residence of non-Crow Indians on the reservation contributed to the continuation of patterns of intermarriage between Crows and members of other tribes. It appears, from the available evidence, that Crow men were far more likely to marry non-Crow women than the reverse, a pattern that fits well with Crow traditions of patrilocal residence and the fact that in prereservation days women were most often adopted and married into the tribe after being captured in war or as a means of formalizing political and economic relationships between Crows and other tribes. Three of Last Bull's daughters (Strikes Twice, Walks in the Night, and Bear Woman) married Crow men, as did Jules Seminole's daughter, Maggie.[33] At least seven Cree women had married Crow men by 1912, five of whom lived with their spouses in the Pryor district.[34] Although in the early

1900s several Crow men sought formal approval in the form of a marriage license from the agent before marrying a non-Crow woman, for the most part, these unions were concluded without input or likely even the knowledge of agency officials at the time.[35]

As was the case with socially disruptive reservation residents, inevitably agents found themselves forced to delve more deeply into the social backgrounds of the tribal members they supervised. At Crow and elsewhere, the main factor driving this process was the tangled legacy of allotment. As members of the original generation of allottees began to die, usually without wills, in the early 1900s, agents faced the problem of determining an allottee's legal heirs in order to either divide the land or distribute the monies from the property if it were sold. In numerous cases, agents discovered that legal heirs included individuals who belonged to other tribes and lived on other reservations. In 1909 Crow agent Reynolds notified his counterpart at Fort Berthold that there were several estates at Crow in which Berthold Indians possessed an interest, and promised to write more "as soon as the family history work is done." Crow Agency records from this period also contain references to heirs to Crow allottees at Wind River, Fort Belknap, and numerous other reservations.[36] Heirship ties could, of course, run in the other direction as well, as happened in 1905 when a Mrs. Mouse, a Crow woman married to a Gros Ventre Indian and living on the Fort Belknap Reservation, returned to Crow after being notified of the death of her father and his bequeathal to her of a number of horses and other property (presumably including a portion of an allotment).[37]

The "family history work" Reynolds referred to was an ambitious, ongoing project begun by his office in response to the mounting complexities of inheritance issues. Reynolds's goal was to produce a full genealogical database of individual Crows to simplify and streamline the heirship process. However, simply compiling information and translating genealogical data from Crow cultural and social norms to Anglo-American legal ones proved to be a time-consuming, almost insurmountable task. In January 1907, Special Allotting Agent John Rankin reported back to the commissioner of Indian Affairs regarding the project. Rankin complained that "the work was not as far advanced as I had reason to expect," but admitted that "it is hard to get any one who can understand the scope of inquiry, and genealogical lines, as defined by the Montana law, required to successfully do this particular work." Despite his criticism, Rankin confessed that he knew of "no available way by which it could have been accelerated."[38] As it turned out, the work took considerably longer than the sixty days Edward Becker had estimated in 1899.[39] Two and a half years after Rankin's visit, Reynolds reported that he had five people working full time on the project—three elderly Crows, one interpreter, and one "educated Indian girl"—but as the work was still nowhere near complete, heirship cases continued to be handled on an ad hoc, piecemeal basis.[40] Two years later, in 1911, OIA officials in Washington questioned Crow agent W. W. Scott's continuing expenditure of funds for "two assistant historians and an interpreter" in heirship cases. Defending his practice, Scott explained the different connotations of Crow kinship terminology and asserted that "only Indians trained in this kind of work avoid the error of making affidavit that a certain person is a brother or sister instead of cousin, and uncle instead of a father, or an aunt instead of a mother. The old women employed in this office as assistant historians understand this perfectly."[41] Ironically, in delegating responsibility for determinations of heirship to two elderly Crow women, Scott deferred to superior Crow knowledge of genealogy in order to settle inheritance issues according to Anglo-American norms of descent and kinship.

Although a final copy of the family history project does not exist in Crow Agency records, if indeed it was ever completed, one record does provide at least a partial picture of the complex social makeup of the Crow community around the turn of the century—that being a family register of households with members carried on Crow tribal rolls completed in 1902. Unlike federal census returns, allotment registers, and tribal enumerations gathered by OIA officials, the 1902 family register lists not just members of families, their ages, and their relationship to each other, but also individuals' natal tribal affiliation, thus making it possible to determine how many Crows in 1902 were Crow by birth and how many were outsiders of foreign parentage or origin who were either adopted or married into the tribe at some point.[42]

Seven hundred sixty-seven different families are listed on the 1902 register. Of these 767 households, forty-three contained individuals of non-Crow ancestry or origin. They included a fifty-year-old man named Sioux who lived alone, whose ancestry was listed as Sioux, and who was noted as having been adopted into the Crow tribe; the fifty-five-year-old Bird Tail That Rattles, a Sioux man married to a Crow woman whose name was given only as "Old"; Big Man, whose "nationality" was listed as Gros Ventre but whose "tribe or allegiance by citizenship" was listed as Crow, married to the Crow woman Swamp Flag; and other families containing adopted (or unadopted) Cree, Cheyenne, Cherokee, Arapaho, Piegan, Assiniboine, Chippewa, or Yanktonais spouses, children, or individuals.[43]

Forty-three households represents less than 6 percent of the families listed on the register. But if anything, the register actually understates the degree of ethnic diversity both within the Crow tribe itself and within the Indian community on the Crow Reservation as a whole. For one thing, the register failed to note the mixed ancestry of many individuals born within the Crow tribe (such as Plenty Coups, whose mother was a Shoshoni captured and adopted by the Crows). And because it was a register only of families with enrolled tribal members, it did not include non-Crow families such as that of Jules Seminole or Last Bull (though it did include their offspring who had married Crows), or any of the families of Crees or other Indians who resided at Crow, regardless of their official enrollment status.[44]

Even as an incomplete picture of the Crow tribal and reservation community, however, the register provides strong evidence of the persistence and vitality of ties between Crows and other Indians and other reservations. But despite its origin in information either self-reported by individuals or supplied by native informants, the register cannot answer many fundamental questions regarding the multiethnic community that existed on the Crow Indian Reservation around the turn of the century. Non-Crow individuals, families, and even groups of families could live, work, and survive comfortably at Crow with little interference or objection from government officials or, seemingly, Crows themselves. But what was the nature of these people's relationship with Crows and the Crow tribe? How could it happen that a single individual like the fifty-year-old Sioux, with no apparent marital or biological ties to real Crows, could be adopted and regarded as being Crow? What differences were there between himself and individuals like Jules Seminole, who, though Indian, apparently remained outside the boundaries of the officially recognized Crow community? Were markers of inclusion and exclusion such as tribal enrollment simply bureaucratic constructions created by the OIA, or did they represent basic Crow concepts regarding the nature and limits of community? What did it mean to be a Crow Indian or an Indian who was not Crow on the Crow Reservation in the early 1900s?

In the 1880s and 1890s, Young Man Afraid of His Horses, Sitting Bull, and others had invoked the concept of an Indian identity, suggesting that the ties that linked Indian peoples to each other, including their shared cultural and social values as well as their common subjection to the United States, were every bit as important as the tribal lines that divided them. Building on traditional models of community that emphasized fluid and permeable boundaries, they explored the potential for intertribal communication and cooperation in the new world of the reservation era, as did literally thousands of ordinary Native peoples across the Northern Plains, whose travels, visits, movements, work, and intermarriages contributed to the creation and persistence of poly-ethnic reservation communities such as that at Crow. At the same time, how-ever, countervailing forces were pulling Crows and other Indians in the oppo-site direction: toward a more narrowly drawn, parochial vision of community. As the relative prosperity of the late 1800s and early 1900s declined with the sale of allotments, the end of irrigation construction and the burdens of annual irrigation fees, and the finite resources of per-capita payments from land sales as they either came to an end or were divided among a tribal popu-lation no longer in decline, pressures would mount to limit the number of indi-viduals who could lay claim to Crow tribal resources. The conflicts that ensued would divide Crows against one another as they debated the limits of com-munity and identity as Crows and as Indians. The outcome of this struggle would help shape the boundaries and conceptions of tribalism on the North-ern Plains, and its potential for serving as a basis for intertribal cooperation, for the remainder of the twentieth century.

CHAPTER SIX

The Limits of Community

Throughout the 1800s, Crows had cultivated relationships both with other Indians and with the United States. Though radically different in the way those relationships were structured and the way they functioned, the two would not collide until the end of the nineteenth century.

Crow relations with other Indians, either as communities or as individuals, were shaped by the norms of Crow society and culture. As a nonstate society lacking a centralized government, political decisions regarding relations with other groups—defining them as enemies, allies, or somewhere in between— were made at the band level, not the tribal level. Whether a River Crow band decided to follow the lead of a Mountain Crow band in its attitude toward the Blackfeet, or the Cheyenne, or the Lakota was entirely up to the leaders of that band—the band chief, the *batse'tse*, and the heads of families. The decision could not simply be imposed from above; it had to be reached by consensus. Nor could the band leader coerce or compel compliance beyond a very limited degree. Though the camp police (members of a warrior society chosen each spring to regulate hunts, supervise camp movements, and maintain order in the camp) acting under his direction could discipline individuals who set out on war parties at inappropriate times or against inappropriate targets, families and individuals still had the option of simply leaving the group and affiliating themselves with another band.[1]

Similar dynamics governed the treatment of outsiders either joining the Crows or simply seeking to establish contact with a Crow community for the purposes of diplomacy or trade. One did not "become" Crow by passing some citizenship test and gaining the imprimatur of a tribal leader. Instead, rather than being constructed from the top down, Crow society was constructed from the bottom up. Individuals became Crow not by fiat from above, but through being accepted as a member by a Crow family and thus acquiring the clan membership, kin relationships, and other affiliations that rippled outward from that family through a particular band to all Crow bands and tribal divisions. Such structures facilitated the addition of individuals to Crow society; they also created openings through which individuals who were not Crow themselves but who had relatives among the Crow, such as Young Man Afraid of His Horses, could gain access to Crow society and speak to Crows not as an outsider, but as one who possessed a tie to the larger Crow community.

As suggested in previous chapters, establishing such relationships actually became easier, rather than more difficult, during the early decades of the reservation era. Although reservations were surprisingly ineffective at restricting Indians' ability to travel, communicate, and meet with members of other tribes, they did seemingly eliminate many of the sources of tension that had previously produced hostility between different Indian communities. The well-defined and much reduced boundaries of reservations ended conflicts over territory, while the reservation system itself, as well as the policies that government officials attempted to enforce, increasingly enabled Indians of different tribes to see each other not as strangers but as people who shared common values and cultural beliefs (even in the case of individuals without kin ties to another community), and who faced similar difficulties in dealing with an increasingly intrusive non-Indian society. This newly emergent sense of Indianness was more than just a product of reservation life, however. It built on older patterns of intertribal contact, exchange, and communication in which culture, politics, religion, and society were often intertwined. It was these features of Indian, not just Crow, life that enabled people like Sitting Bull, Sword Bearer, Finds Them and Kills Them, Jules Seminole, Leonard Tyler, and others to cross community boundaries with such dexterity and apparent ease.

Crow relations with the United States, on the other hand, were guided by an entirely different set of principles and premises, and moved, over time, in an entirely different direction. Since 1825, Crows and the United States had signed treaties and agreements with each other. From the perspective of the U.S. government, these accords were legally binding on all Crows, not just the signatories and their followers. In this, the United States was following centuries of precedent dating back to colonial times in treating the Crow and other tribes as corporate entities with centralized leadership structures similar to that of the United States and other European states—nations, in other words. Though the facade of equality between tribes and the U.S. government was eroded over time both by the Supreme Court and by Congress (which in 1871 officially abolished the treaty-making process, though the government continued to negotiate legally binding agreements with tribes), the legal fiction of treating tribes as corporate entities served the interests of both the U.S. government and Indians in various ways.[2] For the government, the treaty system created at least the illusion of a single, unitary governing structure in each tribe analogous to that of the United States, and provided a pretext for punitive action whenever members of a Native community violated an agreement signed by their leaders. For Native Americans, treaties and agreements confirmed rights to territory and pledges for payments or benefits due signatories and their followers made by U.S. officials at treaty councils.[3]

Ironically, the reservation system itself brought these two understandings into conflict. Even as it fostered peaceful interaction and greater understanding between Crows and other Indians, the creation of the Crow Indian Reservation also led to disputes among Crows themselves over what it meant to be and who was to be considered Crow. To be sure, the United States played a critical role in the process of making the modern Crow nation, but the requirement that Crows speak with a single voice in the new, more confined context of the reservation did not produce internal unity. Instead, the consolidation of previously independent bands and families into a single tribal body in a single location exposed fault lines within the community.[4]

The Treaty of 1868 set the stage for future conflicts. Previous treaties the Crows had signed with the United States in 1825 and 1851 amounted to little more than expressions of amity and goodwill.[5] Though the latter treaty provided for the distribution of annuity goods to tribal members, the actual distribution remained largely ad hoc and informal. Agents sometimes stored annuities at trading posts to be handed out to individual families as they came in, or issued them to band leaders for distribution to their followers; sometimes they were distributed to entire camps.[6] No headman was in a position to exercise a veto power over who was eligible to receive annuities, beyond members of his own band. Because agents did not maintain itemized lists of who received (or did not receive) annuities, their receipt conferred no permanent tribal status or set of rights from the perspective of the Office of Indian Affairs. Similarly, though the Treaty of 1851 did demarcate formal boundaries for Crow territory, the government was in no position to actively enforce those boundaries.[7] Most importantly, the Crow homeland itself remained large enough and rich enough for most Crow bands to subsist themselves without falling into dependency on annuities or other resources provided through the U.S. government.

Beyond sharply reducing the territory acknowledged as belonging to the Crows, the Treaty of 1868 also restricted its occupancy to Crows "and such other friendly tribes or individual Indians as from time to time they may be willing, with the consent of the United States, to admit amongst them."[8] Beyond implying the existence of a unified Crow tribe possessing the structure and authority to decide who could live on the reservation, the treaty also—in the phrase "with the consent of the United States"—for the first time arrogated the right of the United States to exercise a veto power over such questions. As such, the treaty both asserted the sovereignty of the Crow tribe—though a Crow tribe that, as of 1868, did not exist in the form necessary to exercise such power—and undermined that sovereignty in the same breath. Moreover, the treaty also provided for the survey of Crow lands and established the right of "any individual belonging to said tribe of Indians, or legally incorporated with them" to select up to 320 acres of land that could be withdrawn from common tribal ownership and held as private property.[9] This provision for the individual ownership of land (what would later become known as an allotment) constituted a radical departure from the existing system of annuities. In place of the episodic and unregulated distribution of annuities, the issuance of an allotment conveyed an official and essentially permanent recognition of one's tribal status.

It would be several decades before the full implications of these provisions became clear, and it is doubtful whether the Crow leaders who signed the Treaty of 1868 recognized their significance at the time. However, recognized or not, the treaty established new parameters and standards for the determination of tribal membership. With its references to legal incorporation and federal authority, it implied that the determination of an individual's status as a Crow would shift from the domain of households to the purview of U.S. officials and federally recognized tribal leaders, a change from the historic Crow framework of kinship and society to a reliance on Euro-American legal and genealogical norms. The treaty language also suggested a change in the meaning of membership away from that of an individual's willingness to fulfill his or her duties to an extended network of relatives and community members toward an entitlement to permanent tribal rights and privileges, including the right to land ownership and a share of tribal assets and income.

Nor were U.S. officials any more prescient. Although the government relied on the fiction of tribes with centralized sources of authority to negotiate and enforce treaties, federal Indian policy in the mid- to late nineteenth century did not aim at the creation of unitary, centralized Native communities, at least not in a permanent sense. Instead, the goal of American policy was to break tribes apart, to individualize Indians and separate them from their culture and fellow tribal members. In part this would be accomplished though the criminalization of Native social and cultural practices (including the banning of indigenous religion rituals, polygamy, and the practice of redistributing property and wealth to extended family members and the larger community through giveaways); in part though increasingly coercive education policies; but mainly through the introduction of concepts of private property and capitalism exemplified by allotment.[10] In this respect, the Treaty of 1868 constituted an opening salvo in the U.S. government's efforts to demolish the Crow tribe entirely and assimilate Crows into the individualistic norms of American society.

So long as Crow retained their economic autonomy, however, many of the provisions in the Treaty of 1868 remained a dead letter. During the 1870s, conflicts with the Lakotas and Blackfeet and the treaty provisions concerning annuities held more immediate relevance than arcane articles on the selection of lands and determination of tribal membership. However, the destruction of livelihoods dependent on the buffalo and federal determination to assign lands in severalty during the 1880s lent new urgency to questions of individual and group identity for both Crows and government officials. Ration lists, census rolls, and allotment registers—artifacts of what Frederick Hoxie calls "the Crows' arrival in the land of bureaucratic record keeping"—illustrated a new resolution on the part of the Crows' federal overseers to determine who belonged to or held rights as Crow.[11]

The process of limiting, bounding, and administratively circumscribing Native communities, eventually through the imposition of minimum blood quantum standards in many cases, has led some scholars to assert that federal officials unilaterally imposed standards of ethnic or racial purity as a criteria for tribal membership.[12] However, as Alexandra Harmon has suggested in her analysis of tribal enrollment councils on the Colville Reservation, the reality was more complicated.[13] For federal officials, the problems posed by generations of intermarriage, adoption, and other forms of inter- and intratribal demographic exchange, together with expansive concepts of kinship, became apparent in the allotment process itself. Shortly after beginning his work as an allotment agent in 1885, George Milburn protested that the system used to allot Crows was "wrong—radically." Confused by the proliferation of fathers and mothers among the Crows, Milburn alleged, erroneously, that "no one knows who is the father of a Crow Indian." Even determining motherhood was difficult, he claimed, "on account of the practice of giving away children, even before they are born, who being adopted are declared by the foster-parents to be their own." Milburn suggested that the existing system of assigning different-sized allotments on the basis of European lines of descent be abandoned, and "so much land, no more and no less, say 120 acres, should be given to each person, irrespective of age, sex, or family ties."[14] Though Milburn's confusion stemmed largely from demographic exchanges occurring within the Crow community, his recommended remedy potentially had much farther-reaching ramifications. Taken at face value, his suggestion implied that anyone living among the Crows and accepted by them as a Crow was entitled to an allotment, regardless of origins among the Crow or elsewhere.

However, though agents continued to adopt an essentially laissez-faire attitude toward Indians who came to Crow to live and work, they almost immediately adopted a harder line toward individuals who came to Crow seeking adoption into the Crow tribe—and the allotment and share of tribal benefits that now came with adoption. In cases like that of Good Owl, who possessed family at Crow who could vouch for her identity, agents permitted individuals to return to Crow and claim their share of the tribal estate. In other cases, they cast a more jaundiced eye at applicants. Thus, when Aliss Parker, a women from Sun River, Montana, just outside Great Falls, wrote to Agent J. W. Watson, claiming Crow ancestry and inquiring about the possibility of adoption, Watson recommended she not come to the reservation. Adoption, Watson replied, would require both the consent of a majority of the Crow tribe gathered in council and that of the agent. "I would not consider it for the best interests of the tribe to adopt a large family," he wrote, adding that even if a tribal council approved the adoption, he would not endorse its action.[15]

Agents were particularly concerned about the potential for abuse of the allotment process by individuals they called squaw men: white men married to Indian women. After surveys for allotment began in 1885, Agent Henry Williamson exercised a veto power over white men seeking to marry Crow women, prohibiting such marriages until the groom had supplied proof of his "good character, industry, and willingness to support" his bride.[16] Williamson's seemingly heavy-handed exercise of authority had some justification. As Tom Leforge (who himself married four Crow women at different points during his residence with the tribe) remarked, "Every Indian had treaty claims for rations, for annuity money payments, for supplies of various kinds. Hence, the Indian wife of a white man could be the family breadwinner without being heavily burdened if the white husband was the sort of human being who was satisfied to live without ambition."[17]

Several years after Williamson's prohibition, Agent E. P. Briscoe evicted Barney Bravo and a man named Morrison, both white men married to Crow women, from the reservation. According to Briscoe, Bravo was a bigamist married to two Crow women who had illegally killed stock issued to one of his wives, and abandoned his first wife without obtaining a divorce. The agent also charged Bravo with bribing a Crow in an attempt to influence the assignment of allotments. After twice failing to remove Bravo from the reservation, Briscoe finally had him taken into custody and evicted by a U.S. marshal. Morrison, meanwhile, was removed on the considerably vaguer charge of "disobeying the agent's orders." In general, Briscoe opined in a letter on the affair to Commissioner of Indian Affairs John Oberly, white men married to Crow women sought to use the reservation resources they gained access to through their wives for their own selfish purposes and cavalierly defied agency regulations.[18] Briscoe's comments imply that he was as interested in preserving his own authority and control over reservation affairs as in protecting Crow interests, but his pursuit of Bravo, and the eventual postscript to the case, illustrates the ways in which the commodification of identity increasingly posed difficulties both for agents and Crows themselves.

Taken by themselves, neither Bravo's bigamy nor his separation from his first wife were censorious acts by Crow standards. Indeed, Briscoe's failed attempts to apprehend Bravo suggest that Bravo enjoyed the assistance of at least some Crows in his efforts to avoid arrest. The agent's disparaging comments aside, Bravo had lived among the Crows for more than twenty years since deserting from Fort C. F. Smith in 1867. During the 1870s, Bravo had worked as a courier and interpreter for the government, even serving with a detachment of Crow scouts for the army during the 1876 campaign against the Lakota.[19] Even after his eviction from the reservation, Bravo still possessed an heirship interest in an allotment after the death of one of his Crow wives. Whatever the current agent's attitude, Bravo might well have expected to find greater sympathy from the Crows among whom he lived. Yet in 1904, when Bravo sought to be formally adopted and enrolled as a Crow, his application was rejected by a council of chiefs and headmen, who dismissed Bravo as a white man who "has never been any particular good to the Crow tribe."[20]

The tribal council that rejected Bravo's attempt to claim status as a Crow was just one of numerous tribal councils between 1887 and 1921 that collectively considered the application of more than 200 individuals for adoption and enrollment in the Crow tribe. An outgrowth of the councils of headmen that met with U.S. delegates at treaty negotiations in 1825, 1851, and 1868, agents and Crows alike increasingly turned to tribal councils in the 1880s and 1890s to ratify decisions regarding reservation affairs, including grazing leases with local white cattlemen, right-of-way grants to railroad companies, or proposed land cessions.[21] In this process, the line between purely internal Crow affairs and those that implicated or involved the U.S. government blurred or simply vanished. Eventually, as allotment and the question of rights to reservation resources grew in importance, these councils became forums in which not just people's qualifications to be considered Crow were debated, but on the meaning and significance of "being Crow" itself. The decisions councils and federal officials reached in answering these questions sheds light on the conflicts and pressures that shaped these debates: collisions between traditional understandings and modern reservation realities; between competing interests of bands, districts, and families; and between the specific cultural, economic, and bureaucratic benefits of Crow tribal membership and the more intangible significance of belonging to a broader, more diffuse Indian community that spanned the entire Northern Plains.

When Yellow Leggings adopted a young Tom Leforge into his family in 1868, and thus into his band and into the larger Crow community, neither race nor ethnicity played a role in the process. Unlike in Bravo's case in 1904, in 1868 Leforge's biological ancestry and origins in Anglo-American society were irrelevant. Ironically, however, race most likely did play a significant role in the first formal tribal council adoption proceedings at Crow. In the winter of 1887, a council voted to adopt Addison Quivey, the government farmer in the Pryor district, and Crow Agency farmer Richard Cummings.[22] Quivey and Cumming's status as not only white but also government employees was a key factor in the Crows' request that both be enrolled as tribal members. It is, in fact, entirely possible that the decision to adopt the two men originated with the Crows themselves rather than Quivey or Cummings.

As government farmers (who were expected to direct and provide assistance to Crows in adapting to an agricultural mode of subsistence), neither Quivey nor Cummings was responsible for formulating Office of Indian Affairs policy, but both were responsible for implementing those policies and held positions that brought them into close daily contact with individual Crows and community leaders. Coming barely a month after the Sword Bearer episode sparked armed conflict between Crows and U.S. troops, the adoptions bear the mark of a strategic move by a community increasingly in need of trusted individuals to mediate (and provide a buffer) between Crows and the agents, army officers, ranchers, and other whites who were becoming an increasingly intrusive presence in Crow life.

Besides being government employees, both Quivey and Cummings possessed other qualities that made them good candidates for adoption. Though unmarried, Quivey had lived with the Crows since 1872, spoke Crow fluently, and likely possessed at least some fictive kin ties to members of the community. Cummings, a more recent arrival to Crow Agency, was married to a Sioux woman with whom he had three children. Quivey's long tenure with the tribe and linguistic proficiency, and Cummings's long, stable marriage to a Native American woman likely indicated to Crow leaders a potential willingness to not only be part of the community but also to be sensitive to and sympathetic to tribal needs. According to members of the council, Crows valued and trusted Quivey as an interpreter who would defend their interests. If white ranchers illegally grazed cattle on Crow land, Plenty Coups explained, "we can tell him and he will put them off. He can help us in many ways." Similarly, Cummings's adoption received the "unanimous consent" of the council of nearly 100 chiefs and headmen. "We all like Mr. Cummings as one of our own people," Big Shoulder Blade stated. "I would like to have Mr. Cummings stay with us as he has been doing." Plenty Coups added that Cummings and his family should have all the rights on the reservation that Crows possessed, including an allotment.[23]

The use of adoptions to forge strategic alliances with outsiders was hardly a new feature of Crow life. Such adoptions, usually brokered by band leaders, had been used routinely to open trade with other communities, or for purposes of defense against a common enemy. Unlike adoptions of individuals by Crow families, such strategic adoptions did not make a person a permanent part of the Crow community.[24] Instead, they created links between two distinct and separate communities that might last no more than a day, or might persist for years. In many respects, the Quivey and Cummings adoptions bear many of the hallmarks of these earlier strategic adoptions. The adoption of both was brokered and undertaken by Crow leaders rather than individual families—indeed, neither man apparently possessed any formal ties to a specific Crow family. And though both Quivey and Cummings would now legally be considered Crows, their adoption would presumably not alter their status as employees and representatives of the U.S. government, but put them in a unique position to serve as intermediaries in the relationship between their community and their employer.[25]

The request that Quivey and Cummings be issued allotments and given full rights as Crows complicates this picture, however. Allotment and tribal rights took the Quivey and Cummings adoptions beyond the realm of purely strategic or limited adoptions. Besides acknowledging and reciprocating for Quivey and Cummings's past services, adoption—and the tangible economic benefits that went with it—represented for Big Shoulder Blade and Plenty Coups not only a means to forge alliances but to give both men a vested interest in the Crow tribe by tying their future and that of the Crows together.

The Quivey and Cummings adoptions demonstrate that Crows (or at least the Crows who participated in the council) had not yet internalized Anglo-American notions of race.[26] To members of the council, the evident willingness of both men to act in the best interests of the Crow community and fulfill their obligations to members of that community far outweighed their biological or social origins, as evidenced by the reference to Cummings as being "one of our own people." This did not mean that Quivey and Cummings's whiteness was altogether irrelevant, however. Council participants appear to have recognized that Quivey and Cummings's racial status, at least in the eyes of other whites, would give their statements and opinions more authority and influence than those of ordinary Crows, thus playing off Anglo-American racial constructions in the cause of protecting the interests of the Crow community.

The complex interplay of identity, strategic maneuvering, emerging Crow ideas about race, and older conceptions of community would become apparent in later councils, including the one that rejected Barney Bravo's application. In 1904 and 1905, Crow councils considered twenty-seven applicants, recommending fourteen for adoption and rejecting thirteen.[27] As in the Quivey and Cummings adoptions, race continued to be elusive, at times rising into view and at other times disappearing, but still governed by uniquely Crow notions of identity and community. In addition to Bravo, the 1904 councils considered two other non-Indian applicants, Charles "Smokey" Wilson and Arthur White, both African Americans. The councils rejected White's application but endorsed that of Wilson. Wilson, like Quivey, possessed no formal kin ties to Crows (at least in an Anglo-American sense) but had lived with the Crows for more than thirty years, had served as an interpreter at Crow Agency, and spoke "more Crow than English." White, in contrast, had been with the tribe for about ten years and had a Crow wife, but the council noted that he did not "get along with" her (and, presumably, her family). Apparently to council members the close ties generated by Wilson's years of residence and linguistic affinity overrode his lack of Crow heritage or marital ties, while White, like Bravo, had evidently failed to fulfill his familial and community responsibilities.[28]

However, even Wilson's adoption met with some opposition. As agency interpreter, Wilson's closest ties would naturally have been with those Crow communities located closest to Crow Agency. But Wilson had also served as an agency policeman, a job that may have brought him into conflict with various Crows, sparking animosity and raising questions about his cultural and political allegiances. Support for Wilson's adoption also diminished with distance; the Crows in the Pryor district, on the west end of the reservation and farthest from the agency, initially objected to the adoption of Bravo, White, and Wilson, calling them all "white boys." As the district farmer at Pryor put it, "They would object to them as they haven't any Indian blood in them."[29] However, by the time the councils took place, the Pryor representatives agreed to endorse Wilson's adoption, apparently swayed by the arguments of Crows from other districts.

The argument that a lack of Indian blood invalidated the applications of White, Wilson, and Bravo represented a departure from the Quivey and Cummings proceedings some seventeen years earlier and exposed the multiple lines of the evolution of concepts of race in Crow thought. In 1887, race as a qualifier for tribal membership had not been an important barrier to the incorporation of Quivey and Cummings. In contrast, by 1904 the idea of race—or, to put it in a different sense, Indianness—had crystallized sufficiently among some Crows to pose a fundamental obstacle to the adoption of "white boys"—even white boys who were actually black. For most Crows, however, race appears to have been less of a factor, even in 1904, than the manner in which applicants' social behavior toward other Crows revealed their true identities and affiliations.

The other twenty-four applicants considered for adoption in 1904 and 1905 all possessed (or claimed to possess) the Indian blood that Bravo, Wilson, and White lacked. However, only thirteen out of this group received the councils' endorsement. The rejection of nearly half the applicants suggests that a generalized notion of Indian identity alone was not enough to earn the councils' recommendation. What qualities separated the thirteen successful applicants from those whose requests were denied?

Significantly, only five of the twenty-four had any Crow relatives in a European, biological sense. However, all but one of the approved adult applicants were linked to the Crow community by marriage. Bear Woman, Strikes Twice, and Walks in the Night were all Northern Cheyenne women who had married Crow men. They and their children by former Cheyenne husbands were all recommended for adoption. The Canadian Cree Stands on a Cloud had lived with a Crow man named Rock for eight years and had had several children with him, while the Cree man Kills With the Horses had lived with the Crow woman Fish Bird for ten years. Amelia Frost, variously identified as either a Cree or a Minnesota Chippewa, was recommended for adoption on the basis of her marriage to John Frost, a Crow with whom she had had four children.[30] Mark Wolfe and Mary Wolfe-Farwell, Eastern Cherokee siblings who worked for the OIA, were also recommended by virtue of their marriages to Crows.[31] Thomas Medicine Horse, a Lakota allottee from Rosebud who had met the Crow woman Julia High Hawk at boarding school and later married her, also received the councils' endorsement. Out of all the successful applicants, only Shot Twice, a Pine Ridge Lakota who had resided on the Crow reservation for three years, lacked marital ties to the Crows. Shot Twice had left a wife and two children at Pine Ridge but testified that he did not know whether he had been allotted there. At the time of the councils, he was living at Crow with a Lakota woman who had come to Montana from Pine Ridge the previous summer.[32]

Among the unsuccessful applicants, nine—including the Lakotas Wolf Trail and Baby in the Mouth and the Shoshonis Bow Legs and Dog With His Eyes Closed—already had allotments on other reservations. The applicants endorsed by the councils either had not received an allotment on their original reservation (or, in the case of Shot Twice, claimed not to know if they had) or had agreed to relinquish their allotments and their tribal rights with their former community. The council also noted that neither Wolf Trail, Baby in the Mouth, Bow Legs, or Dog With His Eyes Closed had relatives living on the Crow Reservation.[33] The tenth applicant, a woman from Mendocino County, California, named Nancy Hall, claimed in an affidavit to be the daughter of a fur trader named Johnson Gardiner and the Crow woman Red Berry, and a sister of a Crow named Spotted Horse. Hall claimed to have been orphaned about 1848 at age seven when her parents died in a smallpox epidemic, and to have been subsequently taken to St. Louis by a sister named White Berry and her husband, a white man named Caleb Greenwood. Upon White Berry's death, Hall claimed to have been adopted by foster parents, with whom she moved to California. Despite the genealogy Hall supplied (including her claim to kinship with the prominent Crow headman Spotted Horse, who had died in 1902), the council denied her application, stating bluntly, "None of our old Indians have any recollection of Mrs. Nancy Hall or any of the relatives mentioned by her."[34]

The final applicant was the Northern Cheyenne mixed blood Jules Seminole, who had taken refuge on the Crow Reservation after fatally shooting a fellow Northern Cheyenne at Tongue River in the 1890s. Seminole sought enrollment for himself, his Northern Cheyenne wife, and their eight children, but was rejected. One of the councils deliberating Seminole's application cited his history as a "disturbing element" and commented, "If this family is fit to remain on a reservation they should be on the one with their relatives. They have no Crow blood in them." Although the council rejected Seminole's application for enrollment as a Crow, it is worth noting that until this time, Seminole's right to live at Crow as a non-Crow Indian apparently had never been challenged, at least by the Crows themselves.[35]

From the evidence available, it is clear that the Crow councils of 1904–1905 adhered to a set of standards in evaluating the qualifications of individuals for tribal membership. However, the decisions also reveal Crows struggling to reconcile older community values with new complications introduced via treaties and emerging concepts of race and ethnicity. Questions of land ownership, for example, appear to have been central to council decisions, with people possessing allotments on other reservations being seen as having permanent interests and connections to a community other than that of the Crows. The problem of allotment rights posed other problems as well. In a matrilineal society such as that of the Crows, it would be natural to adopt a woman who had married into the community to give her and her children clan and kin status. Conversely, it would not be necessary for a man who had married into the tribe to be adopted, because the father's outsider standing would not affect his children. However, in the new era of the reservation foreign fathers, such as the Lakota Thomas Medicine Horse and the Cree Kills With the Horses, had to be officially incorporated into the community in order to be eligible for the allotments that, as heads of households, they would need to support their families.

Kin ties also played a central role in council decisions. Viewed in isolation, the verdicts on Shot Twice and Nancy Hall's applications—one without any biological or marital Crow ties yet recommended for adoption, the other with a specific genealogical account yet rejected—seem anomalous. However, here too, distinctly Crow notions of community and identity seem to have governed council decisions, just as they did with Bravo and White, men whose conflict-ridden marriages to Crow women made them unfit for enrollment, and Wilson, whose lack of Crow kin and Indian blood was offset by his cultural qualifications and demonstrated history of community affiliation. From a Euro-American perspective (and that of the Office of Indian Affairs, as it turned out), Shot Twice may have lacked any real ties to the Crow Reservation, certainly compared to his ties to Pine Ridge, where he had a family and, despite his testimony, an allotment. However, the councils' endorsement of Shot Twice's adoption was not based on genealogy or marriage, but on the fictive (in an anthropological sense) ties that Shot Twice had established with a middle-aged Crow named Young Hairy Wolf. Young Hairy Wolf had a deceased son whom Shot Twice resembled, and the Crow had decided to adopt the younger Lakota as a replacement for his dead offspring.[36] In ratifying his adoption, whatever his prior personal history, the councils were following generations of Crow history in deferring to the adoption of an outsider by a Crow family.

The endorsement of Shot Twice's adoption by the nearly 600 Crows who participated in the 1904 councils represented a striking reaffirmation of traditional Crow conceptions of community. Though Shot Twice was otherwise lacking in the qualities other applicants were measured against, Young Hairy Wolf's sponsorship, and his willingness to accept the Lakota as his son, out-weighed all other deficiencies.[37] In the case of Nancy Hall, despite her claims to kinship, the failure of any Crow families to recognize and embrace her as a relative doomed her application. Hall's temporal and geographic distance also weighed against her, as did her failure to appear personally at Crow and her reliance on an affidavit—a culturally foreign, Euro-American means of estab-lishing her identity.

Both the Shot Twice and Nancy Hall cases produced consensus, at least among Crows, regarding questions of identity and community. However, with another set of applicants—five brothers named Charles, George W., Robert B., Eugene, and Frank Means—those ideas collided with the new meanings attached to tribal membership.

The Means brothers' case was unique in that a previous Crow council in 1901 had already approved their adoption. Like Nancy Hall, the Meanses' con-nection to the Crows was temporally distant. Unlike Hall, their Crow ancestry was unquestioned. According to Pretty Eagle, a prominent leader in the Bighorn district, Hairy Old Woman, the Meanses' mother, had traveled to Fort Laramie with soldiers in 1872 and later married a white man and settled at Pine Ridge. Although the sons remained at Pine Ridge, where they were enrolled and allotted, their mother returned to the Crow Reservation in 1888 and died there, apparently unallotted, in 1892.[38]

Charles Means first appears in Crow Reservation records in the summer of 1900, when he worked as a laborer on the Crow Irrigation Survey.[39] In March 1901, Eugene wrote to Crow agent John Edwards, requesting a transfer from Pine Ridge to Crow.[40] During the 1901 Fourth of July celebration at Lodge Grass, Edwards held a council with leaders from the Bighorn, Lodge Grass, Reno, and Black Lodge districts to consider the Meanses' adoption. Medicine Crow, Old Dog, and Spotted Horse, all band leaders from Lodge Grass, endorsed the petition, as did Pretty Eagle. Big Medicine, a Black Lodge River Crow and chief of the agency police, and Plain Owl and Shot in the Arm also approved the adoption.[41]

The Meanses' strongest support appears to have come from Mountain Crows in the Reno, Lodge Grass, and Bighorn districts. Spotted Horse and Plain Owl testified that they were half-brothers of Hairy Old Woman, while Shot in the Arm said he was her brother.[42] According to the council proceed-ings, "All of the older men that spoke . . . are willing that the sons of 'Hairy Old Woman' should come to the Crow Reservation and be permitted to have all the rights of the Crow Indians," while the younger men apparently deferred to their elders' knowledge and wishes.[43]

Less willing to defer were OIA officials, including Edwards's successor, the authoritarian Samuel Reynolds, and the Crows from the Pryor district on the west end of the reservation. In January 1904, representatives from Pryor, absent from the initial Means council, demanded that the brothers explain what they were doing at Crow and what they wanted before their adoption was approved. Later that spring, several of the Means brothers traveled to Pryor. Their explanation apparently satisfied Plenty Coups and the other Pryor leaders, for Plenty Coups informed the government farmer in his district that the Pryor Crows would also vote in favor of the adoption.[44]

Given the apparent earlier approval of all the Crow districts, it remains a mystery why the councils held in the fall of 1904 rescinded their prior approval of the Means brothers' enrollment. Apparently after gaining consent to their enrollment, the Means brothers requested that their wives and children also be enrolled as Crows. The only explanation given in the council records is that as the adoption "would admit to the Crow tribe nine more persons already enjoying the benefits of the Pine Ridge Sioux, and as the five brothers are themselves enrolled their [*sic*], we not only refuse to consent to the adoption of the wives and children but withdraw the consent given" for the brothers themselves.[45] One possible answer for the reversal is that the Means brothers' efforts to have their families (and particularly their spouses) enrolled sparked opposition. Given the maternal nature of Crow kinship structures, extending enrollment to the Means brothers' Lakota wives might have opened up a Pandora's box by giving the women's Lakota relatives a loophole through which they could claim Crow rights.

Reynolds's opposition to the Meanses' enrollment probably also played a role in turning Crow sentiment against the adoptions. At times, as in his support of the family history project, Reynolds relied on Crow community knowledge and values. However, Reynolds also engaged in energetic (if less than completely successful) campaigns to run foreign Indians off the Crow Reservation and bring a sense of order and propriety to what he viewed as the messy administration and social environment of the reservation. In Reynolds's eyes, the Means brothers, as allotted and enrolled Pine Ridge Indians, didn't belong at Crow, regardless of their ancestry. Reynolds also claimed that at least one of the Means brothers had a checkered personal history akin to that of Barney Bravo. After the council rejected his application, Reynolds would order George Means expelled from the reservation after he failed to leave voluntarily.[46]

Nor was the Meanses' case the only occasion where Reynolds exerted his authority over Crow membership matters. In 1907, eighteen family heads from Pryor signed a petition requesting the enrollment of Emma Upshaw, a white woman married to the Crow Alex Upshaw. In response, Reynolds passed the petition along to the OIA with his negative endorsement without even calling a tribal council. According to Reynolds, the Upshaws had been married for five years but had separated once or twice during that time. "I cannot see any reason why a proposal to adopt her should be considered," he wrote.[47]

Reynolds's offhand rejection of Emma Upshaw's proposed adoption further illustrates the collision between Crow and Euro-American concepts of identity and community. From a Crow perspective, the children of a non-Crow mother and a Crow father lacked a social identity; indeed, they might not have been regarded as Crow at all, given their lack of clan membership, which could only come from the mother. Emma Upshaw's adoption, then, was a necessity, not only to give her children clan membership (which could have been accomplished via her informal adoption into a Crow family), but also to cut off any questions as to their rights as Crow tribal members. To Reynolds, coming from an Anglo-American perspective, a child's social identity derived from the father, rendering Emma Upshaw's adoption superfluous. There is also a hint here that Reynolds may have been less willing to countenance the legal transformation of a white woman into a Crow Indian than in cases where an Indian woman from another tribe married a Crow man and sought enrollment, given his approval of the 1904 council decisions.

Reynolds also acted to block consideration of the adoption of Crazy Bear, the head of a Lakota *tiyospaye* at Pine Ridge. Crazy Bear made his first visit to Crow in 1893 and returned several times thereafter.[48] In August 1900, Crazy Bear's son, Brave Heart, died during a visit to Crow and was buried on the Crow Reservation.[49] In subsequent years, Crazy Bear made regular trips to visit his son's grave and in 1903, claiming that Crows had agreed to give him a house and land, requested permission for himself and eight other Pine Ridge households to be transferred to Crow. In a letter to the commissioner of Indian Affairs, Crazy Bear stated that he had "brothers" at Crow and wanted to be buried there near his son. "I am 71 years of age," he wrote, "I want to move over there to die there."[50] Surprisingly, the agent at Pine Ridge endorsed Crazy Bear's request, writing, "The transfer of these parties to Crow Agency from this reservation would be satisfactory to this office and the Indians of this reservation."[51] Reynolds, however, refused to bring Crazy Bear's request before a Crow council. Writing to the Pine Ridge agent, Reynolds doubted that "the relationship claimed by Crazy Bear is as close as he claims, and also do not credit the statement made by him that he has been given a house and land."[52]

Despite Reynolds's objections, Crazy Bear did not give up. Instead, in subsequent requests, he raised the number of families seeking a transfer with him to twelve. He also stated that he had already given up his land at Pine Ridge, and he asked Reynolds to check with a number of Crows (including chief of police Big Medicine, Medicine Crow, and Two Leggings) to verify "the truth of what I say about having long ago obtained the consent of your people."[53] Reynolds replied by citing the previous Crow rejection of Lakota applicants, by stating (falsely) that there was no available surplus land available for allotment, and finally by claiming that the Crows themselves had refused to consider his adoption.[54] Reynolds's claims to the contrary, there is no evidence that Crazy Bear's request for a transfer was ever placed before a Crow council. Yet even with the support of Medicine Crow, Two Leggings, and others, it is unclear whether Crazy Bear's attempts to bring an extended network of relatives and followers with him to Crow would have gathered the broad community consensus necessary to win approval from a tribal council.

Despite Reynolds's interference in the Crazy Bear case, councils continued to be the main venue for adoptions into the tribe. In August 1906, a Crow council approved the enrollment of twenty individuals. Most of those adopted were either spouses of Crows or children of marriages between white men and Crow women whose original allotments were now located outside reservation boundaries as a result of subsequent land cessions. The remaining adoptions—eight in all—were of agency employees, their spouses, and their children.[55]

The adoption of government employees, either because of a genuine affiliation with and sympathy for the community or as a calculated strategic maneuver, was not unprecedented. However, unlike the previous adoptions of Wilson, Cummings, and Quivey, all the 1906 adoptions of agency workers and their relatives involved people of Indian (though not Crow) heritage. Among those adopted were Harry Throssel, a Cree–Metis agency clerk, his part-Shawnee wife, Myrtle, and their two children; Harry's brother, Richard, also an agency clerk, and his daughter; and Myrtle's sister, Emma, the wife of agency clerk Fred Miller, and the Miller's part-Shawnee daughter Hilda. The Throssel brothers were relatively recent arrivals to the reservation, having come to Crow in 1902, while Fred Miller had lived and worked at Crow Agency since 1898. Significantly, even though his wife and daughter were adopted, Fred Miller, the only person in the three families not of Native ancestry, was not even considered for enrollment. Despite his longer tenure at Crow, presumably yielding at least some friendships or acquaintances, and the value of cultivating a useful government ally, Miller's lack of Indian blood apparently posed an insuperable barrier to his adoption.[56]

In the past, the willingness of Crows to adopt outsiders, whether of Indian or non-Indian ancestry, had reflected a confidence in the community's ability to incorporate and remake individuals as Crows. The metaphor of tangled driftwood to describe Crow clans and the large Crow community provides a useful illustration. The interwoven network of branches not only lent resiliency and strength to the whole, but also provided any number of openings within which a new branch could find a secure place.[57] By the early years of the twentieth century, however, that confidence was being eroded. The 1906 Miller and Throssel adoptions marked the last time the Crows would adopt individuals lacking either Crow ancestry, marital ties, or lengthy affiliation and residence in the community.[58] Ironically, as the structure of the Crow tribe shifted away from a network of socially and culturally linked but politically autonomous bands toward a single, unified political entity, it became more difficult to fit outsiders into Crow society. The increasing difficulty of achieving consensus would become even more visible in cases where the old technique of using adoption to augment the numbers and power of a particular community was perceived as posing a potential threat to the status, power, and resources available to other communities within the Crow tribe. Nowhere would this new reality become more evident than in the increasingly contentious debate over the place of Cree Indians on the Crow Reservation.

By the early 1900s, Crees in varying numbers had been a presence on the Crow Reservation for nearly a decade.[59] Although not all Crees remained permanently on the reservation, many returned to Crow on an annual basis to live and work. In 1908, Agent Reynolds reported that Crees "came on the reservation by the hundreds."[60] Crees served as a reserve labor pool for the reservation economy, useful at different times and in different ways to Crows and government officials alike. Occasionally, when work was scarce, when Crees were perceived as a burden on the Crows, when Crees were blamed for poaching or smuggling liquor, or simply when the mood struck, agents attempted to evict them from the reservation.[61] Such efforts were generally unsuccessful, however. When troops from Fort Custer rounded up several hundred Crees and shipped them from Billings to Canada in the late 1890s, it was recorded that "the Indians got back to this part of the country as soon as the troops did."[62] Despite Reynolds's characterization of them as transient visitors, for many Crees, the Crow Reservation was becoming more and more a permanent home.

By the latter half of the first decade of the 1900s, however, the position of

Crees on the Crow Reservation was becoming tenuous, as the Crow economy began to deteriorate. After 1905, the pace of construction on the Crow Irrigation Survey slowed, removing a formerly dependable source of income for both Crows and Crees. Instead of providing income, the massive irrigation network became a burden for many Crows, who were now saddled with high annual maintenance charges whether they used the system or not. Cash-strapped Crow agriculturalists often found themselves forced to sell or lease their allotments to better-capitalized white farmers. At the same time, white settlement and the lure of agriculture increased pressure on the tribe to sell off its remaining "surplus" unallotted lands. In the 1890s, the Crows had been one of the most prosperous tribes in Montana; by 1910, the tribe was sliding steadily into economic dependency.[63] It is against these twin poles of a decaying economy and increasing white demands for land that efforts to adopt Crees into the Crow tribe must be viewed.

As already noted, the closest ties between Crees and Crows developed in the Pryor district on the west end of the reservation. Although Cree women married to Crow men were typically adopted via tribal councils—and their adoptions approved by the OIA—in 1909 Plenty Coups proposed the adoption of not only Cree women married to Crows, but also their extended families. Most Crows in other districts apparently opposed the move, as did Agent Reynolds. "If these Indians, however, started into adopting the relatives there would be no end to Cree adoptions into this tribe," he informed the commissioner of Indian Affairs.[64] Writing to subordinates in the Bighorn district, Reynolds proclaimed not only his opposition to the proposed adoptions but also his plans to round up all the Crees either not married to Crows or actively employed and "run them off the reservation." "These are the Indians that Plenty Coups and the Pryor people have wanted to adopt," he added. "I understand that they told them to go over on Muddy Creek and take up land and that they could have it."[65]

Years later, an elderly Cree named Jim Gopher remembered an episode that may match Plenty Coups's proposal: "My father worked for the Crow Chief at Pryor in the Crow Reservation (Chief Plenty Coups). One day we were told that we were going to get enrolled in [the] reservation, eight families, so my father continued working for the Chief for a long time—in fact, where he is buried now, we lived there at the time."[66]

According to Gopher, the Cree families began building homes and putting in gardens in anticipation of their adoption. However, Gopher's father also received letters from Browning on the Blackfeet Reservation, allegedly promising land and provisions there. Gopher's family eventually traveled to Browning, only to find when they returned to Crow that the other Crees were gone. "I regret now, that my father left that place," Gopher said; "we could have been still there today."[67]

The defeat of Plenty Coups's 1909 proposal and Reynolds's subsequent roundup of Crees did not settle the issue, however. Within three years there were again at least 119 Crees living at Crow, most of them in the Pryor district. In 1912, Plenty Coups broached the subject of Cree adoptions again, this time with Reynolds's successor, Superintendent (as agents were now called) W. W. Scott. As it turned out, Scott was no more enthusiastic about enrolling the Crees than Reynolds had been. Writing to his superiors, Scott sought to downplay the depth of ties between Crees and Crows. Of the 119 Crees documented in a recent census, Scott wrote, only six women (actually seven) were married to Crows. However, of the 119 Crees listed on the census, fifty-eight were children under the age of eighteen, and at least sixteen were over fifty. Of the twenty-five women between the ages of eighteen and fifty, nearly one-third were married to Crows, while fifteen were married to Crees and three were single. Nor did Scott's census include several Crees married to Crows who had already been adopted and enrolled at Crow. Finally, of the fifty-eight children listed on the census, nine were offspring of Crow–Cree marriages.[68]

Both the Crees and the Pryor Crows had a vested interest in pursuing adoption. For the Crees, unrecognized by either the U.S. or Canadian governments, enrollment would signal the end of a generation of wandering and insecurity with the opportunity to rebuild their lives in a permanent home. Of equal significance, it would allow the relatives of those Crees already married to Crows (and in some cases, already adopted) the opportunity to remain with their kin. While Crow marriage patterns tended to be fairly flexible (with a slight preference for patrilocal residence near the groom's family), Crees were firmly matrilocal, with newly married couples living with or near the bride's parents. Cree culture also typically included a year's worth of service by the groom to the in-laws after marriage.[69] In lieu of the adoption of in-laws, Crow–Cree couples might have to leave the reservation, where the groom presumably already had an allotment. Instead of a Crow man leaving the reservation to follow his essentially homeless in-laws, it would have made more sense from a Cree and a Crow perspective to adopt the in-laws as well, providing them with a home and the husband with a chance to meet his marital obligations.

If enrollment represented the attainment of a permanent home for Crees, for Pryor Crows it meant something else. For Plenty Coups and other Crows in the Pryor district, incorporating Crees represented a recourse to a traditional strategy for strengthening their community in the face of potential threats. The relationship between Pryor Crows, agents, and even other Crows had frequently been marked by tension. Agents resented the ability and willingness of Crows in the Pryor district to assert their independence and repeatedly sought to bring the district under a greater degree of government control. In December 1912, Scott disgustedly wrote that the Pryor Crows had "grown impatient of all restraint" and proposed putting a new subagent "with a somewhat heavy hand" at Pryor to get the Crows there "started on the upgrade."[70] The influence and relative autonomy of Plenty Coups and his community also grated on some Crows from other districts. "It seems that Plenty Coups and his aggregation seem to take a road off from the tribe, and do not keep in touch with the tribe," commented Sees With His Ears, a Crow from Black Lodge.

Along with placing a more discipline-minded subagent in Pryor, Scott suggested another remedy to both bring the Pryor community under closer control and feed the land hunger of white settlers. "It has frequently occurred to me that it would be in the interest of all concerned to sell quite a large body of land in that territory," he wrote the commissioner of Indian Affairs, "and with the proceeds purchase and equip farms for those Indians [that is, the Pryor Crows] on the Big Horn valley among their people." Given the small size of the Pryor community and the availability of land elsewhere on the reservation, Scott suggested that relocation would not be difficult: "There are about 55 families in the Pryor District, comprising 46 able-bodied men, and, all told, 219 persons. There is in the Big Horn valley 'dead land' enough to supply these fifty-five families several times over."[71]

Despite being "fine land . . . under a very complete and costly irrigation system," Bighorn valley land had been slow to sell to non-Crow settlers because it lacked schools, churches, and railroad connections. However, the lack of such amenities would not bother the Crows, according to Scott. With a straight face, Scott claimed that both the Crows living in Pryor and in other districts would support his scheme, predicting, "The fact that practically all of them would profit from the sale of the land, in both localities, would prove a powerful factor."[72]

Scott may have been half right in his analysis. The 1891 land cession had already pushed the reservation boundary to within a few miles of Pryor. For many Crows in other districts, the sale of the Pryor district would not have affected them personally and would have represented an infusion of cash into increasingly empty pockets. It is unlikely that many Pryor residents would have shared such an attitude, however. The sale would have entailed the loss of a generation's worth of work in building the community and the loss of sacred and historic sites in the Pryor Mountains and along Pryor Creek.[73]

An obvious strategy to head off such threats to the Pryor community was to augment the strength and size of the community, a tactic much like that used by Crow bands during the nineteenth century. Such a strategy likely accounts for both the 1909 proposal by Plenty Coups and the invitation extended in 1913 for Little Bear and his band of sixty-six Crees to settle on the Crow Reservation. The exact source of the invitation is unclear because news of the offer came not from Plenty Coups but from members of Little Bear's band, then encamped around Missoula, where they were being supplied with aid and informed the provisioning officer of the proposal.[74] The circumstances and later events, however, strongly suggest that the invitation again originated from Pryor. If the intent was to sidestep Scott, the ploy succeeded. The Indian Office ordered Scott to verify the information and find out whether the offer applied only to Little Bear's Crees or if it extended to all of the estimated 500 nonreservation Indians in the state. Additionally, at the earliest possible moment, Scott was to "present to the Indians, in tribal council or to their Business Committee . . . the question of the allotment of the non-reservation Indians in Montana, on the Crow Reservation."[75]

Scott responded on Thursday, March 28, by calling a meeting of the tribal business committee for Saturday, March 31. The business committee, first created in 1910, was an elective body consisting of three representatives from each of the six districts on the reservation. Whether the creation of the business committee was a Crow initiative or suggested (or imposed) by the OIA officials is unclear, though there were clearly advantages to superintendents in empowering a smaller group that could respond more quickly to summons to meet (and potentially be influenced more easily) than large, unwieldy gatherings of all the headmen and heads of households on the reservation. Even with this, notice for the March 31 meeting was so short that only five of the eighteen committee members were present. None of the representatives from Pryor were able to make the trip to Crow Agency in time for the meeting. Despite this, the rump committee passed a resolution denying that any "official or authorized invitation has ever been extended to Little Bear and his band, or to any other non-reservation Indians, to remove to and make a home on the Crow Reservation." The council further resolved "that we are unanimously and earnestly opposed to such an arrangement, and we are confident that in this sentiment we represent the almost unanimous wish of the tribe." The resolution was signed by Looks [Sees] With His Ears, Two Leggings, and Frank Shane, with George Hogan and Charles Yarlott refusing to sign.[76]

In his report to the commissioner of Indian Affairs, written the same day as the business committee meeting, Scott acknowledged that, as a result of the haste of calling the meeting, the committee "members living in the outlying districts failed to appear." However, Scott said he had issued two reports to each district: one approving the proposed resolution and one rejecting it. Five representatives from Lodge Grass signed the report supporting the resolution, as did three committee members from the new Wyola district on the south end of the reservation. Scott blithely noted that the vote included "returns from all except the Pryor district."[77]

It bears repeating that the ties between Crees and Crows, particularly in the Pryor district, were not illusory. But if the needs of Crees seeking a home and Pryor Crows seeking to protect and preserve their homes merged, so too did the interests of Crows in other districts and those of Superintendent Scott. Before the reservation era, the addition of new members to a band not only strengthened that band, but also the entire Crow community by increasing the number of relatives individual Crows could call on for support. It also augmented the tribe's ability to assert control of and defend its homeland and hunting grounds, a vital concern for all Crow bands. However, from a treaty rights (and reservation) perspective, an increase in tribal population merely reduced each individual's potential share of tribal resources, a matter of growing concern on a reservation of fixed size and saddled with a declining economy. As Crows became more dependent on income from grazing and other land leases and annuity payments, tribal members in locations other than Pryor had a vested interest in keeping tribal enrollment down.[78] With a tribal population of 1,740 in 1910, the addition of sixty-six individuals would have represented an almost 4 percent increase in enrollment, to say nothing of Plenty Coups's earlier proposal that might have added upwards of several hundred people. Merging all 500 nonreservation Indians in Montana into the Crow tribe would have resulted in a nearly 30 percent increase in population—and a concomitant decrease in the annual payments many Crows increasingly relied on to survive.[79] In these circumstances, the interests of a majority of Crows outside Pryor converged with the narrowly drawn, Euro-American definition of kinship, identity, and tribe held by Scott.

Thus, by the early 1900s, the need to protect and conserve resources had a constraining effect on the manner in which Crows thought about community—its boundaries, who was excluded and who was included, and the degree to which those boundaries remained flexible and permeable—at least in the sense of one's legal, official identity. This constriction was not an outgrowth of old, nineteenth-century ideas about tribalism, nor was it an inevitable consequence of the creation of reservations. Had the Crow Reservation remained a place of (relative) prosperity and stable economic horizons, incorporating

Crees might not have proved to be such a divisive issue. However, the forces that led to the rejection of proposals for wholesale adoptions of Crees would have ripple effects on Crow relations with other Native peoples. As with Crees, these effects would have the greatest impact on those people with whom the Crows had cultivated the closest relations.

Throughout the late nineteenth and early twentieth centuries, Northern Cheyennes and Crows had been more than neighbors. Northern Cheyennes came to Crow to work and to trade, and people from each reservation traveled to the other to celebrate holidays both sacred and secular. Social connections inevitably led to personal connections; between 1895 and 1920, at least five Northern Cheyenne women married Crow men and were formally adopted into the Crow tribe, along with their children from former marriages to Northern Cheyennes.[80]

The relationship between the two communities was not completely symmetrical, however. In the late 1900s, grinding poverty at Tongue River meant that the Crow Reservation was more important for Northern Cheyennes than vice versa. Beginning in 1903, Northern Cheyenne agents began to reduce the amount of rations issued, based on the amount of work available for Northern Cheyenne men. However, unlike at Crow, conditions at Tongue River even in 1903 were not conducive to the elimination of rations as a major source of subsistence. In 1904, ethnologist George Bird Grinnell wrote that due to high prices at traders' stores, one dollar in wages at Tongue River had only half the purchasing power it did off the reservation. Even worse, he noted, Northern Cheyenne workers typically had to wait three to six months for payment, even for government work. "Since I have been on this reservation," he wrote, "I have seen children and old people more emaciated from hunger than I have ever before seen living human bodies. Unless prompt action is taken, this winter here will see many deaths from starvation."[81]

As at Crow, government-run labor projects provided a critical source of income, however insufficient it might be. After an executive order issued by President William McKinley in 1900 expanded reservation boundaries and confirmed Northern Cheyenne ownership by withdrawing reservation land from sale and settlement, agents had employed Northern Cheyenne labor in building more permanent reservation infrastructure, including buildings and facilities, roads and bridges, and a 6.8-mile irrigation ditch in the Tongue River valley near the community of Birney. Despite these projects, the number of Cheyennes dependent on rations never dropped below 50 percent before 1920.[82]

Ironically, the pace of government work projects at Tongue River acceler-ated just as projects at Crow began to tail off, leading, in some cases, to a rever-sal of previous labor-movement patterns. Where Northern Cheyennes had formerly gone to Crow to work, now some Crows were traveling east to Tongue River. Under the circumstances, Northern Cheyennes were reluctant to see any outsiders infringing on labor opportunities. In 1907, Big Head Man wrote to the Crow agent protesting the presence of Crow workers at Tongue River. Big Head Man claimed Crows might kill Cheyenne cattle and "get into trouble," but the heart of his complaint involved competition for work, most likely on the Birney ditch. "Please don't let the Crow Indians go over to Tongue River to work," he wrote. "Don't let them come."[83] Crows living near the boundary of the two reservations proved equally tenacious of their rights, accusing Cheyennes of trespassing on the Crow side of the Wolf Mountains, gathering Crow berries, and killing Crow cattle.[84]

Tensions also emerged (or were manufactured) whenever government offi-cials proposed consolidating the Crows and Northern Cheyenne on a single reservation. In 1885, 1890, and 1898, federal officials seriously contemplated relocating the Northern Cheyenne at Crow, both as a way of resolving the tan-gled legal status of the Tongue River Reservation and as a solution to the Northern Cheyennes' lack of (and the Crows' perceived surplus of) suitable agricultural land.[85] Understandably alarmed by renewed relocation proposals after their long struggle to stay in Montana, Northern Cheyennes generally couched their objections by reiterating their close ties to the Tongue River region and the promises previously made by Miles and others. "We don't want to live among the Crows," Round Stone stated. "Don't bother yourself about the Crow country," Medicine Bear added, expressing his people's desire to "live and die in a country in which [they] were born and grew up in."[86]

Crows were less restrained in their opposition. Playing on durable white per-ceptions of Cheyennes and Crows as implacable enemies, they portrayed their Cheyenne friends and neighbors to an 1890 commission as "bad and crazy peo-ple" who would likely "do something to get the Crows in trouble" if located on the same reservation.[87] The head of the 1898 commission, former Stand-ing Rock agent James McLaughlin, accepted these claims at face value, noting in his report that "although they are neighbors, there is not the most cordial feel-ing between them." According to McLaughlin, the Crows regarded the North-ern Cheyenne as "uncivilized and aggressive," while the Cheyennes "hold the Crows in contempt [as] inferior to themselves." It should be noted that during all this time, Crows and Cheyennes continued to exchange friendly visits, but the contrived animosity had its intended effect. Concluding that "it would be useless to attempt to get the consent of the Crow Indians to dispose of any part of their reservation up on which the Northern Cheyenne could be located," McLaughlin recommended instead that the Cheyennes' own reservation be enlarged and their title confirmed—as it was in 1900.[88]

The defeat of government efforts to relocate the Northern Cheyennes to the Crow Reservation, and of efforts by some Crows to adopt large numbers of Crees into the tribe, did not end either threats to Crow land or debates about the meaning and significance of tribal identity. Beginning in 1907, members of Montana's congressional delegation introduced a spate of bills that proposed opening unallotted land on the reservation to homesteading. For more than a decade Crow leaders, aided by Washington attorneys, the Indian Rights Association, and the workings of partisan politics, managed to stave off passage of a bill. Finally, in 1919 the Crows agreed to a proposal that provided for the distribution of all unallotted land in equal shares to tribal members. The bill, which became known as the Crow Act of 1920, passed the Senate in October 1919, the House in April 1920, and was signed into law that June.[89]

As a result, the Crow Act became the stage for the final debate over Crow tribal membership. The act called for completion of a final roll, consisting of all living tribal members as of January 4, 1921. After 160-acre allotments were given to all heads of families not yet allotted, the remaining lands (and tribal funds) would be divided equally among individual members on the roll.[90] Preparation of the final roll spurred Crow councils to consider the adoption of twenty individuals in the two years before the deadline. In January 1919, a tribal council of approximately fifty Crows approved the adoption of seven people: three part-Crow children, the wives of three Crow men, and the divorced Sioux wife of former agency farmer Richard Cummings. Only one candidate was not approved; Ralph Emmet Throssel's adoption was defeated by a vote of 40 to 1.[91] In the spring of 1920 another council recommended the adoption of eight more people. The eight included Maggie Seminole, wife of Eugene Long Ears and the daughter of Northern Cheyenne Jules Seminole; Joseph Dillon, a half-blood Cree who had been adopted as a child and raised by Knows the Ground and his wife; and six elderly white men (including Barney Bravo) who had at one time been married into the tribe.[92] Finally, in January 1921 a council advanced four more names, including Emma Rides a Sorrel Horse and Juanita Ketosh (both of whom had been previously recommended for adoption but rejected by the OIA); Ketosh's brother, Lewis Walters (previously considered and rejected by a Crow council); and Nellie

Wyman, a forty-six-year-old white field matron married to the twenty-year-old Crow David Bad Boy.[93]

The 1919–1921 adoptions generated controversy. Although 108 Crows participated in the 1921 council, Emma Rides a Sorrel Horse and Nellie Wyman received only 52 and 51 votes, respectively. However, only four Crows voted against Rides a Sorrel Horse and five against Wyman, with the remainder abstaining. Both women's adoptions were rejected by the OIA. Emma Rides a Sorrel Horse already possessed tribal rights at the recently established Rocky Boy's Reservation, and both the OIA and Superintendent Calvin Asbury looked askance at the age difference between Nellie Wyman and her Crow husband. Suspicion also attached to the adoption of the six elderly white men, with the OIA remanding the question of enrollment to Asbury for further investigation. Asbury himself regarded the adoptions as a scheme by the men's part-Crow children, all of whom were already enrolled, to get more land.[94]

Crows were also divided. After the January 1921 council voted on Ketosh, Wyman, Walter, and Rides a Sorrel Horse, council member James Carpenter noted cryptically that "other names were presented." Faced with a potentially endless list of possible adoptees, the council passed a resolution opposing more adoptions by a vote of 70 to 5.[95] Other Crows believed the council should not have considered any adoptions. Ninety-five Crows, headed by the redoubtable Plenty Coups, signed a petition to the commissioner of Indian Affairs protesting the adoptions. Admitting that the council had a "fairly good representation" of Crows, the dissenters argued "by no means were all the adult Indians who were entitled under law to cast a vote on the question of adoptions present." The protesters cited the Treaty of 1868's provision that their reservation was set aside for the "absolute and undisturbed occupation" of the Crows "and for such other friendly tribes or individual Indians as from time to time they may be willing" to admit. "It is now desired by us," the petitioners continued, "that this letter serve as a minority report and also a protest against the adoption of any further outsiders including those submitted by the last council."[96] Plenty Coups's opposition was particularly noteworthy. Just eight years after attempting to incorporate landless Crees into the Crow tribe, the Pryor leader now stood against any more adoptions under any circumstances. In the absence of a threat to Crow landholdings—and, indeed, given that all remaining reservation land was to be divided up among already enrolled Crows—it made no sense to add more people to the enrollment lists and further reduce the size of the shares of land to be assigned to existing tribal members.

The crux of the petitioners' complaint was the acquisition of Crow land

and rights by individuals whose ties to the Crow community were regarded as suspect. They noted that "by the provisions of the Crow Bill just recently past [*sic*], all Crow children born six months after June 4th last, cannot share in the division of tribal lands." The petitioners argued against what they saw as the illogic of taking in outsiders but shutting out the future children of established Crow families: "Until the children of the members of the Crow tribe shall have been provided for, then if we find that we have any surplus of land, money, and other gifts to bestow upon foreigners who continually seek entrance into the Crow Tribe only for the benefits that might accrue to them, we might then look with more favor upon this method of taking that that should go to our children and ourselves and give to others."[97]

The adoptions associated with the Crow Act and the disputes they engendered illustrate the sweeping changes that had occurred in both the meaning and determination of tribal membership and identity. By Crow tradition, Plenty Coups and the other petitioners had little ground to object to the adoptions. Historically, if an individual was accepted as part of a household by a Crow family, others in the community had no room to question that person's status. In fact, the councils had hewed fairly close to Crow tradition in endorsing the adoption of Bravo and the other elderly white men, regardless of their race. Similarly, despite Asbury's suspicions of the May–September marriage of David Bad Boy and Nellie Wyman, an overwhelming majority of Crows meeting in council had either voted for or at least refused to block her adoption. Yet there was also considerable irony in the council decisions themselves. Given Bravo's past failures to live up to his family and community obligations, there is considerable room to argue (as Asbury did) that the men's adoptions were motivated by factors other than kinship. The fact that none of the men (except Bravo) had even been brought up for adoption before 1920 suggests that the upcoming land distribution was the primary motivation behind their applications.

Indeed, questions of land and tribal rights rather than kinship and place in the community dominated many, if not all, of the council decisions regarding adoption in the 1910s. During the nineteenth century, the bottom-up construction of community had defused questions of identity and had actually contributed to the overall strength of the community. In keeping kin networks broad and open, Crows had ensured that no individual would be without relatives one could turn to in times of need. Rather than conferring abstract rights, inclusion rewarded one with relatives and required one to meet his or her obligations to them. However, the transformation of communally held land and resources into private property threatened to turn this formulation upside down. Instead of adding strength and support to the community, the addition of outsiders depleted available resources, while the shift in authority in questions of membership from families to the tribe itself led to dissension. Although individual families and groups, such as the Pryor Crows, still had vested and often valid reasons for advancing adoption proposals, the shift led many Crows to cast a jaundiced eye on adoptions that would not immediately benefit, and might actually harm, their own interests.

It remained possible, of course, for outsiders to become part of the Crow community socially or culturally, whether through intermarriage, residence, or simple affiliation. The social adoption of individuals by Crow families, giving them clan and kin affiliations within the community, continues to the present. However, after the closing off of tribal adoptions after the Crow Act, it would no longer be possible for individuals of non-Crow birth to receive political rights as a member of the tribe. Finally, the redefinition of tribal membership and Crow identity that occurred between 1887 and 1920 encouraged Crows to look inward rather than outward. Many of the social and cultural connection with other Native peoples that had flourished during the previous thirty-three years would continue, but they would now take place in an environment dominated by discourses on treaty rights, tribal identity, and the Crows exclusive relationship with the United States.

The divisiveness of debates over community boundaries and membership during the early twentieth century was matched by controversy over peyotism on the Crow Reservation. Though one scholar has dubbed peyotism "the pan-Indianism of the reservation," consensus over the place of the religion—and its sacrament—at Crow would prove difficult to achieve.[98]

Although Leonard Tyler and Ed Black had planted the first seeds of peyotism in the Bighorn ditch camps in the late 1890s, the new faith either did not immediately take root or else required a long germination. Most Crows credit Frank Bethune, a mixed-blood Crow from Reno district, with becoming the first Crow roadman to conduct ceremonies at Crow around 1910.[99] Bethune's home near the Wolf Mountains on the eastern edge of the reservation placed him in close contact with Northern Cheyennes, and Bethune regularly traveled the twenty miles to the Northern Cheyenne community of Busby to attend meetings.[100] However, peyotism at Crow did not attract official notice until 1918, when Superintendent Calvin Asbury noted that "the use of peyote is just being started on this reservation."[101]

Despite its slow start, peyotism soon acquired more converts through the efforts of Bethune and others. A meeting at Tom Stewart's home in Lodge Grass in 1919 attracted thirty-five people, including fifteen Cheyennes.[102] Although the district farmer in the Bighorn district claimed its use was unknown there, the field matron at St. Xavier (between Bighorn and Black Lodge) said peyote had been in use for at least two years by 1919, and a Baptist missionary complained that Bethune, Albert Anderson, and Curley were actively proselytizing in Reno and Black Lodge.[103] Robert Yellowtail, later to become the first Crow superintendent for the Crow Reservation and a delegate to the 1950 Native American Church national convention, remembered Bethune's efforts: "There was a horse race south of Hardin in 1914. We were all up on a hill watching a horse race and Bethune was down below someplace beating a drum in a tipi and singing peyote songs. Everybody thought he was nuts in those days. There was a lot of opposition at first, but Bethune and Anderson said when you understand this thing you'll all belong to it."[104]

As Yellowtail suggested, peyote attracted opposition not only from government officials and Christian missionaries, but also from Crows themselves. Peyotism tended to be embraced most readily by younger, Anglo-educated Crows, many of them mixed bloods, and opposed by more culturally conservative older leaders such as Plenty Coups.[105] "The old medicine men and those that believed in it [the old medicine] didn't like it," Frank Takes Gun said. "This gave the missionaries ground to argue that even the Indians were against peyote. The medicine men were against it."[106] In January 1921, thirty-one St. Xavier residents signed a petition urging that peyote "be kept out of our reservation." The following month, 113 Pryor Crows, led by Plenty Coups, filed a similar petition, citing "the evil effects of the peyote eating as it is indulged in by other tribes."[107]

Although missionaries and federal officials such as Asbury certainly played a role in stimulating antipeyote sentiment, much of the Crow opposition was undoubtedly genuine.[108] Once again, however, there was no small degree of irony in the source of much of the opposition, particularly that of Plenty Coups, the former patron and patient of a Cree shaman. It is difficult to determine how much of the opposition was generated by fears of the effects of peyote, either physical or moral, versus the reluctance to embrace a religious ritual foreign to Crow tradition. Crows themselves wrestled with these questions. At a 1922 meeting in St. Xavier, a vote was held "on whether the peyote should be abolished or not." Seventeen people voted in favor of banning peyote, two opposed the motion, and four abstained.[109] When Asbury wrote and circulated an antipeyote regulation for tribal judges, police, and tribal council members to sign, James Carpenter of Lodge Grass refused to do so, asserting that he needed the approval of district residents to do so. According to the district farmer, Carpenter admitted taking part in peyote ceremonies in the past but claimed he had not done so recently. The farmer added that Carpenter "dwelt largely on the religious element of the peyote séances" and defended Crows' right to free expression of religion.[110]

As the 1919 meeting at Tom Stewart's home suggests, intertribal contact continued to be critical to the existence and growth of peyotism at Crow. Crows often obtained peyote on the Northern Cheyenne Reservation, either from Northern Cheyennes themselves or from a white-owned drugstore in Ashland that sold peyote over the counter. Other Crows apparently traveled to Oklahoma to obtain it.[111] Asbury informed his counterpart on the Northern Cheyenne Reservation, O. M. Bogguss, that "it seems a good many of the peote [*sic*] eaters have been down here holding their meetings around Ionia and Reno and that a rather vigorous missionary campaign is being made by them."[112] Bogguss replied helplessly, "We have so many peyote eaters here that the presence of a few guests from your reservation would not make any shortage in the supply at our banquet, and hence if we run them off it will simply be because we hope to get them to take it back to Crow."[113] In addition to Crow and Northern Cheyenne roadmen, Lakota, Kiowa, Southern Cheyenne, and Winnebago peyotists traveled to the Crow Reservation in the 1920s, and Crow peyotists visited the Comanches, Kiowas, and Osages in Oklahoma, as well as Shoshonis (probably at Wind River in Wyoming).[114]

In February 1923 Asbury succeeded at getting a bill outlawing peyote through the Montana legislature. That fall, Big Sheep, a Lodge Grass Crow, was arrested near Hardin on the property of Austin Stray Calf and charged with possession of peyote. Despite a defense effort mounted by Crow peyotists, Big Sheep was found guilty and fined $100. The conviction was upheld at the district court level but overturned by the Montana state supreme court as a result of questions regarding Big Sheep's citizenship and the jurisdiction of the state on fee patent land.[115] Though the Supreme Court decision gave peyotists some protection on reservation land (and by extension the supply route from Oklahoma and Texas, because packages could cross by rail directly from Wyoming onto the Crow Reservation), it did not overturn the state law itself. Nor did the court accept the argument that peyote was protected as a religious sacrament. Crow and Northern Cheyenne peyotists would still be vulnerable if they left their reservations to travel to other Montana reservations where peyote had not yet been established.

The Big Sheep case thus gave Crow and Northern Cheyenne peyotists additional incentive to create a formal organization to aid their quest for legitimacy.

Several years earlier, Crow and Northern Cheyenne peyotists had obtained a copy of the charter of the Native American Church incorporated by Oklahoma peyotists in 1918. According to the Northern Cheyenne William Hollowbreast, "We studied the charter and couldn't see how we would be protected here in Montana. Some Crows were fighting it out here. The Big Sheep thing for instance. We had an organization at Busby—called it the Native American Church of Montana. We copied from the Oklahoma charter and incorporated at Montana."[116]

On March 26, 1926, while the Big Sheep case was awaiting a hearing by the Montana supreme court, three Northern Cheyenne and nine Crow peyotists (including Thomas Stewart, Childs, Big Sheep, Holman Caesley, Erick Bird Above, Austin Stray Calf, Arnold Costa, Harry Whiteman, and Frank Bethune for the Crows and Thaddeus Redwater, Dallas Wolf Black, and Frank Waters for the Northern Cheyenne) signed articles of incorporation for what they called the Native American Church of Hardin, Montana. Stewart was named president and Ceasley secretary.[117] Despite its incorporation, years of struggle still lay ahead before peyotism received legal protection in Montana.[118]

Anthropologist Omer Stewart has suggested that the incorporation of the Native American Church in Montana represented a "bringing together [of] two tribes that had been historic enemies."[119] Although accurate in a purely literal sense, Stewart's broad characterization, like that of James McLaughlin in 1898, ignored decades of peaceful contact, exchange, and cooperation between Crows and Northern Cheyenne, even before the introduction of peyote. Tensions between Crows and Northern Cheyennes tended to emerge only in specific contexts, usually ones not related to intertribal hostilities during the pre-reservation era, but instead when one group (or actions taken by the government on behalf of one group) was seen as threatening the interests of the other. In circumstances where shared interests were involved, however, cooperation was the norm, not the exception. This legacy helps explain some of the seeming anomalies of early peyotist activism in Montana. The number of Northern Cheyenne peyotists dwarfed the number of their Crow coreligionists, so much so that the superintendent at the Northern Cheyenne Reservation was apparently resigned to the existence of peyotism, yet Crows outnumbered Northern Cheyennes three to one among signers of the Montana Native American Church charter and claimed both leadership positions.[120]

One explanation is that Crow peyotists faced much greater repression, both from the state in the Big Sheep case and from their staunchly antipeyote reservation superintendent. This repression, however, was as threatening to Northern Cheyennes as it was to Crows. Lacking the Crows' direct rail connections to Wyoming, Northern Cheyennes were much more dependent on the rail line running to Crow Agency, especially after antipeyote legislation made access to off-reservation suppliers such as the Ashland druggist problematic. Northern Cheyenne superintendent Bogguss, in fact, claimed that Crows were the main supplier of peyote to the Northern Cheyennes, rather than vice versa.[121] After the prohibition law passed, even Crows were reluctant to bring peyote in by rail. The Crow peyotists Martin He Does It recalled that peyote would be mailed from Texas to Parkman, Wyoming: "We used to ride through the hills on horseback and sneaked over there to pick it up. At that time the pressure was really on."[122]

If the debates over identity, group membership, and adoption revealed the limitations of concepts of community among Crows and other Indians on the Northern Plains, peyotism seemed to demonstrate its infinite possibilities. While still retaining individual tribal identities, peyotists were able to collaborate, mobilize, and act across community boundaries. Their accomplishment raises the question: why weren't Crows and other Northern Plains peoples able to do the same at the tribal level in other areas?

In fact, peyotism hardly represented an unqualified success as a source of Indian identity. The regional growth of peyotism came at a price at the local level, as disputes over the legitimacy of the religion insinuated themselves into tribal politics. Robert Yellowtail, not yet a convert, declared that in the 1920s peyotists "declared war on him" and conspired to defeat his candidacy for tribal chairman because of his opposition to peyote. Yellowtail, a Republican, also claimed that peyote influenced county and state politics as its supporters lined up behind the Democrats.[123]

As divisive as peyote could be at the tribal level, internally, the movement was essentially apolitical and heterodox. Without an ecclesiastical head, believers were free to develop new versions of the ritual, provided they could attract converts and followers. Not only was individual variation permissible, but tribal variations also emerged without harming religious harmony.[124] Even with local differences, a Crow peyotist could participate in a Cheyenne or Cree meeting or vice versa. Initially, the institutionalization of peyotism was designed purely to protect the movement and its adherents from external threats and to secure legal recognition, not to police the internal workings of the movement or enforce some notion of orthodoxy in practice, ritual, or membership. In arguing for religious freedom, peyotists based their claims not on treaty rights specific to any one tribe, but on universal constitutional guarantees and peyotism's equivalence to Anglo-American forms of Christianity.

In contrast, politics on the tribal level was becoming increasingly regularized and unable to accommodate the varying interests of different tribes. Although displays of generosity by individuals toward members of other communities remained common at social events such as powwows, fairs, and other gatherings that brought visitors to Crow from other reservations, tribal politicians were reluctant to sacrifice resources belonging to the entire tribe to assist members of another community. In making the transition from a decentralized community where membership was based on mutual obligation to one another to a tribal nation based on individual rights, Crows steadily turned away from political involvement with other native peoples. This process was not unique to Crow. In his analysis of the remaking of Blackfeet politics, Paul Rosier has noted that "full-bloods in particular did not want the Blackfeet Nation linked to other tribes for fear that its already limited pool of money would be stretched even thinner with the support of tribes less well off."[125] At Crow, full bloods and mixed bloods, progressives and traditionalists agreed that politically, being Crow took precedence over being Indian.

Peyotism, of course, also emphasized rights—at least the right to use peyote—but also placed an emphasis on the fulfillment of obligations to the wider community of peyotists that no longer existed under the narrow legal definition of Crow tribal membership. The charter of the Native American Church of Montana described itself not only as a religious body but also a "benevolent association." The charter added that the purpose of the corporation was to "teach the Christian religion with morality, sobriety, industry, kindly charity and right living and to cultivate a spirit of self-respect and brotherly union among the members of the Native race of Indians."[126] The status of peyotists, either as believers or officiants at meetings, did not depend on confirmation by some higher body; rather, it depended on older conventions of participation and fulfillment of obligations. Although a roadman could not be expelled from the church or have his authority to lead meetings taken away, a roadman who abused his position or failed to live up to his moral and ethical responsibilities risked losing his followers.[127]

At Crow, the decline in political intertribalism was not matched by a decline in social or cultural intertribalism. Joe Ten Bear Jr. recalled the entire period from 1910 to 1930 as a time when there was "lots of foreign Indians on the reservation."[128] The 1924 Fourth of July celebration in Pryor saw visitors from Pawhuska, Oklahoma, Northern Cheyennes from Lame Deer, and Lakotas from Pine Ridge.[129] Crees also remained a presence on the reservation. Although many Crees left Crow after the creation of Rocky Boy's Reservation near Havre in 1915, others remained or returned to Crow occasionally to work.[130] The Cree William Denny introduced peyote at Rocky Boy's in 1934 after spending two years on the Crow Reservation, working part of the time on Civilian Conservation Corps timber projects.[131]

A few Crow leaders attempted to continue older traditions of intertribal political contact and activity. Most notable among these was the young politico Robert Yellowtail. In 1920, during a period of active oil exploration at Crow, Yellowtail traveled to Oklahoma to discuss oil leases with Osages and reported on his trip to the Crow business committee.[132] Even Yellowtail, however, drew distinctions between intertribal communication and cooperation in areas of political policy and the internal structure of the Crow community. Both before and after his appointment as the first Crow to serve as superintendent of the Crow Reservation, Yellowtail would unsuccessfully petition for the revocation of the Miller and Throssel adoptions (and the allotments of Crow land those individuals had received) on the basis of the applicants' lack of Crow ancestry and alleged irregularities in the adoption process.[133]

For the most part, however, the narrowing of Crow community boundaries was mirrored in intertribal political affairs. On October 6, 1926, the Crow tribal council heard a petition presented by Robert Hamilton calling for a Senate investigation of the Bureau of Indian Affairs. Hamilton, a mixed-blood Piegan political activist and Carlisle graduate, had been involved in a running battle with the bureau over its management and supervision of the Blackfeet Reservation.[134] Hamilton's petition requested "a thorough and impartial investigation be made of said Indian Bureau, relating particularly to the administration of the property and rights of the Indians and the conduct of the Bureau and its officers, inspectors, agents, and employees."[135] In support of his petition, Hamilton cited a statement by Commissioner of Indian Affairs E. B. Meritt that the government held $35,000,000 in bank accounts in trust for Indians, but Hamilton said, "The Indians do not get the interest and not a solitary Indian has a bank account that shows the ownership of this money." Hamilton also recited his unsuccessful efforts to get an accounting of the funds held by the superintendent of the Blackfeet Reservation and the lack of accountability in the government's handling of heirship matters:

> When an Indian dies, an Examiner of Inheritance comes to this or that reservation to determine the heirs to that Indian's property. When the heirs are determined, they do not know the kind of a report the

Examiner makes. The Examiner makes a confidential report, deciding the case before it leaves the reservation and then such funds are held by the officials, placed on deposit in some bank to the credit of the Superintendent and is drawing interest, but the heirs do not get that interest.[136]

"If the Crows can walk into this office here, get this information that they want, then you have no complaints to make," Hamilton told the council. "If you should think it affects your Tribesmen or other Tribes of Montana, then you should give the matter some consideration. You could give the matter your moral support for the benefit of other tribes of Indians who are asking, seeking such legislation."[137]

The council heard Hamilton out but refused to support his petition. "We have a good standing with the Department and the President and with Congress and we do not want to affiliate ourselves with any movements like the one just offered us," Charles Yarlott commented. "We are going to do our own business as a tribe and it is best for the tribe to look after its own affairs," George No Horse added. Even Frank Bethune and Ralph Saco, both prominent peyotists, refused to endorse this sort of intertribal political activism. "In the early days when we were boys we used to have lots of trouble on the Crow Reservation and there were many grievances we thought we had, but at the present time we have been educated in such a way that we can look after our own affairs," Saco said. "I do not agree with a man from another Tribe coming here and bothering us." If the petition had come earlier, Bethune noted, "we would have considered it, but we now have our own attorneys."[138]

Of all the council members, only Walks With a Wolf spoke in favor of Hamilton's proposal. "Whenever the Indians have any inheritance money or whenever they have any money, they never can find out anything from this office. It looks like we never get anywhere with our own business here." Walks With a Wolf added, "Many times I go over the hills here thinking of what has been done to us, often wishing that some higher power in authority, like Washington, would come here and investigate and give us redress for all that was done against us. I am certainly in accord with the petition."[139]

Instead, the council unanimously endorsed a resolution introduced by Yarlott. It began by stating baldly that as "the Crow Tribe of Indians have for many years transacted their own business without outside interference or the help of any so-called Indian organizations, we feel that it is in our best interest to continue the policy of the past." The resolution expressed sympathy for any problems affecting other tribes but reserved "our right of independent action so far as matters affecting the Crow Indians. Therefore, we cannot endorse said petition or become affiliated with outside interests."[140]

Fifty-eight years had passed since the Crows successfully backed Lakota demands that the United States abandon the Bozeman Trail; forty years since Sitting Bull had invited Crows to look upon "the work of our people" at the Little Bighorn and Young Man Afraid of His Horses had described the need for tribes to meet and discuss "what is best for our common welfare"; and thirty-six years since Young Man Afraid of His Horses had sat down with his Crow hosts to discuss the dangers of land cessions. In the intervening time, shifts in the determination and meaning of Crow identity and the hardening and reification of tribal boundaries had led Crows to draw a sharp distinction between their interests and that of other tribes. Ultimately, efforts to build a sustainable, pantribal Indian political identity on the Northern Plains during the early 1900s failed not because of the legacies of nineteenth-century tribalism, but in spite of them.

History, Memory, and Community

> Paul Smith, a Comanche guy with a weird history, said, "In this century the story of any Indian is a typical Indian story, no matter how different." Which means to me that in this allotted century of life in dispersed parcels, we are still the people, with a common thread.
>
> [Allotment] invented Indians. Before, we were strictly Cherokee or Sioux or Apaches. When they legislated that we were all "Indians" and homeless, they lumped us all together, and this century has seen us trying to pull all those fingers into a fist.
>
> —*Jimmie Durham (Wolf Clan Cherokee), "Those Dead Guys for a Hundred Years"*

In *I Tell You Now*, a collection of autobiographical essays by Native American writers, Cherokee author Jimmie Durham noted the ambiguities of being an Indian in the twentieth century. "It doesn't matter to me that there are contradictions that are irresolvable, because they are irresolvable," he wrote. "To be an Indian writer today means being on no path, contradicting yourself at every turn."[1]

Durham's comments on the contradictions of being "the people, with a common thread" and the perception of Indians as a foreign invention, a Euro-American imposition, serve as an appropriate coda for this study. Before the arrival of Europeans and Africans in America, Native peoples did not possess a shared, common identity. However, though indigenous peoples eventually became Indians as part of a historical process that began in 1492, they were hardly passive bystanders in this development. Just as Europeans (and later Americans) constructed an imagined Indian identity that matched their needs and desires, so too did Native peoples on the Northern Plains engage in their own project of reimagining what it meant not just to be members of tribal communities, but Indians.[2] At different times and in different places, this process would replicate itself across the entire North American continent.[3]

On the Northern Plains, Native peoples entered the reservation era beset by common problems and seeking common goals, including the preservation of tribal resources, land, culture, and identity. They also entered this era with a legacy of contact and communication that they could use to confront these problems and pursue solutions. Decades of exchanges—social, cultural, material, and demographic—had encouraged Native peoples to look to one another for ideas and support in times of need. During the late nineteenth century, a host of individuals, including prominent leaders like Young Man Afraid of His Horses and Plenty Coups, rebels like Sword Bearer, and ordinary (and not so ordinary) people like Finds Them and Kills Them and Leonard Tyler, turned to those legacies in their efforts to chart a path through the new contours of Native American life.

It may be possible to make too much of all this, to suggest that rather than symbolizing the crystallization of an otherwise inchoate sense of Indian identity, the experiences of these individuals might just have been business as usual in terms of protocols and procedures for dealing with people outside one's own community. Certainly, in many ways the activities of people like Young Man Afraid of His Horses in reaching out to or asserting ties to members of another community were not new, either on the Northern Plains or elsewhere. Historians have documented numerous instances in which Native Americans from different communities succeeded in coming together politically and militarily to resist European and, later, American expansion, from the alliance of Wampanoags, Narragansetts, and other New England Indians during King Philip's War to the pan-Indian resistance movements against the English and Americans in the Great Lakes region during the late 1700s and early 1800s to the Lakota–Northern Cheyenne–Northern Arapaho coalition that spearheaded resistance to the United States on the northern Great Plains in the 1860s and 1870s. Under the right circumstances, even Native American communities that were normally rivals could come together to pursue common goals, as in the case of Crow cooperation with the Lakota during the Bozeman Trail conflict. Likewise, it is also true that Native Americans of differing communities came together regularly before the reservation era to trade, conduct diplomacy, or engage in exchanges of people through intermarriage or adoption.

However, in a larger sense, that is precisely the point of this book. Its argument is that the structures of tribalism on the Northern Plains during the early to mid-nineteenth century—its fluidity, openness to outsiders, and use of kinship and families as basic building blocks for constructing community from the bottom up—were actually ideally suited to building a larger sense of community after the prereservation contests over territory, resources, and trade that had once divided Indians of different communities from one another had ended. Tribalism enabled people at both individual and community levels to craft entirely new senses of self and peoplehood, and to conceive of their relationships with other Indians, both inside their tribal community and across tribal communities, in new ways.[4] At the same time, reservations provided a setting within which the cultural meanings of being Crow, and the new meanings of being Indian, could be "revalued as they [were] practically enacted," in the words of Marshall Sahlins.[5] During the 1880s, 1890s, and even into the early 1900s, this new identity, one shared with other Indians and other tribes but which also coexisted with rather than replaced existing tribal identities, actually strengthened the ability of and provided new avenues for peoples like the Crow, Lakota, and Northern Cheyenne to resist U.S. colonial policies.[6]

Over time, the determination of Northern Plains peoples to continue to move and communicate with each other outlasted the determination of their overseers to keep their charges fixed in place. As crucial as the social dimensions of visiting proved to be in enabling Native Americans to retain elements of their culture, the economic and political dimensions of visiting, often inextricably intertwined with the social, were equally important. Whether in the form of temporary visits or permanent relocations, travels for work or trade, or exchanges of people, culture, and ritual, the contacts and connections made between peoples from different reservations and different communities suggest both the limitations of traditional tribal histories and the opportunities that exist for broader regional studies that link rather than separate the pre-reservation and reservation eras. In places, this work is already being done. Wendy Wickwire and Paul Tennant, in studying pantribal political activism in British Columbia during the early 1900s, have found evidence that Native leaders from different communities across the province sought to organize collectively to assert land claims and protest provincial Indian policies. Tennant labels this new form of leadership and engagement "neo-traditional." "Able to choose between tradition and assimilation," he writes, "they chose tradition, but they sought to widen it, to adapt it."[7] The widening of tradition Tennant speaks of seems an apt description for the activities of people like Plenty Coups, Sitting Bull, and Young Man Afraid of His Horses.[8]

Reservations played a key role in this process. Though reservations have generally been portrayed as institutions that limited and confined Native Americans, ironically, they could also liberate Indians to pursue these new conceptions of identity and community in much the same way that Indian students in boarding schools turned those institutions from sites of cultural genocide to become sources of strength and unity.[9] Reservations in effect leveled the playing field between formerly powerful communities like the Lakota and smaller tribes like the Crow. In the 1870s, Crows had allied themselves with the United States against the Lakota; by the 1880s, Crows and Lakotas could once again see one another as equals—as they had, briefly, during the Bozeman Trail conflict—in confronting similar threats emanating from a single source. As they did so, Crows, Lakotas and other Native peoples utilized shared cultural values promoting communalism and generosity, as well as the fulfillment of kin and social obligations toward others to reaffirm old ties and create new ones. These distinctly Indian values were counterpoised to perceived Anglo-American cultural values.

Yet if the creation of reservations aided this process, another aspect of reservations, their role as harbingers of modernity, would gradually erode and ultimately doom efforts to forge a sense of pantribal Indian identity, at least in a political sense. During the early reservation period, Native communities on the Northern Plains found themselves pushed in opposite directions. On the one hand, reservations promoted a sense of commonality and unity among Native peoples from differing tribes. On the other hand, the bureaucratic creation of atomized individuals, the introduction of new concepts of land ownership, the threats to finite and geographically bounded tribal resources, and the delineation of specific individual and group rights via the treaty process encouraged movement toward a more rigid, legalistic construction of community.[10] What George Castile has described as "the commodification of Indian identity" pushed tribes and the people who belonged to them to protect themselves from outsiders who sought inclusion "only for the benefits that might accrue to them."[11]

This redefinition of community and identity—originating from outside agencies and forces but internalized and participated in by Crows and other Native peoples—divided tribes from each other. As the Crow tribal enrollment councils demonstrated, Crows played an active role in shaping, and indeed sometimes dictated, the rules governing this redefinition of tribalism, as the terrain on which matters of community membership were determined gradually shifted from cultural and social markers of identity to strictly biological and legal standards.[12] Though federal officials in theory possessed (and sometimes did exercise) a veto power over Crow adoptions, more often than not this power was not necessary, particularly as Crow standards moved closer to (and sometimes even beyond) Euro-American notions of race and ethnicity.[13] Ultimately, the new world of the reservation, with its emphasis on individual property and rights, and its rigid bureaucratic markers of membership and belonging, could not accommodate the multiple, fluid, and open identities that traditional nineteenth-century tribalism permitted and even encouraged.

One reflection of this shift was the Crow business committee's rejection of Blackfeet politician Robert Hamilton's petition calling for an investigation of the Bureau of Indian Affairs' handling of Indian monies in 1926. Eight years later, Crow leaders would reaffirm their commitment to political isolationism by rejecting the Indian Reorganization Act (IRA) put forth by the Bureau of Indian Affairs under Commissioner John Collier. The Indian Reorganization Act represented Collier's attempt to restore a greater degree of self-government to Native American communities. Introduced into Congress as the Wheeler–Howard Bill (after sponsors Senator Burton K. Wheeler of Montana and Representative Edgar Howard of Nebraska), the initial bill contained provisions for the establishment of tribal governments with powers of a municipal corporation (including supervision and power of removal over BIA personnel); for the establishment of a national court of Indian affairs; for expanded education and training programs for Indians; and for ending allotment and allocating money to purchase land and consolidate fragmented landholdings on reservations. Though considerably watered down in Congress, the bill nonetheless represented a significant shift in federal Indian policy, perhaps most notably in its provision that tribes would decide for themselves whether or not to accept the act in referendums after its passage in Congress.

In part, the Crow rejection of the IRA was due to, as Frederick Hoxie has put it, "pure political rivalry" within the Crow tribe itself, most notably the controversial appointment of Crow politician Robert Yellowtail as superintendent of the Crow Reservation—the first Indian ever appointed by the BIA to supervise his own reservation agency.[14] However, the issue of the Crows' separate status apart from other tribes, and the fear that they would be lumped in with other, poorer tribes if they accepted the IRA, also played a role in the Crows' rejection of the act. At a May 2, 1934, meeting of the Crow business council, Harry Whiteman expressed the belief that the reorganization act might be beneficial for some tribes, but that the Crow tribe had already "through its own efforts secured from Congress legislation which tends to give us more privileges and rights than other tribes of the United States enjoy." He added, "The bill may be very good for some of the Indians—landless Indians—but so far as the Crow tribe is concerned we are satisfied with the present status."[15] In the eventual referendum on May 17, 1935, Crows voted down the reorganization act 689–112.[16]

It bears repeating that the Crows' rejection of intertribal political activism did not spell the end of Crow social and cultural contact and exchange with other Northern Plains communities. But this process did affect the way Crows thought about themselves and other Native peoples, as well as the way Crow history (and that of other tribes) would be told by scholars and by Native peoples themselves. Though the interethnic roots of many Crow families would continue to be remembered, the increasing emphasis on Crows as a politically and socially distinct people would shape the actions of not only Crow tribal business committee members in the 1920s and of Crow voters in 1935, but also later Crow memories of the early reservation period.

In 1979, seventy-three-year-old Crow John Bulltail was interviewed as part of an oral history project sponsored by the Montana Historical Society. In the interview, Bulltail discussed the development of the modern Crow Sun Dance, describing it as the result of continuing visits and friendship during the 1930s and 1940s between the Crows and Shoshonis at the Wind River Indian Reservation in Wyoming. "The present-day Sundance as we know it today was brought over from the Shoshone and we were given the right to adopt it their way," he said. Bulltail also recalled the continuing influence of Crees on the reservation, including their role as construction workers in the Pryor district and as builders of Plenty Coups's house.[17]

However, Bulltail was also careful to draw sharp distinctions between Crows and other Indians. He described the French Canadian Crees, for example, as living "right among us [Crows] here on the reservation, most of them came from Rocky Boy's Reservation." The old Crow fair was also recalled as being completely different from the modern Crow fair's status as the "tipi capital of the world" with visitors from tribes all over the United States and Canada:

> There used to be no visitors from other Reservations either, maybe a
> carload or two from Fort Berthold, North Dakota, some Gros Ventre
> people and usually a couple of Northern Cheyennes used to come and
> also camped and that was all the visitors we had. There was no influence
> from the other Reservations until very recently when they started
> advertising the fair by naming it "Tipi Capital of the world" and this drew
> the visitors around [the] 1950s.[18]

As in Charles Yarlott's version of Crow history, in which Crows acted in political affairs without input or influence from outsiders, Bulltail's memories enacted strict definitions of place, belonging, and community. While acknowledging the roles of Shoshones and Crees in Crow affairs, he distinguished between the presence of other Native peoples at Crow and the places where those people belonged: Wind River for the Shoshones and Rocky Boy's for the Cree. Though Bulltail's comment that the Crees "came from Rocky Boy's" suggested that Crees possessed a separate place where they belonged, before the creation of Rocky Boy's in 1915 (when Bulltail was nine years old), the Crow Reservation came closer to being a home for many Crees than anyplace else. To Bulltail, however, Crees may have lived and worked among Crows, but they did not belong at Crow and could not become or be considered Crow. Similarly, the Crow acquisition of the Shoshoni Sun Dance entailed a distinction between separate peoples, requiring a transfer of the right to perform the ritual from one group to the other. Finally, the Crow fair was remembered as a uniquely and exclusively Crow event, with the impact and participation of other Native peoples before the 1950s minimized.

As Peter Nabokov has noted, Native American conceptions of the past, like those of Europeans—or, indeed, any people—tend to be unabashedly and unapologetically ethnocentric.[19] The versions of Crow history put forth by Yarlott in 1926 and by Bulltail in 1989 illustrate this point. Both conveyed a vision of the past in which Crow social and political distinctiveness, not only from Euro-Americans but other Native peoples, was enshrined, affirmed, and even celebrated. Over time, this interpretation became dominant both in scholarly and tribal traditions, not just for Crows but in the broader corpus of Native American tribal histories.

To a certain degree, it must be said, this version is accurate. Historically, Crows had and have been a distinct people, with a particular relationship to the United States confirmed by a series of treaties and agreements dating back to 1825. From another perspective, however, this narrative is, if not inaccurate, at least overstated. Just as Crows possessed diplomatic ties to the United States, so too they possessed social, cultural, and diplomatic ties to numerous other Native communities throughout the nineteenth century. These ties did not disappear with the arrival of reservations, but they all too rarely appear in tribal histories of the reservation era.[20] The activities of Plenty Coups, Young Man Afraid of His Horses, Leonard Tyler, Sword Bearer, and Finds Them and Kills Them do not fit easily within this historiography. In many cases, the narrative balkanization of tribal (or reservation) histories has little room for such fluidity, shape-shifting, and boundary crossing, what colonial scholar Homi Bhabha has called the "lived perplexity" of human experience.[21]

Yarlott and Bulltail's statements were as much a reflection of contemporary circumstances as they were of the past. They recalled the past in a way that confirmed and legitimized what the Crow tribe had become, instead of drawing a contrast against what the Crow community had been. Rather than being an artifact of the past, the fixed and reified boundaries of the Crow tribe and most other contemporary tribes are actually a product of modernity, and their projection back into the past an example of what Eric Hobsbawm has termed "the invention of tradition." Such invention, Hobsbawm suggests, normally takes place when "a rapid transformation of society weakens or destroys the social pattern for which 'old' traditions had been designed . . . or when such old traditions and their institutional carriers and promulgators no longer proved sufficiently adaptable and flexible."[22] For Crows and other Indians on the Northern Plains, ironically, it was the flexibility of identity ingrained in tribal tradition, not just the hegemony of the federal government, that forced change when it came to questions of individual and group identity. Only the centralization of such matters in the hands of tribal councils or business committees could meet the new conditions of modern reservation life and the demands for totalizing, legally binding determinations of identity. In a sense, Crows had to be distinct from other Indians, not just to preserve their own community, but to preserve the reservation that belonged to them, perhaps most notably in efforts to prevent the government from relocating the Northern Cheyenne to Crow in the late 1890s.

The issue of identity is of more than just abstract historical interest. The shift in U.S. Census Bureau procedures from ascription to self-identification in 1960 led to an explosion in the number of people claiming an Indian identity, while migration and urbanization have resulted in a majority of Indians (tribally enrolled or not) living off reservations. As Angela Gonzales notes, "Questions of individual identity and ethnic 'authenticity' have become particularly contentious when these individuals are seen as accruing benefits earmarked for American Indians," whether in the form of Indian-targeted scholarships, increased profits or visibility as producers of Indian art, or per capita payments.[23] It has also led to corrosive infighting between federally recognized tribes and those communities seeking federal acknowledgment.[24]

The need for both individuals and groups to prove their "authenticity" has led many tribes to rely on direct descent or minimum blood quantum requirements to define membership. As a result, many tribes today find themselves on the horns of a demographic and cultural dilemma. Tribes with more restrictive definitions of community, often based on minimum blood quantum, are faced with the possibility that as intermarriage with outsiders continues, fewer and fewer people will meet the qualifications for membership, until the tribe eventually disappears (at least in a legal sense).[25] Conversely, those tribes in which membership is determined via descent from a previous tribal roll regardless of blood quantum (as in the Cherokee Nation) face the problem of cultural and social fragmentation, as tribal membership is passed along as a birthright to individuals regardless of their cultural orientation or participation in the community.[26] Neither standard allows for the inclusion of individuals who may not be able to meet measurements of blood quantum or descent but who may be more socially or culturally integrated into the community than many officially recognized members.

The ability to define membership is an inherent prerogative of tribal sovereignty. However, modern tribes' reliance on the mystical qualities of blood or linear descent calls to mind Paul Gilroy's warnings about the use of "ethnic absolutisms." "Too often in this century," he writes, "those folk have found only the shallowest comfort and short-term distractions in the same repertory of power that produced their sufferings in the first place."[27] As Frederick Hoxie has noted, regulations such as the 1990 American Indian Arts and Crafts Act (which make it a federal crime for anyone not a member of a federal- or state-recognized tribe to produce Indian art) "amounts to a codification by the tribes themselves of racial classification schemes":

> By relying on blood quantum to define membership, tribes are forced to equate "blood" with sovereignty. A defense of sovereignty, then, requires a defense of one's "blood." The sad consequence of that logic is that the tribes' lobbying has produced an American law that can penalize people whose lives violate an official ethnohistory.[28]

Gonzales adds, "Markers of ethnic authenticity are a result of American Indians having reified the criteria used by the federal government and stereotypes that exist within larger society. As a litmus test for identity, the extent to which individuals meet these criteria is used as a measure of their Indianness. The internalization of stereotypes creates expectations of how 'real' Indians are supposed to act, talk, and dress, but also creates norms with which individuals must conform."[29]

Adopting such methods imposed costs beyond individuals, however. In the early twentieth century, the hardening of tribal boundaries and definitions of identity closed off possibilities for intertribal cooperation. "Mixedness," suggests historian Laurie Mengel, can provide "a link between people . . . legitimate and viable panethnicity—a group response to collective racial categorization."[30] Unlike emancipated African Americans, who would engage in their own project of social and political mobilization during this period, not until the IRA congresses of the 1930s, the appearance of the National Congress of American Indians in the 1940s, and the civil rights movements of the 1950s and 1960s would Native Americans on the Northern Plains return to the strategies of collective activism Plenty Coups and others had pursued.[31]

Few people are more heavily burdened by the past than Native Americans.

As Ward Churchill (who has faced challenges to his own degree of Indian authenticity) notes, the question of identity holds "an obvious and deeply important bearing not only upon the personal sense of identity inhering in millions of individuals scattered throughout the continent, but in terms of the degree to which some form of genuine self-determination can be exercised by indigenous nations in coming years."[32] Indeed, Native Americans are not so much people without history as they are people trapped by history—a history without regard for the lived realities of the past or present.

There are other options. The Oglala Lakota of Pine Ridge Reservation have abandoned the use of blood quantum and have incorporated other standards such as residency, community affinity, knowledge of tribal culture, and service to the community.[33] Tribes might also choose to recognize dual or multitribal citizenship for individuals of mixed heritage. Native leaders in Minnesota have discussed the possibility of sharing casino revenue among state tribes.[34] As Nez Perce author W. S. Penn notes, "American Indian people themselves, along with their cousins on a North-South axis, have the most difficult job of all":

> They have to find a way to get serious and aim the argument, not at the ownership of the past but of the future; not at the images themselves, but at what the images mean; at the process, not the artifact. They have to be careful not to revise history or tradition, and at the same time allow it to reveal itself—and tradition, like history, reveals itself not by mannered manifestations of artifactuality that try to tell us what we have been, but by humorous suspicions of how we can continue to be.

Otherwise, as a speaker in Penn's *Feathering Custer* warns, "the separation of one from another, the discrete description of one as fixedly different from the other" may become "the death of both."[35]

NOTES

ABBREVIATIONS

ARCIA   Annual Report, Commissioner of Indian Affairs
CCF   Central Classified Files (National Archives)
CIA   Commissioner of Indian Affairs
LR-OIA   Letters Received, Office of Indian Affairs
NARA-Denver   National Archives and Records Administration, Denver, Colo.
NARA-DC   National Archives and Records Administration, Washington, D.C.
OPA   Oregon Province Archives
RG   Record Group (National Archives)
SC   Special Collection (National Archives)

INTRODUCTION. YOUNG MAN AFRAID OF HIS HORSES'S LETTER

1. For information on Young Man Afraid of His Horses, see Agonito, "Young Man Afraid of His Horses"; Hyde, *Red Cloud's Folk,* 117–118, 122–124. On the role of shirtwearers and *itancans,* see Price, *Oglala People,* 8–11, 17.

2. 1st Lt. W. M. Day to General George Crook, January 26, 1889, RG 75, LR-OIA, 5119–1889, NARA-DC.

3. Although scholars like Morton Fried and Raymond Fogelson have commented on the essentially fictive nature (or at least origins) of the Western concepts of tribalism and tribes themselves, this has done little to staunch the outpouring of historical and anthropological studies that use the notion of tribe as an organizational framework. See Fried, *Notion of Tribe;* Fogelson, "Perspectives on Native American Identity," 51.

4. Colson, "Political Organization in Tribal Societies," 5.

5. Stocking, *Race, Culture, and Evolution;* see also Kuper, *Invention of Primitive Society.*

6. The standard work on pan-Indian identity in the late 1800s and early 1900s remains Hazel W. Hertzberg's *Search for an American Indian Identity.*

7. Wolf, *Europe and the People sithout History.* I take my concept of modernity from Anthony Giddens, *The Consequences of Modernity,* 21–36.

8. Powers, *War Dance,* 87.

9. On Indian Territory/Oklahoma, see Howard, "Pan-Indian Culture of Oklahoma"; Hamill, *Going Indian,* x, xii–xiii. For an opposing view on the development of an Indian ethnicity in Indian Territory/Oklahoma in the 1800s, see David La Vere, *Contrary Neighbors,* 200–229.

10. McBeth, *Ethnic Identity,* 141. The literature on boarding schools is extensive. For the schools' impact on identity, see Adams, *Education for Extinction,* 336; Child, *Boarding School Seasons,* xiv, 2, 4, 73; and Coleman, *American Indian Children at School,* 142.

11. Gonzales, "Urban (Trans)formations," 172–173. For more on urban Indian communities, see Weibel-Orlando, *Indian Country, L.A.,* 7–8, 40–43, 58–60; Waddell and Watson, eds., *American Indian in Urban Society,* 62; Fixico, *Urban Indian Experience,* 6, 140, 187–188.

12. Cowger, *National Congress of American Indians,* 25–26.

13. Nagel, *American Indian Ethnic Renewal,* 159–160. Similarly, while acknowledging the existence of intertribal ties and alliances prior to the 1880s and social ties between tribes on reservations afterward, Stephen Cornell suggests that on reservations, Indians' world "remained a tribal one" and that the development of a sense of Indianness was primarily a "product of the incorporative process" occurring outside reservation boundaries. Cornell, *Return of the Native,* 107, 117–118.

14. Roosens, *Creating Ethnicity.*

15. Albers, "Symbiosis, Merger, and War," 96.

16. Richter, *Ordeal of the Longhouse,* 32–35, 65–73; Hyde, *Pawnee Indians,* 157–164, 198–199; Murie, *Ceremonies of the Pawnee,* 114–125; Saunt, *New Order of Things,* 51–54, 273–274; and Mulroy, "Ethnogenesis and Ethnohistory."

17. See, for example, Powers, *Andean Journeys;* Anderson, *Indian Southwest,* 4; James Merrell, *Indians' New World;* Wright, *Creeks and Seminoles;* White, *Middle Ground.*

18. For the impact of horses, see Holder, *The Hoe and the Horse,* 112; Ewers, *The Horse in Blackfoot Indian Culture,* 302–308. On trade, see Ewers, *Indian Life on the Upper Missouri,* 14–33; Wood, "Plains Trade," 98–103; Wishart, *Fur Trade,* 18–21, 53–64.

19. Sharrock, "Crees, Cree-Assiniboines, and Assiniboines"; Albers, "Changing Patterns of Ethnicity." Moore has described a similar process in the formation of the Cheyenne Indians in *Cheyenne Nation,* 86–87.

20. Binnema, *Common and Contested Ground,* xi–xii. For other works that emphasize hybridity and the heterogeneous nature of Indian communities, see Hamalainen, *Comanche Empire,* 170–180, 300–303, 326; Brooks, *Captives and Cousins,* 179–193.

21. Agonito, "Young Man Afraid of His Horses," 119–121; Valentine T. McGillycuddy to CIA, June 26, 1883, RG 75, LR-OIA, 11905–1883, NARA-DC. For more on McGillycuddy's conflicts with Red Cloud, see James C. Olson, *Red Cloud and the Sioux Problem,* 264–305, and Nancy J. Hulston, "Federal Children."

22. Agonito, "Young Man Afraid of His Horses," 129.

23. Thomas, *Colonialism's Culture,* 60–61.

24. Scott, *Weapons of the Weak,* 289–293. Scott argues against a limited definition of resistance as "(a) organized, systematic, and cooperative, (b) principled or selfless, (c) that has revolutionary consequences, and/or (d) embodies ideas or intentions that negate the basis of domination itself." Scott elucidates a broader, more inclusive definition that includes acts that "evade the state and the legal order" as well as those that confront them directly.

25. Ostler, *Plains Sioux,* 144–145.

26. Thompson, "Primary Sources," 138–139.

27. Ostler, *Plains Sioux,* 289–360.

28. Greenwald, *Reconfiguring the Reservation,* 143–145; Moses, *Wild West Shows,* 44, 70–71; Marquis, *Wooden Leg,* 366–369.

29. For peyotism, see Stewart, *Peyote Religion;* Steinmetz, *Pipe, Bible, and Peyote;* Aberle, *Peyote Religion among the Navaho;* Maroukis, *Peyote and the Yankton Sioux;* Couch and Marino, "Chippewa–Cree Peyotism," 7–15. On the Ghost Dance, see Andersson, *Lakota Ghost Dance of 1890;* Kehoe, *Ghost Dance;* Hittman, *Wovoka and the Ghost Dance;* Vander, *Shoshone Ghost Dance Religion;* and Smoak, *Ghost Dance and Identity.*

30. Ironically, despite its title, one notable exception to this trend is the seminal original work on the Ghost Dance, James Mooney's "The Ghost Dance Religion and the Sioux Outbreak of 1890." Though not all specific to the Northern Plains, other more recent examples include Mellis, *Riding Buffaloes and Broncos;* Meredith, *Dancing on Common Ground;* Ellis, *A Dancing People;* and Harmon, *Indians in the Making.*

31. For representative recent tribal histories see Ostler, *Plains Sioux;* Stamm, *People of the Wind River;* Rosier, *Rebirth of the Blackfeet Nation;* Thompson, *Kiowa Humanity.*

32. For Crow tribal history, see Hoxie, *Parading through History,* and Algier, *The Crow and the Eagle.*

33. Berkhofer, "Political Context," 358.

34. Dowd, *Spirited Resistance,* xiii–xv.

35. Anderson, *Imagined Communities.*

36. See Binnema, *Common and Contested Ground,* 13–16, for a similar discussion. Though Binnema generally avoids using the term "tribe," he does use tribal identifers such as Gros Ventre, Cree, Crow, and Blackfeet for various Native communities, even when those groups were allied with or residing with members of a different ethnic group.

PART ONE. INTIMATE ENEMIES

1. Nabokov, *Two Leggings,* 32–33.

CHAPTER ONE. SYMBIOTIC ENEMIES: CROWS AND
BLACKFEET, 1800–1885

1. Ewers, *Blackfeet,* 6–8, 22–30; Binnema, *Common and Contested Ground,* 23, 74–75, 179–180, 182–184. Brian Reeves and Sandy Peacock have argued against the Blackfeet migration thesis in *"Our Mountains Are Our Pillows,"* 7–12, 75–83, in favor of long-term Blackfeet residence in northern Montana and southern Alberta, and sustained contact between Crows and Blackfeet well before 1800. However, several of their tribal locations during this period (notably placing the Lakota and Cheyenne in the vicinity of the Black Hills as early as 1500) are suspect, and their evidence for close Crow–Blackfeet contact before 1800 is not conclusive. The possibility does exist that Blackfeet groups inhabited the region before the 1700s but were briefly driven north by Shoshonean peoples after the Shoshonean acquisition of horses.

2. Scholars have debated whether the Crow–Hidatsa split involved a single separation or multiple migrations by different Crow groups, as well as the timing, with most dates falling in a range between the mid-1500s and the mid-1700s. Peter Nabokov summarizes the evidence surrounding the Crow separation from the Hidatsa in "Cultivating Themselves," 111–123. See also Wood and Downer, "Notes on the Crow–Hidatsa Schism."

3. Hoxie, *Parading through History,* 41.

4. For an exceptionally good description and analysis of these changes, see Binnema, *Common and Contested Ground,* chaps. 4 and 5; Flores, "Great Contraction," 12–13; see also Isenberg, *Destruction of the Bison,* 33–47. Elliot West describes a similar process for the central Plains in *Contested Plains,* 64–76. See also Vickers, "Cultures of the Northwestern Plains," 26–33, Gregg, "Archaeological Complexes," 88–95, and Schlesier, "Commentary: A History of Ethnic Groups," 313–316, 321–323, 328–330, 335–346; Wedel, *Central Plains Prehistory,* 43–46.

5. For culture areas, see A. L. Kroeber, "Cultural and Natural Areas." For critiques of the culture area concept, see Howard, "Culture Area Concept"; Foster, introduction to Jablow, *Cheyenne in Plains Indian Trade Relations,* v–xvi; and Scaglion, "Plains Culture Area Concept," 31.

6. Sturtevant, *Handbook of North American Indians,* 61, 329, 349, 365–366, 695, 718–719, 863, 907.

7. M'Gillivray, *Journal;* Henry and Thompson, *New Light;* Ewers, "Intertribal Warfare." W. Raymond Wood and Thomas Theissen note that the only recorded mention of Crows in Hudson Bay Company journals during the early to mid-1700s was when a party of Mandan or Hidatsa Indians arrived at York Fort on Hudson's Bay accompanied by a group of Crow slaves in 1716. Wood and Theissen, *Early Fur Trade,* 18–19. For the first recorded extended contact between Crows and Europeans, see Hoxie, *Parading through History,* 31–53.

8. Binnema notes that Crow–Shoshoni relations remained generally peaceful during this time but that Crow movement westward "may well have caused friction with some Shoshoni bands." Binnema, *Common and Contested Ground,* 93–94, 179–183; quotation at 93.

9. Henry and Thompson, *New Light,* 525–526. Ewers compared the relative wealth in horses of the Blackfeet to other Plains tribes in *The Horse in Blackfoot Indian Culture,* 20–31.

10. Binnema, *Common and Contested Ground,* 133–135; Ewers, *Blackfeet,* 32.

11. Wood, "Plains Trade," 100–103; Henry and Thompson, *New Light,* 399; Larocque, "Yellowstone Journal," 213–215.

12. Larpenteur, *Forty Years a Fur Trader,* 1:45.

13. Hamalainen, "Rise and Fall of Plains Indian Horse Cultures," 846–847, 851–854; West, *Contested Plains,* 86–88. Hamalainen suggests that part of the explanation for Crow and Piegan horse wealth lay in their location close to the Rocky Mountains, where warm Chinook winds provided a more favorable environment for wintering horses.

14. For a general discussion of band societies on the Northern Plains, see Binnema, *Common and Contested Ground,* 11–15; for the Crow, see Hoxie, *Parading through History,* 57–59; for the Blackfeet, see Ewers, *Blackfeet,* 96–98.

15. Lowie, *Crow Indians,* 5.

16. For descriptions of early Blackfeet leadership structures and warfare, see Thompson, *David Thompson's Narrative,* 240–245, 252–253. Writing of Blackfeet culture in the early 1900s, Clark Wissler stated that "no Blackfoot can aspire to be looked upon as a head man unless he is able to entertain well, often invite others to his board, and make a practice of relieving the wants of his less fortunate band members." Wissler, "Social Life," 22–23, 25; quote at 23.

17. For community structures and Blackfeet culture, see Wissler, "Societies and Dance Associations," 436–440; Wissler and Duvall, *Mythology,* 121; Binnema, "Old Swan, Big Man, and the Siksika Bands," 5–7; Nugent, "Property Relations," 343–350; Conaty, "Economic Models," 404–407; Ewers, *Blackfeet,* 94–96; Lewis, *Effects of White Contact,* 34–46, 52–59; and McGinnis, *Counting Coup,* 7–12.

18. Wishart, *Fur Trade,* 29–30.

19. Hoxie, *Parading through History,* 71–72; Ewers, *Blackfeet,* 63–64.

20. Hickerson, "Virginia Deer."

21. Albers, "Symbiosis, Merger, and War," 94–132.

22. Hoxie, *Parading through History,* 67–68.

23. For Blackfeet relations with traders, see Judy, "Powder Keg," 129–144; Church, "Blackfeet and Fur Traders"; and Lewis, *Effects of White Contact,* 16–30. For the establishment of Fort Piegan, see Bradley, "Affairs at Fort Benton," 201–207.

24. Conaty, "Relationships, Power, and Sacred Objects."

25. Lowie, *Crow Indians,* 7–8, 248–250.

26. Wood, "Plains Trade," 100, 103–107; Ewers, *Indian Life on the Upper Missouri,* 15–30; Holder, *The Hoe and the Horse,* 84–85, 130–131.

27. Henry and Thompson, *New Light,* 399. For a good discussion of this subject, see Harrod, *Becoming and Remaining a People,* 6–9. Karl Schlesier has argued that the Sun Dance originated with the Sutaios, an Algonquian group that later assimilated with the Cheyenne. Schlesier, "Rethinking the Midewiwin and the Plains Ceremonial," 1–26. Accepting Schlesier's thesis does not invalidate the theory that horticultural groups were seen as possessing not only superior material wealth but also spiritual power; the Cheyenne were also horticulturalists until the late 1700s. Hoebel, *Cheyennes,* 3–9; Moore, *Cheyenne Nation,* 129–138.

28. Linderman, *Pretty Shield,* 83.

29. In particular, historians and anthropologists have debated the impact of horses on gender roles and the social status of men and women. See Liberty, "Hell Came with Horses," 10–19; Foster, "Of Baggage and Bondage." For more general discussions of the impact and influence of horses, see Ewers, *The Horse in Blackfoot Indian Culture,* 299–322; West, *Contested Plains,* 49–54

30. Henry and Thompson, *New Light,* 399.

31. Perhaps significantly, the information on the Crow–Blackfeet trade in Crow war shields comes not from the records of resident European traders but from the account of European traveler Alexander Philip Maximilian, Prince of Wied. Maximilian, *Travels in the Interior of North America,* 117–118, 161. On shield designs, see Lowie, *Crow Indians,* 86.

32. Most estimates of Crow population during the early to mid-1800s fall in the range of 3,500 to 5,000 people. Hoxie, *Parading through History,* 131. Blackfeet population figures range from Alexander Henry's estimate of 5,200 people (2,800 Piegan, 1,600 Siksika, and 800 Blood) in 1809 to Maximilian's estimate of 18,000 to 20,000 for all three divisions combined in 1833. Ewers, *Blackfeet,* 37, 60. The consensus among scholars is that the Lakota population actually increased in the early 1800s, with the most careful student estimating an increase from 8,500 in 1805 to 12,845 in 1849. Bray, "Teton Sioux Population History," 170–177.

33. Wishart, *Fur Trade,* 42–48, 54–66, 86–87. For a more detailed discussion of Crow trading difficulties, see Chapter 2.

34. Nabokov, "Cultivating Themselves," 320, 395.

35. Precise dating of the Blackfeet adoption of Crow tobacco and medicine water ceremonialism is nearly impossible. Wissler believed that the Medicine Water ceremony did not reach the Blackfeet until at least 1860. The planting of sacred tobacco has been completely integrated into the Blackfeet Beaver Bundle origin stories, but both James Willard Schultz and Edward Curtis reported that the sacred tobacco elements came from the Crows. McClintock, *Old North Trail,* 104–112; Wissler and Duvall, *Mythology,* 74–81; Curtis, *North American Indian,* 6:68–69, 76–79; Schultz, *Blackfeet and Buffalo,* 344–345. Wissler described the Beaver Bundle complex as "a kind of nucleus around which are found a number of more or less related ceremonies" and suggested that the Beaver Bundle itself was one of the earliest rituals developed by the Blackfeet. Though individually owned, Beaver Bundles and their powers could be called upon by all members of the community and were perhaps the most important bundle type among the Blackfeet. Wissler, "Ceremonial Bundles," 168–175, 281–282; quotation at 169. One of Wissler and Duvall's Blackfeet informants told them that the Crow Medicine Water ceremony "has great power. If any one wishes a horse, he calls in some of the Crow-water-medicine people." Wissler and Duval, *Mythology,* 80. The ritual was also credited with having the power to avert the fulfillment of bad dreams and to cure the sick. Along with Wissler, Edward Curtis and James Willard

Schultz also stated that the Blackfeet obtained the tobacco planting portion of the Beaver Bundle ritual complex from the Crows. Schultz, *Blackfeet and Buffalo*, 344–346; Curtis, *North American Indian*, 6:68–69, 76–79.

36. Wissler, "Societies and Dance Associations," 451, 459–460; Lowie, *Crow Indians*, 4. Ewers notes the relative poverty of the Cree, Gros Ventre, and Assiniboine in terms of horses in *The Horse in Blackfoot Indian Culture*, 23–24.

37. Maximilian, *Travels in the Interior of North America*, 121.

38. Larpenteur, *Forty Years a Fur Trader*, 2:401.

39. Denig, *Five Indian Tribes*, 144–145.

40. Curtis, *North American Indian*, 4:51–52.

41. Leonard, *Narrative*, 237.

42. The Houghton Running Rabbit winter count (Siksika) lists 1838 as the year a Crow was killed and the Siksika held war dances, while the Teddy Yellow Fly count (Siksika) lists 1838 as "the year of the Crow victory dances." The Joe Little Chief count (Siksika) contains the reference to the Crow–Siksika Sun Dance. Houghton Running Rabbit, Teddy Yellow Fly, and Joe Little Chief winter count transcripts held at the Glenbow-Alberta Institute, Calgary.

43. Cut Nose's visit is recorded in the Houghton Running Rabbit and Joe Little Chief counts for 1840. The Teddy Yellow Fly count lists 1841 as the year a Crow chief "without a nose" was killed. Walking Crow's death is from the Bad Head (Blood) count in Dempsey, *Blackfoot Winter Count*, 11.

44. Bradley, "Affairs at Fort Benton," 219. The Jesuit missionary Pierre-Jean De Smet noted a similar peace with a near-identical end during the 1840s. There is the possibility that both authors were describing the same event. Chittenden and Richardson, *Life, Letters, and Travels*, 3:1037–1043.

45. Maximilian, *Travels in the Interior of North America*, 161. For Maximilian's ethnographic sensibilities, see Liebersohn, *Aristocratic Encounters*, 137–163.

46. Marquis, *Memoirs*, 99. In this case, Leforge was referring to contacts between Crows and Lakotas during the 1870s and 1880; however, the evidence suggests that Leforge's analysis may also be extended to Crow contacts with other peoples earlier in the nineteenth century.

47. Bradley, "Affairs at Fort Benton," 221–26; Denig, *Five Indian Tribes*, 169–70.

48. Denig, *Five Indian Tribes*, 204; Catlin, *Letters and Notes*, 42–43.

49. Denig, *Five Indian Tribes*, 163–64.

50. Chittenden and Richardson, *Life, Letters, and Travels*, 1:524.

51. Dempsey, *Vengeful Wife*, 142.

52. Ibid., 139–150.

53. Linderman, *Pretty Shield*, 173.

54. Denig, *Five Indian Tribes*, 148.

55. Frey, *The World of the Crow Indians*, 3–4.

56. For discussions of the role of kinship in structuring Native societies, see Fogelson, "Perspectives on Native American Identity," and DeMallie, "Kinship," 44–45, 52–53, 323–330.

57. Hoxie, *Parading through History*, 169–170.

58. Lowie, *Crow Indians*, 7, 18–32.

59. Ibid., 212.

60. Although I see no reason to question the account of Leforge's adoption, it is colored somewhat by the fact that Leforge never mentions which clan he belonged to in his memoirs. Writing of life after his marriage to the Crow woman Cherry, Leforge refers to the Burnt Mouths as his people. However, given that he identifies Cherry as a Burnt Mouth, Leforge him-

self could not have belonged to that clan, given Crow prohibitions on marriages between members of the same clan. It is probable that Leforge was referring only to patterns of residency (i.e., traveling and camping with other Burnt Mouth families) rather than his own clan affiliation. Marquis, *Memoirs,* 25–27, 36–37, 148–149. Lowie makes clear that individuals adopted into Crow families (as opposed to purely ceremonial or social adoptions) automatically became members of their new mother's clan. Lowie, *Crow Indians,* 9.

61. Linderman, *Plenty Coups,* 6–7; Wagner and Allen, *Blankets and Moccasins,* 238. See also Bradley, "Manuscript—Book F," 210.

62. Binnema, *Common and Contested Ground,* 14.

63. Significantly, the information on Medicine Prairie Chicken comes from a Blackfoot winter count. Dempsey, *Blackfoot Winter Count,* 13.

64. Pierre-Jean De Smet to Charles Mix, acting Superintendent of Indian Affairs, November 1, 1862, Records of the Montana Superintendency of Indian Affairs, 1861–1871, Small Collection 889, Montana State Historical Society, Helena. Unfortunately, De Smet did not record the outcome of the negotiations. Given the fact that dating of winter counts is sometimes not exact, the winter count and De Smet's letter may even refer to the same event.

65. Lowie, *Crow Indians,* 229, 312.

66. Bradley, "Manuscript—Book F," 242.

67. For mid-nineteenth-century cultural attitudes and ideas regarding "savage" Indians, see Berkhofer, *White Man's Indian,* 51–61, 95–96; Dippie, *Vanishing American,* 25–43, 82–86; and Saum, *Fur Trader.*

68. Denig, *Five Indian Tribes,* 148.

69. Schultz and Donaldson, *Sun God's Children,* 228–229.

70. Bedford, "The Fight at 'Mountains on Both Sides,'" 20.

71. Wissler, "Societies and Dance Associations," 436–437. On the role of Crow women in religion in general, see Lowie, *Crow Indians,* 60–61.

72. Denig, *Five Indian Tribes,* 146–147.

73. Ibid., 145–146.

74. Kappler, *Indian Affairs,* 594–596.

75. According to U.S. treaty commissioners, the Crows were unable to attend because a recent measles outbreak had scattered the tribe. "Report of Commissioners Alfred Cummings and Isaac I. Stevens on council with Blackfoot, October 22, 1855," Small Collection 895, Montana State Historical Society, Helena.

76. Partoll, "Blackfoot Indian Peace Council," 10–11; Kappler, *Indian Affairs,* 736–739.

77. Joe Little Chief and Teddy Yellow Fly winter counts, Glenbow Archives, Calgary, Alberta. A journal kept at Fort Benton in the 1850s does seem to indicate a reduction (though not a complete cessation) in the number of war parties passing the post after the Judith treaty council. McDonnell, "Fort Benton Journal," 1–99.

78. Ewers, *Blackfeet,* 227.

79. Bradley, "Manuscript—Book F," 281. Moore describes the process of new bands "hiving off" from existing bands, as occurred for the Cheyenne, in *Cheyenne Nation,* 50–54, 205–250, 266–275.

80. Wissler, "Social Organization," 21–22; Alfred J. Vaughn to A. B. Greenwood, Commissioner of Indian Affairs, August 31, 1860, *Annual Report of the Commissioner of Indian Affairs, 1861,* Senate Exec. Doc. 1, 36th Congress, 2nd session, Serial 1078, 308–309. Ewers suggested that Wissler's list of Piegan bands may have been inaccurate; an 1870 report listed fifteen Piegan bands compared to nine Blood and nine Siksika bands. Ewers, *Ethnological Report,* 13.

81. Ewers, *The Horse in Blackfoot Indian Culture*, 20–21, 29–30, 319. In the Blackfeet, Ewers notes that the ability of American fur trade companies to send steamboats up the Missouri gave them a considerable advantage over the Hudson's Bay Company in fur trade volume, an advantage the Piegan (the southernmost Blackfeet group) were best positioned to benefit from. Ewers, *Blackfeet*, 63–64.

82. In 1865, the Biters band of Siksika split over the question of who would assume band leadership after the death of Three Suns. Eventually the band split, with about twenty-seven lodges following the leadership of Three Suns's son (also named Three Suns), and about twenty-one lodges following the leadership of Crowfoot. Crowfoot's group eventually became a separate band in its own right, known as the Big Pipes. Dempsey, *Crowfoot*, 46–47.

83. Vaughn to Greenwood, August 31, 1860, *ARCIA, 1861*, 308.

84. Although some scholars have suggested that the division between the Mountain Crows and River Crows may mark two separate migrations away from the Hidatsa, on a cultural and individual level, the distinction between the two was largely academic; both spoke the same dialect, and River Crows could and did live among the Mountain Crows and vice versa. Lowie, *Crow Indians*, 3–17; Bowers, *Hidatsa Social and Ceremonial Organization*, 13–25; Wood and Downer, "Notes on the Crow–Hidatsa Schism." For mixed residency patterns, see Nabokov, *Two Leggings*, 143–144; Hoxie, *Parading through History*, 93. Wissler noted that in Plains sign language, there were separate signs for the Piegan, Blood, and Siksika, but there was apparently no universal sign for the Blackfeet as a single group, and there was no tradition of Piegan, Blood, or Siksika camp circles ever being combined. Wissler, "Social Life," 7–8, 22.

85. For a general discussion of the vision quest, see Dugan, *Vision Quest*, and Benedict, "The Vision in Plains Culture." The rite among the Blackfeet is discussed in Schultz, *Blackfeet and Buffalo*, 145–154; Ewers, *The Horse in Blackfoot Indian Culture*, 178–180; and Ewers, *Blackfeet*, 162–163.

86. Catlin, *Letters and Notes*, 37–38.

87. Ewers, *Blackfeet*, 167–173; Wissler and Duvall, *Mythology*, 74–78, 89–90.

88. Conaty, "Relationships, Power, and Sacred Objects," 3.

89. Ewers, *The Horse in Blackfoot Indian Culture*, 178–179.

90. Conaty, "Economic Models," 407.

91. Benedict, "The Vision in Plains Culture," 12.

92. Curtis, *North American Indian*, 6:79.

93. Wildschudt, *Crow Indian Medicine Bundles*, 7.

94. Nabokov, *Two Leggings*, 23–26, 43, 45–51, 61–65. Edward Curtis stated that Crow men were undergoing multiple vision quests as early as the mid-nineteenth century. Curtis, *North American Indian*, 4:45–46, 53–54.

95. Linderman, *Plenty Coups*, 34–44, 57–67; Nabokov, *Two Leggings*, 56–57, 62–65.

96. Wildschudt, *Crow Indian Medicine Bundles*, 14–15, 40. Wildschudt believed that the number and variety of Crow bundles exceeded that of other comparable Plains tribes. Wildschudt, *Crow Indian Medicine Bundles*, 12.

97. Ewers, *Blackfeet*, 11–14; Medicine Crow, *From the Heart of the Crow Country*, 86–99.

98. Ewers, *Indian Life on the Upper Missouri*, 162–168. Buffalo drives or jumps survived slightly longer among the Blood. According to Hugh Dempsey, Seen From Afar's band conducted the last Blood buffalo drive in 1868. Dempsey, *Vengeful Wife*, 112.

99. Curtis, *North American Indian*, 6:17–29.

100. Hoxie, *Parading through History*, 84. Hoxie notes that the warrior societies "helped the

Crows defend themselves from outside aggression by checking the traditional tendency toward fragmentation and providing networks to hold scattered band members in line."

101. Ibid., 172–173; Lowie, *Crow Indians,* 172–173, 200–202.

102. Hoxie, *Parading through History,* 92–93, McGinnis, *Counting Coup,* 122, 136–137; Milloy, *Plains Cree,* 103–118.

103. Flores, "Great Contraction," 14–17; Isenberg, *Destruction of the Bison,* 130–143; Ostler, *Plains Sioux,* 53.

104. Dobak, "Killing the Canadian Buffalo," 38–49.

105. Denig, *Five Indian Tribes,* 93–95; Chittenden and Richardson, *Life, Letters, and Travels,* 3:3, 948, 1187–1189.

106. Farr, "Going to Buffalo," 33–36.

107. Chittenden and Richardson, *Life, Letters, and Travels,* 3:948.

108. Henry Armstrong to Price, February 24, 1884, Record Group 75, Letters Received, Commissioner of Indian Affairs, 4127–1884, NARA-DC.

109. Marquis, *Memoirs,* 47.

110. *ARCIA 1870,* House Exec. Doc. 1, 43rd Congress, 1st session, Serial 1449, 654, 662–664.

111. Mahlon Wilkinson to A. J. Faulk, July 15, 1867, *ARCIA 1867,* House Exec. Doc. 1, 40th Congress, 2nd session, Serial 1326, 236–237; *Montana Post,* November 13, 1866.

112. Report of the Commission to Negotiate with the Crow Tribe of Indians, August 15, 1873, *ARCIA 1873,* House Exec. Doc. 1, 43rd Congress, 1st session, Serial 1601, 506.

113. Wissler, "Social Organization," 26. The Big Brave winter count from which this information is taken does not contain dates, but a rough approximation of the year can be gained by keying the other events noted in the winter count, such as the 1855 and 1866 treaty councils and the 1856 "slippery winter" to their proper calendar years.

114. Dempsey, *Blackfoot Winter Count,* 17.

115. Dempsey, *Vengeful Wife,* 220–221.

116. For a description of the Crow–Piegan council, see Hoxie, *Parading through History,* 140–141. Hoxie echoes the views of American officials in terming the meeting a "turning point" in Crow–Piegan relations. The last officially recognized horse raid between Crows and Blackfeet took place in 1889, when a Blood war party stole some forty horses from a Crow camp. McGinnis, *Counting Coup,* 191.

117. Nabokov, *Two Leggings,* 193.

118. For what would later be dubbed "salvage" ethnography, see Dippie, *Vanishing American,* 222–223, 231–236; and Smith, *Reimagining Indians.* More recent scholars are not immune to this train of thought. In his study of intertribal warfare, Anthony McGinniss suggested that the collapse of intertribal raiding "paralleled the entire defeat of a culture." McGinnis, *Counting Coup,* 192.

CHAPTER TWO. CROWS, LAKOTAS, AND THE BOZEMAN TRAIL, 1863–1868

1. Denig, *Five Indian Tribes,* 139.

2. Bradley, "Arapooash," 306–307.

3. See, for example, Carrington, *Ab-sa-ra-ka,* 13; Chittenden, *American Fur Trade,* 2:855. For a discussion of the actual meaning of the term, see Lowie, *Crow Indians,* 3.

4. Fuller, *River of the West,* 83, 96.

5. Kappler, *Indian Affairs,* 595.

6. Hoxie, *Parading through History,* 72; Colin Calloway, "Inter-tribal Balance of Power," 28–29, 44–46.

7. Upper Platte Agent Thomas Twiss to Commissioner of Indian Affairs A. B. Greenwood, August 5, 1859, and Twiss to Greenwood, May 23, 1860, both in Letters Received, Upper Platte Agency, RG 75, NARA Microform 234, roll 890; White, "The Winning of the West," 333–334.

8. Lt. Col. C. A. May to Acting Assistant Adjutant General, Department of the Platte, November 6, 1858, and Twiss to Commissioner of Indian Affairs Charles Mix, February 25, 1861, both in Letters Received, Upper Platte Agency, RG 75, NARA Microform 234, roll 890.

9. Sunder, *Fur Trade,* 45, 59–60. Even for fur traders, the posts in the Yellowstone Valley were widely regarded as the most dangerous on the Northern Plains. Fur trader Charles Larpenteur once turned down $1,000 to take over management of Fort Alexander on the Yellowstone, preferring the safer surroundings of Fort Union. Larpenteur, *Forty Years a Fur Trader,* 2:277. Denig commented that the Crow trade was never very profitable as a result of the dangers of the area and the Crows' demand for high prices for their furs and robes. Denig, *Five Indian Tribes,* 200–204.

10. John Hutchinson to Commissioner of Indian Affairs William P. Dole, September 23, 1863, and Samuel N. Latta to Dole, August 27, 1863, both in *Annual Report of the Commissioner of Indian Affairs, 1863,* House Exec. Doc. 1, 38th Congress, 1st session, serial 1182, 273, 288–289.

11. Henry W. Reed to Dole, n.d., *ARCIA, 1864,* House Exec. Doc. 1, 38th Congress, 1st session, serial 1220, 415.

12. Maj. Mahlon Wilkinson to Gov. Newton Edwards, August 31, 1864. *ARCIA, 1864,* 406–407; testimony of Mahlon Wilkinson at Vermillion, D.T., September 12, 1865, in Commissioner of Indian Affairs, *Report on the Condition of Indian Tribes,* Senate Record 156, 39th Congress, 2nd session, Serial 1279, 416.

13. Linderman, *Plenty Coups,* 49.

14. Ewers, *Blackfeet,* 230.

15. Report of 1st Lt. John Mullins, *Exploration of the Yellowstone River,* Senate Exec. Doc. 77, 40th Congress, 2nd session, serial 1317, 166–67.

16. Historian George E. Hyde and John F. Kinney, a member of a commission sent to contact the Crows in 1867, both dated the final expulsion of the Crows from the Powder River country as occurring in 1859. Hyde, *Red Cloud's Folk,* 91–92; Kinney to N. G. Taylor, June 4, 1867, *ARCIA, 1867,* House Exec. Doc. 1, 40th Congress, 2nd session, Serial 1326, 126–128. The diaries of emigrants who traveled the Bozeman Trail before the onset of the Bozeman Trail conflict are conspicuous for their lack of references to encounters with Crows south and east of the Bighorn River. See Richard Lockey, "Diary on the Bozeman Trail, 1866," and Theodore Bailey, "Diary, 1866," both typescripts at the Montana State Historical Society, Helena, and Ellen Fletcher, "Letters," Merrill G. Burlingame Department of Special Collections, Montana State University, Bozeman. William Emory Atchison's 1864 party, which took the Bridger Cutoff west of the Bighorn Mountains, did encounter Crows, but not until they reached Clark's Fork of the Yellowstone. Atchison, *Epic of the Middle West.* See also Lt. George M. Templeton, "Diary, 1866–1868," July 26, 1866, typescript copy, Newberry Library, Chicago.

17. Marquis, *A Warrior Who Fought Custer,* 2–5; Simonin, *Rocky Mountain West,* 115; Nabokov, *Two Leggings,* 201; Curtis, *North American Indian,* 4:51.

18. Bray, "Lone Horn's Peace," 29–32.

19. Ibid., 37–44; Hoxie, *Parading through History,* 83; Carrington, *Ab-sa-ra-ka,* 17.

20. Gray, "Blazing the Bozeman and Bridger Trails"; Doyle, "Journeys to the Land of Gold," 56–59.

21. For a description of these conflicts, see Utley, *Frontiersmen in Blue,* 281–297, 300–332; Hyde, *Red Cloud's Folk,* 101–133; and Hyde, *Life of George Bent,* 118–266.

22. Eli Ricker, "Tablets," interview with Baptiste Pourier, reel 3, Nebraska State Historical Society; see also Brian Jones, "John Richard Jr.," 238, for a list of traders who arrived in Montana in the mid-1860s. For an account of powder being traded to the Crows, see the *Montana Post,* March 30, 1867.

23. Report of Lt. Col. W. F. Raynolds, *Exploration of the Yellowstone River,* Sen. Exec. Doc. 77, 40th Congress, 2nd session, Serial 1317, 16–17.

24. Johnson, *Bloody Bozeman,* 30–43.

25. Gen. Alfred Sully to Secretary of the Interior O. H. Browning, April 4, 1867, *Investigation of the Fort Phil Kearny Massacre,* RG 75, NARA Microform 740, roll 1; Robert M. Utley, *The Lance and the Shield,* 62.

26. Col. Henry Maynadier to Commissioner of Indian Affairs, March 24, 1866, in Letters Received, Upper Platte Agency, RG 75, NARA Microform 234, roll 891. In reporting his efforts to arrange a treaty council, Maynadier wrote that he was attempting to contact the Lakota and Northern Cheyenne, but since the Arapahos had joined the Crows, "it is useless to send for them." Implicit in Maynadier's statement is the idea that the Crows no longer possessed title to or an interest in the region. Similarly, mention of Crows is absent from correspondence among government officials in the area during preparations for the council. U.S. officials did conclude a separate treaty (mainly with River Crow representatives) in 1866 at Fort Benton, Montana, just below Great Falls on the Upper Missouri River, that established a right of way running up the Yellowstone River in return for annuities and the establishment of an agency, but the Senate failed to ratify the treaty. *ARCIA, 1866,* House Exec. Doc. 1, 39th Congress, 2nd session, serial 1284, 13–14; Smith, "Politics and the Crow Indian Land Cessions," 24–37.

27. For events surrounding the 1866 Fort Laramie councils and Carrington's arrival, see Gray, *Custer's Last Campaign,* 36–48; Carrington, *Indian Operations on the Plains, 1866,* Senate Exec. Doc. 33, 50th Congress, 1st session, serial 2504, 5–6; Carrington, *Ab-sa-ra-ka,* 72–80.

28. Carrington, *Indian Operations on the Plains,* 20; Bradley, "Manuscript—Book F," 223.

29. Gray, *Custer's Last Campaign,* 49–51; Carrington, *Indian Operations on the Plains, 1866,* 20.

30. George Templeton, "Diary, 1866–1868." The identity of Smith and Leighton is drawn from Gray, *Custer's Last Campaign,* 53. Templeton spelled the interpreter's last name as Shane; Gray lists it as Chene, while Hoxie, in *Parading through History,* 91, gives the name as Chien.

31. Carrington, *Indian Operations on the Plains,* 22.

32. Testimony of Col. Henry C. Carrington, extract of report from Carrington to Assistant Adjutant General Maj. H. G. Litchfield, November 5, 1866, *Investigation of Fort Phil Kearny Massacre.*

33. Carrington, *Indian Operations on the Plains,* 22.

34. Templeton, "Diary, 1866–1868," October 31, 1866.

35. Carrington, *Indian Operations on the Plains,* 20–22.

36. Templeton, "Diary, 1866–1868," October 31 and November 2, 11, 15, 19, and 23, 1866.

37. Ibid., November 11 and 23, 1866.

38. Doyle, "Indian Perspectives on the Bozeman Trail."

39. Spotted Blue Body, a Minniconjoux Lakota, said four Crows were present among the Lakota, Cheyenne, and Arapahos at the battle. Testimony at Fort Laramie, May 9, 1867, *Investi-*

gation of Fort Phil Kearny Massacre. In 1876, the Crow Half Yellow Face told Army Lt. James H. Bradley that the Crow participants consisted of three men and one woman. Bradley, "Manuscript—Book F," 223.

40. Capt. N. C. Kinney to the Governor of Montana, February 8, 1867. RS 250, Montana Secretary of State Records, Box 3, folder 9, Montana State Historical Society, Helena.

41. Templeton, "Diary, 1866–1868." In the December 28, 1866, entry, Templeton recorded that the Fetterman fight was a major subject of discussion among the Crows, and he speculated whether the Crows were wondering whether the army would abandon the trail. The December 31, 1866, entry contains the order from the Lakota to the Crows to move away from Fort C. F. Smith because the Lakota did not want to fight them.

42. Ibid., January 2, 1867.

43. Report of Capt. N. C. Kinney, February 9, 1867, in *Investigation of Fort Phil Kearny Massacre*.

44. Bradley, "Manuscript—Book F," 223.

45. Report of Capt. N. C. Kinney, February 9, 1867, in *Investigation of Fort Phil Kearny Massacre*. None of the available sources give a reason for the move, but Lowie, in *Crow Indians*, 4, states that the Wind River was a traditional wintering spot for the Mountain and Kicked-in-the-Belly Crows.

46. Report of Capt. N. C. Kinney, February 9, 1867, in *Investigation of Fort Phil Kearny Massacre*.

47. Returns from U.S. Military Posts, Fort C. F. Smith, January 1867, RG 98, U.S. Army Commands, NARA Microform 617, roll 1190; *Montana Post*, March 16, 1867.

48. Templeton, "Diary, 1866–1868," entries for January 23, February 5, 6, 15, 18, 27, and March 6, 1867.

49. *Montana Post*, April 22, 1868; Templeton, "Diary, 1866–1868," March 18 and 25, 1867.

50. Returns from U.S. Military Posts, Fort C. F. Smith, May, 1867, RG 98, NARA Microform 617, roll 1190.

51. Templeton, "Diary, 1866–1868," June 25, 1867.

52. For meetings in Bozeman, see the *Montana Post*, April 27, 1867. The report on Bozeman's death is in the May 4 issue.

53. August H. Chapman to N. G. Taylor, Commissioner of Indian Affairs, July 5, 1867. *ARCIA, 1867*. House Exec. Doc. 1, 40th Congress, 2nd session, serial 1326, 259–260.

54. *Montana Post*, May 11, 1867.

55. *Montana Post*, July 20 and 27, 1867.

56. For proposals to arm friendly Indians while taking their families hostage, see *Montana Post*, April 13, 1867. Meagher's letter appears in *Montana Post*, June 8, 1867. The charge that the Crows were sheltering Bozeman's killers does have some support from another source. On May 6, Templeton recorded Bozeman's death in his diary, along with information that the Blackfeet who killed him were living in a Crow village camped within fifteen miles of Fort C. F. Smith. "Diary, 1866–1868."

57. For examples of reports of gold in Crow lands, see *Montana Post*, February 3, 1866, September 9, 1867, and March 7, 1868.

58. Thomas Francis Meagher to Commissioner of Indian Affairs, December 14, 1865, and April 20, 1866, both in *ARCIA, 1866*, House Exec. Doc. 1, 39th Congress, 2nd session, serial 1284, 196–97, 200.

59. Meagher to Commissioner of Indian Affairs, April 20, 1866, *ARCIA, 1866*, House Exec. Doc. 1, 39th Congress, 2nd session, serial 1284, 200.

60. Templeton, "Diary, 1866–1868," June 18, 1867.

61. Tom Leforge, who briefly served in the militia in the summer of 1867, noted that it was composed "largely of ex-ruffians of the Missouri–Kansas border" and that several officers were killed by their own men in disputes. Marquis, *Memoirs,* 16–20; quotation at 19.

62. *Montana Post,* July 13, 1867. Templeton recorded that the militia members were so undisciplined that when they reached Fort C. F. Smith, they were required to camp on the opposite side of the Bighorn. "Diary, 1866–1868," June 14, 1867.

63. *Montana Post,* August 31, 1867.

64. *Montana Post,* September 7, 1867.

65. *Secretary of War Annual Report, 1867,* House Exec. Doc. 1, 40th Congress, 2nd session, serial 1324, 33. For a fuller examination of Sherman's response to the war scare, see Athearn, *William Tecumseh Sherman,* 133–148. For Sherman's attitude toward Indians and the Office of Indian Affairs, see Marszalek, *Sherman,* 379–383.

66. Chapman to Taylor, *ARCIA, 1867,* 259–260; *Montana Post,* February 8, 1868.

67. Commissioner of Indian Affairs, *Letter on Indian Hostilities,* Senate Exec. Doc. 13, 40th Congress, 1st session, serial 1308, 55–56.

68. Gen. Alfred Sully to Secretary of the Interior O. H. Browning, April 4, 1867, *Investigation of Fort Phil Kearny Massacre.*

69. Templeton, "Diary, 1866–1868," April 12, 1867.

70. Wessells to Assistant Adjutant General, April 26, 1867, Department of the Platte, Register of Letters Received, microform copy in the Nebraska State Historical Society, Lincoln, RG 533, reel 5.

71. Gen. C. C. Augur to Sully, April 26, Sully to Gen. N. G. Palmer, April 26, Wessells to Sully, April 22, 1867, and Palmer to Sully, April 30, 1867, all in *Investigation of Fort Phil Kearny Massacre.*

72. Kinney report, June 4, 1867, *Investigation of Fort Phil Kearny Massacre.*

73. Ibid.

74. Dunlay, *Wolves for the Blue Soldiers.* 39.

75. Mattes, *Indians, Infants, and Infantry,* 131–132; Dunlay, *Wolves for the Blue Soldiers,* 39.

76. Templeton, "Diary, 1866–1868," July 15 and 17, 1867. The warning Templeton recorded came from an Indian named The Swan. The warning was clouded by The Swan's claim that the Crows were sheltering 600 Lakotas in their camp, but this may have been a reference to a Lakota trading expedition to Crazy Head's camp. Templeton did not identify The Swan's tribal affiliation, but Kappler, *Indian Affairs,* 1011, lists The Swan as one of the signers of the May 7, 1868, treaty between the United States and the Mountain Crows. The *Montana Post* did allege (in its September 7, 1868, edition) that Crows participated in the Hayfield Fight, but this claim is not corroborated by any other source.

77. Wessells to Assistant Adjutant General, June 7, 1867, Department of the Platte, Register of Letters Received.

78. Kinney to Secretary of the Interior Orville H. Browning, October 7, 1867, *Investigation of Fort Phil Kearny Massacre.* Templeton, "Diary, 1866–1868," July 11, 1867.

79. Testimony of Raphael Gallegos, Fort Phil Kearny, August 4, 1867, *Investigation of Fort Phil Kearny Massacre.*

80. Ibid.

81. Templeton, "Diary, 1866–1868," July 11, 12, 14, 16, and 18, 1867.

82. Gallegos testimony, *Investigation of Fort Phil Kearny Massacre.*

83. Ibid.

84. Kinney to Taylor, June 17, 1867, Letters Received, Upper Platte Agency, RG 75, NARA Microform 234, roll 892.

85. Taylor to Kinney, July 9, 1867, *Letter on Indian Hostilities*, Senate Exec. Doc. 13, 40th Cong., 1st session, serial 1308, 55–56.

86. *ARCIA, 1868*, House Exec. Doc. 1, 40th Cong., 3rd session, serial 1366, 486.

87. *New York Times*, August 11, 1867. There has been confusion over the identity of the agent sent to the Crows, with some authors listing him as Dr. Washington Matthews. However, the records of the commission and the agents' own reports conclusively identify him as Dr. Henry Matthews, who had previously served as post surgeon at Fort C. F. Smith. See also Gray, *Custer's Last Campaign*, 74–75.

88. Templeton, "Diary, 1866–1868," September 12, 1867; Matthews to Taylor, September 13, 1867, RG 48, Department of the Interior, Records of the Indian Division, Entry 663, Box 3, NARA-DC.

89. Lt. Col. Luther Bradley to Sanborn, October 17, 1867, RG 48, Department of the Interior, Records of the Indian Division, Entry 663, Box 3, NARA-DC.

90. Templeton, "Diary, 1866–1868," September 21, 23, 24, and 27, 1867; Returns from U.S. Military Posts, Fort C. F. Smith, September, 1867, RG 98, NARA Microform 617, roll 1190.

91. Bradley to Matthews, January 10, 1868, Letters Received, Montana Superintendency, 1864–68, RG 75, NARA Microform 234, roll 488.

92. Matthews to Taylor, February 18, 1868, RG 48, Department of the Interior, Indian Division, Entry 663, Box 4, NARA-DC.

93. Templeton, "Diary, 1866–1868," September 26, October 23 and 26, 1867.

94. The main sources for information on the November 1867 Laramie councils are the reports by a correspondent for the *New York Times* and the account by a French mining engineer named Louis Simonin who was touring the Plains and happened to be at Laramie at the time. See in particular the *New York Times* issue for December 23, 1867, and Simonin, *Rocky Mountain West*. The official report of the Peace Commission devoted just two paragraphs to the November council.

95. Simonin, *Rocky Mountain West*, 109–110.

96. Templeton, "Diary, 1866–1868," August 7 and 21, 1866.

97. Lt. Col. Luther Bradley to Dr. H. M. Matthews, January 10, 1868, Letters Received, Montana Superintendency, RG 75, NARA Microform 234, roll 488. Ironically, given the relatively small number of emigrants who dared use the trail during the conflict, it seems likely that much of the diminution of buffalo and other game was due to increased hunting pressure by Indians themselves. The lack of hostilities between Crows and Lakotas allowed both groups to make more intensive use of a region that had increasingly become a game-rich buffer zone between the two (but that neither dared inhabit or exploit on a full-time basis) during the late 1850s and early 1860s.

98. Simonin, *Rocky Mountain West*, 105–109. The December 23, 1867, *New York Times* article contains the same speech with a slightly different translation but the same meaning, including an explicit reference to the Bozeman Trail.

99. Simonin, *Rocky Mountain West*, 104–105, 111.

100. Gemien P. Beauvais to O. H. Browning, December 14, 1867, Letters Received, Upper Platte Agency, RG 75, NARA Microform 234, roll 892.

101. *New York Times*, December 23, 1867; Simonin, *Rocky Mountain West*, 115–116. Tom Leforge noted that Blackfoot "knew fairly well the Sioux language, having perhaps acquired it from his wife," and that Blackfoot's Lakota wife occasionally interpreted for visiting Lakotas. Marquis, *Memoirs*, 180–181.

102. *New York Times,* December 23, 1867; Simonin, *Rocky Mountain West,* 115–116.

103. Simonin, *Rocky Mountain West,* 107–108, 115–117.

104. Greene, "Lt. Palmer Writes from the Bozeman Trail," 27–29.

105. Kappler, *Indian Affairs,* 998–1003.

106. Ibid., 1008–1011. The Mountain Crow and Kicked-in-the-Belly representatives were Pretty Bull, Mountain Tail, Blackfoot, White Horse, Poor Elk, Shot in the Jaw, White Forehead, Pounded Meat, Bird in the Neck, and The Swan. The lone River Crow signer was Wolf Bow, who spent much time with his Mountain Crow kin. See also Humphrey, "Crow Indian Treaties," 82–84, and Hoxie, *Parading through History,* 92–93.

107. Calloway, "Army Allies or Tribal Survival?," 71–76.

108. Linderman, *Plenty Coups,* 78, 154.

Part Two. Reimagining Community

1. Dixon, *Vanishing Race.* On Dixon and Wanamaker, see Lindstrom, "Not from the Land Side," 209–212.

2. Dixon, *Vanishing Race,* 5, 9–10.

3. Ibid., 39, 192, 194–195.

4. Barsh, "American Heart of Darkness," 91–94, 108–111.

Chapter Three. The Politics of Visiting

1. Henry J. Armstrong to Commissioner of Indian Affairs, November 13, 1883, RG 75, Crow, Box 1, book 16, NARA-Denver.

2. For efforts to stop intertribal warfare, see McGinnis, *Counting Coup,* 174–192.

3. Armstrong to CIA, November 13, 1883, RG 75, Crow, Box 1, book 16, NARA-Denver.

4. Ibid.

5. There can hardly even be said to be a literature on the topic of intertribal visiting; I am unaware of any article or monograph devoted to the subject. Most tribal histories make casual reference to intertribal visiting, but most fall into the mode of Ewers's *Blackfeet.* Ewers devotes one page to the subject, confined mostly to the exchange of gifts, storytelling, and social practices such as the Grass Dance. Ewers, *Blackfeet,* 312. Many more recent tribal histories, such as Paul C. Rosier's *Rebirth of the Blackfeet Nation* and Stamm's *People of Wind River,* make no reference to visiting at all.

6. For the pass, see Valentine T. McGillycuddy to CIA, June 26, 1883, RG 75, LR-OIA, 11905–1883, NARA-DC.

7. Ibid.

8. For more on the divided nature of colonial projects, see Thomas, *Colonialism's Culture,* 60–61; Thompson, "Primary Sources," 138–139.

9. Agonito, "Young Man Afraid of His Horses." See also Hulston, "Federal Children"; Larson, "Lakota Leaders," 50.

10. McGillycuddy to CIA, June 2, 1884, RG 75, LR-OIA, 10836–1884, NARA-DC.

11. Armstrong to CIA, June 4, 1884, RG 75, Crow, Box 10, book 17, and Armstrong to Gen. A. A. M. Dudley, September 11, 1885, RG 75, Crow, Box 12, book 19, both NARA-Denver. For more on the contentious relationship between the military and Office of Indian Affairs

during this period, see Mardock, *Reformers,* 159–169; Prucha, *Great Father,* 1:549–560; Wooster, *Military and United States Indian Policy,* 77–84, 88–89, 210–211.

12. Armstrong to Col. George B. Sanford, August 25, 1884, and September 7, 1884; Armstrong to CIA, September 20, 1884, and December 2, 1884, all RG 75, Crow, Box 10, book 17, NARA-Denver.

13. See, for example, the comment of Standing Rock Agent J. A. Stephens in 1880: "As a general thing, it is the indolent and more worthless class of Indians who are the most clamourous for passes, seeking to escape work during the summer time, and appearing promptly when fall comes for their rations and annuity goods." *ARCIA, 1880,* House Exec. Doc. 1, 46th Congress, 3rd session, Serial 1959, 178.

14. Armstrong to H. Price, February 26, 1885, RG 75, Crow, Box 10, book 20, NARA-Denver; Hoxie, *Parading through History,* 112.

15. Armstrong to Gen. John P. Hatch, May 16, 1884, RG 75, Crow, Box 10, book 17, NARA-Denver.

16. Marquis, *A Warrior Who Fought Custer,* 2–5, 96.

17. Armstrong to Gen. John P. Hatch, May 16, 1884, RG 75, Crow, Box 10, book 17, NARA-Denver.

18. Armstrong to E. P. Ewers, June 26, 1884, RG 75, Crow, Box 10, book 17, NARA-Denver.

19. For the background of and establishment of the Tongue River Reservation, see Svingen, *Northern Cheyenne Indian Reservation,* 11–45.

20. James C. Clifford to U.S. Indian Agent, March 7, 1898, RG 75, Crow, Box 36, NARA-Denver. For Northern Cheyenne service as army scouts, see Dunlay, *Wolves for the Blue Soldiers,* 143–145.

21. L. S. Spencer to Williamson, May 30, 1887, RG 75, Crow, Box 2, book 4, NARA-Denver.

22. Williamson to Atkin, June 8, 1887, RG 75, Crow, Box 2, book 4, NARA-Denver.

23. For passes issued to Crows to find stolen stock, see C. H. Barstow pass to Plenty of Writing, September 22, 1882, RG 75, Box 9; Armstrong to Price, November 20, 1883, RG 75, Crow, Box 1, book 16; Armstrong to Hatch, November 14, 1884, RG 75, Crow, Box 11, book 12; Barstow pass to Spotted Tail, June 8, 1884, RG 75, Crow, Box 11, book 14, all NARA-Denver.

24. Armstrong to S. R. Anislie, June 18, 1884, RG 75, Crow, Box 10, book 17, NARA-Denver.

25. Armstrong to Gen. J. F. Oakes, August 18, 1884, RG 75, Crow, Box 10, book 17, NARA-Denver.

26. M. L. Black to Abram J. Gifford, July 3, 1886, RG 75, Crow, Box 13, book 3, NARA-Denver.

27. See Armstrong to James McLaughlin, August 14, 1885, RG 75, Crow, Box 12, book 21; Armstrong to McGillycuddy, October 8, 1885, RG 75, Crow, Box 12, book 19; Williamson to Sir, August 20, 1886, RG 75, Crow, Box 13, book 3; Williamson to Reuben A. Allen, September 9, 1886, RG 75, Crow, Box 13, book 4, all NARA-Denver.

28. Henry Williamson to CIA, June 8, 1887, RG 75, Crow, Box 2, book 4, NARA-Denver.

29. Clow, "General Philip Sheridan's Legacy." Estimates of the number of horses seized ranged from an army figure of 4,277 to an 1891 Indian Office figure of 7,261.

30. *ARCIA, 1881,* House Exec. Doc. 1, 47th Congress, 1st session, Serial 2018, 116.

31. For estimates of horse numbers, see *ARCIA, 1880,* House Exec. Doc. 1, 46th Congress, 3rd session, Serial 1959, 229, 388–389, 394–395; *ARCIA, 1881,* House Exec. Doc. 1, 47th Congress, 1st session, Serial 2018, 171, 358–359, 364–365; *ARCIA, 1882,* House Exec. Doc. 1, 47th

Congress, 2nd session, Serial 2100, 416–417; *ARCIA, 1883*, House Exec. Doc. 1, 48th Congress, 1st session, Serial 2191, 352–353, 358–359.

32. *ARCIA, 1884*, House Exec. Doc. 1, 48th Congress, 2nd session, Serial 2287, 82.

33. McGillycuddy to Price, June 6, 1883, RG 75, LR-OIA, 11908–1883; McGillycuddy to Price, June 2, 1884, RG 75, LR-OIA, 10836–1884; McGillycuddy to Atkins, July 20, 1885, RG 75, LR-OIA, 17987–1885, all NARA-DC; Williamson to Atkins, June 8, 1887, RG 75, Crow, Box 2, book 4, NARA-Denver. Ironically, when Cheyenne River Lakotas requested permission to come to Crow to trade for horses in 1886, Crow Agent Williamson urged that the pass be denied, citing recent horse raids against the Crows by the Piegan and Yankton Sioux. In his letter, Williamson failed to explain how preventing peaceful trade would contribute to stopping hostile raiding. Charles E. McChesney to CIA, August 9, 1886, RG 75, LR-OIA, 21738–1886; Williamson to Atkins, August 29, 1886, RG 75, LR-OIA, 23145–1886; H. Heth to Williamson, August 30, 1886, RG 75, LR-OIA, 24401–1886, all NARA-DC.

34. "Number Head Domestic Animals on Cheyenne River Indian Reservation," November 10, 1878, RG 75, LR-OIA, M235, roll 130; *ARCIA, 1887*, House Exec. Doc. 1, 50th Cong., 1st session, Serial 2542, 100, 465; *ARCIA, 1889*, House Exec. Doc. 1, 51st Cong., 1st session, Serial 2725, 156.

35. Spotted Elk to E. H. Becker, April 9, 1899, RG 75, Crow, Box 37, NARA-Denver.

36. Armstrong to Atkins, August 3, 1885, RG 75, LR-OIA, 18128–1885, NARA-DC.

37. Hyde, *Sioux Chronicle,* 53–54; Ostler, *Plains Sioux,* 154–156.

38. "Proceedings of a Council, held April 15, 1890, between Major Henry Carroll and certain Cheyenne Chiefs at Tongue River Agency," RG 75, LR-OIA, 19493–1890, NARA-DC.

39. Upshaw to CIA, June 19, 1890, RG 75, LR-OIA, 19377–1890; John Tully to CIA, October 31, 1890, RG 75, LR-OIA, 34627–1890, both NARA-DC.

40. Hazel Hertzberg makes this point in her discussion of the spread of the Ghost Dance: "Ghost Dancers lived in a practical, everyday world as well as an ecstatic one. They carried their ideas with them over railroads and highways, wrote letters, and discussed problems in the English which was beginning to replace sign language as the lingua franca of the Plains." Hertzberg, *Search for an American Indian Identity,* 14.

41. McGinnis, *Counting Coup,* 174–177, 180–182, 185,

42. Lt. Col. C. C. Compton to Commanding Officer, District of Montana, March 17, 1885, LR-OIA, 9697–1885, NARA-DC. I have been unable to find any further reference to this rumored meeting.

43. Ibid.

44. Capt. Carroll H. Potter to 1st Lt. Robert R. Bates, March 19, 1885, RG 75, LR-OIA, 9697–1885, NARA-DC.

45. Gallagher to Williamson, June 5, 1887, RG 75, LR-OIA, 16978–1887, NARA-DC.

46. For a good discussion of the problematic nature of concepts such as traditionalist and progressive (not only for contemporaries but for modern scholars), see Lewis, "Reservation Leadership."

47. Utley, *The Lance and the Shield,* 251, 254–255; Rickey, *History of Custer Battlefield,* 72–73; Burdick, *David F. Barry's Indian Notes,* 21.

48. Wiliamson to Atkins, August 29, 1886, RG 75, LR-OIA, 23145–1886, NARA-DC; Williamson to McLaughlin, September 7, 1886, RG 75, Crow, Box 13, book 4, NARA-Denver.

49. Charles McChesney to CIA, August 9, 1886, RG 75, LR-OIA, 21738–1886; Capt. W. Bell to J. D. C. Atkins, September 3, 1886, RG 75, LR-OIA, 23842–1886, both NARA-DC.

50. Williamson to Atkins, August 29, 1886, RG 75, LR-OIA, 23145–1886, NARA-DC; Williamson to Heth, August 21, 1886, RG 75, Crow, Box 13, book 3, NARA-Denver.

51. Heth to CIA, September 26, 1886, RG 75, LR-OIA, 25673–1886; Heth to Williamson, August 30, 1886, RG 75, LR-OIA, 24410–1886, both NARA-DC; Williamson to Heth, September 7, 1886, RG 75, Crow, Box 13, book 4, NARA-Denver.

52. Williamson to McLaughlin, September 7, 1886, RG 75, Crow, Box 13, book 4, NARA-Denver.

53. The agency policeman accompanying Sitting Bull's party was Bull Head, who in 1890 would lead the police detachment that arrested and killed Sitting Bull. Marquis, *Cheyennes of Montana,* 103–104; Utley, *The Lance and the Shield*, 300–306.

54. Billings *Gazette,* June 10, 1887.

55. Utley, *The Lance and the Shield*, 122–123, 202, 204–205; Dempsey, *Crowfoot*, 88–92.

56. Utley, *The Lance and the Shield*, 204–205.

57. Hoxie, *Parading through History,* 116–121, 144–145, 150–151.

58. For early attempts to break up the Great Sioux Reservation, see Utley, *The Lance and the Shield*, 257–258, and Ostler, *Plains Sioux,* 218–221.

59. James R. Howard to CIA, September 27, 1886, RG 75, LR-OIA, 26352–1886, NARA-DC.

60. Ibid. Crow Agent Williamson used the effect of Sitting Bull's visit to once again urge a blanket prohibition on interreservation visits. Williamson to Atkins, September 27, 1886, RG 75, LR-OIA, 26353–1886, NARA-DC. Despite a promise to return to the Crow Reservation the next year, Sitting Bull never traveled to Montana again. Billings *Gazette*, June 10, 1886.

61. For Crow enthusiasm for allotments, see Williamson to Atkins, September 27, 1886, RG 75, LR-OIA, 26353–1886, NARA-DC. Milburn's troubles are in Milburn to Commissioner, February 25, 1886, RG 75, LR-OIA, 6429–1886, NARA-DC.

62. Brig.-Gen. Thomas Ruger to Assistant Adjutant General, November 30, 1887, RG 75, LR-OIA, 33393–1887, NARA-DC.

63. For more extended accounts, see Calloway, "Sword Bearer"; Jones, "Battle at Little Bighorn"; Hoxie, *Parading through History,* 154–164.

64. Hoxie, *Parading through History,* 155–156; Alfred H. Terry to Assistant Adjutant General, July 19, 1887, RG 75, LR-OIA, 20534–1887, NARA-DC.

65. Brig.-Gen. Thomas Ruger to Adjutant General, November 30, 1887, RG 75, LR-OIA, 33393–1887, NARA-DC.

66. James R. Howard to CIA, October 7, 1887, LR-OIA, 27964–1887, NARA-DC. Crow oral history states that Wraps Up His Tail received (or found) his sword during a visionary experience in the Bighorn Mountains. Hoxie, *Parading through History,* 155.

67. Afton et al., *Cheyenne Dog Soldiers,* 28, 80, 114, 128, 138, 194, 262.

68. Lowie, *Crow Indians,* 297–298. Perhaps because of the decline in intertribal warfare, the traditional Crow Sun Dance appears to have ended before strenuous government efforts to prohibit "barbaric" rituals took effect. The last known performance of the nineteenth-century Crow Sun Dance took place in 1875. The modern Crow Sun Dance was adopted from the Shoshonis in the twentieth century. Voget, *Shoshoni–Crow Sun Dance,* 77–78.

69. Moore, *Cheyenne Nation,* 11, 38.

70. For an example of the Sun Dance as a means to cement social and political ties, see Utley, *The Lance and the Shield*, 122–124.

71. Stands in Timber and Liberty, *Cheyenne Memories,* 249–250. Interestingly, Stands in Timber agreed with Crow oral history in stating that Sword Bearer got his power from fasting in

the Bighorn Mountains and does not mention his participation in a Cheyenne Sun Dance. It is impossible to determine whether this account is in any way influenced by the ultimate failure of Sword Bearer's power and the desire to keep the spiritual power of the Cheyenne Sun Dance untainted by Sword Bearer's failure.

72. Spencer to CIA, October 20, 1887, RG 75, LR-OIA, 27900–1887, NARA-DC.

73. Frank C. Armstrong to Secretary of the Interior, October 25, 1887, RG 75, LR-OIA, 28539–1887; Edwin Fields to CIA, October 22, 1887, RG 75, LR-OIA, 29178–1887, both NARA-DC.

74. Williamson to CIA, October 12, 1887, RG 75, Crow, Box 2, book 6, NARA-Denver; Armstrong to Secretary of the Interior, October 25, 1887, RG 75, LR-OIA, 28539–1887, NARA-DC; Armstrong to Secretary of the Interior, October 27, 1887, RG 75, LR-OIA, 28777–1887, NARA-DC.

75. Armstrong to Secretary of the Interior, October 19, 1887, RG 75, LR-OIA, 27964–1887; Armstrong to CIA, November 4, 1887, RG 75, LR-OIA, 30413–1887; Upshaw to CIA, October 21, 1887, RG 75, LR-OIA, 28087–1887; Ruger to Assistant Adjutant General, November 30, 1887, RG 75, LR-OIA, 33393–1887; R. C. Drum to Commanding General, Division [of the] Missouri, October 24, 1887, RG 75, LR-OIA, 28583–1887, all NARA-DC.

76. See, for example, Hoxie, *Parading through History,* 158. Colin Calloway comments that "the Cheyenne were unlikely to make common cause with their long-time Crow enemies." Calloway, "Sword Bearer," 43–44.

77. Svingen, *Northern Cheyenne Indian Reservation,* 30–31, 34–36, 40–42, 50–53, 57–60.

78. Dusenberry, "Northern Cheyennes."

79. In addition to the Sword Bearer episode, army units were sent to Tongue River in July and November 1885 and August 1887. Armstrong to Atkins, July 16, 1885, RG 75, LR-OIA, 16585–1885; T. H. Logan to Post Adjutant, July 22, 1885, RG 75, LR-OIA, 18052–1885, all NARA-DC; Armstrong to Atkins, November 22, 1885, Maj. Henry Carroll to Post Adjutant, November 25 and November 28, 1885, and Col. George Gibson to Adjutant General, September 4, 1887, all RG 75, SC 137, NARA-DC.

80. In "Northern Cheyenne," Schrems suggests White Bull's comments may have been based on early knowledge of the Ghost Dance, which would add another layer of complexity to Sword Bearer's spiritual biography.

81. Major Simon Snyder to Lt. O. F. Long, September 3, 1887, RG 75, SC 137, NARA-DC.

82. Dusenberry, "Northern Cheyennes," 26–27.

83. DeMontravel, *A Hero to His Fighting Men,* 83–84, 152–153, 226–228. In a conversation with an army officer in 1885, White Bull claimed that the soldiers had been the Cheyennes' best friends because "General Miles and all soldiers tell the truth," in contrast to government agents. Capt. T. H. Logan to Post Adjutant, July 22, 1885, RG 75, SC 137, NARA-DC.

84. Dusenberry, "Northern Cheyennes," 33.

85. "Talk of John Two Moons," in Upshaw to Atkins, June 4, 1887, SC 137, NARA-DC.

86. Two Moons, American Horse, and White Bull to Our Great Father in Washington, July 5, 1887, and Col. George Gibson to Adjutant General, September 4, 1887, both RG 94, LR–Office of the Adjutant General, NARA Microform 689, roll 537.

87. Dusenberry, "Northern Cheyennes," 33.

88. The Ghost Dance did gain a strong cadre of supporters among the Northern Cheyenne at Tongue River, but their ties to the military (including service as scouts and their relationship with Nelson Miles) meant that the government response to the Ghost Dance at Tongue River would be very different from the heavy-handed approach the military took with the Lakota—

one that led eventually to Wounded Knee. See Ostler, *Plains Sioux,* 289–290; Svingen, *Northern Cheyenne Indian Reservation,* 78–86; Weist, "Ned Casey," 36–39; Wooster, *Nelson A. Miles,* 188; Dusenberry, "Northern Cheyennes," 37–40.

89. Hoxie, *Parading through History,* 166, 171–172.

90. On the breakup of the Great Sioux Reservation, see Ostler, *Plains Sioux,* 228–239. On the Ghost Dance, the basic source remains James Mooney's "Ghost Dance Religion." For demographic explanations for participation or nonparticipation in the Ghost Dance, see Thornton, *We Shall Live Again;* for the Ghost Dance as a response to allotment, see Landsman, "Ghost Dance," 162–166.

91. It may be worth noting that Sitting Bull also stopped at Tongue River on his way to Crow in 1887. However, though the Northern Cheyenne had been allies of the Lakota at Little Bighorn (in contrast to the Crows), his stop there apparently generated much less controversy and unrest. Marquis, *Cheyennes of Montana,* 21, 104.

92. For correspondence regarding passes and visiting during this period, see RG 75, Crow, Box 14, book 11, NARA-Denver. Specific references are E. P. Briscoe to Upshaw, June 20, 1888, Briscoe to Upshaw, December 31, 1888, Briscoe to Upshaw, July 21, 1888, Briscoe to J. L. Summerville, October 20, 1888, and Briscoe to W. D. Pickett, October 15, 1888, all RG 75, Crow, Box 14, book 11, NARA-Denver.

93. M. P. Wyman to Upshaw, October 17, 1889, RG 75, Crow, Box 14, book 2, NARA-Denver.

94. Wyman to P. Ronan, January 28, 1890 (Flathead), Wyman to A. J. Simon, July 2, 1890 (Fort Berthold), both RG 75, Crow, Box 14, book 2, NARA-Denver; Wyman to F. H. Marsh, May 20, 1891 (Nez Perce and Flathead), Wyman to Whom It May Concern, May 22, 1891 (Nez Perce), Wyman to U.S. Indian Agent, Fort Belknap, September 12, 1891 (Assiniboine and Gros Ventre), Wyman to U.S. Indian Agent, Shoshoni Agency, October 27, 1891, and Wyman to U.S. Indian Agent, Nez Perce Agency, March 14, 1892, all RG 75, Crow, Box 15, NARA-Denver.

95. Wyman to Conductor, November 10, 1889 (Hidatsas), Wyman to H. D. Gallagher, February 4, 1890 (Pine Ridge), RG 75, Crow, Box 14, book 2; Wyman to Maj. A. C. Timbers, August 11, 1890 (Fort Belknap), RG 75, Crow, Box 14, book 4; Wyman to Col. A. K. Arnold, December 9, 1890 (Pine Ridge), RG 75, Crow, Box 15, book 5; Wyman to Capt. John Tully, July 29, 1891 (Northern Cheyenne), Wyman to Whom It May Concern, November 3, 1891 (Pine Ridge), RG 75, Crow, Box 15; Wyman to Charles H. Thompson, July 6, 1892 (Cheyenne River), Wyman to Maj. C. R. A. Scobey, August 23, 1892 (Fort Peck), Wyman to Whom It May Concern, March 24, 1893 (Cheyenne River), Wyman to Capt. George LeRoy Brown, May 25, 1893 (Pine Ridge), RG 75, Crow, Box 16, book 38; Wyman to Capt. Charles Perry, August 21, 1893 (Pine Ridge), Wyman to G. P. Connor, October 4, 1893 (Pine Ridge), Wyman to Capt. P. H. Roy, September 23, 1893 (Shoshonis), Wyman to Capt. Charles R. Robe, October 4, 1893 (Fort Belknap), C. H. Barstow to Capt. Thomas Sharp, August 16, 1893 (Northern Cheyenne), RG 75, Crow, Box 16, book 39, all NARA-Denver.

96. Edwards to Charles E. McChesney, February 2, 1900, RG 75, Crow, Box 20, book 19, NARA-Denver.

97. Wyman to Tully, September 5, 1891, and Wyman to Whom It May Concern, September 12, 1891, both RG 75, Crow, Box 15, NARA-Denver.

98. Wyman to U.S. Indian Agent, Nez Perce Agency, March 14, 1892, and Wyman to Northern Pacific Railroad Conductor, March 14, 1892, both RG 75, Crow, Box 15, NARA-Denver. For Deaf Bull's involvement with Sword Bearer, see Hoxie, *Parading through History,* 158–159, 164–166.

99. Wyman to Conner, October 4, 1893, RG 75, Crow, Box 16, book 39, NARA-Denver.

100. W. H. Clapp to U.S. Indian Agent, September 17, 1898, RG 75, Crow, Box 36, NARA-Denver. For an example of such a directive, see Acting Commissioner A. C. Tonney to John E. Edwards, August 24, 1900, RG 75, Box 34, NARA-Denver. This is not to say that agents condoned or necessarily liked the proliferation of visiting. In 1902, Wind River agent H. G. Nickerson wrote to Crow agent Samuel Reynolds that "the pass nuisance is the curse of the Indian Service and I should like to see it prohibited." Reynolds sympathized, replying, "The pass system has certainly been a nuisance this summer; this place is flooded with visitors from the day I came here until the present time." Nickerson to Reynolds, October 13, 1902, RG 75, Crow, Box 40; Reynolds to Nickerson, October 31, 1902, RG 75, Crow, Box 21, book 27, both NARA-Denver.

101. Edwards to Charles E. McNichols, June 2, 1902, RG 75, Crow, Box 21, book 26, NARA-Denver.

102. Riebeth, *J. H. Sharp*, 106–107. Sharp, an artist, painted several scenes depicting intertribal visiting, including a painting of Crow teepees at Lame Deer on the Northern Cheyenne Indian Reservation and a picture of Blackfeet playing an arrow-throwing game during a winter visit to Crow.

103. Wyman to Col. A. Arnold, September 4, 1891, and Wyman to Frank Lillibridge, November 5, 1892, RG 75, Crow, Box 16, book 38, both NARA-Denver.

104. Wyman to Capt. French, January 7, 1891, RG 75, Crow, Box 15, book 5; Wyman to Whom It May Concern, January 8, 1891, both RG 75, Crow, Box 15, book 5, NARA-Denver.

105. Wyman to Arnold, December 9, 1890, RG 75, Crow, Box 15, book 5, NARA-Denver.

106. Agonito, "Young Man Afraid of His Horses," 126.

107. For the circumstances of the 1890 council, see Hoxie, *Parading through History,* 228–232.

108. The report and minutes of the commission are in RG 75, Entry 310, Irregularly Shaped Papers, Box 23, Item 42, NARA-DC.

109. "Report of the Proceedings in Council," Crow Commission of 1890, RG 75, Entry 310, Irregularly Shaped Papers, Box 23, Item 42, NARA-DC.

110. Ibid. For the Sioux Agreement of 1889 and its aftermath, see Mooney, *Ghost Dance Religion,* 824–842; Utley, *The Lance and the Shield,* 271–284; and Ostler, *Plains Sioux,* 230–239. Young Man Afraid's actions in 1890 apparently had no long-term effect on his ability to visit the Crows. He traveled to Montana again the following year with sixty Lakotas, and the group earned Wyman's approval for conducting themselves in a "commendable manner." Wyman to Whom It May Concern, November 3, 1891, RG 75, Crow, Box 15, NARA-Denver.

111. Voget, *They Call Me Agnes,* 3.

112. The Long Lodge Dance is still performed by the Crow Ree and Night Hawk societies. Ibid., 181–184.

113. Hoxie, *Parading through History,* 294. For efforts to ban giveaways, see Reynolds to Charles D. Curtis, February 23, 1903, RG 75, Crow, Box 22, book 28, NARA-Denver.

114. Stands in Timber and Liberty, *Cheyenne Memories,* 282–283. In later years, Crows gave away thoroughbred racehorses and even cars. Ibid. The Northern Cheyenne woman Belle Highwalking recalled visits to Crow Agency and a trip to Pryor on the west end of the reservation, where gifts were "heaped in the middle of the dance ground," including shawls, quilts, dress goods, and horses. Weist, *Belle Highwalking,* 2.

115. Red Cloud, Spotted Elk, Young Man Afraid of His Horses, Poor Elk, and Charging Cat to Plenty Killer [Plenty Coups], Old Man, Crane Bull, Old Whiteman, and Deaf Bear, January 6, 1906, Plenty Coups Papers, Plenty Coups State Park, Pryor, Mont.

116. Stands in Timber and Liberty, *Cheyenne Memories,* 281.

117. Thomas B. Marquis diary, June 22, 1926, Microform copy in possession of Margot Liberty, Sheridan, Wyoming. It should be noted that neither the Bannock nor the Nez Perce had any special connection to the battle or its anniversary; they just happened to be visiting Crow at the time of the event.

118. Wyman to Brown, May 25, 1893, RG 75, Crow, Box 16, book 38, NARA-Denver.

119. J. W. Watson to U.S. Indian Agent, June 11, 1894, Watson to Capt. Charles G. Perry, August 13, 1894, both RG 75, Crow, Box 16, book 40, NARA-Denver.

120. Watson to Perry, May 31, 1895, RG 75, Crow, Box 16, book 40, NARA-Denver.

121. Watson to U.S. Indian Agent, Cheyenne River, May 5, 1896, Watson to Chief Standing Bear, May 9, 1896, Watson to Spotted Elk, June 22, 1896, Watson to Capt. George Stouch, June 26, 1896, all RG 75, Crow, Box 17, book 44, NARA-Denver. Earlier in the spring, Watson had complained to an agency farmer that the Crows on the southern portion of the reservation needed a "thorough shaking up." "They should do 6 days work out of 7 but are more likely to do 1 of 7," he wrote. "Let them know there is a guard house here for all who won't or don't work." Wyman to A. A. Campbell, April 8, 1896, RG 75, Crow, Box 17, book 43, NARA-Denver.

122. Watson to Henry Keiser, June 24, 1897, RG 75, Crow, Box 18, book 46, NARA-Denver. By 1900, at least eight American holidays were celebrated by the Crows, including Christmas/New Year's, George Washington's birthday, Easter, spring planting, Decoration Day, the Fourth of July, harvest, and Thanksgiving. Hoxie, *Parading through History,* 210. Holidays could also be used as a cover for otherwise prohibited or restricted activities. At Tongue River, the Cheyenne Sun Dance (often referred to obliquely as Willow Dance) was often held in conjunction with the Fourth of July, even though the ritual was officially proscribed by the Indian Office. John R. Eddy to CIA, November 11, 1911, RG 75, Northern Cheyenne, Box 13; "Council Proceedings, Lame Deer, Montana," October 22, 1914, RG 75, Northern Cheyenne, Box 29, both NARA-Denver.

123. Samuel R. Reynolds to J. C. Clifford, December 20, 1902, RG 75, Crow, Box 21, book 27, NARA-Denver.

124. Reynolds to Rev. William A. Petzholdt, December 10, 1904, RG 75, Crow, Box 23, book 33; Reynolds to CIA, March 13, 1906, RG 75, Crow, Box 7, book 2, both NARA-Denver; Hoxie, *Parading through History,* 207. For Catholic missionary activity at Tongue River, see Schrems, "Northern Cheyenne," 18–33; and Sr. Saint Angela Louise Abair, "Mustard Seed."

125. Annual Report of St. Xavier's Industrial Boarding School, November 4, 1891, St. Francis Xavier Collection, Box 768, OPA, Society of Jesus, Gonzaga University, Spokane, Washington. For Prando's work at Crow, see Engh, "Peter Paul Prando," 24–31.

126. St. Francis Xavier House diaries for 1893–1898 and 1898–1908, Box 767, OPA, Gonzaga University. Until priests became proficient in Crow (and Crows in English), there is evidence they used other languages that members of their congregations were familiar with; the St. Xavier house diary for June 18, 1893, notes that Father Peter Bandini preached "in English and Nez Perce." The activity of Indian lay missionaries deserves further study. Pine Ridge was a center of lay missionary travel to other reservations; a Jesuit there argued that Indian proficiency in sign language would speed transmission of the Gospel, stating, "I think they could do more good in a way than many a priest." Oglala Catholic lay missionaries visited the Wind River, Winnebago, Sisseton, and other Lakota reservations in the early 1900s; however, I have been unable to determine whether any made official trips to Crow. For a good summary of the lay missionary activities of the Oglala holy man Nicholas Black Elk, see Demallie, *Sixth Grandfather,* 16–24. Baptist missionaries also brought converts from other tribes to meetings at Crow, according to Agnes Yellowtail Deernose. Voget, *They Call Me Agnes,* 197.

127. Thomas B. Marquis diary, December 24, 1925.

128. Hoxie, *Parading through History,* 198–208,

129. Sam Lapointe, Farmers Weekly Report, December 2, 1922, RG 75, Crow, Box 87, folder 139, NARA-Denver.

130. Charles H. Burke to Rev. William Hughes, n.d., RG 75, Crow, Box 83, folder 131; E. B. Meritt to Charles H. Asbury, March 8, 1924, and Asbury to CIA, January 29, 1924, both RG 75, Crow, Box 92, folder 200, all NARA-Denver.

131. Demallie, *Sixth Grandfather,* 19.

132. Reynolds to Capt. C. G. Hall, December 20, 1906, RG 75, Crow, Box 24, book 37, NARA-Denver; *ARCIA, 1906* (Washington, D.C.: Government Printing Office, 1906), 16–23.

133. Reynolds to CIA, September 29, 1908, RG 75, Box 8, book 20; Reynolds to Crazy Bear, June 30, 1908, RG 75, Box 25, book 45, both NARA-Denver.

134. Hoxie, *Parading through History,* 306–307.

135. Mrs. E. A. Richardson, "The Crow Indian Fair," *Yellowstone Monthly,* December 1907, copy in Eloise Whitebear Pease Collection, Box 8, folder 3, Little Big Horn College Archives, Crow Agency, Montana.

136. Hoxie, *Parading through History,* 307. In 1914, an assistant commissioner of Indian affairs recommended to the Crow superintendent that he coordinate the date of the Crow fair with Lakota fairs in South Dakota to discourage members of each tribe from attending the others' fair. E. B. Meritt to Evan W. Estep, July 31, 1914, RG 75, Central Classified Files, Crow, file 47, 80454–1914, NARA-DC. Thomas Yellowtail (Crow) noted that it became "harder to get together in the late 1910s and 1920," but attributed this development to World War I. Fitzgerald, *Yellowtail,* 25–26.

137. Woodenlegs, *Northern Cheyenne Album,* contains numerous pictures of Crows and Northern Cheyennes at Busby and Lame Deer (both on the Northern Cheyenne Reservation) and at the Crow fair, including photos of hand game competitions, horse races, and camp scenes. In many pictures, Crows and Northern Cheyennes can be distinguished by their different hair styles and modes of dress. See also Superintendent's Diary, September 30, and October 2 and 3, 1916, RG 75, Crow, Box 156; Asbury to Farmers, September 22, 1921, and C. F. Russell to Crow Indian Agent, August 9, 1924, both RG 75, Crow, Box 82, folder 129, all NARA-Denver.

138. Fitzgerald, *Yellowtail,* 25.

139. Marquis diary, September 5, 1925. Marquis also noted intertribal baseball matches between Northern Cheyenne and Crow teams. Ibid., April 26, 1926.

140. Stands in Timber and Liberty, *Cheyenne Memories,* 284–285. On hand games, see Lowie, *Crow Indians,* 98–99.

141. Agonito, "Young Man Afraid of His Horses," 129.

142. Wissler, *Indian Cavalcade,* 344.

143. Letters (both in English and in languages such as Lakota) were a key contributor to the spread of the Ghost Dance. Mooney, *Ghost Dance Religion,* 780–782, 788.

144. Red Cloud, Spotted Elk, Young Man Afraid of His Horses, Poor Elk, and Changing Cat to Plenty Killer [Plenty Coups], Old Man, Crane Bull, Old Whiteman, and Deaf Bear, January 6, 1906, Plenty Coups Papers, Plenty Coups State Park, Pryor, Montana.

145. Heap of Bears to Dear Friend Plenty Coups, May 1, 1909, Plenty Coups Papers, Plenty Coups State Park, Pryor, Montana.

146. Bull Calf to Plenty Coups, February 10, 1905, Plenty Coups Papers, Plenty Coups State Park, Pryor, Montana.

147. Bull Calf to Plenty Coups, March 5, 1906, Plenty Coups Papers, Plenty Coups State Park, Pryor, Montana.

148. There were occasions when intertribal coordination and treaty rights did prove compatible. One example that deserves further study is that of the Black Hills Treaty Council, comprising signatories to the Fort Laramie Treaty of 1868 affected by the United States' seizure of the Black Hills in 1875. Participants in the Treaty Council included representatives from the Rosebud, Pine Ridge, Lower Brule, Crow Creek, Cheyenne River, and Standing Rock Lakota reservations; the Northern Cheyenne; the Northern Arapaho from Wind River Reservation; and the Santee Sioux. One of the few discussions of the Council's activities is Lazarus, *Black Hills, White Justice*, 119–149.

149. Calvin H. Asbury to Superintendent, January 19, 1925, Finds Them and Kills Them to Asbury, February 2, 1925, and Dan C. Pettibone to Asbury, February 28, 1925, all RG 75, Crow, Box 91, folder 153, NARA-Denver.

150. Asbury to Superintendent, January 19, 1925, RG 75, Crow, Box 91, folder 153, NARA-Denver.

151. Williams, *The Spirit and the Flesh*, 178–180; Lowie, *Crow Indians*, 48.

152. Roscoe, "That Is My Road," 54.

153. Ibid., 47–48, 54.

154. Ibid., 55.

CHAPTER FOUR. A NEW WORLD OF WORK

1. Marquis, *A Warrior Who Fought Custer*, 348–349.

2. Ibid., 353–354.

3. Ibid., 356. Despite his response to Crows at the 1909 council, Wooden Leg may have attended the fiftieth anniversary commemoration of the Battle of the Little Bighorn in 1926. Woodenlegs, *Northern Cheyenne Album*.

4. John E. Edwards to James C. Clifford, November 22, 1899, RG 75, Crow, Box 20, book 18, NARA-Denver; "Report of Irregular Employees at Crow Irrigation Survey, September 1897," RG 75, LR-OIA, 43628–1897, NARA-DC. Wooden Leg may also appear as "Strong Legs" in the irrigation reports for May and June 1897 and August 1896, and as "Woman Leggings" in the irrigation report for October 1896. "Report of Irregular Employees at Crow Irrigation Survey, May 1897," RG 75, LR-OIA 24498–1897; "Report of Irregular Employees at Crow Irrigation Survey, June 1897," RG 75, LR-OIA 28840–1897; "Report of Irregular Employees at Crow Irrigation Survey, August 1896," RG 75, LR-OIA 36315–1896; "Report of Irregular Employees at Crow Irrigation Survey, November 1896," RG 75, LR-OIA 48088–1896, all NARA-DC.

5. Smits, "Squaw Drudge," 281. The failure to consider Indians' productive activities as work is another example of what Robert H. Berkhofer called the "deficient Indian." Berkhofer, *White Man's Indian*, 25–30. See also Usner, *Indian Work*, 10–23. For Indian participation in the fur trade, see Jablow, *Cheyenne in Plains Indian Trade Relations;* Ray and Freeman, *"Give Us Good Measure";* Wishart, *Fur Trade*, 92–100.

6. Lewis, *Neither Wolf nor Dog;* Carlson, *Indians, Bureaucrats;* Thomas R. Wessel, "Agent of Acculturation: Farming on the Northern Plains Reservations, 1880–1910," *Agricultural History* 60, 2 (Spring, 1986), 233–245. For specific reservations see Thomas R. Wessel, "Agriculture on the Reservations: The Case of the Blackfeet, 1885–1930," *Journal of the West* 18, 4 (Octo-

ber, 1979), 17–23; Svingen, "Reservation Self-Sufficiency"; Hoxie, *Parading through History,* 278–281.

7. Vicki Page, "Reservation Development in the United States: Peripherality in the Core," *American Indian Culture and Research Journal* 9, 3 (1985), 21–35; Thomas D. Hall, "Peripheries, Regions of Refuge, and Nonstate Societies: Toward a Theory of Reactive Social Change," *Social Science Quarterly* 64, 3 (September, 1983), 587–591; Thomas D. Hall, "Native Americans and Incorporation: Patterns and Problems," *American Indian Culture and Research Journal* 11, 2 (1987), 1–23; White, *Roots of Dependency,* xv–xix; Littlefield and Knack, *Native Americans and Wage Labor,* 11–12

8. On World War II, see Bernstein, *American Indians and World War II,* 86–88, 171–175; Townsend, *World War II and the American Indian,* 170–193, 215–228. For relocation and urban work experiences see Fixico, *Urban Indian Experience,* 123–124, 172–189. On Wild West shows, see Moses, *Wild West Shows,* and Ellis, "Five Dollars a Week."

9. See, for example, O'Neill, *Working the Navajo Way;* Hosmer, *American Indians in the Marketplace;* Littlefield and Knack, *Native Americans and Wage Labor;* Bauer, *"We Were All Like Migrant Workers Here."*

10. Although agents continued to encourage the Northern Cheyenne to plant crops, the results were usually disappointing. In 1902, for example, Agent James C. Clifford reported that planting had been delayed by the late arrival of seed. Those crops that were planted were then damaged by a summer dry spell and a killing frost on June 20 that "destroyed almost all of the gardens and most of the corn." On August 8, a hailstorm destroyed crops on the Rosebud, and a storm one week later destroyed half the alfalfa and grass on the reservation, while grasshoppers consumed all the grass in the Tongue River Valley. As a result, Clifford wrote with considerable understatement, the condition of the Northern Cheyenne was "not what it should be if the climatic conditions during the past summer had been more favorable." Clifford to CIA, October 10, 1902, RG 75, Northern Cheyenne, Box 10, book 3, NARA-Denver; Upshaw to CIA, August 24, 1886, *ARCIA, 1886,* House Exec. Doc. 1, 49th Congress, 2nd session, Serial 2467, 403; Upshaw to CIA, August 18, 1888, *ARCIA, 1888,* House Exec. Doc. 1, 50th Congress, 2nd session, Serial 2637, 165–166; Campbell, "Changing Patterns," 344.

11. Upshaw to CIA, August 18, 1888, *ARCIA, 1888,* 165–166.

12. Upshaw to J. D. C. Atkins, July 13, 1888, RG 75, Northern Cheyenne, Box 10, book 2, NARA-Denver. For efforts to have the Tongue River Reservation disestablished, see Svingen, *Northern Cheyenne Indian Reservation,* 49–75.

13. Upshaw to CIA, August 24, 1886, *ARCIA, 1886,* 403; Upshaw to CIA, August 19, 1889, *ARCIA, 1889,* House Exec. Doc. 1, 51st Congress, 1st session, Serial 2725, 235; Upshaw to CIA, August 24, 1887, *ARCIA, 1887,* House Exec. Doc. 1, 50th Congress, 1st session, Serial 2542, 229–230.

14. George W. H. Stouch to CIA, September 21, 1895, *ARCIA, 1895,* House Doc 5, 54th Congress, 1st session, Serial 3382, 197–199.

15. Ibid.

16. Ibid.

17. See, for example, Upshaw to CIA, August 18, 1888, *ARCIA, 1888,* 165–167.

18. The Northern Pacific Railroad reached Billings in 1883. The Chicago, Burlington, and Quincy (sometimes locally called the Burlington and Missouri) reached Huntley on the Missouri River (then the northern border of the Crow Reservation) in 1894. Hoxie, *Parading through History,* 174; Overton, *Burlington Route,* 229.

19. For the preference for Crow Agency as a freight terminus, see C. F. Larrabee to Super-

intendent, Tongue River School, June 22, 1905, RG 75, Northern Cheyenne, Box 9; and Eddy to CIA, April 3, 1911, RG 75, Northern Cheyenne, Box 13, both NARA-Denver.

20. C. F. Larrabee to Superintendent, Tongue River School, June 22, 1905, RG 75, Northern Cheyenne, Box 9.

21. For samples of lists of Cheyenne freighters, see Becker to Clifford, May 12, 1899, RG 75, Crow, Box 19, book 16; Edwards to U.S. Indian Agent, July 10, 1899, and Edwards to Clifford, November 22, 1899, both RG 75, Crow, Box 20, book 18; Edwards to Clifford, February 13, 1900, RG 75, Crow, Box 20, book 19, all NARA-Denver. On Porcupine, see Eddy to CIA, July 24, 1909, RG 75, Northern Cheyenne, Box 13, NARA-Denver. In 1900, Agent Clifford ordered Porcupine arrested for leaving the reservation to allegedly conduct Ghost Dance meetings at Wind River Reservation. As a result, Porcupine was jailed at Fort Keogh from October 22, 1900, until March 28, 1901. However, his continued alleged involvement with the Ghost Dance was apparently not seen as an obstacle to his work as a teamster. Clifford to U.S. Indian Agent, June 23, 1900, RG 75, Northern Cheyenne, Box 16, book 2, NARA-Denver. For Wooden Leg, see, "Request for Leave," n.d., RG 75, Northern Cheyenne, Box 5, NARA-Denver; and Marquis, *A Warrior Who Fought Custer.* For Willis Rowland, see Eddy to CIA, May 6, 1907, RG 75, Northern Cheyenne, Box 11, book 2, NARA-Denver.

22. John A. Buntin to W. M. Barnhart, August 25, 1915, RG 75, Northern Cheyenne, Box 10, NARA-Denver.

23. Clifford to Agent, Burlington and Missouri Railroad, April 12, 1901, and Clifford to A. J. Davidson, Montana Hide Company, July 24, 1901, both RG 75, Northern Cheyenne, Box 16, book 2, NARA-Denver.

24. See Eddy, "Transported Lumber to Crow Agency," n.d., RG 75, Northern Cheyenne, Box 14, NARA-Denver. In 1908, the Northern Cheyenne sold 50,000 board feet of lumber to Crow Agency at $24 per 1,000 board foot. An Indian Office official noted there was "no margin of profit on the deal but the Indians will get the benefit of logging the timber and hauling the freight." Cross to Forester, October 14, 1908, RG 75, Northern Cheyenne, Box 19, book 1; see also Eddy to Samuel G. Reynolds, December 14, 1906, RG 75, Northern Cheyenne, Box 19, both NARA-Denver. In 1912, Northern Cheyenne sawmills produced 500,000 board feet of lumber. Eddy to CIA, January 29, 1914, RG 74, Box 27, NARA-Denver.

25. For links between freighting and visiting, see Clifford to Edwards, October 4, 1901, Northern Cheyenne, Box 16, book 2, NARA-Denver. On trading, see Eddy to E. A. Richardson, June 18, 1912, RG 75, Northern Cheyenne, Box 23, and Eddy to E. A. Richardson and Co., October 4, 1912, RG 75, Northern Cheyenne, Box 24, both NARA-Denver.

26. Eddy to CIA, November 19, November 27, and December 3, 1907, all RG 75, Northern Cheyenne, Box 17; Eddy to CIA, December 8, 1908, RG 75, Northern Cheyenne, Box 12; Eddy to Maj. M. Gray Zelinki, December 17, 1909, Eddy to W. H. H. Garritt, March 12, 1909, and "Agreement with Bearcomesout and Abram Yelloweyes," March 26, 1909, RG 75, Northern Cheyenne, Box 20, all NARA-Denver.

27. Eddy to W. W. Scott, June 4, 1913, RG 75, Northern Cheyenne, Box 26, NARA-Denver.

28. Eddy to J. A. Nelson, July 25, August 7, and August 17, 1907, all RG 75, Northern Cheyenne, Box 11, book 1, NARA-Denver.

29. *ARCIA, 1890*, House Exec. Doc. 1, 51st Congress, 2nd session, Serial 2841, 454–455; *ARCIA, 1891*, House Exec. Doc. 1, 52nd Congress, 1st session, Serial 2934, 763; *ARCIA, 1892*, 789–790; *ARCIA, 1893*, House Exec. Doc. 1, 53rd Congress, 2nd session, Serial 3210, 699; *ARCIA, 1894*, House Exec. Doc. 1, 53rd Congress, 2nd session, Serial 3306, 573–574; *ARCIA,*

1895, 569–570, *ARCIA, 1896*, House Doc. 5, 54th Congress, 2nd session, Serial 3489, 524–525; *ARCIA, 1897*, House Doc. 5, 55th Congress, 2nd session, Serial 3641, 487; *ARCIA, 1898*, House Doc. 5, 55th Congress, 3rd session, Serial 3757, 603–604.

30. Hoxie, *Parading through History,* 230–231, 282–285.

31. M. P. Wyman to CIA, October 22, 1891, *ARCIA, 1891,* 269.

32. Hoxie, *Parading through History,* 273–280; Edward H. Becker to William A. Jones, September 17, 1898, RG 75, Crow, Box 5, book 1; Becker to Jones, January 14, 1899, RG 75, Crow, Box 5, book 10; John E. Edwards to CIA, August 27, 1900, RG 75, Crow, Box 5, book 11, all NARA-Denver.

33. Eddy to John Small, November 5, 1910, RG 75, Northern Cheyenne, Box 22; John A. Buntin to W. M. Barnhart, August 25, 1915, RG 75, Northern Cheyenne, Box 10, both NARA-Denver.

34. Henry J. Armstrong to CIA, August 31, 1884, *ARCIA, 1884*, House Exec. Doc. 1, 48th Congress, 2nd session, Serial 2287, 154; Armstrong to CIA, November 22, 1884, RG 75, LR-OIA, Special Case 190, Crow Irrigation, NARA-DC.

35. Hoxie, *Parading through History,* 274–275; Clyde E. Lewis to E. B. Linen, August 27, 1914, RG 75, Crow, Box 221, NARA-Denver.

36. Hoxie, *Parading through History,* 274–280, describes the impact and expense of irrigation. For maintenance charges, see Lewis to B. A. Achenbach, August 2, 1915, RG 75, Crow, Box 222, NARA-Denver.

37. Wessel, "Agriculture on the Reservations," 19, describes reservation irrigation projects as irrational exercises that eventually "became an end in itself without direction and without discernable benefit to the Tribe." See also Pisani, "Irrigation, Water Rights"; Carlson, "Economics and Politics."

38. The literature on Indian attitudes toward irrigation is comparatively sparse. McMillen's "Rain, Ritual, and Reclamation" argues that irrigation failed to convert the Navajo from a pastoral to an agricultural economy because "Indians would not accommodate Progressive Era reclamation efforts on religious, cultural, and material grounds" (437). Peterson, in "Headgates and Conquest," also emphasizes Indian reluctance to force massive changes upon nature, rather than Indian attitudes toward the actual work of irrigation construction.

39. See, for example, "Report of Irregular Employees at Crow Irrigation Survey for Month Ending June 30, 1893," RG 75, LR-OIA, 32785–1893, NARA-DC.

40. Funding for irrigation construction did not come from federal largesse; the money came from funds already due the tribe from land sales and other sources. Hoxie, *Parading through History,* 274–278.

41. Wage rates are from the 1893 monthly reports of irregular employees. By 1900, wages had risen to $4 for a team wheel scraper, $3.50 for a team drag scraper, and $1.75 for common day labor.

42. "Verbatim Report of a Council Held at the Irrigation Ditch Camp, Big Horn Valley, Crow Indian Reservation, Montana, October 28, 1895," RG 75, LR-OIA, SC 190 Crow Irrigation, NARA-DC.

43. Walter Graves to CIA, August 9, 1895, RG 75, LR-OIA, SC 190, Crow Irrigation, NARA-DC.

44. "Verbatim Report of a Council Held at the Irrigation Ditch Camp, Big Horn Valley, Crow Indian Reservation, Montana, October 28, 1895," RG 75, LR-OIA, SC 190 Crow Irrigation, NARA-DC.

45. Watson to CIA, September 18, 1895, *ARCIA, 1895*, 183–184.

46. John Lewis to Thomas P. Magee, August 20, 1910, RG 75, Crow, Box 47, folder 1; Richard Sanderville to W. W. Scott, July 25, 1910, RG 75, Crow, Box 47, folder 2, both NARA-Denver.

47. Hoxie, *Parading through History,* 267.

48. See, for example, "Report of Irregular Employees at Crow Irrigation Survey for Month Ending April 30, 1898," RG 75, LR-OIA, 23746–1898, NARA-DC.

49. The monthly irrigation labor reports are found scattered throughout RG 75, Letters Received, Office of Indian Affairs, NARA-DC.

50. "Report of Irregular Employees at Crow Irrigation Survey for Month Ending September 30th, 1897," RG 75, LR-OIA, 43628–1897, NARA-DC.

51. "Report of Irregular Employees at Crow Irrigation Survey for Month Ending July 31st, 1893," RG 75, LR-OIA, 41782–1893, NARA-DC.

52. Walter H. Graves to CIA, October 25, 1892, RG 75, LR-OIA, SC 190, Crow Irrigation, NARA-DC.

53. For Red Hat, see Powell, *People of the Sacred Mountain,* 1019, 1074. "Report of Irregular Employees at Crow Irrigation Survey for Month Ending October 31st, 1894," RG 75, LR-OIA, 45874–1894, and "Report of Irregular Employees at Crow Irrigation Survey for Month Ending November 30th, 1894," RG 75, LR-OIA, 3792–1895, both NARA-DC.

54. "Report of Irregular Employees at Crow Irrigation Survey for Month Ending April 30th, 1895," RG 75, LR-OIA, 25407–1895, NARA-DC; Tongue River Indian Census, 1891, RG 75, Indian Census Rolls, NARA Microform 595, roll 574. An Arthur and Eugene Standing Elk are also listed among the Cheyenne freighters hauling flour from Crow in 1899. John E. Edwards to James C. Clifford, November 22, 1899, RG 75, Crow, Box 20, book 18, NARA-Denver. On Standing Elk, see Marquis, *Cheyennes of Montana,* 72–73; Svingen, *Northern Cheyenne Indian Reservation,* 18–19, 22, 92. For St. Labre and Eugene Standing Elk, see Schrems, "Northern Cheyenne," 21–22, and Woodenlegs, *Northern Cheyenne Album,* 144.

55. "Report of Irregular Employees at Crow Irrigation Survey for Month Ending August 31st, 1896," RG 75, LR-OIA, 36315–1896; "Report of Irregular Employees at Crow Irrigation Survey for Month Ending October 31st, 1896," RG 75, LR-OIA, 48088–1896; "Report of Irregular Employees at Crow Irrigation Survey for Month Ending November 30th, 1896," RG 75, LR-OIA, 48441–1896, all NARA-DC. For Limpy and Mrs. Limpy, see Liberty, *A Northern Cheyenne Album,* 50–51. For Wild Hog, see Powell, *People of the Sacred Mountain,* 1149–1152; Epps, *"State of Kansas"*; Svingen, *Northern Cheyenne Indian Reservation,* 18–24. Woman Leggings appears on an 1899 list of Northern Cheyenne freighters. See Edwards to Clifford, November 22, 1899, RG 75, Crow, Box 20, book 18, NARA-Denver.

56. "Report of Irregular Employees at Crow Irrigation Survey for Month Ending September 30th 1897," RG 75, LR-OIA, 43628–1897; "Report of Irregular Employees at Crow Irrigation Survey for Month Ending October 31st 1897," RG 75, LR-OIA, 51601–1897; "Report of Irregular Employees at Crow Irrigation Survey for Month Ending November 30, 1897," RG 75, LR-OIA, 2368–1898, all NARA-DC. Unfortunately the monthly employee report for August 1897 is missing. An eighteen-year-old Charles Roman Nose and a twenty-one-year-old Frank Standing Elk are listed on the 1891 Tongue River Indian Census, RG 75, Indian Census Rolls, NARA Microform 595, roll 574. For Howling Wolf, see Stands in Timber and Liberty, *Cheyenne Memories,* 223, 257.

57. "Report of Irregular Employees at Crow Irrigation Survey for Month Ending October 31st, 1896," RG 75, LR-OIA, 48088–1896; "Report of Irregular Employees at Crow Irrigation

Survey for Month Ending November 30th, 1896," RG 75, LR-OIA, 48441–1896; "Report of Irregular Employees at Crow Irrigation Survey for Month Ending September 30th 1897," RG 75, LR-OIA, 43628–1897, all NARA-DC.

58. "Report of Irregular Employees at Crow Irrigation Survey for Month Ending February 29th 1896," RG 75, LR-OIA, 10966–1896; "Report of Irregular Employees at Crow Irrigation Survey for Month Ending May 31st, 1896," RG 75, LR-OIA, 24084–1896; "Report of Irregular Employees at Crow Irrigation Survey for Month Ending October 30th, 1896," RG 75, LR-OIA, 48088–1896; "Report of Irregular Employees at Crow Irrigation Survey for Month Ending November 30st, 1896," RG 75, LR-OIA, 48441–1896; "Report of Irregular Employees at Crow Irrigation Survey for Month Ending Dec. 31st, 1896," RG 75, LR-OIA, 800–1897; "Report of Irregular Employees at Crow Irrigation Survey for Month Ending May 31st, 1897," RG 75, LR-OIA, 24498–1897; "Report of Irregular Employees at Crow Irrigation Survey for Month Ending June 30th, 1897," RG 75, LR-OIA, 28840–1897; "Report of Irregular Employees at Crow Irrigation Survey for Month Ending July 31st, 1897," RG 75, LR-OIA, 33506–1897; "Report of Irregular Employees at Crow Irrigation Survey for Month Ending May 31st, 1898," RG 75, LR-OIA, 28266–1898; "Report of Irregular Employees at Crow Irrigation Survey for Month Ending June 30th, 1898," RG 75, LR-OIA, 32362–1898; "Report of Irregular Employees at Crow Irrigation Survey for Month Ending July 31st, 1898," RG 75, LR-OIA, 37568–1898; "Report of Irregular Employees at Crow Irrigation Survey for Month Ending June 30, 1900," RG 75, LR-OIA, 34397–1900; "Report of Irregular Employees at Crow Irrigation Survey for Month Ending July 31st, 1900," RG 75, LR-OIA, 39076–1900; "Report of Irregular Employees at Crow Irrigation Survey for Month Ending September 30th, 1900," RG 75, LR-OIA, 49651–1900; "Report of Irregular Employees at Crow Irrigation Survey for Month Ending May 31st, 1901," RG 75, LR-OIA, 30977–1901; "Report of Irregular Employees at Crow Irrigation Survey for Month Ending April 30th, 1902," RG 75, LR-OIA, 29034–1902; "Report of Irregular Employees at Crow Irrigation Survey for Month Ending June 30th, 1902," RG 75, LR-OIA, 42146–1902; "Report of Irregular Employees at Crow Irrigation Survey for Month Ending May 31st, 1903," RG 75, LR-OIA, 35795–1903, all NARA-DC. Between 1896 and 1903 the only year in which Seminole is not listed as doing ditch work is 1899; however, only three monthly reports for that year (October, November, and December) survive. For Seminole's background, see the correspondence in file 75540–1906, RG 75, LR-OIA, NARA-DC.

59. S. L. Taggart to CIA, March 6, 1905, RG 75, LR-OIA, 19413–1905, NARA-DC. For more on the Rowland family see Stands in Timber and Liberty, *Cheyenne Memories*, 238–239; and Liberty, *A Northern Cheyenne Album*, 254–255.

60. "Report of Irregular Employees at Crow Irrigation Survey for Month Ending September 30th 1897," RG 75, LR-OIA, 43628–1897; "Report of Irregular Employees at Crow Irrigation Survey for Month Ending October 31st 1897," RG 75, LR-OIA, 51601–1897; "Report of Irregular Employees at Crow Irrigation Survey for Month Ending November 30, 1897," RG 75, LR-OIA, 2368–1898, all NARA-DC.

61. For samples of Cheyenne freighters who also appear on irrigation employee reports, see Edwards to U.S. Indian Agent, Tongue River, July 10, 1899 (William Rowland and Howling Wolf), and Edwards to Clifford, November 22, 1899 (Wooden Leg, Frank Standing Elk, Willis Rowland, Woman Leggings, Arthur Standing Elk, and Eugene Standing Elk), both RG 75, Crow, Box 20, book 18, NARA-Denver.

62. John E. Edwards to J. W. Collins, January 8, 1900, RG 75, Crow, Box 20, book 19; "Historical Data on Canals and Ditches," n.d., RG 75, Crow, Box 244, both NARA-Denver.

63. W. W. Scott to CIA, February 5, 1912, RG 75, Crow, Box 54, NARA-Denver.

64. Hogue, "Disputing the Medicine Line"; Burt, "Nowhere Left to Go" and "In a Crooked Piece of Time."

65. Dusenberry, *Montana Cree*, 34–41. Dusenberry notes that the Blackfeet, for one, made the Crees feel "inferior and unwanted" (43).

66. Superintendent's Annual Report, 1910, RG 75, NARA Microform 1011, roll 30.

67. Samuel G. Reynolds to CIA, August 28, 1908, RG 75, Crow, Box 8, book 20; John E. Edwards to J. W. Collins, January 8, 1900, RG 75, Box 20, book 19, both NARA-Denver.

68. Reynolds to Dr. W. A. Allen, August 6, 1903, RG 75, Crow, Box 22, book 29; Reynolds to J. H. Young, November 5, 1909, RG 75, Crow, Box 26, book 51, both NARA-Denver.

69. W. W. Scott to CIA, February 5, 1912, RG 75, Crow, Box 54, NARA-Denver.

70. Ira R. Bauker to Joseph Dussome, August 16, 1910, RG 75, Crow, Box 47, folder 4, NARA-Denver.

71. J. W. Watson to Gov. John E. Edwards, May 2, 1896, and Watson to Richards, May 16, 1896, both RG 75, Crow, Box 17, book 44; Reynolds to CIA, August 22, 1908, RG 75, Crow, Box 8, book 20, all NARA-Denver.

72. In 1909, before another sweep of the reservation, Reynolds told the district farmer at St. Xavier that he had no intention of removing Crees doing work from the reservation, "only those merely stopping here and there with no visible means of support." Reynolds to J. H. Young, November 5, 1909, RG 75, Crow, Box 26, book 51, NARA-Denver. For more on Crees at Crow, see Chapter 5.

73. Spotted Rabbit to Mr. Edwards, April 18, 1900, RG 75, Crow, Box 37, NARA-Denver.

74. "Report of Irregular Employees at Crow Irrigation Survey for Month Ending June 30th, 1900," RG 75, LR-OIA, 34397–1900; "Report of Irregular Employees at Crow Irrigation Survey for Month Ending July 31st, 1900," RG 75, LR-OIA, 39076–1900. For Charles Means's background, see Chapter 6.

75. For the percentage of work done and wages paid to Native Americans, see Graves to CIA, October 10, 1894, and W. B. Hill to CIA, February 20, 1902, both RG 75, LR-OIA, SC 190, Crow Irrigation, NARA-DC.

76. "Verbatim Report of a Council Held at the Irrigation Ditch Camp, Big Horn Valley, Crow Indian Reservation, Montana, October 28, 1895," RG 75, LR-OIA, SC 190, Crow Irrigation, NARA-DC.

77. "Transcript of Council at Crow Agency, May 31, 1899," RG 75, LR-OIA, 27761–1899; see also Plenty Coups to CIA, June 10, 1899, RG 75, LR-OIA, 22111–1899, both NARA-DC.

78. "Verbatim Report of a Council Held at the Irrigation Ditch Camp, Big Horn Valley, Crow Indian Reservation, Montana, October 28, 1895," RG 75, LR-OIA, SC 190, Crow Irrigation, NARA-DC.

79. See, for example, Thomas Sharp to CIA, August 18, 1893, RG 75, LR-OIA, 32142–1893, NARA-DC. For more on the proposals to relocate the Northern Cheyenne to Crow, see Chapter 6, "The Limits of Community."

80. "Report of Irregular Employees at Crow Irrigation Survey for Month Ending September 30, 1897," RG 75, LR-OIA, 43628–1897, NARA-DC.

81. For a full discussion of proposals to adopt Crees into the Crow tribe, see Chapter 6.

82. Stewart, *Peyote Religion*, 3, 17–30, 45–106.

83. Stewart, "Peyotism in Montana," 6–7; Stewart, *Peyote Religion*, 104–105, 183; La Barre, *Peyote Cult*, 114–115. In the 1956 reissue of *The Crow Indians*, Robert H. Lowie dated the arrival of peyote at Crow to about 1912. Lowie, *Crow Indians*, vii.

84. Stewart, "Peyotism in Montana," 7. Frederick Hoxie accepts Stewart's date of 1910 for the arrival of peyote at Crow but does not discuss the reason for the apparent twenty-year gap between its arrival at Tongue River and at Crow. Hoxie, *Parading through History,* 219.

85. John A. Buntin to John H. Wilson, October 5, 1917, RG 75, Northern Cheyenne, Box 38, folder 102, NARA-Denver.

86. An obituary of Leonard Tyler in the January 2, 1913, edition of the *Indian Helper* (Carlisle, Pa.), contained in the Omer Stewart Papers, gives the maiden name of Tyler's wife as Jennie Black. Omer C. Stewart Papers, Box 51, Southern Cheyenne folder, University of Colorado, Boulder. For a reference to Ed Black being in the ditch camp in 1897, see Watson to Graves, September 1, 1897, RG 75, Crow, Box 18, book 46, NARA-Denver. In 1898, Black worked as a laborer for four and a half days in May, and he drove a drag scraper for nine days in June and sixteen days in July. Tyler is listed as a laborer for ten days in July. The Northern Cheyenne Jules Seminole is also listed as a ditch worker during the summer of 1898. "Report of Irregular Employees at Crow Irrigation Survey for Month Ending May 31, 1898," RG 75, LR-OIA, 28266–1898; "Report of Irregular Employees at Crow Irrigation Survey for Month Ending June 30, 1898," RG 75, LR-OIA, 32362–1898; "Report of Irregular Employees at Crow Irrigation Survey for Month Ending July 31, 1898," RG 75, LR-OIA, 37568–1898, all NARA-DC. Black's first name is listed as both Ernie and Ed in correspondence and ditch records. I have been unable to locate the employee report for August 1898.

87. Watson to Graves, September 1, 1897, RG 75, Crow, Box 18, book 46; George Stouch to Clifford, June 17, 1898, RG 75, Crow, Box 19, both NARA-Denver.

88. Clifford to Becker, July 16, 1898, RG 75, Crow, Box 36, NARA-Denver.

89. Clifford to Becker, July 21, 1898, RG 75, Crow, Box 36, NARA-Denver.

90. Clifford to Becker, August 29, 1898, RG 75, Crow, Box 36, NARA-Denver.

91. Graves to CIA, November 2, 1897, RG 75, LR-OIA, 46699–1897, NARA-DC. Graves made no reference to the use of teepees or tents by Indian workers.

92. Thomas P. Smith to CIA, August 7, 1893, RG 75, LR-OIA, 30378–1893, NARA-DC.

93. For gambling, see Watson to CIA, December 22, 1894, RG 75, LR-OIA, 50726–1894, NARA-DC. Watson complained that gamblers "make their money by plying their nefarious trade among the Indians. Their operations are confined principally to workers, Indians and others, on the system of Irrigation Ditches now in process of construction. A very large percentage of the money disbursed to those ditch workers goes, every day, into the pockets of these 'tin horn' gamblers, whose position in the social scale and the scale of usefulness is at the very bottom." See also He Does It to Dear Sir, November 2, 1902, RG 75, Box 40, NARA-Denver. The card games He Does It described involved the transfer of horses and sacks of wheat between players. On whiskey, Inspector Smith stated that "whiskey and drunkenness have prevailed in the ditch camp and bootlegging is said to be growing up to a wholesale business." Smith to CIA, August 8, 1893, RG 75, LR-OIA, 30378–1893, NARA-DC. On prostitution, see W. B. Hill to CIA, May 25, 1900, RG 75, LR-OIA, SC 190, Crow Irrigation, NARA-DC. In response to charges of prostitution, Hill, the superintendent in charge of irrigation construction at the time, carefully enumerated all the white women present in the camp, but notably failed to mention whether any Indian women were in the camp or their activities.

94. Stewart, "Peyotism in Montana," 5.

95. Slotkin, *Peyote Religion,* 71.

96. E. Black to U.S. Indian Agent, August 22, 1898, RG 75, Crow, Box 36; Becker to Black, August 31, 1898, RG 75, Crow, Box 19, both NARA-Denver.

97. Becker to W. A. Jones, November 17, 1898, RG 75, Crow, Box 5, book 1, NARA-Denver.

98. Becker to Jones, November 21, 1898, RG 75, Crow, Box 5, book 1, NARA-Denver. I have been unable to locate any of the related correspondence from Jones to Becker, either in the letters received portion of the Crow Agency files at the Federal Records Center in Denver or in the OIA files at NARA-DC.

99. Bethune is credited with having received the ritual from the Northern Cheyenne. Stewart, "Peyotism in Montana," 7. Robert C. Kiste states that members of a small group of Crow peyotists (between six and twelve) were attending peyote meetings on the Northern Cheyenne Reservation in 1905 and 1906. Kiste, "Crow Peyotism," 1. Leroy White, a Crow peyotist, stated in an interview with Timothy McCleary that Crows occasionally held peyote for Northern Cheyennes before its adoption by the Crows. Leroy White interview with Timothy P. McCleary, December 27, 1995, in Timothy P. McCleary files, Hardin, Mont. Tyrone Ten Bear, another Crow peyotist, states that Austin Stray Calf, one of the early Crow peyotists, experienced a peyote vision sometime during the 1890s and participated in his first peyote meeting approximately five years later. Tyrone Ten Bear interview with Frank Rzeczkowski, August 8, 2001. Stray Calf's name does not appear on irrigation employee reports during any of the months in which Tyler and Black are listed. None of the first-generation Crow peyotists appear to have been asked whether they were acquainted with either Tyler or Black.

100. W. B. Hill to CIA, April 21, 1905, RG 75, LR-OIA, SC 190, Crow Irrigation, NARA-DC; Lewis to W. H. Code, February 22, 1909, RG 75, Crow, Box 220; Lewis to H. L. Oberlander, February 24, 1913, RG 75, Crow, Box 211, both NARA-Denver.

101. John McLeod, "Special Officer's Weekly Report," February 20, 1926, RG 75, Crow, Box 86, folder 139a; Charles H. Asbury to farmers, December 4, 1925, RG 75, Crow, Box 91, folder 153, both NARA-Denver.

102. For irrigation at Tongue River, see Clifford to U.S. District Attorney, Helena, May 13, 1903, RG 75, Northern Cheyenne, Box 16, book 4; Clifford to CIA, October 10, 1903, RG 75, Northern Cheyenne, Box 10, book 3; and Eddy to M. A. Carleton, October 21, 1907, RG 75, Northern Cheyenne, Box 18, all NARA-Denver. Unlike at Crow, Tongue River agents actively discouraged non-Cheyenne Indians from coming to Tongue River to work. In response to an inquiry from James Long, a Lakota from Cheyenne River, Agent John Eddy replied that work was only available for Northern Cheyennes. Eddy to Long, April 6, 1909, RG 75, Northern Cheyenne, Box 20, NARA-Denver. For off-reservation work, see Eddy to CIA, January 15, 1907, RG 75, Northern Cheyenne, Box 11, book 2; Eddy to E. E. McKean, March 13, 1909, and Eddy to Charles Daganett, March 13, 1909, both RG 75, Northern Cheyenne, Box 20, all NARA-Denver (beets); Eddy to E. E. Young, May 10, 1913, RG 75, Northern Cheyenne, Box 26; Clifford to F. G. Mattoon, July 7, September 5, and November 20, 1906, all RG 75, Northern Cheyenne, Box 17, book 6, NARA-Denver (railroad work); Eddy to Nelson, August 17, 1907, RG 75, Northern Cheyenne, Box 11, book 1, NARA-Denver (irrigation).

103. Eddy to Keiser, July 23, 1907, RG 75, Northern Cheyenne, Box 11, book 1, NARA-Denver; Eddy to George Farr, July 8, 1909; Eddy to Keiser, July 31, 1909; Eddy to Keiser, September 22, 1909; and Eddy to Daganett, n.d., all RG 75, Northern Cheyenne, Box 20, NARA-Denver.

104. Hoxie, *Final Promise,* ix–xiii.

105. Svingen, *Northern Cheyenne Indian Reservation,* 132–147.

106. As late as 1901, all the agency buildings at Tongue River were constructed of logs, with the exception of the agent's house, office, warehouse, and granary. "All the buildings need more or less repair," Agent James Clifford reported. The walls of the day school were settling, mak-

ing it impossible to fully open the doors. The blacksmith and wagon shops, Clifford wrote, "are in rather dangerous condition, having earth-covered roofs, which are rather heavy for the walls, causing them to press out; making it necessary to brace inside to keep the walls from falling; wagon sheds are in same condition. New shops and sheds should be built." Clifford to CIA, August 5, 1901, *ARCIA, 1901*, House Doc. 5, 57th Congress, 1st session, Serial 4290, 267.

107. Clifford to Roger C. Spooner, February 17, 1904, RG 75, Northern Cheyenne, Box 16, book 4; Farmer's Annual Report, O. D. District, May 25, 1915, RG 75, Northern Cheyenne, Box 19, folder 114, both NARA-Denver.

108. Superintendent to CIA, April 19, 1921, RG 75, Northern Cheyenne, Box 12, folder 243, NARA-Denver.

109. Eddy to CIA, May 31, 1907, RG 75, Northern Cheyenne, Box 11, book 2, NARA-Denver. Tongue River agents' continued attempts to cut ration rolls during the early 1900s met with little success. In January 1910, Eddy proclaimed his intention to cut all able-bodied Northern Cheyennes from the ration rolls by the end of the year. However, eight months later, only seventy-three "half-bloods" and three full bloods had been stricken from the list. Eddy cited the lack of local work in explaining the difficulty of removing able-bodied Cheyennes from the roll. Two years later, all the Northern Cheyenne remained dependent on rations, and in the early 1920, field matrons described the Cheyennes as suffering from malnutrition and "eating any old thing they find to eat." Eddy to Daganett, January 29, 1910, RG 75, Northern Cheyenne, Box 21, book 1; Eddy to CIA, September 14, 1910, RG 75, Northern Cheyenne, Box 13; Eddy to CIA, November 23, 1912, RG 75, Northern Cheyenne, Box 14; Reports of Field Matron, RG 75, Northern Cheyenne, Box 40, folder 372, all NARA-Denver.

110. Littlefield and Knack, *Native Americans and Wage Labor*, 14.

111. Hoxie, *Parading through History*, 219–220.

112. The subject of Indian wealth (as opposed to Indian poverty) and its role in the cultural construction of concepts such as that of Indianness has only recently begun to be systematically explored by scholars. For a good introduction to the topic, see Harmon, *Rich Indians*, 3–14.

Chapter Five. The Multiethnic Reservation

1. Edward H. Becker to William A. Jones, January 7, 1899, RG 75, Crow, Box 5, book 10, NARA-Denver.

2. Ibid.

3. For a vivid example of the difficulties of census takers among the Lakota, see Biolsi, "The Birth of the Reservation," 28–29.

4. The first formal census of Crows taken in 1887 revealed a population of 2,456 individuals in 630 families. Henry Williamson to Commissioner of Indian Affairs, June 30, 1887, RG 75, LR-OIA 17921–1887, NARA-DC. While Frederick Hoxie expresses confidence in the overall accuracy of censuses taken among the Crows, he too acknowledges the likelihood of errors in the enumeration of individuals. Hoxie, *Parading through History*, 131–133. On Crow kinship and naming practices and reluctance to refer to deceased individuals by name, see Lowie, *Crow Indians*, 19, 43–44, 68–69.

5. A partial exception to this is the histories of reservations that were home to more than one tribe, such as Loretta Fowler's *Arapaho Politics, 1851–1978: Symbols in Crises of Authority*, which, despite its name, also deals extensively with Arapaho relations with the Eastern Shoshone

with whom they share the Wind River Indian Reservation. The same is true of Fowler's *Shared Symbols, Contested Meanings,* which studies the Fort Belknap Reservation shared by Gros Ventres and Assiniboines, and Fowler's *Tribal Sovereignty and the Historical Imagination,* which examines the Cheyenne–Arapaho Reservation in Oklahoma. A more recent example is William J. Bauer's *"We Were All Like Migrant Workers Here."*

6. M. P. Wyman to Thomas J. Morgan, July 12, 1889, RG 75, Crow, Box 2, book 1, NARA-Denver.

7. Ibid.

8. Ibid.

9. Edward H. Becker to U.S Indian Agent, September 7, 1898, RG 75, Crow, Box 19; Becker to Thomas Richards, September 10, 1898, and Becker to U.S. Indian Agent, September 12, 1898, all RG 75, Crow, Box 19, NARA-Denver. Stevenson may have eventually moved to Fort Berthold permanently, for in 1903 the Crow agent gave his permission for a Fort Berthold Indian of the same name to come to Crow to visit relatives. See Reynolds to Amzi W. Thomas, May 29, 1903, RG 75, Crow, Box 22, book 28, NARA-Denver.

10. Wyman to U.S. Indian Agent, Shoshoni Agency, October 27, 1891, and Wyman to Whom It May Concern, November 11, 1891, both RG 75, Crow, Box 15, NARA-Denver. During a period of hostilies between Crows and Shoshonis, Washakie captured Bull Rises Up's sister and subsequently married her. The son mentioned here likely does not refer to an offspring of this union, but to one of Washakie's Crow "relatives." In Crow kinship reckoning, the husband of a person's aunt, either maternal or paternal, is referred to as "father." Lowie, *Crow Indians,* 19. Agnes Yellowtail Deernose, a granddaughter of Bull Rises Up, mentions visiting between her family and her Shoshoni relatives in her memoir. Voget, *They Call Me Agnes,* 51–52.

11. Eagle Elk to U.S. Indian Agent, Crow Agency, October 20, 1901, RG 75, Crow, Box 39, NARA-Denver.

12. Edward H. Becker to William A. Jones, October 19, 1898, RG 75, Crow, Box 5, book 1, and Becker to Jones, March 17, 1899, RG 75, Crow, Box 5, book 10, both, NARA-Denver. Over time, the question of tribal enrollment would become considerably more complex. See Chapter 6.

13. Cott, *Public Vows,* 1–7, 106–123. For a good discussion of the difficulties missionaries and government officials experienced in attempts to extend Anglo-American concepts of marriage to Native Americans, see Wall, "Gender and the 'Citizen Indian,'" 203–205, 215–218.

14. Lowie, *Crow Indians,* 50–51, 54–59; Hoxie, *Parading through History,* 188–190.

15. Lowie, *Crow Indians,* 53–58.

16. For Eaton's effort to have his wife returned from Tongue River, see F. G. Mattoon to U.S. Indian Agent, May 31, 1905, RG 75, Crow, Box 21, book 23, NARA-Denver. For Eaton's move to Crow, see Charles Briscoe to Harry Eaton, January 21, 1886, RG 75, Crow, Box 12, book 19, NARA-Denver.

17. Reynolds to Capt. J. Z. Dare, August 24, September 16, and October 21, 1907, all RG 75, Crow, Box 24, book 38, and Reynolds to CIA, December 24, 1907, RG 75, Crow, Box 7, book 19, all NARA-Denver.

18. See Reynolds to Ed Schroeder, September 15, 1909, and Reynolds to A. A. Campbell, October 12, 1909, both RG 75, Crow, Box 29; and Reynolds to W. E. Wadsworth, September 15, 1909, RG 75, Crow, Box 26, book 51, all NARA-Denver.

19. Charles S. McNichols to CIA, January 10, 1905, RG 75, LR-OIA, 5224–1905, NARA-DC. For Reynolds's personal background, see Riebeth, *J. H. Sharp,* 12. For the Crows' conflicts with Reynolds, see Hoxie, *Parading through History,* 239–253. For Plenty Dogs, see Reynolds to

Amzi Thomas, April 5, 1905, RG 75, Crow, Box 23, book 34, NARA-Denver. When Reynolds asked (not ordered) him to leave Crow, Plenty Dogs refused, pleading poverty. The resolution of this particular case is unknown.

20. Samuel G. Reynolds to CIA, December 20, 1906, RG 75, Crow, Box 7, book 17, NARA-Denver.

21. See the correspondence in RG 75, LR-OIA, 75540–1905, NARA-DC.

22. Powell, *Sweet Medicine,* 95–96, 151–169. See also Grinnell, *Fighting Cheyennes,* 362–382; and Stands in Timber and Liberty, *Cheyenne Memories,* 214–218.

23. K. N. Llewellyn and E. Adamson Hoebel, *Cheyenne Way,* 119–122; Powell, *Sweet Medicine,* 96, 392–395; Stands in Timber and Liberty, *Cheyenne Memories,* 86–88. Last Bull apparently moved to Crow in the mid-1890s. J. R. Eddy to Reynolds, February 21, 1907, RG 75, Crow, Box 46, folder 1, NARA-Denver.

24. According to Agent John Edwards, Little Horse came to the Crow Reservation around 1894, living "among the Crows" for four years, and then "left for parts unknown" without ever receiving annuities or being regarded as possessing Crow tribal rights. Edwards to CIA, October 9, 1900, RG 75, Crow, Box 5, book 11, NARA-Denver.

25. After taking over as agent in 1902, for example, Samuel Reynolds only gradually became aware of Jules Seminole's background. In correspondence with Northern Cheyenne Agent James Clifford, Reynolds stated that he had been inquiring into Seminole's history and didn't think he was really a Crow. "I think he must be some kind of outcast," Reynolds concluded. Reynolds to Clifford, December 20, 1902, RG 75, Crow, Box 21, book 27, NARA-Denver.

26. W. W. Scott to CIA, May 7, 1919, RG 75, Crow, Box 54, NARA-Denver.

27. W. W. Scott to CIA, June 1, 1913, RG 75, Crow, Box 48, NARA-Denver; Hoxie, *Parading through History,* 176–178.

28. Reynolds to Dare, September 16, 1907, RG 75, Crow, Box 24, book 38, NARA-Denver.

29. "Historical Data on Canals and Ditches," n.d., RG 75, Crow, Box 244; John Lewis to W. H. Code, February 22, 1909, RG 75, Crow, Box 220; John Lewis to Dr. H. L. Oberlander, February 24, 1913, RG 75, Crow, Box 221, all NARA-Denver.

30. George Stouch to A. A. Campbell, April 16, 1898, RG 75, Crow, Box 28, book 14, NARA-Denver.

31. F. Glenn Mattoon to CIA, March 17, 1898, RG 75, Crow, Box 5, book 1, and Scott to CIA, February 5, 1912, RG 75, Crow, Box 54, both NARA-Denver.

32. *ARCIA, 1912,* 79; Reynolds to CIA, March 4, 1907, Box 7, book 2, NARA-Denver.

33. For Last Bull's daughters, see Reynolds to CIA, February 25, 1905, and James C. Clifford to CIA, May, 29, 1905, both RG 75, LR-OIA, 65863–1905, NARA-DC. For Maggie Seminole, see Superintendent to CIA, May 26, 1920, and "Certificate of Action by Crow Tribal Council," May 3, 1920, both RG 75, Crow, Box 77, folder 121, NARA-Denver.

34. H. L. Oberlander to Scott, November 22, 1912, RG 75, Crow, Box 10, book 22, NARA-Denver.

35. For examples of agents issuing marriage licenses, see Reynolds to J. P. Van Hoose, January 13, 1908 (Gets Down marriage to Spotted Sky [Cree]), RG 75, Crow, Box 29, book 44; Reynolds to Fr. Aloysius Vrebosch, October 8, 1907 ("Mike" marriage to unnamed Cree woman), RG 75, Crow, Box 24, book 38; Reynolds to Clifford, September 7, 1906 (Big Man to "Woman Bear" [Northern Cheyenne]), most likely Jules Seminole's daughter, Bear Woman, aka Maggie Seminole, RG 75, Crow, Box 24, book 37, all NARA-Denver.

36. Reynolds to Charles W. Hoffman, January 9, 1909, RG 75, Crow, Box 25, book 49, NARA-Denver.

37. W. M. Logan to Reynolds, October 5, 1905, RG 75, Crow, Box 43, folder 3, NARA-Denver.

38. See Reynolds to CIA, January 8, 1908, RG 75, Crow, Box 7, book 19, NARA-Denver; John K. Rankin to CIA, January 24, 1907, RG 75, LR-OIA 9405–1907, NARA-DC.

39. I have been unable to locate a copy of the family history project (even an incomplete version) in any of the extant Crow Agency files.

40. Reynolds to CIA, June 22, 1909, RG 75, Box 8, book 20, NARA-Denver.

41. W. W. Scott to CIA, October 18, 1911, RG 75, Crow, Box 56, NARA-Denver.

42. "Family Register, 1902," RG 75, Crow, Box 155a, NARA-Denver. Hoxie uses federal census returns to argue for a high level of ethnic homogeneity in the Crow community, asserting that census data proved that Crows "continued to marry within the tribe" and that 98 percent of reservation residents were Crows. Hoxie, *Parading through History,* 189. Both these claims are misleading, if not actually in error. Census returns list only a person's race, not tribal affiliation. Thus, while 98 percent of the reservation residents in 1910 were Indian (and most marriages tended to be between Indians), this does not necessarily mean that all these people were born Crow or married other Crows, as the 1902 register makes evident.

43. The register actually contains 768 households, but the Crow man Gros Ventre is listed twice, once as the head of household number 63 (including his wife, Kills Twice, an adopted Cheyenne woman, and a two-year-old adopted Cheyenne daughter named Twin Woman or Emma Flies Away), and once as a single individual with no family, listed in household number 265. "Family Register, 1902," RG 75, Crow, Box 155a, NARA-Denver.

44. Ibid.

CHAPTER SIX. THE LIMITS OF COMMUNITY

1. Lowie, *Crow Indians,* 4–6; Marquis, *Memoirs,* 105–106.

2. Harring, *Crow Dog's Case,* 4–5.

3. Demallie, "American Indian Treaty Making" and "Touching the Pen."

4. Hoxie, *Parading through History,* 115–122, 150–154, 228–233.

5. For the text of both treaties, see Kappler, *Indian Affairs,* 244–246, 594–596.

6. Samuel N. Latta to William P. Dole, August 27, 1863, *ARCIA, 1863,* House Exec. Doc. 1, 38th Congress, 1st session, Serial 1182, 288–289; Henry Reed to Dole, n.d., *ARCIA, 1864,* House Exec. Doc. 1, 38th Congress, 1st session, Serial 1220, 415.

7. For a discussion of the limitations of the Treaty of 1851, see Hoxie, *Parading through History,* 86–88; McGinnis, *Counting Coup,* 85–91.

8. Kappler, *Indian Affairs,* 1008–1009.

9. Ibid., 1009.

10. For summaries of federal Indian policy in the 1870s and 1880s, see Prucha, *Great Father,* 1:593–596, 2:621–624, 2:646–648, 2:659–671, 2:687–707; Otis, *Dawes Act,* 8–16; Adams, *Education for Extinction,* 10–24; and Hoxie, *Final Promise.*

11. Hoxie, *Parading through History,* 126.

12. Jaimes, "Federal Indian Identification Policy," 124, 126, 129; Edmunds, "Native Americans, New Voices," 733–734. Melissa Meyer suggests that the use of blood quantum by modern tribal governments represents "the combined influence of Euroamerican scientific racism and conflated ideas about 'blood' and 'peoplehood.'" Meyer, "American Indian Blood," 244.

13. Harmon, "Tribal Enrollment Councils," 177–179, 199–200.

14. George Milburn to CIA, February 25, 1886, RG 75, LR-OIA, 6429–1886, NARA-DC.

15. J. W. Watson to Aliss J. Parker, August 15, 1896, RG 75, Crow, Box 17, book 44, NARA-Denver.

16. Henry Williamson to Frank Sucher, July 30, 1886, RG 75, Crow, Box 13, book 3, NARA-Denver.

17. Marquis, *Memoirs,* 34–37, 58, 139–140, 202–203, 279–280,

18. E. P. Briscoe to John H. Oberly, February 14, 1889, RG 75, LR-OIA, 4888–1889, NARA-DC.

19. Gray, *Custer's Last Campaign;* Marquis, *Memoirs,* 50, 53–54, 202, 207–211.

20. "Proceedings of a Council with the Crow Tribe by S. G. Reynolds, United States Indian Agent, at Crow Agency, Montana, Relative to the Adoption of Certain Indians Desiring Adoption into the Crow Tribe," n.d., RG 75, LR-OIA, 40084–1905; S. G. Reynolds to CIA, September 19, 1904, and Acting Secretary of the Interior Thomas Ryan to CIA, August 18, 1905, both RG 75, LR-OIA, 65863–1905, all NARA-DC.

21. Hoxie, *Parading through History,* 150–154, 165–166, 226–238.

22. Henry Williamson to CIA, December 9, 1887, and "Report of Council with Crows," December 31, 1887, both RG 75, Crow, Box 2, book 6, NARA-Denver. Interestingly, Cummings's Sioux wife was not presented for adoption until 1919, after she divorced Cummings. In the 1890 tribal census, in fact, every individual listed is identified as either "Crow" or "half-breed," with the exception of Mrs. Cummings, who is listed as "Sioux." M. P. Wyman, "Enumeration of Crow Indians for 11th Census of the United States," September 18, 1890, RG 75, Crow, Box 2, book 3, NARA-Denver.

23. Henry Williamson to CIA, December 9, 1887, and "Report of Council with Crows," December 31, 1887, both RG 75, Crow, Box 2, book 6, NARA-Denver.

24. For examples of such adoptions, see Wood and Theissen, *Early Fur Trade,* 168, 172.

25. A considerable literature on individuals variously termed intermediaries, culture brokers, negotiators, or transculturites has emerged. For examples of such individuals, see Szasz, *Between Indian and White Worlds;* Merrell, *Into the American Woods;* Hallowell, "American Indians, White and Black"; Richter, "Cultural Brokers and Intercultural Politics"; Fausz, "Middlemen in Peace and War"; Hagedorn, "A Friend to Go Between Them."

26. For the development of late nineteenth-century concepts of race, see Stocking, *Race, Culture, and Evolution,* and, as it relates to Anglo-American perceptions of Native Americans specifically, Dippie, *Vanishing American,* 82–106, 252–262.

27. The exact dates of the 1904 and 1905 councils are uncertain. In September 1904, agency officials held councils during annuity payments at Crow Agency, Saint Xavier, and Pryor to consider the adoption of twenty-four individuals. A total of 572 heads of families were reported as participating. An additional council was subsequently held to consider the adoption of three children whose mothers had been adopted in the September councils. "Proceedings of a Council with the Crow Tribe of Indians by S. G. Reynolds, United States Indian Agent, With the Heads of Families of the Crow Tribe of Indians Relative to Adoption of Certain Indians Desiring to be Enrolled as Members of the Crow Tribe of Indians," n.d., and Acting Secretary of the Interior Thomas Ryan to CIA, August 18, 1905, both RG 75, LR-OIA, 65863–1905, all NARA-DC.

28. "Proceedings of a Council with the Crow Tribe of Indians by S. G. Reynolds, United States Indian Agency at Crow Agency, Montana, Relative to the Adoption of Certain Indians Desiring Adoption into the Crow Tribe," n.d., RG 75, LR-OIA, 40084–1905, NARA-DC.

29. J. P. Van Hoose to Samuel G. Reynolds, April 18, 1904, RG 75, Crow, Box 42, NARA-Denver.

30. By European reckoning, John Frost was actually not Crow at all but a quarter-blood Pie-gan. However, Frost, a Carlisle graduate, had been raised on the Crow reservation, was listed on the tribal rolls, and had received an allotment during the 1890s. M. P. Wyman to CIA, May 8, 1891, RG 75, SC 147, NARA-DC.

31. The Wolfes both worked in the government schools at Crow Agency. Mark Wolfe to J. E. Edwards, January 29, 1901, RG 75, LR-OIA, 7127–1901, NARA-DC.

32. S. G. Reynolds to CIA, February 25, 1905, RG 75, LR-OIA, 65863–1905, NARA-DC.

33. "Proceedings of a Council with the Crow Tribe of Indians by S. G. Reynolds, United States Indian Agency at Crow Agency, Montana, Relative to the Adoption of Certain Indians Desiring Adoption into the Crow Tribe," n.d., RG 75, LR-OIA, 40084–1905, NARA-DC. For Thomas Medicine Horse's relinquishment of his Rosebud allotment, see Reynolds to CIA, December 23, 1905, RG 75, Crow, Box 7, book 17, and Edward B. Kelley to U.S. Indian Agent, November 24, 1906, RG 75, Crow, Box 44, folder 2, both NARA-Denver.

34. Secretary of the Interior E. A. Hitchcock to CIA, May 25, 1905, Affidavit of Nancy Hall, Mendocino County, Calif., March 27, 1903, and "Proceedings of a Council with the Crow Tribe of Indians by S. G. Reynolds, United States Indian Agency at Crow Agency, Montana, Relative to the Adoption of Certain Indians Desiring Adoption into the Crow Tribe," n.d., all RG 75, LR-OIA, 40084–1905, NARA-DC.

35. "Proceedings of a Council with the Crow Tribe of Indians by S. G. Reynolds, United States Indian Agency at Crow Agency, Montana, Relative to the Adoption of Certain Indians Desiring Adoption into the Crow Tribe," n.d., RG 75, LR-OIA, 40084–1905, NARA-DC.

36. Samuel G. Reynolds to CIA, May 15, 1908, RG 75, Crow, Box 7, book 19, NARA-Denver. According to Crow census rolls, Young Hairy Wolf was fifty-six years old in 1904. RG 75, Indian Census Rolls, Crow, National Archives Microform Publication M685, rolls 79–80.

37. Despite the councils' endorsement, the OIA ultimately rejected Shot Twice's application for enrollment, citing his enrollment at Pine Ridge and the presence of his wife, children, and allotment there, ordering the Crow agent to take him into custody and return him to Pine Ridge. Ryan to CIA, August 18, 1905, RG 75, LR-OIA, 40084–1905, NARA-DC; Reynolds to CIA, May 15, 1908, RG 75, Crow, Box 7, book 19, and Reynolds to CIA, December 23, 1905, Box 7, book 17, both NARA-Denver. In an ironic twist, as a younger man, Young Hairy Wolf orig-inally belonged to the Fox warrior society but was selected by the rival Lumpwoods to take the place of a deceased member whom Young Hairy Wolf resembled. According to Edward S. Cur-tis, Young Hairy Wolf was "compelled by custom to join the rival organization." Curtis, *North American Indian,* 6:209.

38. Edwards to CIA, September 4, 1901, RG 75, Crow, Box 6, book 12, NARA-Denver. In his autobiography, the Lakota activist/actor Russell Means, a grandson of Eugene Means, notes that his great-grandmother was a full-blood Crow. Means, *Where White Men Fear to Tread,* 17.

39. "Report of Irregular Employees at Crow Irrigation Survey for Month Ending June 30, 1900," RG 75, LR-OIA 34397–1900, and "Report of Irregular Employees at Crow Irrigation Survey for Month Ending July 31, 1900," RG 75, LR-OIA 39076–1900, both NARA-DC. It should be noted that it is entirely possible that Charles Means had traveled to the Crow Reser-vation before 1900, most likely to visit his mother, without it being noted in agency corre-spondence.

40. E. C. Means to Edwards, March 14, 1901, RG 75, Crow, Box 38, NARA-Denver.

41. "Proceedings of a Council Held With the Crow Tribe of Indians," n.d., RG 75, Crow, Box 48, NARA-Denver; Hoxie, *Parading through History,* 175–181.

42. "Proceedings of a Council Held With the Crow Tribe of Indians," n.d., RG 75, Crow,

Box 48, NARA-Denver. According to Robert Lowie, Shot in the Arm (and, by extension, Hairy Old Woman) belonged to the Greasy Mouth clan. As children of a Greasy Mouth woman, the Means brothers may also have received support from this source. Lowie, *Crow Indians,* 14–15. After being turned down for adoption in 1904, George Means lived for a time in the Bighorn district. Reynolds to James R. Brennan, March 28, 1905, RG 75, Crow, Box 23, book 34, Reynolds to T. J. Connelly, December 15, 1906, RG 75, Crow, Box 29, book 41, and Reynolds to Brennan, December 20, 1906, RG 75, Crow, Box 24, book 39, all NARA-Denver.

43. "Proceedings of a Council Held With the Crow Tribe of Indians," n.d., RG 75, Crow, Box 48, NARA-Denver.

44. J. P. Van Hoose to Reynolds, April 19, 1904, RG 75, Crow, Box 42, NARA-Denver.

45. "Proceedings of a Council with the Crow Tribe of Indians by S. G. Reynolds, United States Indian Agent, with the Heads of Families of the Crow Tribe of Indians Relative to Adoption of Certain Indians Desiring to be Enrolled as Members of the Crow Tribe of Indians," n.d., RG 75, LR-OIA, 65863–1905, NARA-DC.

46. Reynolds to Brennan, March 28, 1905, RG 75, Crow, Box 23, book 34, Reynolds to Connelly, December 15, 1906, RG 75, Crow, Box 29, book 41, and Reynolds to Brennan, December 20, 1906, RG 75, Crow, Box 24, book 39, all NARA-Denver.

47. Bell Rock, Old Crane, Hides, Coyote That Runs, Fights Well Known, Young Swallow, John Push, Foolish Man, Old Coyote, Bull Well Known, Shows a Little, Old White Man, Hears All Over, The Crane, Bull Snake, Comes Up, Bird All [Over] the Ground, and Smalls to CIA, February 20, 1907, and Reynolds to CIA, March 20, 1907, both RG 75, LR-OIA, 29055–1907, NARA-DC.

48. In addition to his 1893 visit, Crow Agency records also indicate that Crazy Bear visited the Crow Reservation in 1896 and 1897, and possibly in 1898. M. P. Wyman to G. P. Conner, October 4, 1893, RG 75, Crow, Box 16, book 39, J. W. Watson to Crazy Bear, September 21, 1897, RG 75, Crow, Box 18, book 46, and Crazy Bear to Indian Agent, September 12, 1898, RG 75, Crow, Box 36, all NARA-Denver. For Crazy Bear's claimed status as a band leader, see Crazy Bear to U.S. Indian Agent, May 31, 1905, RG 75, Crow, Box 44, folder 1, NARA-Denver.

49. Edwards to U.S. Indian Agent, August 5, 1900, RG 75, Crow, Box 20, book 22, and Edwards to Crazy Bear, April 22, 1901, RG 75, Crow, Box 21, book 23, both NARA-Denver.

50. Crazy Bear to CIA, March 23, 1903, RG 75, LR-OIA, 33683–1903, NARA-DC.

51. Brennan to U.S. Indian Agent, April 10, 1903, RG 75, LR-OIA, 33683–1903, NARA-DC.

52. Reynolds to Brennan, May 20, 1903, RG 75, LR-OIA, 33683–1903, NARA-Denver. Reynolds did add that "in view of his son being buried at this place, he will have my permission to visit here at any time he desires."

53. Crazy Bear to Dear Friend, October 4, 1904, and Crazy Bear to U.S. Indian Agent, October 17, 1904, both RG 75, Crow, Box 42, NARA-Denver.

54. Reynolds to Crazy Bear, October 10, and November 18, 1904, RG 75, Crow, Box 23, book 33, and Reynolds to Crazy Bear, June 6, 1905, RG 75, Crow, Box 23, book 34, all NARA-Denver.

55. Reynolds to CIA, December 11, 1906, RG 75, Central Classified Files, Crow, Decimal 053, 93867–1907, NARA-DC.

56. For a detailed discussion of the Throssel and Miller adoptions, see Albright, *Crow Indian Photographer,* 7–8, 17–24. Albright notes that "the council indicated the non-Crow Indians were eligible for adoption because they lived among the Crows but lacked official tribal affiliation of their own," and that the adoptees' parents had "failed to keep up [their own] tribal relationship

to the extent of securing allotments or enrollments." Albright, *Crow Indian Photographer,* 21–22. Though perhaps a justification, the failure of other Crees not connected to the OIA to secure adoption suggests that the Throssel adoptions were at least partially politically motivated. A recent work by Fred Miller's granddaughter, Nancy Fields O'Connor, claims that Fred Miller was also adopted by the Crows. Though Miller may have been socially adopted by a Crow family, there is no indication in Crow Agency records that Miller was ever officially adopted and enrolled as a Crow. O'Connor, *Fred E. Miller,* 12.

57. In 1939, Crow historian Joseph Medicine Crow depicted a similar process in describing how Crow clan and kinship networks helped reclaim students who had been exposed to the assimilative environments of off-reservation boarding schools: "School children who had been away would return and try to disassociate themselves from tribal customs and traditions, but invariably would be reclaimed through the kinship route. It is so affectionate, so real and embracing that before they know, it has melted their individualist tendencies into the Indian nature, which is sympathetic, understanding, and philanthropic." Medicine Crow, "Effect of European Culture," 25.

58. In January 1910, a Crow council consisting of thirty-five headmen and community leaders voted to adopt seventeen individuals. Among those adopted were Charles Dillon, a half-blood Lakota from Pine Ridge; Bear Woman, a Northern Cheyenne; Rainbow Woman, a Cree; Pauline Pickett, a half-blood Cree; Mrs. Mike Two Belly, a Cree; Josephine White (listed as a "Metlakatha" Indian); Ollie Yarlott, a Pottawatomi from Oklahoma; Mollie Keiser, a Piegan; and Mrs. Andrew Fog, a Cree, all of whom had Crow spouses. Also adopted were Dahlia and John Anderson, children of a quarter-blood Crow woman and a white man; and Florence and Bertha Williams, also children of a half-blood Crow woman and a white man, who were enrolled as Crows but had never been allotted; Emma Barrett, quarter-blood Gros Ventre and quarter-blood Crow, who had been raised off the reservation but had an uncle at Crow named Cut Ear, and her son; and John Wesley Milliken and Juanita Ketosh, both Piegans who had been raised on the Crow Reservation. Ketosh had been allotted but never placed on the tribal roll, and Milliken had been dropped from the roll after moving to Canada but had returned to the reservation. The council rejected the wife of Sam Davis "because she is a full-blood white woman" despite her marriage to a Crow man. The council also rejected Mrs. Old Lodge Pole, a Cree woman formerly married to a Crow, who had separated from her husband and moved to Canada; Henry Ketosh, the Chippewa husband of Juanita Ketosh; and Lewis Walters, the brother of Juanita Ketosh. Walters, like his sister, had an allotment, but he was not on the tribal roll; his application was rejected by a majority of the council as a result of his alleged involvement in the theft of some cattle belonging to Crows and their sale to a white man. Reynolds to CIA, May 2, 1910, RG 75, Crow, Box 74, folder 112–2, NARA-Denver. In 1915, a council voted to adopt two children, one the offspring of a Crow father and a Cree mother, and the other a half-Omaha/half-Yankton ward of the state who had been adopted by a Crow couple. See correspondence in RG 75, CCF, Crow, file 53, 1329229–1914 and 35595–1915, both NARA-DC.

59. The first recorded mention of Crees at Crow was in 1896, when Agent J. W. Watson apprehended and evicted a party of twenty-nine Crees under Little Bear. Watson to Gov. John E. Richards, May 2, 1896, RG 75, Crow, Box 17, book 44, NARA-Denver.

60. Reynolds to CIA, August 22, 1908, RG 75, Crow, Box 8, book 20, NARA-Denver.

61. For removals of Crees see Watson to Richards, May 2, 1896, RG 75, Crow, Box 17, book 44, Edwards to Van Hoose, January 16, 1902, RG 75, Crow, Box 28, book 25, Reynolds to Connelly and Van Hoose, November 2, 1905, RG 75, Crow, Box 29, book 30, Reynolds to CIA,

August 22, 1908, RG 75, Crow, Box 8, book 20, all NARA-Denver. For complaints against Crees, see Scott to CIA, July 17, 1912, RG 75, Crow, Box 54, NARA-Denver.

62. Reynolds to CIA, August 22, 1908, RG 75, Crow, Box 8, book 20, NARA-Denver.

63. For an analysis of the decline of the Crow economy, see Hoxie, *Parading through History,* 266–294. For a general assessment of the impact of market forces and competition on Indian farming, see Carlson, *Indians, Bureaucrats,* and "Federal Policy."

64. Reynolds to CIA, October 7, 1909, RG 75, Crow, Box 10, book 22, NARA-Denver.

65. Reynolds to W. T. Foster, June 18, 1909, RG 75, Crow, Box 29, and Reynolds to J. H. Young, November 5, 1909, RG 75, Crow, Box 26, book 21, both NARA-Denver.

66. Interview with Jim Gopher, n.d., Oral History Collection 542, Montana State Historical Society, Helena.

67. Ibid. Gopher placed this incident in the spring of 1904, although he would have been only two years old at the time. The evidence suggests Gopher may have been recalling the 1909 episode, although the movement of Cree families to Browning also fits a subsequent incident in 1912.

68. Scott to CIA, December 20, 1912, RG 75, Crow, Box 54, NARA-Denver.

69. Lowie, *Crow Indians,* 58; Dusenberry, *Montana Cree,* 95.

70. Scott to CIA, December 24, 1912, RG 75, Crow, Box 54, NARA-Denver. See also Hoxie, *Parading through History,* 176, 216–217, 232–233.

71. Scott to CIA, June 1, 1913, RG 75, Crow, Box 54, NARA-Denver. Intentionally or not, Scott apparently underestimated Pryor's Crow population. District population estimates in both 1903 and 1907 gave the district a population of 400. According to these figures, somewhere between one-fifth and one-quarter of the Crow tribe lived in the district. Hoxie, *Parading through History,* 176. Such estimates most likely did not count the district's Cree population.

72. Ibid.

73. The Pryor region contains numerous vision quest, offering, and other sacred sites, as well as places significant in Crow tribal history. Loendorf, "Results of Archeological Survey— 1970," 14–101; Loendorf, "Results of the Archeological Survey—1971," 8–92; Medicine Crow, *From the Heart of the Crow Country,* 43, 82, 84; Loendorf and Nabokov, "Every Morning of the World." Julie Francis and Lawrence Loendorf have commented on the Crows' "great reverence" for the Pryor Mountain region and their belief "that the spirits made the petroglyphs and pictographs that occur in and around the Pryor and Bighorn Mountains." Francis and Loendorf, *Ancient Visions,* 17.

74. C. F. Hawke to Scott, May 24, 1913, RG 75, Crow, Box 50, NARA-Denver.

75. Ibid.

76. Scott, "Minutes of meeting of the Crow Business Committee, Crow Agency, Montana, May 31, 1913," RG 75, Crow, Box 50, NARA-Denver. Looks (or Sees) With His Ears and Two Leggings were River Crows from Black Lodge; Frank Shane represented the Reno (agency) district. Charles Yarlott was from Bighorn and George Hogan from Reno. Superintendent to CIA, April 20, 1911, RG 75, Crow, Box 50, and Calvin H. Asbury to CIA, January 2, 1917, RG 75, Crow, Box 77, folder 121, both NARA-Denver. Hoxie, *Parading through History,* 331.

77. Signing from Wyola were Red Wolf, Pretty Horse, and Knows His Coups; signing from Lodge Grass were Ed Wolf-Lays-Down, Medicine Crow, Plain Owl, Bull Don't Fall Down, and The Wet (Scott claimed six Lodge Grass representatives signed, but listed only five names in his report). Scott also failed to explain why there were five signers from Lodge Grass rather than just three business council members. Scott to CIA, May 31, 1913, RG 75, Crow, Box 50,

NARA-Denver. Perhaps not coincidentally, Scott made his proposal to sell off the Pryor district the day after the business council meeting.

78. Hoxie, *Parading through History,* 270.

79. *ARCIA, 1910,* 63.

80. Northern Cheyenne adoptees included Strikes Twice, who married Horse; Walks in the Night, wife of Dust; and Bear Woman, wife of Clifford White Shirt, all of whom were adopted in 1904; another Bear Woman (also known as Black Beaver), who married Big Man and was adopted in 1910; and Maggie Seminole (daughter of Jules Seminole), who married Ben Long Ears and was adopted in May 1920. "Proceedings of a Council with the Crow Tribe of Indians by S. G. Reynolds, United States Indian Agency at Crow Agency, Montana, Relative to the Adoption of Certain Indians Desiring Adoption into the Crow Tribe," n.d., RG 75, LR-OIA, 40084–1905, NARA-DC; Reynolds to CIA, May 2, 1910, RG 75, Crow, Box 74, folder 112–2, NARA-Denver; Superintendent to CIA, May 26, 1920, and "Certificate of Action by Crow Tribal Council," May 3, 1920, both RG 75, Crow, Box 77, folder 121, NARA-Denver.

81. Campbell, "Health Patterns," 65–70; George Bird Grinnell to William A. Jones, October 20, 1904, RG 75, LR-OIA, 7996–1905, NARA-DC.

82. The 1900 executive order also changed the name of the reservation from Tongue River to Northern Cheyenne. Svingen, *Northern Cheyenne Indian Reservation,* 144–147, 174–175; Campbell, "Health Patterns," 68–69.

83. Big Head Man to Agent, October 6, 1907, RG 75, Crow, Box 46, NARA-Denver. Construction on the Birney ditch began in 1906 and was completed in 1910. Thomas D. Weist, introduction to Marquis, *Cheyennes of Montana,* 16.

84. Reynolds to James Clifford, August 10, 1904, RG 75, Crow, Box 23, book 33, NARA-Denver.

85. Svingen, *Northern Cheyenne Indian Reservation,* 53–56, 74–75, 88–89, 130–136. Among the locations proposed for the resettlement of the Northern Cheyennes was the northeast corner of the Crow Reservation and the Pryor district. It should be noted that the resettlement did not involve a merger of the two tribes; the Pryor proposal would have entailed the resettlement of the Pryor Crows in the Bighorn and Little Bighorn valleys. J. D. C Atkins to Secretary of the Interior, October 5, 1885, SC 137, Northern Cheyenne, NARA-DC; *Condition of Northern Cheyenne Indians,* Senate Exec. Doc. 121, 51st Cong., 1st session, Serial 2686, 7–8.

86. *Proposed Removal of the Northern Cheyenne Indians,* House Doc. 15, 55th Cong., 3rd session, Serial 3807, 2–5, 86–87.

87. Svingen, *Northern Cheyenne Indian Reservation,* 87–88.

88. *Proposed Removal of the Northern Cheyenne Indians,* House Doc. 15, 55th Cong., 3rd session, Serial 3807, 2–5, 86–87, 97–99.

89. Hoxie, *Parading through History,* 253–263.

90. Public Law 239, *U.S. Statutes at Law* 41, pt. 1, 751–752.

91. Besides Mrs. Cummings, those recommended for adoption included Charles Anderson, Peter William Dawes, and Owen B. Williams Jr., all children; Emma Rides Sorrel Horse, the Cree wife of Stanley Rides the Horse; Many Necklaces, Cree wife of The Wet; and Mrs. L. Whitebear. "Report of Tribal Council Meeting, January 22, 1919," and E. B. Meritt to Secretary of the Interior, January 12, 1920, both RG 75, Crow, Box 77, folder 121, NARA-Denver.

92. Superintendent to CIA, May 26, 1920, and "Certificate of Action by Crow Tribal Council," May 3, 1920, both RG 75, Crow, Box 77, folder 121, NARA-Denver.

93. James Carpenter to CIA, January 8, 1921, and Superintendent to CIA, January 16, 1921, both RG 75, Crow, Box 77, folder 121, NARA-Denver.

94. Carpenter to CIA, January 8, 1921, Meritt to Robert Half and Walks With a Wolf, February 26, 1921, Supt. to CIA, May 26, 1920, and Meritt to Asbury, July 24, 1920, all RG 75, Crow, Box 77, folder 121, NARA-Denver.

95. Carpenter to CIA, January 8, 1921, RG 75, Crow, Box 77, folder 121, NARA-Denver.

96. Plenty Coups et.al. to CIA, January 8, 1921, RG 75, CCF, Crow, file 53, 10094–1921, NARA-DC.

97. Ibid.

98. Hertzberg, *Search for an American Indian Identity,* 239.

99. Hoxie, *Parading through History,* 219–220; Stewart, "Peyotism in Montana," 7; Ed Little Light, interview by Omer C. Stewart, n.d., and James Big Lake, interview by Omer C. Steward, n.d., both in folder 52, Omer C. Stewart Collection, University of Colorado at Boulder Archives. Robert C. Kiste has stated that Crows were attending peyote meetings on the Northern Cheyenne Reservation as early as 1905 or 1906. Kiste, "Crow Peyotism," 2. Tyrone Ten Bear states that Austin Stray Calf attended a peyote meeting at Tongue River sometime in the 1890s. Tyrone Ten Bear interview with Frank Rzeczkowski, August 8, 2001.

100. McCleary, "Legal History of Peyotism"; Kiste, "Crow Peyotism," 3–4. For an example of Bethune's contact with Northern Cheyennes, see Reynolds to Clifford, May 29, 1904, RG 75, Crow, Box 22, book 32, NARA-Denver.

101. Hoxie, *Parading through History,* 219.

102. O. P. Cope to Asbury, April 14, 1919, RG 75, Crow, Box 79, folder 122–2, NARA-Denver.

103. T. J. Burbank to Asbury, April 11, 1919, Bridgett C. Keogh to Asbury, April 12, 1919, and G. A. Vennick, "Answers to Questions on Peyote," n.d. but probably 1919, all RG 75, Box 79, folder 122–2, NARA-Denver.

104. Kiste, "Crow Peyotism," 3.

105. Hoxie, *Parading through History,* 220.

106. Kiste, "Crow Peyotism," 5.

107. Thomas Gardner and others to CIA, January 23, 1921, and "A Resolution of the Pryor District Crow Indian Council," February 12, 1921, both RG 75, Crow, Box 79, folder 122–2, NARA-Denver.

108. Hoxie, *Parading through History,* 220–221; Stewart, "Peyotism in Montana," 11.

109. "Minutes of Meeting on Peyote, St. Xavier, February 28, 1922," RG 75, Crow, Box 79, folder 122–2, NARA-Denver. One of the abstainers, Good Horse, had signed the January 1921 antipeyote petition.

110. Cope to Asbury, February 13, 1922, RG 75, Crow, Box 79, folder 122–2, NARA-Denver. An anonymous informant told the Indian Rights Association that several government employees, including interpreters and policemen, were peyotists, claiming, "The first thing we know they will be running the agency." An Indian Friend to M. K. Sniffen, July 12, 1922, and Asbury to Sniffen, July 26, 1922, both RG 75, Crow, Box 79, folder 122–2, NARA-Denver.

111. Stewart, *Peyote Religion,* 186; Nellie Bad Boy to CIA, April 30, 1919, and O. P. Cope to Asbury, February 7, 1921, both RG 75, Crow, Box 79, folder 122–2, NARA-Denver.

112. Asbury to O. M. Bogguss, May 6, 1920, RG 75, Crow, Box 79, folder 122–2, NARA-Denver.

113. Bogguss to Asbury, May 15, 1920, RG 75, Crow, Box 79, folder 122–2, NARA-Denver.

114. Sam Lone Bear, a Lakota roadman from Pine Ridge, reportedly was the first to introduce peyote in the Pryor district around 1926. Kiste, "Crow Peyotism," 6–12; Stewart, *Peyote*

Religion, 186–189; Robert Yellowtail to Commissioner Burke, January 2, 1927, RG 75, CCF, Crow, file 126, 1024–1927, NARA-DC.

115. McCleary, "Legal History of Peyotism," 3–4. The prosecution was dropped after the Supreme Court's reversal and remand of the case. Stewart, "Peyotism in Montana," 11–12.

116. Kiste, "Crow Peyotism," 15. In June 1921, Asbury mailed a copy of the Oklahoma NAC charter to the Commissioner of Indian Affairs with a cover note stating that "this copy came into our hands somewhat accidentally" from a Cheyenne. Asbury to CIA, June 6, 1921, RG 75, Crow, Box 83, folder 131, NARA-Denver.

117. Stewart, "Peyotism in Montana," 12; Stewart, *Peyote Religion*, 231.

118. McCleary, "Legal History of Peyotism," 5–11.

119. Stewart, *Peyote Religion*, 231.

120. A 1924 article by Dr. Robert Newberne in the *Indian School Journal*, published at the Chilocco, Oklahoma, Indian boarding school, claimed there were only thirty-four peyotists at Crow out of a population of 1,703, while an estimated 35 percent of Northern Cheyenne (515 out of 1,470) were peyotists. Dr. Robert E. L. Newberne, "Peyote," RG 75, Box 79, folder 122–2, NARA-Denver.

121. Bogguss to Asbury, March 14, 1923, RG 75, Crow, Box 79, folder 122–2, NARA-Denver.

122. Kiste, "Crow Peyotism," 16.

123. Robert Yellowtail to Commissioner Burke, January 2, 1927, RG 75, CCF, Crow, file 126, 1024–1927, NARA-DC.

124. Verne Dusenberry noted that Crow ceremonies tended to have more emphasis on form than Northern Cheyenne meetings, while Cree meetings featured weeping, which one of his informants called "a Cree trait." Dusenberry, *Montana Cree*, 176–177.

125. Rosier, *Rebirth of the Blackfeet Nation*, 280.

126. Stewart, *Peyote Religion*, 148.

127. Sam Lone Bear, who brought the New Way peyote rite to Crow and introduced peyote in Pryor, is perhaps the best example. Omer Stewart described Lone Bear as "lawless, immoral, exploitative, overbearing, acquisitive, and dishonest." A Cheyenne peyotist remarked that Lone Bear "really abused" his position, perhaps referring to his taking a teenage girl off the Crow Reservation in the 1920s. Joe Ten Bear Jr. (Crow) commented that Lone Bear "was not what he was supposed to be" and that "Crows turned against him because of his misuse of peyote." Although Lone Bear was discredited in the eyes of many, the ritual he introduced survived at Crow until after World War II. Stewart, *Peyote Religion*, 6–9; Joe Ten Bear Jr. interview with Omer Stewart, n.d., and Ed Little Light interview with Stewart, n.d., both folder 52, Omer C. Stewart Collection, University of Colorado Library Archives, Boulder.

128. Joe Ten Bear Jr. interview with Omer Stewart, folder 52, Omer C. Stewart Collection, University of Colorado Library Archives, Boulder.

129. Sam LaPointe, Weekly Farmer's Report, July 5, 1924, RG 75, Crow, Box 87, folder 139, NARA-Denver.

130. Burt, "Nowhere Left to Go," 206–207. The Superintendent's Diary for May 1917 comments on the activities of OIA inspector James McLaughlin at Crow enrolling Crees as Rocky Boy Indians. Superintendent's Diary, RG 75, Crow, Box 156, NARA-Denver. The superintendents' diaries, weekly farmers' reports, and special officers' reports contain numerous references to Crees. RG 75, Crow, Boxes 86 and 87 (Farmers' Reports), 88 (Special Officers' Weekly Reports), and 156 (Superintendent's Diary), NARA-Denver.

131. Couch and Marino, "Chippewa–Cree Peyotism," 8–10; Kiste, "Crow Peyotism," 19.

132. James Carpenter to CIA, January 12, 1921, RG 75, Crow, Box 77, folder 121, NARA-Denver; Hoxie, *Parading through History,* 315–319.

133. Albright, *Crow Indian Photographer,* 23.

134. "Minutes of a Council Held at Crow Agency, Montana, October 6, 1926," RG 75, Crow, Box 77, folder 121, NARA-Denver. For Hamilton's activities on the Blackfeet Reservation, see Rosier, *Rebirth of the Blackfeet Nation,* 15–53.

135. "Minutes of a Council Held at Crow Agency, Montana, October 6, 1926," RG 75, Crow, Box 77, folder 121. NARA-Denver.

136. Ibid.

137. Ibid.

138. Ibid.

139. Ibid.

140. Ibid.

CONCLUSION. HISTORY, MEMORY, AND COMMUNITY

1. Durham, "Those Dead Guys for a Hundred Years," 163.

2. For white constructions of Indians, see Berkhofer, *White Man's Indian;* Deloria, *Playing Indian;* Bird, *Dressing in Feathers;* Lepore, *The Name of War.*

3. In the Southeast, this process began as early as the early 1700s, when Cherokees and other Native Americans began classing themselves as "red," in contrast to "white" Europeans. Shoemaker, "How Indians Got to Be Red," 627–629.

4. The concept of peoplehood has sometimes been advanced as a terminological replacement for tribe and has been linked to concepts of shared language, sacred history, religion, and land. Holm, Pearson, and Chavis, "Peoplehood," 11–15. In my formulation, peoplehood would constitute a form of supratribal identity based on shared cultural values and a common relationship to the United States.

5. Sahlins, *Islands of History,* vii.

6. For a discussion of the strategic uses of ethnicity, see Stephan and Stephan, "What Are the Functions of Ethnic Identity?," and Burroughs and Spickard, "Ethnicity, Multiplicity, and Narrative."

7. Wendy Wickwire, "We Shall Drink from the Stream," 200–202, 210; Tennant, *Aboriginal Peoples and Politics,* 84–85.

8. In contrast, in his account of the meeting between Plains and Southeastern Indians in Indian Territory, David La Vere suggests that cultural differences between the two groups actually inhibited the emergence of a shared sense of Indian ethnicity. La Vere, *Contrary Neighbors,* 226–229.

9. Lomawaima, *They Called It Prairie Light,* 167.

10. For an insightful discussion of this process, see Biolsi, "The Birth of the Reservation."

11. Castile, "Commodification of Indian Identity."

12. Currently, Crow tribal membership qualifications include the ability to demonstrate descent from an individual listed on a previous tribal roll or census, and having at least one-quarter Crow blood. Personal communication from Timothy P. McCleary, Little Big Horn College.

13. This trend is not limited to the Crow tribe. According to Kristy Gover, in recent decades, an increasing number of tribes have begun to require not just a particular quantum of Indian blood to qualify for tribal membership, but a particular degree of tribally specific blood quantum. As Gover points out, the concept of tribal blood quantum "is a tribal innovation, not a federal one." Gover, "Genealogy as Continuity," 244–252.

14. Hoxie, *Parading through History,* 328–331, 335–342. Officially Yellowtail's appointment as Crow superintendent and the IRA were separate issues, but both Crow supporters and opponents of the bill often lumped both issues together,

15. "Minutes of the Crow Tribal Council Held May 2, 1934," RG 75, Records Concerning the Wheeler-Howard Act, 1933–1937, Entry 1011, Box 4, folder 1, 4894–1934, NARA-DC.

16. Ultimately the Crow and the Assiniboine and Sioux tribes of the Fort Peck Reservation were the only Montana tribes to reject the IRA. Haas, *Ten Years of Tribal Government,* 17.

17. John Bulltail, interview by Carson Walks Over Ice, June 13, 1989, Typescript, Oral History Collection 1165, Montana State Historical Society, Helena. For another description of the transmission of the Shoshoni Sun Dance to the Crows, see Voget, *Shoshoni–Crow Sun Dance,* 129–162.

18. Ibid.

19. Nabokov, *Forest of Time,* 97.

20. For an examination of nineteenth-century Crow intertribal diplomacy, see Weist, "Ethnohistorical Analysis."

21. Bhabha, "Dissemination," 307.

22. Hobsbawm and Ranger, *Invention of Tradition,* 4–5; see also Geertz, *Invention of Prophecy,* 7.

23. Angela Gonzales, "(Re)Articulation of American Indian Identity," 200. Gonzales adds that the definition of Indian tribes as "static, rigidly bound, and identifiable entities" is "a dated model not applicable to urban Indian communities": a statement equally applicable to pre-reservation communities. Ibid., 199.

24. Jaimes, "Federal Indian Identification Policy," 129–130.

25. On the Rosebud Reservation in South Dakota, Thomas Biolsi notes that "many older Lakota people are concerned because their grandchildren do not possess the 'one-fourth (1/4) or more Sioux Indian blood' required for tribal enrollment." Biolsi, *Deadliest Enemies,* 5.

26. In the Cherokee Nation of Oklahoma, nearly 90,000 of the 175,000 enrolled members (as of 2002) have less than 1/16 Cherokee blood. Sturm, *Blood Politics,* 2–3.

27. Gilroy, *Between Camps,* 6.

28. Hoxie, "Ethnohistory for a Tribal World," 599.

29. Gonzales, "(Re)Articulation of American Indian Identity," 210–211. Ironically, Jimmie Durham, whose words open this chapter, has had his own Indianness challenged. In Durham's case, his refusal to obtain a certificate of authenticity under the Indian Arts and Crafts Act led to cancellations of showings of his work at the Centre for Contemporary Art in Santa Fe and at the American Indian Contemporary Arts Festival in San Francisco in 1991. Turney, *"Ceci n'est pas* Jimmie Durham," 426–428.

30. Quoted in Burroughs and Spickard, "Ethnicity, Multiplicity, and Narrative," 248.

31. Hahn, *A Nation under Our Feet.* A partial exception to this statement would be the activities of Lakota and Cheyenne councils protesting the 1875 seizure of the Black Hills in the early 1900s (which Young Man Afraid of His Horses suggested also concerned the Crows). Lazarus, *Black Hills, White Justice,* 119–149. To date, no historian has specifically examined the activities of the Black Hills Council.

32. Churchill, "Crucible of American Indian Identity," 39.

33. Jaimes, "Federal Indian Identification Policy," 134.

34. Pat Doyle, "Tribal Leader Suggests a Robin Hood Scenario: If Wealthier Bands Shared Gambling Profits with Poorer Ones, There Wouldn't Be a Need for a State-Sanctioned Casino, He Said," (Minneapolis) *Star-Tribune*, February 2, 2002.

35. Penn, *Feathering Custer*, 44, 90.

BIBLIOGRAPHY

ARCHIVAL MATERIALS

Bailey, Theodore. "Diary, 1866." Typescript at the Montana State Historical Society, Helena.

Big Lake, James. Interview with Omer C. Steward, n.d. Folder 52, Omer C. Stewart Collection, University of Colorado at Boulder Archives.

Bulltail, John. Interview with Carson Walks Over Ice, June 13, 1989. Oral History Collection 1165, Montana State Historical Society, Helena.

Commissioner of Indian Affairs. *ARCIA, 1906*. Washington, D.C.: Government Printing Office, 1906.

————. *ARCIA, 1910*. Washington, D.C.: Government Printing Office, 1911.

————. *ARCIA, 1912*. Washington, D.C.: Government Printing Office, 1912.

Congressional Serial Set. *Annual Report of the Commisioner of Indian Affairs, 1861*. Senate Exec. Doc. 1, 36th Congress, 2nd session, Serial 1078.

————. *ARCIA, 1863*, House Exec. Doc. 1, 38th Congress, 1st session, serial 1182.

————. *ARCIA, 1864*, House Exec. Doc. 1, 38th Congress, 1st session, serial 1220.

————. *ARCIA, 1866*, House Exec. Doc. 1, 39th Congress, 2nd session, serial 1284.

————. *ARICA, 1867*, House Exec. Doc. 1, 40th Congress, 2nd session, Serial 1326.

————. *ARCIA, 1868*, House Exec. Doc. 1, 40th Congress,, 3rd session, serial 1366.

————. *ARICA, 1870*, House Exec. Doc. 1, 43rd Congress, 1st session, Serial 1449.

————. *ARCIA, 1873*, House Exec. Doc. 1, 43rd Congress, 1st session, Serial 1601.

————. *ARCIA, 1880*, House Exec. Doc. 1, 46th Congress, 3rd session, Serial 1959.

————. *ARCIA, 1881*, House Exec. Doc. 1, 47th Congress, 1st session, Serial 2018.

————. *ARCIA, 1882*, House Exec. Doc. 1, 47th Congress, 2nd session, Serial 2100.

————. *ARCIA, 1883*, House Exec. Doc. 1, 48th Congress, 1st session, Serial 2191.

————. *ARCIA, 1884*, House Exec. Doc. 1, 48th Congress, 2nd session, Serial 2287.

————. *ARCIA, 1886*, House Exec. Doc. 1, 49th Congress, 2nd session, Serial 2467.

————. *ARCIA, 1887*, House Exec. Doc. 1, 50th Congress, 1st session, Serial 2542.

————. *ARCIA, 1888*, House Exec. Doc. 1, 50th Congress, 2nd session, Serial 2637.

————. *ARCIA, 1889*, House Exec. Doc. 1, 51st Congress, 1st session, Serial 2725.

————. *ARCIA, 1890*, House Exec. Doc. 1, 51st Congress, 2nd session, Serial 2841.

————. *ARCIA, 1891*, House Exec. Doc. 1, 52nd Congress, 1st session, Serial 2934.

————. *ARCIA, 1892*, House Exec. Doc. 1, 52nd Congress, 2nd session, Serial 3088.

————. *ARCIA, 1893*, House Exec. Doc. 1, 53rd Congress, 2nd session, Serial 3210.

————. *ARCIA, 1894*, House Exec. Doc. 1, 53rd Congress, 2nd session, Serial 3306.

————. *ARCIA, 1895*, House Doc. 5, 54th Congress, 1st session, Serial 3382.

————. *ARCIA, 1896*, House Doc. 5, 54th Congress, 2nd session, Serial 3489.

————. *ARCIA, 1897*, House Doc. 5, 55th Congress, 2nd session, Serial 3641.

————. *ARCIA, 1898*, House Doc. 5, 55th Congress, 3rd session, Serial 3757.

————. *ARCIA, 1901,* House Doc. 5, 57th Congress, 1st session, Serial 4290.

————. *Condition of Northern Cheyenne Indians.* Senate Exec. Doc. 121, 51st Congress, 1st session, Serial 2686.

————. *Exploration of the Yellowstone River.* Senate Exec. Doc. 77, 40th Congress, 2nd session, serial 1317.

————. *Indian Operations on the Plains, 1866.* Senate Exec. Doc. 33, 50th Congress, 1st session, serial 2504c

————. *Letter on Indian Hostilities.* Senate Exec. Doc. 13, 40th Congress, 1st session, serial 1308.

————. *Proposed Removal of the Northern Cheyenne Indians.* House Doc. 15, 55th Congress, 3rd session, Serial 3807.

————. *Report on the Condition of Indian Tribes.* Senate Record 156, 39th Congress, 2nd session, Serial 1279c.

————. *Secretary of War Annual Report, 1867.* House Exec. Doc. 1, 40th Congress, 2nd session, serial 1324.

Department of the Platte. Register of Letters Received. Microform copy in the Nebraska State Historical Society, Lincoln, RG 533.

Fletcher, Ellen. "Letters." Merrill G. Burlingame Department of Special Collections, Montana State University, Bozeman.

Gazette (Billings, Mont.)

Gopher, Jim. Interview (n.d.). Oral History Collection 542, Montana State Historical Society, Helena.

Kiste, Robert C. "Crow Peyotism." Unpublished manuscript in Timothy P. McCleary files, Hardin, Mont.

Little Chief, Joe. Winter Count. Typescript held at the Glenbow-Alberta Institute, Calgary.

Little Light, ed. Interview with Omer C. Stewart, n.d. Folder 52, Omer C. Stewart Collection, University of Colorado at Boulder Archives.

Lockey, Richard. "Diary on the Bozeman Trail, 1866." Typescript at the Montana State Historical Society, Helena.

Marquis, Thomas B. Diary. Microform copy in possession of Margot Liberty, Sheridan, Wyo.

Montana Post (Helena)

Montana Secretary of State Records, RS 250, Montana State Historical Society, Helena.

New York Times

Office of the Adjutant General. Record Group 48. Letters Received. National Archives Microform Publication 689.

Plenty Coups. Papers. Plenty Coups State Park, Pryor, Mont.

Records of the Bureau of Indian Affairs, Record Group 75. Central Classified Files, Crow. National Archives, Washington, D.C.

————. Crow Agency Records. National Archives, Denver, Colo.

————. Crow Commission of 1890, Entry 310, Irregularly Shaped Papers. National Archives, Washington, D.C.

————. Indian Census Rolls, Crow. National Archives Microform Publication M595.

————. Letters Received, 1824–1881. National Archives Microform Publication M234.

————. Letters Received, Office of Indian Affairs, 1882–1906. National Archives, Washington, D.C.

————. Letters Received, Special Case 137. Northern Cheyenne. National Archives, Washington, D.C.

————. Letters Received, Special Case 190. Crow Irrigation. National Archives, Washington, D.C.

————. Northern Cheyenne Agency Records. National Archives, Denver, Colo.

————. Records Concerning the Wheeler-Howard Act, 1933–1937. Entry 1011, National Archives, Washington, D.C.

————. Records Relating to the Investigation of the Fort Phil Kearny Massacre. National Archives Microform Publication M740.

Records of the Department of the Interior. Record Group 48. Records of the Indian Division. National Archives, Washington, D.C.

Records of the Montana Superintendency of Indian Affairs, 1861–1871. Small Collection 889. Montana State Historical Society, Helena.

"Report of Commissioners Alfred Cummings and Isaac I. Stevens on Council with Blackfoot, October 22, 1855." Small Collection 895. Montana State Historical Society, Helena.

Returns from U.S. Military Posts. Record Group 98. U.S. Army Commands. National Archives Microform Publication M617.

Ricker, Eli. "Tablets." Nebraska State Historical Society, Lincoln.

Running Rabbit, Houghton. Winter Count. Typescript held at the Glenbow-Alberta Institute, Calgary.

St. Francis Xavier Collection. Oregon Province Archives, Society of Jesus. Gonzaga University, Spokane, Wash.

Star-Tribune (Minneapolis)

Templeton, Lt. George M. "Diary, 1866–1868." Typescript copy at the Newberry Library, Chicago.

Ten Bear, Tyrone. Interview with Frank Rzeczkowski, August 8, 2001.

Ten Bear Jr., Joe. Interview with Omer Stewart, n.d. Omer Stewart Collection, University of Colorado Library Archives, Boulder.

White, Leroy. Interview with Timothy P. McCleary, December 27, 1995. In Timothy P. McCleary files, Hardin, Mont.

Whitebear Pease, Eloise. Collection. Little Big Horn College Archives, Crow Agency, Mont.

Yellow Fly, Teddy. Winter Count. Typescript held at the Glenbow-Alberta Institute, Calgary.

REFERENCES

Abair, Sr. Saint Angela Louise. "'A Mustard Seed in Montana': Recollections of the First Indian Mission in Montana." Edited by Orlan J. Svingen. *Montana: The Magazine of Western History* 34, no. 2 (Spring 1984): 16–31.

Aberle, David. *The Peyote Religion among the Navaho.* Norman: University of Oklahoma Press, 1982.

Adams, David Wallace. *Education for Extinction: American Indians and the Boarding School Experience.* Lawrence: University Press of Kansas, 1995.

Afton, Jean, David Fridtjof Halaas, and Andrew E. Masich with Richard N. Ellis. *Cheyenne Dog Soldiers: A Ledgerbook History of Coups and Combat.* Niwot: University of Colorado Press, 1997.

Agonito, Joseph, "Young Man Afraid of His Horses: The Reservation Years." *Nebraska History* 79, no. 3 (Fall 1998): 116–132.

Albers, Patricia C. "Changing Patterns of Ethnicity on the Northern Plains, 1780–1870." In

History, Power, and Identity: Ethnogenesis in the Americas, 1492–1992, edited by Jonathan D. Hill, 90–118. Iowa City: University of Iowa Press, 1996.

———. "Symbiosis, Merger, and War: Contrasting Forms of Intertribal Relationship among Plains Indians." In *The Political Economy of North American Indians,* edited by John H. Moore, 94–132. Norman: University of Oklahoma Press, 1993.

Albright, Peggy. *Crow Indian Photographer: The Work of Richard Throssel.* Albuquerque: University of New Mexico Press, 1997.

Algier, Kenneth. *The Crow and the Eagle: A Tribal History from Lewis and Clark to Custer.* Caldwell, Idaho: Caxton Printers, 1993.

Anderson, Benedict. *Imagined Communities: Reflections on the Origins and Spread of Nationalism.* New York: Verso, 1983.

Anderson, Gary Clayton. *The Indian Southwest, 1580–1830: Ethnogenesis and Reinvention.* Norman: University of Oklahoma Press, 1999.

Andersson, Rani-Henrik. *The Lakota Ghost Dance of 1890.* Lincoln: University of Nebraska Press, 2008.

Atchison, William Emory. *An Epic of the Middle West: Diary of William Emory Atchison.* Minneapolis: Charles Ramsdell and J. E. Haynes, 1933.

Athearn, Robert G. *William Tecumseh Sherman and the Settlement of the West.* Norman: University of Oklahoma Press, 1956.

Barsh, Russel Lawrence. "An American Heart of Darkness: The 1913 Expedition for American Indian Citizenship." *Great Plains Quarterly* 13, no. 2 (Spring 1993): 91–115.

Bauer, William J., Jr. *"We Were All Like Migrant Workers Here": Work, Community, and Memory on California's Round Valley Reservation, 1850–1941.* Chapel Hill: University of North Carolina Press, 2009.

Bedford, Denton R. "The Fight at 'Mountains on Both Sides.'" *Indian Historian* 8, no. 2 (Fall 1975): 13–23.

Benedict, Ruth. "The Vision in Plains Culture." *American Anthropologist* 24, no. 1 (Winter 1922): 1–23.

Berkhofer, Robert F., Jr. "The Political Context of a New Indian History." *Pacific Historical Review* 40, no. 3 (August 1971): 357–382.

———. *The White Man's Indian: Images of the American Indian from Columbus to the Present.* New York: Alfred A. Knopf, 1978.

Bernstein, Alison R. *American Indians and World War II: Toward a New Era in Indian Affairs.* Norman: University of Oklahoma Press, 1991.

Bhabha, Homi K. "DissemiNation: Time, Narrative, and the Margins of the Modern Nation." In *Nation and Narration,* edited by Homi K. Bhabha, 291–322. New York: Routledge, 1990.

———. *The Location of Culture.* London: Routledge, 1994.

Binnema, Theodore. *Common and Contested Ground: A Human and Environmental History of the Northwestern Plains.* Norman: University of Oklahoma Press, 2001.

———. "Old Swan, Big Man, and the Siksika Bands, 1794–1815." *Canadian Historical Review* 77, no. 1 (March 1996): 1–32.

Biolsi, Thomas. "The Birth of the Reservation: Making the Modern Individual among the Lakota." *American Ethnologist* 22, no. 1 (February 1995): 28–53.

———. *Deadliest Enemies: Law and the Making of Race Relations On and Off Rosebud Reservation.* Berkeley: University of California Press, 2001.

Bird, S. Elizabeth, ed. *Dressing in Feathers: The Construction of the Indian in American Popular Culture.* Boulder, Colo.: Westview Press, 1996.

Blackhawk, Ned. *Violence Over the Land: Indians and Empires in the Early American West.* Cambridge, Mass.: Harvard University Press, 2006.

Bowers, Alfred W. *Hidatsa Social and Ceremonial Organization.* Washington, D.C.: Government Printing Office, 1965.

Bradley, James H. "Affairs at Fort Benton from 1831 to 1869." In *Contributions to the Historical Society of Montana* 3: 201–287. Helena: Rocky Mountain Publishing, 1900; reprint, Boston: J. S. Canner, 1966.

————. "Arapooash." *Contributions to the Historical Society of Montana* 9: 299–306. Helena: Historical Society of Montana, 1923.

————. "Manuscript—Book F." *Contributions to the Historical Society of Montana* 8: 197–250. Helena, Mont.: Rocky Mountain Publishing, 1917; reprint, Boston: J. S. Canner, 1966.

Bray, Kingsley M. "Lone Horn's Peace: A New View of Sioux–Crow Relations, 1851–1858." *Nebraska History* 66, no. 1 (Spring 1985): 28–47.

————. "Teton Sioux Population History, 1655–1881." *Nebraska History* 75, no. 2 (Summer 1994): 165–188.

Brooks, James F. *Captives and Cousins: Slavery, Kinship, and Community in the Southwest Borderlands.* Chapel Hill: University of North Carolina Press, 2002.

Burdick, Usher L., ed. *David F. Barry's Indian Notes on "The Custer Battle."* Baltimore: Wirth Brothers, 1949.

Burroughs, W. Jeffrey, and Paul Spickard. "Ethnicity, Multiplicity, and Narrative: Problems and Possibilities." In *We Are a People: Narrative and Multiplicity in Constructing Ethnic Identity,* edited by Paul Spickard and W. Jeffrey Burroughs, 244–254. Philadelphia: Temple University Press, 2000.

Burt, Larry W. "In a Crooked Piece of Time: The Dilemma of the Montana Cree and the Metis." *Journal of American Culture* 9, no. 1 (Spring 1986): 45–51.

————. "Nowhere Left to Go: Montana's Crees, Metis, and Chippewas and the Creation of Rocky Boy's Reservation." *Great Plains Quarterly* 7, no. 3 (Summer 1987): 195–209.

Calloway, Colin. "Army Allies or Tribal Survival? The 'Other Indians' in the 1876 Campaign." In *Legacy: New Perspectives on the Battle of the Little Bighorn,* edited by Charles E. Rankin, 63–82. Helena: Montana Historical Society Press, 1996.

————. "The Inter-tribal Balance of Power on the Great Plains, 1760–1850." *American Studies* 16, no. 1 (April 1982): 25–47.

————. "Sword Bearer and the 'Crow Outbreak' of 1887." *Montana: The Magazine of Western History* 36, no. 4 (Autumn 1986): 38–51.

Campbell, Gregory R. "Changing Patterns of Health and Effective Fertility among the Northern Cheyenne of Montana, 1886–1903." *American Indian Quarterly* 15, no. 3 (Summer 1991): 339–358.

————. "Health Patterns and Economic Underdevelopment on the Northern Cheyenne Reservation, 1910–1920." In *The Political Economy of North American Indians,* edited by John H. Moore, 60–86. Norman: University of Oklahoma Press, 1993.

Carlson, Leonard A. "The Economics and Politics of Irrigation Projects on Indian Reservations, 1900–1940." In *The Other Side of the Frontier: Economic Explorations into Native American History,* edited by Linda Barrington, 235–258. Boulder, Colo.: Westview Press, 1999.

————. "Federal Policy and Indian Land: Economic Interests and the Sale of Indian Allotments, 1900–1934." *Agricultural History* 57, no. 1 (January 1983): 33–45.

————. *Indians, Bureaucrats, and the Land: The Dawes Act and the Decline of Indian Farming.* Westport, Conn.: Greenwood Press, 1981.

Carrington, Margaret Irvin. *Ab-sa-ra-ka, Home of the Crows.* Philadelphia: J. B. Lippincott, 1868.

Castile, George Pierre. "The Commodification of Indian Identity." *American Anthropologist* 98, no. 4 (December 1996): 743–749.

Catlin, George. *Letters and Notes on the Manners, Customs, and Condition of the North American Indians.* London: David Bogue, 1844.

Child, Brenda J. *Boarding School Seasons: American Indian Families, 1900–1940.* Lincoln: University of Nebraska Press, 1998.

Chittenden, Hiram M. *The American Fur Trade of the Far West.* 2 vols. New York: Francis P. Harper, 1902.

Chittenden, Hiram M., and Alfred T. Richardson, eds. *The Life, Letters, and Travels of Father Pierre-Jean De Smet, S.J.* 3 vols. New York: Francis P. Harper, 1905.

Church, Robert A. "Blackfeet and Fur Traders: Storm on the Northwestern Plains." *Journal of the West* 36, no. 2 (April 1997): 79–84.

Churchill, Ward. "The Crucible of American Indian Identity: Native Tradition Versus Colonial Imposition in Postconquest North America." *American Indian Culture and Research Journal* 23, no. 1 (1999): 39–67.

Clow, Richmond L. "General Philip Sheridan's Legacy: The Sioux Pony Campaign of 1876." *Nebraska History* 57, no. 4 (Winter 1976): 460–477.

Coleman, Michael. *American Indian Children at School, 1850–1930.* Jackson: University Press of Mississippi, 1993.

Colson, Elizabeth. "Political Organization in Tribal Societies." *American Indian Quarterly* 10, no. 1 (Winter 1986): 5–19.

Conaty, Gerald T. "Economic Models and Blackfoot Ideology." *American Ethnologist* 22, no. 2 (May 1995): 403–409.

———. "Relationships, Power, and Sacred Objects." Paper presented at the 12th International Conference on Organizational Symbolism, Calgary, Alberta, Canada, July 1994.

Cornell, Stephen. *Return of the Native: American Indian Political Resurgence.* New York: Oxford University Press, 1988.

Cott, Nancy F. *Public Vows: A History of Marriage and the Nation.* Cambridge, Mass.: Harvard University Press, 2000.

Couch, Carl J., and Joseph D. Marino. "Chippewa–Cree Peyotism at Rocky Boy's." In *Lifeways of Intermontane and Plains Montana Indians,* edited by Leslie B. Davis, 7–15. Bozeman: Montana State University, 1979.

Cowger, Thomas. *The National Congress of American Indians: The Founding Years.* Lincoln: University of Nebraska Press, 1999.

Curtis, Edward S. *The North American Indian.* 20 vols. Norwood, Mass.: Plimpton Press, 1907–1930.

Deloria, Philip J. *Playing Indian.* New Haven, Conn.: Yale University Press, 1998.

DeMallie, Raymond J. "American Indian Treaty Making: Motives and Meanings." *American Indian Journal of the Institute for the Development of Indian Law* 3, no. 1 (January 1977): 2–10.

———. "Kinship: The Foundation for Native American Society." In *Studying Native America: Problems and Prospects,* edited by Russell Thornton, 306–356. Madison: University of Wisconsin Press, 1998.

———. "Touching the Pen: Plains Indian Treaty Councils in Ethnographic Perspective." In *Ethnicity on the Great Plains,* edited by F. C. Luebke, 38–53. Lincoln: University of Nebraska Press, 1980.

———, ed. *The Sixth Grandfather: Black Elk's Teachings Given to John G. Neihardt.* Lincoln: University of Nebraska Press, 1984.

DeMontravel, Peter R. *A Hero to His Fighting Men: Nelson A. Miles, 1839–1925*. Kent, Ohio: Kent State University Press, 1998.

Dempsey, Hugh. *A Blackfoot Winter Count*. Calgary: Glenbow-Alberta Institute, 1965.

———. *Crowfoot: Chief of the Blackfeet*. Norman: University of Oklahoma Press, 1972.

———. *The Vengeful Wife and Other Blackfoot Stories*. Norman: University of Oklahoma Press, 2003.

Denig, Edwin Thompson. *Five Indian Tribes of the Upper Missouri: Sioux, Arickaras, Assiniboines, Crees, Crows*, edited by John C. Ewers. Norman: University of Oklahoma Press, 1961.

Dippie, Brian. *The Vanishing American: White Attitudes and U.S. Indian Policy*. Middletown, Conn.: Wesleyan University Press, 1982.

Dixon, Joseph K. *The Vanishing Race: The Last Great Indian Council*. Garden City, N.Y.: Doubleday, Page, 1913.

Dobak, William A. "Killing the Canadian Buffalo, 1821–1881." *Western Historical Quarterly* 27, no. 1 (Spring 1996): 33–52.

Dowd, Gregory Evans. *A Spirited Resistance: The North American Indian Struggle for Unity, 1715–1815*. Baltimore: Johns Hopkins University Press, 1992.

Doyle, Susan Badger. "Indian Perspectives on the Bozeman Trail." *Montana: The Magazine of Western History* 40, no. 1 (Winter 1990): 56–67.

———. "Journeys to the Land of Gold: Emigrants on the Bozeman Trail, 1863–66." *Montana: The Magazine of Western History* 41, no. 4 (Autumn 1991): 54–67.

Dugan, Kathleen M. *The Vision Quest of the Plains Indians*. Lewiston, N.Y.: Edwin Mellen Press, 1985.

Dunlay, Thomas. *Wolves for the Blue Soldiers: Indian Scouts and Auxiliaries with the United States Army, 1860–1890*. Lincoln: University of Nebraska Press, 1982.

Durham, Jimmie. "Those Dead Guys for a Hundred Years." In *I Tell You Now: Autobiographical Essays by Native American Writers*, edited by Brian Swann and Arnold Krupat, 155–166. Lincoln: University of Nebraska Press, 1990.

Dusenberry, Verne. *The Montana Cree: A Study in Religious Persistence*. Stockholm: Almquist and Wiksell, 1962.

———. "The Northern Cheyennes: All They Have Asked to Do Is to Live in Montana." *Montana: The Magazine of Western History* 5, no. 1 (Winter 1955): 23–40.

Edmunds, R. David. "Native Americans, New Voices: American Indian History, 1895–1995." *American Historical Review* 100, no. 3 (June 1995): 717–740.

Ellis, Clyde. *A Dancing People: Powwow Culture on the Southern Plains*. Lawrence: University Press of Kansas, 2003.

———. "Five Dollars a Week to Be 'Regular Indians': Shows, Exhibitions, and the Economics of Indian Dancing, 1880–1930." In *Native Pathways: American Indian Culture and Economic Development in the Twentieth Century*, edited by Brian Hosmer and Colleen O'Neill, 184–208. Boulder: University Press of Colorado, 2004.

Engh, Michael J., S.J. "Peter Paul Prando, S.J., 'Apostle of the Crows.'" *Montana: The Magazine of Western History* 34, no. 4 (Autumn 1984): 24–31.

Epps, Todd D. "*The State of Kansas v. Wild Hog, et al.*" *Kansas History* 5, no. 2 (Summer 1982): 139–146.

Ewers, John C. *The Blackfeet: Raiders on the Northwestern Plains*. Norman: University of Oklahoma Press, 1958.

———. *Ethnological Report on the Blackfeet and Gros Ventre Tribes of Indians*. New York: Garland, 1974.

————. *The Horse in Blackfoot Indian Culture, with Comparative Material from Other Western Tribes.* Washington, D.C.: Smithsonian Institution Press, 1955.

————. *Indian Life on the Upper Missouri.* Norman: University of Oklahoma Press, 1968.

————. "Intertribal Warfare as a Precursor of Indian–White Warfare on the Northern Plains." *Western Historical Quarterly* 6, no. 4 (October 1975): 397–410.

Farr, William E. "Going to Buffalo: Indian Hunting Migrations across the Rocky Mountains: Part II, Civilian Permits, Army Escorts." *Montana: The Magazine of Western History* 54, no. 1 (Spring 2004): 26–43.

Fausz, J. Frederick. "'Middlemen in Peace and War': Virginia's Earliest Indian Interpreters, 1608–1632." *Virginia Magazine of History and Biography* 95, no. 1 (January 1987): 41–64.

Fitzgerald, Michael Oren. *Yellowtail: Crow Medicine Man and Sun Dance Chief.* Norman: University of Oklahoma Press, 1991.

Fixico, Donald L. *The Urban Indian Experience in America.* Albuquerque: University of New Mexico Press, 2000.

Flores, Dan. "The Great Contraction: Bison and Indians in Northern Plains Environmental History." In *Legacy: New Perspectives on the Battle of the Little Bighorn,* edited by Charles E. Rankin, 3–22. Helena: Montana Historical Society Press, 1996.

Fogelson, Raymond J. Fogelson. "Perspectives on Native American Identity." In *Studying Native America: Problems and Prospects,* edited by Russell Thornton, 40–59. Madison: University of Wisconsin Press, 1998.

Foster, Martha Harroun. "Of Baggage and Bondage: Gender and Status among Hidatsa and Crow Women." *American Indian Culture and Research Journal* 17, no. 2 (1993): 121–152.

Fowler, Loretta. *Arapaho Politics, 1851–1978: Symbols in Crises of Authority.* Lincoln: University of Nebraska Press, 1986.

————. *Shared Symbols, Contested Meanings: Gros Ventre Culture and History, 1778–1984.* Lincoln: University of Nebraska Press, 2002.

————. *Tribal Sovereignty and the Historical Imagination: Cheyenne–Arapaho Politics.* Lincoln: University of Nebraska Press, 2002.

Francis, Julie, and Lawrence L. Loendorf. *Ancient Visions: Petroglyphs and Pictographs from the Wind River and Bighorn Country, Wyoming and Montana.* Salt Lake City: University of Utah Press, 2002.

Frey, Rodney. *The World of the Crow Indians: As Driftwood Lodges.* Norman: University of Oklahoma Press, 1987.

Fried, Morton. *The Notion of Tribe.* Menlo Park, N.J.: Cummings, 1975.

Fuller, Frances Fuller. *The River of the West.* Newark, N.J.: R. W. Bliss, 1870.

Geertz, Armin. *The Invention of Prophecy: Continuity and Meaning in Hopi Indian Religion.* Berkeley: University of California Press, 1994.

Giddens, Anthony. *The Consequences of Modernity.* Stanford, Calif.: Stanford University Press, 1990.

Gilroy, Paul. *Between Camps: Race, Identity, and Nationalism at the End of the Colour Line.* London: Allen Lane, 2000.

Gonzales, Angela A. "The (Re)Articulation of American Indian Identity: Maintaining Boundaries and Regulating Access to Ethnically Tied Resources." *American Indian Culture and Research Journal* 22, no. 4 (1998): 199–225.

————. "Urban (Trans)formations." In *American Indians and the Urban Experience,* edited by Susan Lobo and Kurt Peters, 169–186. Walnut Creek, Calif.: Altamira Press, 2001.

Gover, Kristy. "Genealogy as Continuity: Explaining the Growing Tribal Preference for Descent

Rules in Membership Governance in the United States." *American Indian Law Review* 33 (2008): 243–309.

Gray, John S. "Blazing the Bozeman and Bridger Trails." *Annals of Wyoming* 49, no. 1 (Spring 1977): 23–51.

———. *Centennial Campaign: The Sioux War of 1876.* Fort Collins, Colo.: Old Army Press, 1976.

———. *Custer's Last Campaign: Mitch Boyer and the Little Bighorn Reconstructed.* Lincoln: University of Nebraska Press, 1991.

Greene, Jerome A. "Lt. Palmer Writes from the Bozeman Trail, 1867–68." *Montana: The Magazine of Western History* 28, no. 3 (Summer 1978): 16–35.

Greenwald, Emily. *Reconfiguring the Reservation: The Nez Perces, Jicarilla Apaches, and the Dawes Act.* Albuquerque: University of New Mexico Press, 2002.

Gregg, Michael L. "Archaeological Complexes of the Northeastern Plains and Prairie–Woodland Border, A.D. 500–1500." In *Plains Indians, A.D. 500–1500: The Archaeological Past of Historic Groups,* edited by Karl H. Schlesier, 71–95. Norman: University of Oklahoma Press, 1994.

Grinnell, George B. *The Fighting Cheyennes.* Norman: University of Oklahoma Press, 1956.

Haas, Theodore H. *Ten Years of Tribal Government Under I.R.A.* Chicago: U.S. Indian Service, 1947.

Hagedorn, Nancy L. "A Friend to Go Between Them: The Interpreter as Cultural Broker during Anglo-Iroquois Councils, 1740–1770." *Ethnohistory* 35, no. 1 (Winter 1988): 60–80.

Hahn, Steven. *A Nation under Our Feet: Black Political Struggles in the Rural South from Slavery to the Great Migration.* Cambridge, Mass.: Harvard University Press, 2003.

Hall, Thomas D. "Native Americans and Incorporation: Patterns and Problems," *American Indian Culture and Research Journal* 11, no. 2 (1987): 1–23.

———. "Peripheries, Regions of Refuge, and Nonstate Societies: Toward a Theory of Reactive Social Change." *Social Science Quarterly* 64, no. 3 (September 1983): 282–297.

Hallowell, Irving A. "American Indians, White and Black: The Phenomenon of Transculturation." *Current Anthropology* 4, no. 5 (December 1963): 519–531.

Hamalainen, Pekka. *The Comanche Empire.* New Haven, Conn.: Yale University Press, 2008.

———. "The Rise and Fall of Plains Indian Horse Cultures." *Journal of American History* 90, no. 3 (December 2003): 833–862.

Hamill, James. *Going Indian.* Urbana: University of Illinois Press, 2006.

Harmon, Alexandra. *Indians in the Making: Ethnic Relations and Indian Identities around Puget Sound.* Berkeley: University of California Press, 1998.

———. *Rich Indians: Native People and the Problem of Wealth in American History.* Chapel Hill: University of North Carolina Press, 2010.

———. "Tribal Enrollment Councils: Lessons on Law and Indian Identity." *Western Historical Quarterly* 32, no. 2 (Summer 2001): 175–200.

Harrod, Howard L. *Becoming and Remaining a People: Native American Religions on the Northern Plains.* Tucson: University of Arizona Press, 1995.

———. *Crow Dog's Case: American Indian Sovereignty, Tribal Law, and United States Law in the Nineteenth Century.* New York: Cambridge University Press, 1994.

Hertzberg, Hazel W. *The Search for an American Indian Identity: Modern Pan-Indian Movements.* Syracuse, N.Y.: Syracuse University Press, 1971.

Hickerson, Harold. "The Virginia Deer and Intertribal Buffer Zones in the Upper Mississippi Valley." In *Man, Culture, and Animals: The Role of Animals in Human Adjustments,* edited by A.

Leeds and A. P. Vayda, 43–66. Washington, D.C.: American Association for the Advancement of Science, 1965.

Hittman, Michael. *Wovoka and the Ghost Dance*. Edited by Don Lynch. Lincoln: University of Nebraska Press, 1997.

Hobsbawm, Eric, and Terence Ranger, eds. *The Invention of Tradition*. New York: Cambridge University Press, 1983.

Hoebel, E. Adamson. *The Cheyennes: Indians of the Great Plains*. Fort Worth, Tex.: Harcourt Brace Jovanovich, 1978.

Hogue, Michael. "Disputing the Medicine Line: The Plains Crees and the Canadian–American Border, 1876–1885." *Montana: The Magazine of Western History* 52, no. 1 (Winter 2002): 2–17.

Holder, Preston. *The Hoe and the Horse on the Plains: A Study of Cultural Development among North American Indians*. Lincoln: University of Nebraska Press, 1970.

Holm, Tom, J. Diane Pearson, and Ben Chavis. "Peoplehood: A Model for the Extension of Sovereignty in American Indian Studies." *Wicazo Sa Review* 18, no. 1 (Spring 2003): 7–24.

Hosmer, Brian. *American Indians in the Marketplace: Persistence and Innovation among the Menominees and Metlakatlans, 1870–1920*. Lawrence: University Press of Kansas, 1999.

Howard, James H. "The Culture Area Concept: Does It Diffract Anthropological Light?" *Indian Historian* 8, no. 1 (Spring 1975): 22–26.

———. "The Pan-Indian Culture of Oklahoma." *Scientific Monthly* 81, no. 5 (November 1955): 215–220.

Hoxie, Frederick E. "Ethnohistory for a Tribal World." *Ethnohistory* 44, no. 4 (Autumn 1997): 595–615.

———. *A Final Promise: The Campaign to Assimilate the Indians, 1880–1920*. Lincoln: University of Nebraska Press, 1984.

———. *Parading through History: The Making of the Crow Nation in America, 1805–1935*. New York: Cambridge University Press, 1995.

Hulston, Nancy J. "Federal Children: Indian Education and the Red Cloud–McGillycuddy Conflict." *South Dakota History* 25, no. 2 (Summer 1995): 81–94.

Humphrey, A. Glenn. "The Crow Indian Treaties of 1868." *Annals of Wyoming* 43, no. 1 (Spring 1971): 73–89.

Hyde, George. *Life of George Bent Written from His Letters*. Norman: University of Oklahoma Press, 1968.

———. *The Pawnee Indians*. Norman: University of Oklahoma Press, 1951.

———. *Red Cloud's Folk: A History of the Oglala Sioux Indians*. Norman: University of Oklahoma Press, 1967.

———. *A Sioux Chronicle*. Norman: University of Oklahoma Press, 1956.

Isenberg, Andrew. *The Destruction of the Bison: An Environmental History, 1750–1920*. New York: Cambridge University Press, 2000.

Iverson, Peter. *Carlos Montezuma and the Changing World of American Indians*. Albuquerque: University of New Mexico Press, 1982.

Jablow, Joseph. *The Cheyenne in Plains Indian Trade Relations, 1795–1840*. New York: J. J. Augustin, 1951; reprint, Lincoln: University of Nebraska Press, 1994.

Jaimes, M. Annette. "Federal Indian Identification Policy: A Usurpation of Indigenous Sovereignty in North America." In *The State of Native America: Genocide, Colonization, and Resistance*, edited by M. Annette Jaimes, 123–138. Boston: South End Press, 1992.

Johnson, Dorothy M. *The Bloody Bozeman: The Perilous Trail to Montana's Gold*. New York: McGraw-Hill, 1971.

Jones, Brian. "A Battle at Little Bighorn: Being an Account of the Crow Outbreak of 1887." *Brand Book* 17, no. 3–4 (April–July 1975): 27–55.

———. "John Richard Jr. and the Killing at Fort Fetterman." *Annals of Wyoming* 43, no. 2 (Summer 1971): 237–258.

Judy, Mark A. "Powder Keg on the Upper Missouri; Sources of Blackfeet Hostility, 1730–1810." *American Indian Quarterly* 11, no. 2 (Spring 1987): 127–144.

Kappler, Charles, ed. *Indian Affairs: Laws and Treaties*. Vol. 2. Washington, D.C.: Government Printing Office, 1904.

Kehoe, Alice Beck. *The Ghost Dance: Ethnohistory and Revitalization*. New York: Holt, Rinehart, and Winston, 1989.

Kroeber, A. L. "Cultural and Natural Areas of North America." *University of California Publications in American Archeology and Ethnology* 38 (1939): 1–242.

Kuper, Adam. *The Invention of Primitive Society: The Transformation of an Illusion*. London: Routledge, 1988.

La Barre, Weston. *The Peyote Cult*. New Haven, Conn.: Yale University Press, 1938.

La Vere, David. *Contrary Neighbors: Southern Plains and Removed Indians in Indian Territory*. Norman: University of Oklahoma Press, 2000.

Landsman, Gail. "The Ghost Dance and the Policy of Land Allotment." *American Sociological Review* 44, no. 1 (February 1979): 162–166.

Larocque, Francis Antoine. "Yellowstone Journal." In *Early Fur Trade on the Northern Plains: Canadian Traders among the Mandan and Hidatsa Indians, 1738–1818,* edited by W. Raymond Wood and Thomas D. Theissen, 156–220. Norman: University of Oklahoma Press, 1985.

Larpenteur, Charles. *Forty Years a Fur Trader on the Upper Missouri*. 2 vols. New York: Francis P. Harper, 1898.

Larson, Robert W. "Lakota Leaders and Government Agents: A Story of Changing Relationships." *Nebraska History* 82, no. 2 (Summer 2001): 47–57.

Lazarus, Edward. *Black Hills, White Justice: The Sioux Nation Versus the United States, 1775 to the Present*. New York: HarperCollins, 1991.

Leonard, Zenas. *Narrative of the Adventures of Zenas Leonard*. Chicago: Lakeside Press, 1934; reprint, Lincoln: University of Nebraska Press, 1978.

Lepore, Jill. *The Name of War: King Philip's War and the Origins of American Identity*. New York: Vintage Books, 1999.

Lewis, David Rich. *Neither Wolf Nor Dog: American Indians, Environment, and Agrarian Change*. New York: Oxford University Press, 1994.

———. "Reservation Leadership and the Progressive–Traditional Dichotomy: William Wash and the Northern Utes, 1865–1928." *Ethnohistory* 38, no. 2 (Spring 1991): 124–148.

Lewis, Oscar. *The Effects of White Contact upon Blackfoot Culture, with Special Reference to the Fur Trade*. New York: J. J. Augustin, 1942.

Liberty, Margot. "Hell Came with Horses: Plains Indian Women in the Equestrian Era." *Montana: The Magazine of Western History* 32, no. 3 (Summer 1982): 10–19.

Liebersohn, Harry. *Aristocratic Encounters: European Travelers and North American Indians*. New York: Cambridge University Press, 1998.

Linderman, Frank B. *Plenty Coups: Chief of the Crows*. New York: John Day, 1930; reprint, Lincoln: University of Nebraska Press, 1962.

————. *Pretty-Shield: Medicine Woman of the Crows*. New York: John Day, 1932; reprint, Lincoln: University of Nebraska Press, 1972.

Lindstrom, Richard. "'Not from the Land Side, but from the Flag Side': Native American Responses to the Wanamaker Expedition of 1913." *Journal of Social History* 30, no. 1 (Autumn 1996): 209–227.

Littlefield, Alice, and Martha C. Knack. *Native Americans and Wage Labor: Ethnohistorical Perspectives*. Norman: University of Oklahoma Press, 1996.

Llewellyn, K. N., and E. Adamson Hoebel. *The Cheyenne Way: Conflict and Case Law in Primitive Jurisprudence*. Norman: University of Oklahoma Press, 1941.

Loendorf, Lawrence L. "Results of Archeological Survey in the Pryor Mountain Bighorn Canyon Area, 1970 Field Season." Unpublished manuscript. Grand Forks, N.D.: Loendorf and Associates, 1974.

————. "The Results of the Archeological Survey in the Pryor Mountain Bighorn Canyon Area, 1971 Field Season." Unpublished manuscript. Grand Forks, N.D.: Loendorf and Associates, 1974.

Loendorf, Lawrence L., and Peter Nabokov. "Every Morning of the World: Ethnographic Research Study of the Bighorn Canyon National Recreation Area." Unpublished manuscript. Denver, Colo.: Rocky Mountain Region, U.S. Department of the Interior, National Park Service, 1994.

Lowie, Robert H. *The Crow Indians*. New York: Farrar and Rinehart, 1935; reissued 1956.

Lurie, Nancy Oestreich. "The Contemporary American Indian Scene." In *North American Indians in Historical Perspective*, edited by Eleanor B. Leacock and Nancy Oestreich Lurie, 418–480. New York: Random House, 1971.

M'Gillivray, Duncan. *The Journal of Duncan McGillivray of the North-West Company at Fort George on the Saskatchewan, 1794–1795*. Toronto: Macmillan, 1929.

Mardock, Robert Winston. *The Reformers and the American Indian*. Columbia: University of Missouri Press, 1971.

Maroukis, Thomas Constantine. *Peyote and the Yankton Sioux: The Life and Times of Sam Necklace*. Norman: University of Oklahoma Press, 2004.

Marquis, Thomas B. *The Cheyennes of Montana*. Edited by Thomas D. Weist. Algonac, Mich.: Reference Publications, 1978.

————. *Memoirs of a White Crow Indian*. New York: The Century Company, 1928.

————. *Wooden Leg: A Warrior Who Fought Custer*. Minneapolis: Midwest, 1931.

Marszalek, John. *Sherman: A Soldier's Passion for Order*. New York: The Free Press, 1993.

Mattes, Merrill J. *Indians, Infants, and Infantry: Andrew and Elizabeth Burt on the Frontier*. Denver, Colo.: Old West Publishing, 1960; reprint, Lincoln: University of Nebraska Press, 1988.

Maximilian, Alexander Philip, Prince of Weid. *Travels in the Interior of North America*. Vol. 23 of *Early Western Travels, 1748–1846,* edited by Reuben Gold Thwaites. Cleveland: Arthur H. Clark, 1906.

McBeth, Sally J. *Ethnic Identity and the Boarding School Experience of West-Central Oklahoma Indians*. Lanham, Md.: University Press of America, 1982.

McCleary, Timothy P. "A Legal History of Peyotism in Montana." Paper presented at the 47th Annual Plains Conference, Sioux Falls, S.D., October 18–21, 1989.

McClintock, Walter. *Old North Trail: Life, Legends, and Religion of the Blackfeet Indians*. London: Macmillan, 1910.

McDonnell, Anne, ed. "Fort Benton Journal, 1854–1856." *Contributions to the Historical Society of*

Montana. Vol. 10. Helena, Mont.: Rocky Mountain Publishing, 1940; reprint, Boston: J. S. Canner, 1966.

McGinnis, Anthony. *Counting Coup and Cutting Horses: Intertribal Warfare on the Northern Great Plains.* Evergreeen, Colo.: Cordillera Press, 1990.

McMillen, Christian W. "Rain, Ritual, and Reclamation: The Failure of Irrigation on the Zuni and Navajo Reservations, 1883–1917." *Western Historical Quarterly* 31, no. 4 (Winter 2000): 435–456.

Means, Russell. *Where White Men Fear to Tread: The Autobiography of Russell Means.* New York: St. Martin's Press, 1995.

Medicine Crow, Joseph. "The Effect of European Culture upon the Economic, Social, and Religious Life of the Crow Indians." M.A. thesis, University of Southern California, 1939.

———. *From the Heart of the Crow Country: The Crow Indians' Own Stories.* New York: Orion Books, 1992.

Mellis, Allison Fuss. *Riding Buffaloes and Broncos: Rodeo and Native Traditions in the Northern Great Plains.* Norman: University of Oklahoma Press, 2003.

Meredith, Howard. *Dancing on Common Ground: Tribal Cultures and Alliances on the Southern Plains.* Lawrence: University Press of Kansas, 1995.

Merrell, James. *The Indians' New World: Catawbas and Their Neighbors from European Contact through the Era of Removal.* Chapel Hill: University of North Carolina Press, 1989.

———. *Into the American Woods: Negotiators on the Pennsylvania Frontier.* New York: W. W. Norton, 1999.

Meyer, Melissa. "American Indian Blood Quantum Requirements: Blood Is Thicker Than Family." In *Over the Edge: Remapping the American West,* edited by Valerie J. Matsumoto and Blake Allmendinger, 231–252. Berkeley: University of California Press, 1999.

Milloy, John S. *The Plains Cree: Trade, Diplomacy, and War, 1790 to 1870.* Winnipeg: University of Manitoba Press, 1988.

Mooney, James. "The Ghost Dance Religion and the Sioux Outbreak of 1890." In *Fourteenth Annual Report of the Bureau of American Ethnology,* pt. 2, 645–1136. Washington, D.C.: Government Printing Office, 1896.

Moore, John H. *The Cheyenne Nation: A Social and Demographic History.* Lincoln: University of Nebraska Press, 1987.

Moses, L. G. *Wild West Shows and the Images of American Indians, 1883–1933.* Albuquerque: University of New Mexico Press, 1996.

Mulroy, Kevin. "Ethnogenesis and Ethnohistory of the Seminole Maroons." *Journal of World History* 4, no. 2 (Fall 1993): 287–305.

Murie, James R. *Ceremonies of the Pawnee.* Edited by Douglas R. Parks. Lincoln: University of Nebraska Press, 1981.

Nabokov, Peter. "Cultivating Themselves: The Interplay of Crow Indian Religion and History." Ph.D. diss., University of California, Berkeley, 1989.

———. *A Forest of Time: American Indian Ways of History.* New York: Cambridge University Press, 2002.

———. *Two Leggings: The Making of a Crow Warrior.* New York: Thomas Y. Crowell, 1967.

Nagel, Joane. *American Indian Ethnic Renewal: Red Power and the Resurgence of Identity and Culture.* Berkeley: University of California Press, 1996.

Nugent, David. "Property Relations, Production Relations, and Inequality: Anthropology, Political Economy, and the Blackfeet." *American Ethnologist* 20, no. 2 (May 1993): 336–351.

O'Connor, Nancy Fields. *Fred E. Miller: Photographer of the Crows*. Malibu, Calif.: Carnan Vid-Film, 1984.

Olson, James C. *Red Cloud and the Sioux Problem*. Lincoln: University of Nebraska Press, 1965.

O'Neill, Colleen. *Working the Navajo Way: Labor and Culture in the Twentieth Century*. Lawrence: University Press of Kansas, 2005.

Ostler, Jeffrey. *The Plains Sioux and U.S. Colonialism from Lewis and Clark to Wounded Knee*. New York: Cambridge University Press, 2004.

Otis, D. S. *The Dawes Act and the Allotment of Indian Lands*. Norman: University of Oklahoma Press, 1973.

Overton, Richard C. *Burlington Route: A History of the Burlington Lines*. New York: Alfred A. Knopf, 1965.

Page, Vicki. "Reservation Development in the United States: Peripherality in the Core." *American Indian Culture and Research Journal* 9, no. 3 (1985): 21–35.

Partoll, Albert J. "Blackfoot Indian Peace Council." *Sources of Northwest History*, no. 3. Missoula: Montana State University, 1937.

Penn, W. S. *Feathering Custer*. Lincoln: University of Nebraska Press, 2001.

Peterson, Charles S. "Headgates and Conquest: The Limits of Irrigation on the Navajo Reservation, 1880–1950." *New Mexico Historical Review* 68, no. 3 (July 1993): 269–290.

Pisani, Donald J. "Irrigation, Water Rights, and the Betrayal of Indian Allotment." *Environmental Review* 10, no. 3 (Autumn 1986): 157–176.

Powell, Peter J. *People of the Sacred Mountain: A History of the Northern Cheyenne Chiefs and Warrior Societies, 1830–1879*. San Francisco: Harper and Row, 1981.

———. *Sweet Medicine: The Continuing Role of the Sacred Arrows, the Sun Dance, and the Sacred Buffalo Hat in Northern Cheyenne History*. Norman: University of Oklahoma Press, 1969.

Powers, Karen Viera. *Andean Journeys: Migration, Ethnogenesis, and the State in Colonial Quito*. Albuquerque: University of New Mexico Press, 1995.

Powers, William K. *War Dance: Plains Indian Musical Performance*. Tucson: University of Arizona Press, 1990.

Price, Catherine. *The Oglala People, 1841–1879: A Political and Social History*. Lincoln: University of Nebraska Press, 1996.

Prucha, Francis Paul. *The Great Father: The United States Government and the American Indians*. 2 vols. Lincoln: University of Nebraska Press, 1984.

Rand, Jacki Thompson. *Kiowa Humanity and the Invasion of the State*. Lincoln: University of Nebraska Press, 2008.

———. "Primary Sources: Indian Goods and the History of American Colonialism and the 19th-Century Reservation." In *Clearing a Path: Theoretical Approaches to the Past in Native American Studies,* edited by Nancy Shoemaker, 137–160. New York: Routledge, 2001.

Ray, Arthur J., and Donald B. Freeman. *"Give Us Good Measure": An Economic Analysis of Relations between the Indians and the Hudson's Bay Company before 1763*. Toronto: University of Toronto Press, 1978.

Reeves, Brian, and Sandy Peacock. *"Our Mountains Are Our Pillows": An Ethnographic Overview of Glacier National Park*. Vol. 1. Denver, Colo.: National Park Service, Rocky Mountain Regional Office, 1995.

Richter, Daniel K. "Cultural Brokers and Intercultural Politics: New York–Iroquois Relations, 1664–1701." *Journal of American History* 75, no. 1 (June 1988): 40–67.

———. *The Ordeal of the Longhouse: The Peoples of the Iroquois League in the Era of European Colonization*. Chapel Hill: University of North Carolina Press, 1992.

Rickey, Don, Jr. *History of Custer Battlefield.* Fort Collins, Colo.: Old Army Press, 1967.

Riebeth, Carolyn Reynolds. *J. H. Sharp among the Crow Indians: Personal Memories of His Life and Friendships on the Crow Reservation in Montana.* El Segundo, Calif.: Upton and Sons, 1985.

Roosens, Eugene. *Creating Ethnicity: The Process of Ethnogenesis.* London: Sage, 1989.

Roscoe, Will. "'That Is My Road': The Life and Times of a Crow Berdache." *Montana: The Magazine of Western History* 40, no. 1 (Winter 1990): 46–55.

Rosier, Paul C. *Rebirth of the Blackfeet Nation, 1912–1954.* Lincoln: University of Nebraska Press, 2005.

Sahlins, Marshall. *Islands of History.* Chicago: University of Chicago Press, 1985.

Saum, Lewis O. *The Fur Trader and the Indian.* Seattle: University of Washington Press, 1965.

Saunt, Claudio. *A New Order of Things: Power, Property, and the Transformation of the Creek Indians, 1733–1816.* New York: Cambridge University Press, 1999.

Scaglion, Richard. "The Plains Culture Area Concept." In *Anthropology on the Great Plains,* edited by W. Raymond Wood and Margot Liberty, 23–34. Lincoln: University of Nebraska Press, 1980.

Schlesier, Karl. "Commentary: A History of Ethnic Groups." In *Plains Indians, A.D. 500–1500: The Archaeological Past of Historic Groups,* edited by Karl H. Schlesier, 308–381. Norman: University of Oklahoma Press, 1994.

———. "Rethinking the Midewiwin and the Plains Ceremonial Called the Sun Dance." *Plains Anthropologist* 35, no. 127 (February 1990): 1–26.

Schrems, Suzanne H. "The Northern Cheyenne and the Fight for Cultural Sovereignty: The Notes of Father Aloysius Van Der Velden, S.J." *Montana: The Magazine of Western History* 45, no. 2 (Spring 1995): 18–33.

Schultz, James Willard. *Blackfeet and Buffalo: Memories of Life among the Indians.* Edited by Keith C. Seele. Norman: University of Oklahoma Press, 1962.

Schultz, James Willard, and Jessie Louise Donaldson. *The Sun God's Children.* Boston: Houghton Mifflin, 1930.

Scott, James C. *Weapons of the Weak: Everyday Forms of Peasant Resistance.* New Haven, Conn.: Yale University Press, 1985.

Sharrock, Susan. "Crees, Cree–Assiniboines, and Assiniboines: Interethnic Social Organizations on the Far Northern Plains." *Ethnohistory* 21, no. 2 (Spring 1974): 95–126.

Shoemaker, Nancy. "How Indians Got to Be Red." *American Historical Review* 102, no. 3 (June 1997): 625–644.

———. "Urban Indians and Ethnic Choices: American Indian Organizations in Minneapolis, 1920–1950." *Western Historical Quarterly* 19, no. 4 (November 1988): 431–447.

Simonin, Louis. *The Rocky Mountain West in 1867.* Translated and edited by Wilson O. Clough. Lincoln: University of Nebraska Press, 1966.

Slotkin, J. Stanley. *The Peyote Religion: A Study in Indian–White Relations.* Glencoe, Ill.: The Free Press, 1956.

Smith, Burton M. "Politics and the Crow Indian Land Cessions." *Montana: The Magazine of Western History* 36, no. 4 (Autumn 1986): 24–37.

Smith, Sherry L. *Reimagining Indians: Native Americans through Anglo Eyes, 1880–1940.* New York: Oxford University Press, 2000.

Smits, David D. "The 'Squaw Drudge': A Prime Index of Savagism." *Ethnohistory* 29, no. 4 (Autumn 1982): 281–306.

Smoak, Gregory E. *Ghost Dance and Identity: Prophetic Religion and American Indian Ethnogenesis in the Nineteenth Century.* Berkeley: University of California Press, 2006.

Spickard, Paul, and W. Jeffrey Burroughs, eds. *We Are a People: Narrative and Multiplicity in Constructing Ethnic Identity*. Philadelphia: Temple University Press, 2000.

Stamm, Henry E., IV. *People of the Wind River: The Eastern Shoshones, 1825–1900*. Norman: University of Oklahoma Press, 1999.

Stands in Timber, John, and Margot Liberty. *Cheyenne Memories*. New Haven, Conn.: Yale University Press, 1967.

Steinmetz, Paul. *Pipe, Bible, and Peyote among the Oglala Lakota*. Knoxville: University of Tennessee Press, 1990.

Stephan, Cookie White, and Walter G. Stephan. "What Are the Functions of Ethnic Identity?" In *We Are a People: Narrative and Multiplicity in Constructing Ethnic Identity*, edited by Paul Spickard and W. Jeffrey Burroughs, 229-243. Philadelphia: Temple University Press, 2000.

Stewart, Omer C. *Peyote Religion: A History*. Norman: University of Oklahoma Press, 1987.

———. "Peyotism in Montana." *Montana: The Magazine of Western History* 33, no. 2 (Spring 1983): 2–15.

Stocking, George, Jr. *Race, Culture, and Evolution: Essays in the History of Anthropology*. New York: The Free Press, 1968.

Sturm, Circe. *Blood Politics: Race, Culture, and Identity in the Cherokee Nation of Oklahoma*. Berkeley: University of California Press, 2002.

Sturtevant, William C., ed. *Handbook of North American Indians*. Vol. 13 of *Plains*, edited by Raymond J. Demallie. Washington, D.C.: Smithsonian Institution, 2001.

Sunder, John E. *The Fur Trade on the Upper Missouri, 1840–1865*. Norman: University of Oklahoma Press, 1965.

Svingen, Orlan J. *The Northern Cheyenne Indian Reservation, 1877–1900*. Niwot: University Press of Colorado, 1993.

———. "Reservation Self-Sufficiency: Stock Raising vs. Farming on the Northern Cheyenne Indian Reservation, 1900–1914." *Montana: The Magazine of Western History* 31, no. 4 (Autumn 1981): 14–23.

Szasz, Margaret Connell, ed. *Between Indian and White Worlds: The Culture Broker*. Norman: University of Oklahoma Press, 1994.

Tennant, Paul. *Aboriginal Peoples and Politics: The Indian Land Question in British Columbia, 1849–1989*. Vancouver: University of British Columbia Press, 1990.

Thomas, Nicholas. *Colonialism's Culture: Anthropology, Travel, and Government*. Cambridge: Polity Press, 1994.

Thompson, David. *David Thompson's Narrative, 1784–1812*. Edited by Richard Glover. Toronto: The Champlain Society, 1962.

Thornton, Russell. *We Shall Live Again: The 1870 and 1890 Ghost Dance Movements as Demographic Revitalization*. New York: Cambridge University Press, 1986.

Townsend, Kenneth William. *World War II and the American Indian*. Albuquerque: University of New Mexico Press, 2000.

Turney, Laura. *"Ceci n'est pas* Jimmie Durham." *Critique of Anthropology* 19, no. 4 (December 1999): 423–442.

Usner, Daniel H., Jr. *Indian Work: Language and Livelihood in Native American History*. Cambridge, Mass.: Harvard University Press, 2009.

Utley, Robert. *Frontiersmen in Blue: The United States Army and the Indian, 1848–1865*. New York: Macmillan, 1967.

———. *The Lance and the Shield: The Life and Times of Sitting Bull*. New York: Ballantine Books, 1993.

Vander, Judith. *Shoshone Ghost Dance Religion: Poetry Songs and Great Basin Context.* Urbana: University of Illinois Press, 1997.

Vickers, J. Roderick. "Cultures of the Northwestern Plains: From the Boreal Forest Edge to Milk River." In *Plains Indians, A.D. 500–1500: The Archaeological Past of Historic Groups,* edited by Karl H. Schlesier, 3–33. Norman: University of Oklahoma Press, 1994.

Voget, Fred W. *The Shoshoni–Crow Sun Dance.* Norman: University of Oklahoma Press, 1984.

———. *They Call Me Agnes: A Crow Narrative Based on the Life of Agnes Yellowtail Deernose.* Norman: University of Oklahoma Press, 1995.

Waddell, Jack O., and O. Michael Watson, eds. *The American Indian in Urban Society.* Boston: Little, Brown, 1961.

Wagner, Glendolin Damon, and William A. Allen. *Blankets and Moccasins: Plenty Coups and His People, the Crows.* Caldwell, Idaho: Caxton Printers, 1936.

Wall, Wendy L. "Gender and the 'Citizen Indian.'" In *Writing the Range: Race, Class, and Culture in the Women's West,* edited by Elizabeth Jameson and Susan Armitage, 202–229. Norman: University of Oklahoma Press, 1997.

Wedel, Waldo R. *Central Plains Prehistory: Holocene Environments and Culture Change in the Republican River Basin.* Lincoln: University of Nebraska Press, 1986.

Weibel-Orlando, Joan. "An Ethnohistorical Analysis of Crow Political Alliances." *Western Canadian Journal of Anthropology* 7, no. 4 (1977): 34–54.

———. *Indian Country, L.A.: Maintaining Ethnic Community in Complex Society.* Urbana: University of Illinois Press, 1991.

———. "Ned Casey and His Cheyenne Scouts: A Noble Experiment in an Atmosphere of Tension." *Montana: The Magazine of Western History* 27, no. 1 (Winter 1977): 26–39.

———, ed. *Belle Highwalking: The Narrative of a Northern Cheyenne Woman.* Billings: Montana Council for Higher Education, 1979.

Wessel, Thomas R. "Agent of Acculturation: Farming on the Northern Plains Reservations, 1880–1910." *Agricultural History* 60, no. 2 (Spring 1986): 233–245.

———. "Agriculture on the Reservations: The Case of the Blackfeet, 1885–1930." *Journal of the West* 18, no. 4 (October 1979): 17–24.

West, Elliot. *The Contested Plains: Indians, Goldseekers, and the Rush to Colorado.* Lawrence: University Press of Kansas, 1998.

White, Richard. *The Middle Ground: Indians, Empires, and Republics in the Great Lakes Region, 1640–1815.* New York: Cambridge University Press, 1991.

———. *The Roots of Dependency: Subsistence, Environment, and Social Change among the Choctaws, Pawnees, and Navajos.* Lincoln: University of Nebraska Press, 1983.

———. "The Winning of the West: Expansion of the Western Sioux during the Eighteenth and Nineteenth Centuries." *Journal of American History* 65, no. 2 (September 1978): 319–343.

Wickwire, Wendy. "'We Shall Drink from the Stream and So Shall You': James A. Teit and Native Resistance in British Columbia, 1908–1922." *Canadian Historical Review* 79, no. 2 (June 1998): 199–236.

Wildschudt, William. *Crow Indian Medicine Bundles.* Edited by John C. Ewers. New York: Heye Foundation Museum of the American Indian, 1975.

Williams, Walter L. *The Spirit and the Flesh: Sexual Diversity in American Indian Culture.* Boston: Beacon Press, 1986.

Wishart, David J. *The Fur Trade of the American West, 1807–1840.* Lincoln: University of Nebraska Press, 1979.

Wissler, Clark. "Ceremonial Bundles of the Blackfoot Indians." *Anthropological Papers of the American Museum of Natural History* 7, no. 2 (1912): 65–290.

———. *Indian Cavalcade*. New York: Sheridan House, 1938.

———. "The Social Life of the Blackfoot Indians." *Anthropological Papers of the American Museum of Natural History* 7, no. 1 (1911): 1–64.

———. "Social Organization and Ritualistic Ceremonies of the Blackfoot Indians." *Anthropological Papers of the American Museum of Natural History* 7, no. 2 (1912): 1–64.

———. "Societies and Dance Associations of the Blackfoot Indians." *Anthropological Papers of the American Museum of Natural History* 11, no. 4 (1913): 359–460.

Wissler, Clark, and D. C. Duvall. *Mythology of the Blackfoot Indians*. Lincoln: University of Nebraska Press, 1995.

Wolf, Eric. *Europe and the People without History*. Berkeley: University of California Press, 1982.

Wood, W. Raymond. "Plains Trade in Prehistoric and Protohistoric Intertribal Relations." In *Anthropology on the Great Plains,* edited by W. Raymond Wood and Margot Liberty, 98–109. Lincoln: University of Nebraska Press, 1980.

Wood, W. Raymond, and Alan S. Downer. "Notes on the Crow–Hidatsa Schism." *Plains Anthropologist* 22, no. 78 (November 1977): 83–100.

Wood, W. Raymond, and Thomas D. Theissen. *Early Fur Trade on the Northern Plains: Canadian Traders Among the Mandan and Hidatsa Indians, 1738–1818*. Norman: University of Oklahoma Press, 1985.

Woodenlegs, John. *A Northern Cheyenne Album: Photographs by Thomas B. Marquis*. Edited by Margot Liberty. Norman: University of Oklahoma Press, 2006.

Wooster, Robert. *The Military and United States Indian Policy, 1865–1903*. New Haven, Conn.: Yale University Press, 1988.

———. *Nelson A. Miles and the Twilight of the Frontier Army*. Lincoln: University of Nebraska Press, 1993.

Wright, J. Leitch. *Creeks and Seminoles: The Destruction and Regeneration of the Muscogulge People*. Lincoln: University of Nebraska Press, 1986.

INDEX